MISTRESS OF EVERGREEN PLANTATION
Rachel O'Connor's Legacy of Letters
1823-1845

MISTRESS *of*
EVERGREEN PLANTATION

*Rachel O'Connor's
Legacy of Letters
1823–1845*

Edited by
Allie Bayne Windham Webb

STATE UNIVERSITY OF NEW YORK PRESS
ALBANY

Published by State University of New York Press, Albany

Printed in the United States of America

For information, address State University of New York Press, State University Plaza, Albany, N.Y., 12246

Library of Congress Cataloging in Publication Data
O'Connor, Rachel Swayze, 1774-1846.
  The mistress of Evergreen Plantation.

  Bibliography: p. 000
  Includes index.
  1. O'Connor, Rachel Swayze, 1774-1846. 2. Evergreen Plantation (La.) 3. Plantation life—Louisiana. 4. Slavery—Louisiana. 5. Plantation owners—Louisiana—West Feliciana Parish—Correspondence. 6. West Feliciana Parish (La.)—Biography. I. Webb, Allie Bayne. II. Title.
F379.E930256 1983   976.3'17 [B]   82-7351
ISBN 0-87395-665-6
ISBN 0-87395-666-4 (pbk.)

CONTENTS

Maps
1. *Louisiana* *vi*
2. *Southeast Louisiana* *vii*
3. *Evergreen Plantation and Neighbors* *viii*

Introduction *ix*

Letters *1*

Afterword *275*

Appendixes
1. *Last Will and Testament* *281*
2. *Inventory of Rachel O'Connor's Property, June 4, 1846* *283*
3. *Letter of Rachel O'Connor to David Weeks, February 28, 1830* *287*

Genealogy *289*

Who's Who in the Life of Rachel O'Connor *291*

Bibliography *295*

Index *297*

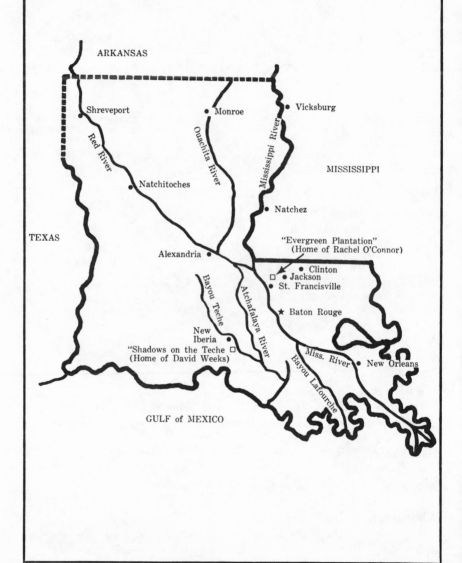

LOUISIANA
Scene of Rachel's Activities
1774-1846

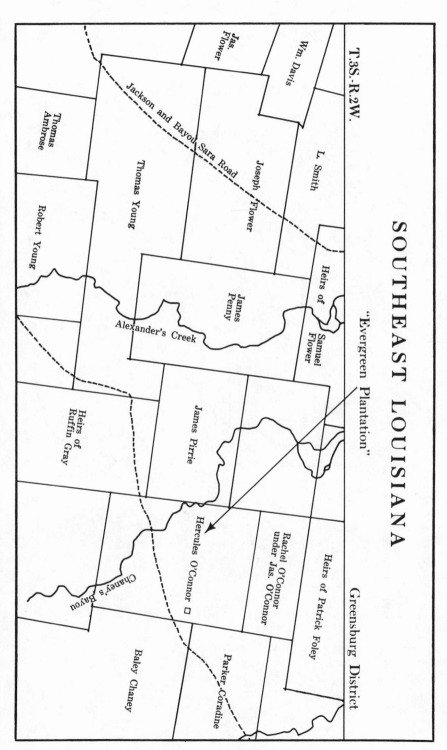

SOUTHEAST LOUISIANA

"Evergreen Plantation"

T.3S.-R.2W.

Greensburg District

Wm. Davis

Jas. Flower

Jackson and Bayou Sara Road

Thomas Ambrose

Joseph Flower

L. Smith

Thomas Young

Robert Young

Heirs of Samuel Flower

James Penny

Alexander's Creek

Heirs of Ruffin Gray

James Pirrie

Hercules O'Connor □

Rachel O'Connor under Jas. O'Connor

Heirs of Patrick Foley

Chaney's Bayou

Baley Chaney

Parker Coradine

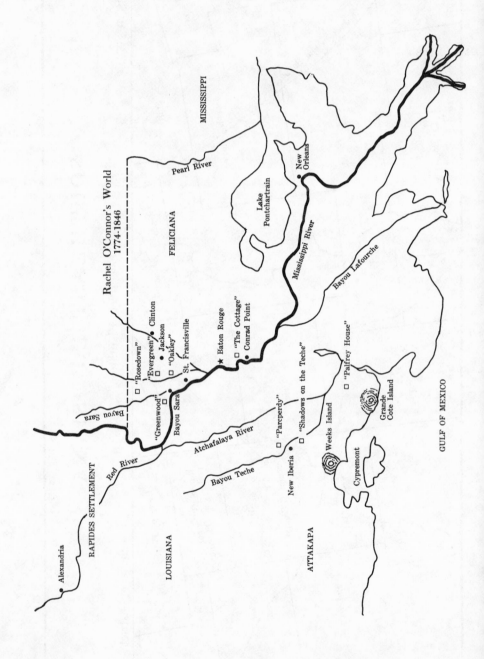

Rachel O'Connor's World
1774-1846

MISSISSIPPI

Pearl River

FELICIANA

Lake
Pontchartrain

New Orleans

Mississippi River

Bayou Lafourche

Clinton
"Evergreen"
"Rosedown"
Jackson
"Oakley"
St. Francisville
Baton Rouge
"The Cottage"
Conrad Point

"Greenwood"
Bayou Sara

Bayou Sara

Atchafalaya River

"Shadows on the Teche"

"Palfrey House"

Weeks Island

Grande
Cote Island

GULF OF MEXICO

RAPIDES SETTLEMENT

Red River

"Parcperdy"

Bayou Teche

New Iberia

Cypremont

ATTAKAPA

LOUISIANA

Alexandria

INTRODUCTION

hen the Feliciana country of Louisiana was being settled in the period following the American Revolution, it was called the "Happy Land."

It was a happy time as well as a happy place, for people in the New World had suddenly become filled with confidence in themselves and in their ability to carve a civilization out of the virgin forests.

Into this happy land, Rachel Swayze was introduced as a four-year-old child in 1778, and in this land she lived all the rest of her seventy-two years. Rachel was an extraordinary woman in her quiet, unassuming way, for she was a successful woman planter in a man's world. She would probably never have been remembered after her death and the passing of her contemporaries were it not for a collection of remarkable letters she wrote to members of her family over a period of twenty-two years. These letters are now deposited in the archives of Louisiana State University, included among the 10,115 items of the Weeks Family Papers, which span the years 1782–1894.

Rachel's letters, evidently treasured by their recipients, are testimony to her unusual character. In addition to making her come alive as a person, the letters re-create the times and places in which she lived and wrote.

Like most frontier settlers, Rachel knew deep sorrows in her life. She accepted these with Christian fortitude as a visitation of God. In early life she suffered the loss of both parents, three brothers and a sister, two husbands, and two sons. Such losses might have caused a weaker woman to become embittered; however, no personal loss ever destroyed her innate faith in herself and in her God.

Rachel's youthful joy later changed into a more sober contentment with her situation. She enjoyed her numerous nieces and nephews, her friends, and her slaves. She never lost her interest and excitement in the various duties of her large plantation.

Rachel was a well-educated woman for her day. Doubtless she wrote personal letters to family members and friends that are not in this collection. She was not prominent in affairs of high finance or cosmopolitan society, so only the esteem in which she was held by her brother David Weeks and his immediate family caused these letters to be preserved.

Apparently, though Rachel treasured her personal correspondence, no answers to her letters exist. Evidently they were destroyed or misplaced after her death. Although an observant person and a prolific letter writer, she seems to have kept no diary. Her letters reveal that she kept a plantation notebook, but it is not to be found among the Weeks papers. One homemade bank book of hers remains. Written on cotton rag paper and sewed together by hand, it registers her account with the Bank of St. Francisville for the years 1822-1825. Her balance on hand for March 3, 1825, the last entry, was $2210, with all debts paid.

In spite of vast property (which by today's values would represent great wealth), Rachel lived a frugal life. Though she owned seventy-seven slaves, she did manual labor as well as the mental labor required to deal with the complicated affairs of her large plantation. Her 157 letters in the Weeks collection portray a busy resourceful woman, who lived a worried but mainly satisfying life in a felicitous land at a time shortly before sectional tragedy divided a nation and people.

The Feliciana country already had a long and interesting history before Rachel Swayze Bell O'Connor lived out her existence as mistress of Evergreen Plantation. The first Europeans who travelled the Feliciana region were Spanish explorers searching for gold and the fountain of youth. Upon the heels of the Spaniards came Frenchmen who participated in a series of daring exploits in their attempt to realize their king's dream of a colonial empire encompassing the entire Mississippi Valley. At intervals during the three-quarter century of French control, Louisiana was governed by Louis XV, king of France; by Antoine Crozat, a merchant; and by John Law, a Scottish gambler with grandiose ideas for developing Louisiana through his Company of the Indies. Indian hostility, poverty, disease, and death tell the story of these early explorers and settlers. The Spanish found neither gold nor a fountain of youth there. The French king, the merchant prince, and the Scottish gambler all spent millions, yet Louisiana remained a wilderness inhabited by Indians and scattered poverty-stricken settlers.

The "river" and the "city" (the Mississippi and New Orleans) were two things that needed no further identification in early Louisiana. The Mississippi has always occupied a unique place in American history. From the date of its discovery, it became important to the Spanish explorers. France and England struggled for control of it throughout much of the colonial period. Following the purchase of Louisiana by the United States in 1803, it has remained of prime importance to the nation. This river has been called by several names. The Choctaw Indians called it *Missah Sippah*, which in their language meant "big strong river." The Algonquin Indians applied the name *Mischipi*, which meant "father of the waters." The Spanish explorers called it *Rio del Espiritu Santo* ("River of the Holy Spirit") or *Rio del Flores* ("River of Flowers"). Father Claude Jean Allouez, an early French missionary, was the first to coin the word *Mississippi*.[1] It was this river that led explorers through the heartland of North America. From this river French explorers envisioned a mighty landed empire and planned a capital city rising from its banks.

In 1718, at a crescent bend near the mouth of the Mississippi, the town of *Nouvelle Orléans* was established through the efforts of the French governor Jean Baptiste Lemoyne, Sieur de Bienville. Under Bienville's direction Adrien de Pauger, a French engineer, planned a town of eight blocks facing the river by five blocks deep. The streets were parallel to each other and were considered to be wide and spacious. A canal was dug to drain the area. (On this site is the present Canal Street, scene of the famous yearly Mardi gras parades.) A low levee held back the river. Centrally located facing the river, a church was built. The Place d'Arms occupied the space between the church and the river. Governor Bienville built his house a short distance down river from the church. A powder magazine, warehouses, and barracks were constructed. Father Pierre François deCharlevoix, a Cathloic priest who visited the city in 1721, stated, "I have the best grounded hopes for saying that this wild and deserted place, at present almost entirely covered with cane and trees, shall one day become the capital of a large and rich colony. Rome and Paris had not such considerable beginnings, were not built under such happy auspices, and their founders met not

1. Edwin Adams, Davis, *Louisiana: A Narrative History* (Baton Rouge: Claitor's Book Store, 1965), pp. 7–8.

with the advantages on the Seine and the Tiber, which we have found on the Mississippi, in comparison of which, these two rivers are no more than brooks."[2]

The priest predicted well. Set in its background of semitropical greenery, this city soon presented a fascination for its residents, settlers of the upriver villages, and foreigners arriving there. By 1721 New Orleans had 370 residents, including sevent-three black slaves and twenty-eight which indentured servants.[3] Its advantageous location for commerce provided the colony a market for produce and a source of imported goods. But men greatly outnumbered women in the city. In 1727, six Ursuline nuns arrived to supply the city's need for education. During the same year, there came a large number of *casket girls* (so called because they carried small hope chests containing necessary items for setting up housekeeping). Upon their arrival the Ursuline sisters took charge of these young women. All were soon wed, even the one who "looked more like a soldier of guard duty than a young lady."[4] A duel for her favor was prevented only by the intervention of the town authorities. Prior to the arrival of the casket girls, most of the female population of New Orleans had been prostitutes seeking clients for their profession. The casket girls as wives for the settlers lent a degree of permanence and dignity to the city. By the beginning of the Spanish colonial period, the population of New Orleans consisted of 3,190 persons, and that of the entire Louisiana colony totaled slightly over 13,500 persons.[5]

The Mississippi River, streams, lakes, and bayous, supplemented by Indian trails, were the only routes for travel in the Louisiana colony. Upriver from New Orleans about 190 miles, the Red River empties into the Mississippi from the northwest. In 1714, four years before the founding of New Orleans, Fort St. Jean Baptiste was established on the Red River by Louis Juchereau de Saint Denis, assisted by a handful of French soldiers. The timely arrival of French settlers assured the permanence of the fort and laid the foundation for Louisiana's first permanent settlement, which was called Natchitoches, and adaptation of the name of the Natchez Indians living in the vicinity. Governor Bienville contributed to the growth of the Louisiana colony by helping to establish

2. Ibid, p. 56.
3. Ibid.
4. Ibid, p. 59.
5. Ibid, p. 104.

settlements on the Quachita River, at the rapids of the Red River, and at St. Francisville in the Feliciana district.[6]

These villages were widely scattered and almost impossible to defend. The political and military situation in Europe made the colony unprofitable. Louis XV of France, determined to waste no more money on Louisiana, gave it to his cousin Charles III of Spain. The transfer of the colony from France to Spain was negotiated by a carefully guarded secret treaty made at Fontainebleau on November 3, 1762. But two years later the secret became public knowledge. French Louisianians bitterly resented the humiliating changes in laws, manners, customs, and government. Their attempted expulsion of the first Spanish governor, Don Antonio de Ulloa, led to his replacement by General Don Alexandre O'Reilly. He became known as "Bloody O'Reilly" because of his ruthless persecution of people connected with the ouster of Ulloa. He had been sent to crush the revolt; when that mission had been accomplished with deliberate and brutal efficiency, Spain recalled O'Reilly.

It was with great relief that Louisiana welcomed Don Louis de Unzaga as governor in 1772. That elderly man was gentle and understanding. His enlightened rule did much to bring about a reconciliation between French and Spanish settlers. For almost the first time, Louisianians were able to enjoy a measure of peace and progress. New settlers began to stake claims to patches of ground already cleared by the Indians. French, Spanish, and English settlers received land grants and established homes along Louisiana's rivers and bayous. These grants usually consisted of a designated number of arpents frontage upon a river or a bayou and extended a greater distance back into the cypress swamps.

Though New Orleans, near the mouth of the Mississippi River, soon became a center of commerce for France and Spain, another settlement almost a hundred miles upriver was rapidly becoming a trading post for the English. Farmers sold their produce for immense profits at the village of St. Francisville, the largest settlement in the Feliciana district. This area, called West Florida by the English, was named Feliciana by the Spanish wishing to attract settlers. The word *feliciana* is derived from the Latin *felix*, meaning "happiness." Spanish governors offered grants comprising as many as five thousand acres to military personnel. Many civilians received grants of one thousand acres provided they agreed to

6. Ibid, p. 65.

occupy and cultivate them, with additional grants of fifty acres for each child or slave.[7]

Into Feliciana came an Englishman named William Weeks. He acquired a land grant from the Spanish government in 1795, married the widow Rachel Hopkins Swayze, Rachel O'Connor's mother, and reared a family whose descendants held most of his landed estate intact until past the middle of the twentieth century. Another prominent settler was Thomas Withers Chinn, a veteran of the War of 1812, who migrated from Kentucky to Feliciana in 1816. He was of English and Scottish ancestry and had the distinction of being closely related through his grandfather to George Washington and through his grandmother to Sir Walter Scott.[8] He is remembered as having donated the land upon which Grace Episcopal Church at St. Francisville was built in 1828. Chinn was appointed a judge in West Feliciana Parish in 1824 but gave up his judicial post to become a cotton and sugarcane planter. His home, Cypress Hall, was destroyed by Union forces during the Civil War.[9] His descendants still live on property he acquired during the 1820s. General Robert Mc-Causland, a veteran of both the Revolutionary War and the War of 1812, established his home in Feliciana. Today the McCausland chapter of the United States Daughters of 1812 honors his memory. An Irish immigrant, Hercules O'Connor, sought his fortune in Feliciana. He acquired property and slaves, married the widow Rachel Swayze Bell (the writer of these letters), and took an active part in the business and farming activities of the region. Perhaps the most illustrious resident of Feliciana during its early years was John James Audubon, the famous naturalist and artist. After a trip upriver from New Orleans, he arrived at Feliciana in June of 1821 to assume his job of tutoring young Eliza Pirrie, a plantation belle, daughter of the wealthy James Pirrie family of Oakley Plantation. Audubon wrote of Feliciana: "The aspect of the Country entirely New . . . distracted My Mind. The rich Magnolia covered with its Odoriferous Blossoms, the Holly, the Beech, the Tall Yellow Poplar, the Hilly ground, even the Red Clay I Looked at with amazement. Such entire change in so Short a time appears often supernatural, and surrounded once more by thousands of Warblers and Thrushes, I enjoyed Nature."[10] These impressions prompted Audubon to refer to Feliciana as his "Happy Land."

7. Ibid, p. 110.
8. Ernest Gueymard, "Notebook," Baton Rouge *State Times*, October 12, 1981.
9. Ibid.
10. Harnett T. Kane, *Plantation Parade* (New York, William Morrow, 1945), p. 290.

The rich Feliciana area had provoked international rivalry during the colonial period. The Spanish government insisted that the area was retained whe Louisiana was retroceded to France in 1802. When the United States purchased Louisiana in 1803, it claimed the disputed area. During the fall 1810, Feliciana settlers, taking matters into their own hands, successfully revolted against Spain and, for seventy-four days, declared themselves to be an independent Republic of West Florida. The leaders of that tiny republic met at St. Francisville on November 19, 1810, elected Fulwar Skipwith as president, and asked United States President James Madison to permit their annexation to the Territory of Orleans. The area soon was taken over by the United States and designated as one county to be known as Feliciana. It was officially joined to the state of Louisiana in 1812 when Louisiana was admitted to statehood. Out of this area were carved the four parishes of Feliciana, East Baton Rouge, St. Helena, and St. Tammany. (Louisiana, after statehood, returned to its earlier system of political divisions called parishes, which corresponded to counties in other states.) Feliciana was later divided into the two parishes of East Feliciana and West Feliciana. Residents of the area were pleased with their boldness and took pride in their settlement. The St. Francisville *Journal* of June 9, 1825, stated that the area was more conducive to permanent settlement than any other section of the republic.

Settlement of Louisiana had increased during the late years of the Spanish colonial period. Spanish governors instituted the empresario system by which recipients pledged themselves to settle families upon land granted to them. The Baron de Bastrop, a German nobleman, received twelve square leagues of land on the Ouachita River in the northeast corner of Louisiana. The revolution in France with its Reign of Terror forced many of the French aristocracy to emigrate to Louisiana. The Marquis de Maison Rouge received a grant of thirty thousand acres south of Bastrop's grant.[11]

One of the most thickly settled areas of the colony was the Attakapa district in southwest Louisiana, so called for the Indians living there. Spaniards from Malaga, Islenos from the Canary Islands, and Acadians expelled from Canada made their homes there. Some settled on the Attakapa prairie and became small farmers and herdsmen. Others settled along the bayous and streams and became fishermen and trappers. In 1779, many of them settled along Bayou Teche and the old Spanish

11. William Scroggs, *The Story of Louisiana* (Bobbs-Merrill, 1935), p. 141.

trail leading from Florida to Texas. Depending upon their nationality, they called their main village either *New Town* or *Nova Iberia* ("New Spain"). This settlement became the present town of New Iberia. (On April 6–8, 1979, ceremonies were held in both New Iberia and Fuengirola to celebrate the bicentennial of the founding of New Iberia. It was from Fuengirola, in the province of Malaga, Spain, that a number of settlers had come to New Iberia in the spring of 1779.)[12]

Americans were also attracted to the rich soil of Attakapa and hastened to apply for land grants. William Weeks acquired two large grants there, one for 800 arpents and another for 2,080 arpents. John Palfrey obtained land along the Gulf of Mexico and called his plantation "Forlorn Hope," but his decendants were to become wealthy planters. (Today the town of Franklin, Louisiana, stands on the site. John's descendants live in Palfrey House, a Greek revival mansion located on the main street of the town.) Such improvements in fortune were then possible in the region.

The Conrads were known in early Louisiana for the size of their family and for their several plantations. Frederick Conrad and his wife Frances Thurston Conrad migrated from Viriginia to Louisiana during the early years of statehood. Their sons became lawyers and planters and their daughters married rich husbands. Alfred Conrad practiced law at New Orleans and late in life became an Attakapa sugar planter. Frederick Conrad was the master of The Cottage Plantation on the Mississippi River a few miles south of the village of Baton Rouge. Charles Magill Conrad practiced law, travelled widely, and became secretary of war in President Millard Fillmore's cabinet. The Conrad daughters were famous for their beauty and charm. Elizabeth married a Mr. Harding, Ann married Dr. John Towles, Sidney married John T. Palfrey, and Mary Clara married David Weeks. Intermarriage of Americans with persons of French or Spanish descent was frowned upon at that time. There were only a few English-speaking families living in Attakapa and several marriages took place among the Weeks, Palfrey, Conrad, and Towles families.

The Spanish had encouraged other nations to settle in Louisiana. Americans from the eastern seaboard needed no inducement. For almost three centuries, the Spanish, French, and English had contended for control of Louisiana, but it was the infant American nation that was to win the struggle. The land drew Americans like a magnet to the

12. *Louisiana Historical Association Newsletter* No. 2 (March 1979).

lower Mississippi valley. The overflowing of the rivers deposited an abundance of silt with soil-enriching properties. The mild winters, the long growing seasons, the abudance of rainfall, and the semitropical climate were conducive to the cultivation of cotton, sugarcane, corn, rice, perique tobacco, rye, oats, and garden vegetables. The soil of the Atlantic seaboard was being depleted through successive crops of indigo and tobacco. Settlers from that area began to drift west and south, bringing their slaves and chattels.

Two events during the late years of the Spanish colonial period revolutionized Louisiana agriculture. These were the invention of the cotton gin and the discovery of a process for granulating sugar. In 1793 Eli Whitney, while living on a Georgia plantation, invented his saw gin, which "set loose the powers of agriculture which was before enchained."[13] Three years later Etienne de Bore, a planter living near New Orleans, succeeded in perfecting sugar granulation.

A phenomenal increase in Louisiana's population came with the cotton gin and sugar granulation. In 1810 the population of the Louisiana territory was 20,845 persons, of whom 3,011 were slaves. By 1820 the population of the state of Louisiana had reached 153,407 persons, of whom 69,046 were slaves; and New Orleans alone had a population of 27,176 persons. The United States census for 1830 revealed 215,739 persons living in Louisiana. The figure increased to 352,411 by the year 1940.

The 1830s and 1840s were characterized by a rapid expansion of the plantation system. Immediately after the cotton gin was invented immense profits from cotton production were made by planters of the Feliciana region, the Red River valley, and the delta parishes along the Mississippi River. Raw cotton exported from Louisiana amounted to five million pounds in 1810, thirty million in 1820, 120 million in 1830, and 164 million in 1834. The price of raw cotton rose from fourteen cents per pound in 1790 to twenty-eight cents in 1800. In the year 1810, the price of cotton dropped to sixteen cents per pound. For the decade 1815–1825 the average price per pound was twenty-one cents. Sales at sixteen cents per pound in 1835 were indicative of the coming panic of 1837. Following that panic, prices remained depressed, but acreage continued to expand. By the year 1840, the parish of Feliciana had

13. Tench Coxe, "A Table (unpaged) of References to Some of the Subject and Matters in this volume." The above quotation included under heading "cotton." Whitney's saw gin is discussed, pp. IX, XXIV. *A Statement of the Arts and Manufacturers of the United States for the Year 1810* (Philadelphia: A. Cornman, 1814).

become one of the chief cotton-producing areas of the state. Of a total parish population of 12,982 persons at that time, 5,802 were engaged in agriculture and made use of the labor of 7,164 slaves.

Immediately after Étienne de Bore had perfected the process for sugar granulation, the sugar country expended widely upriver toward the Baton Rouge settlement, westward into the Attakapa prairie, and south along the Gulf of Mexico. French and Spanish governors had given grants in the Attakapa and neighboring areas on condition that the land be settled within three years. Planters cultivated sugar cane along the rivers and streams for quick profits but often postponed the clearing of the cypress swamps to the rear of their grants. Squatters had entered and had claimed the wooded areas to such an extent that the original grantees petitioned congress in 1805 to confirm their claims to the swamplands. The petitioners stated their belief in the importance of sugar culture to the prosperity and independence of the United States and the fact that its culture was confined exclusively to south Louisiana. Therefore they felt that valid titles to the cypress swamps were necessary for the expansion of the sugar country as well as for the timber for homes and fuel.[14]

Sugar production flourished during the early decades of the nineteenth century. As early as 1802, Louisiana exported nearly 2,500,000 pounds of sugar.[15] In 1810 the value of refined sugar produced in the United States amounted to $1,415,724,[16] most of which was produced in Louisiana. By 1833 production had reached 75,000 hogsheads in Louisiana and it increased fourfold during the 1830s nad 1840s.[17] Both domestic and foreign markets vied for Louisiana sugar. The Attakapa region developed rapidly as a leading sugar-producing area. The population of that region reached 12,063 by 1820, of whom 1643 were engaged in agriculture and utilized the labor of 5707 slaves.

Great landholdings, large numbers of slaves, and unlimited capital were needed to operate Louisiana's plantation system, and adequate supplies of all of these appeared forthcoming. Greek revival mansions rose along the banks of the Mississippi River all the way from New Orleans to Natchez. These homes were located five to ten miles apart depending on the sizes of the grants received by the planters. Perhaps

14. U. S., Congress, *American State Papers*, Public Lands, vol 1., 9th Cong., 1st sess., 1805, Document 113.
15. Davis, *Louisiana A Narrative History*, p. 136.
16. Coxe, "Tabular Statements of the Several Branches of American Manufacturers by States, Territories, and Districts, 1810." *A Statement*, p. 37.
17. Davis, *Louisiana*, p. 204.

not coincidently the distances between plantation mansion houses roughly paralleled the distances between the manor houses of England. And like the manorial system, the southern plantation system exhibited a certain measure of economic self-sufficiency. Within a generation life in the grand manner (symbolized by magnolias, moonlight, and mint juleps) came into being among the wealthy planters of Louisiana. Cotton was king and sugar was white gold.

Of the three components enabling people to live in the grand manner in antebellum Louisiana, land, slaves, and capital, only land was easily acquired. But not all settlers were big land owners and land prices rose rapidly after statehood. Landholdings ranged in size from small farms of a few acres to large plantations consisting of thousands of acres. The single family farm unit greatly outnumbered the large plantation throughout the antebellum period and nonslaveholders greatly outnumbered those who owned slaves. Eleven percent of Louisiana's slaveholders owned less than fifty acres of land; however, thirty percent of the slaveholding planters owned between one thousand and five thousand acres of land.[18]

The southern plantation system was based upon slave labor. Many Negro slaves had been imported into Louisiana during the colonial period. The slave population increased very rapidly in the beginning of the nineteenth century because of the demand for labor to work the cotton and cane fields. New Orleans became the slave trading center of the South and slave auctions were held on specified days in the rotundas of the St. Louis and St. Charles hotels. Prices varied with the age and condition of slaves. Prime field hands and skilled slave artisans sold for between $1000 and $1500. Female slaves could be purchased for from six to eight hundred dollars, and children brought from three to five hundred dollars depending upon age and health. The number of slaves owned by an individual planter varied with the amount of land he owned and the accessibility of capital. The late Walter Prichard, an authority on Louisiana's plantation system, stated that of the slaveholders in antebellum Louisiana, by far the greatest number owned between five and ten slaves. Their slaves, Prichard added, usually consisted of one slave family: a man, his wife, and three to eight children, and altruistic planters tried to keep slave families together by buying entire families or selling them as a family group. It was the ambition of many small farmers and small slaveholders to pass into the planter class and to adopt

18. Ibid, p. 204.

their style of living. Occasionally they succeeded. Rachel O'Connor herself acquired many slaves but preferred to retain her simple life-style.

The overseer system was a necessary accompaniment to slave labor throughout the plantation country. Wages of overseers varied with the size of the plantation and the number of slaves. Small planters with few slaves paid overseers as little as four hundred dollars per year. More affluent planters paid from five to seven hundred dollars annually. In addition to money wages, planters furnished housing and rations to overseers, their families, and slaves, if any. (It was fairly common for overseers to own female slaves as house servants.) Planters also provided stable and food for the overseer's riding horse if he owned one. The overseer class ranked beneath the planter class in antebellum society. The character of an overseer depended upon the individual. Some were good and some were bad, and Rachel O'Connor experienced both kinds. The general tendency of an overseer was to get as much work as possible out of the slaves under his supervision. Sometimes slaves were forced to work extremely hard and some overseers were cruel taskmasters, but this situation was not very common and certainly was not the case on Rachel O'Connor's plantation. Her slaves were her treasured property, which she believed were bestowed on her by the grace of God. Because of her affection for them, they were treated with kindness and generosity.

Rachel's concern for the health of her slaves is an outstanding feature of her letters. Knowledge of medical science was limited in the early nineteenth century, and medicine was scarce and hard to get. The death toll was great in Louisiana. The excessive humidity and moist swamp-lands caused prolific breeding of mosquitoes. One early French priest related that Louisiana's mosquitoes had caused more swearing since the founding of the colony than the world had ever heard before that time. Yellow fever, transmitted by mosquito bite, had appeared in Louisiana during the colonial period and had reached epidemic proportions by 1779. Almost yearly epidemics ravaged the city of New Orleans and spread upriver throughout the plantation region. A particularly serious epidemic occurred in 1810. Another outbreak took place in 1833. The most serious epidemic in the history of Louisiana occurred in 1853 when estimated 12,000 persons died.[19] The disease abated only after sanitation was improved and mesures were taken to control mosquitoes.

One of Rachel's continual troubles was the threat of cholera among her slaves. That very contagious disease reached epidemic stage in

19. Ibid, p. 235.

Louisiana in 1832 and resulted in thousands of deaths during the next decade. Cures and treatment of cholera were primitive. But Rachel's constant attention to sanitation, diet, and nursing resulted in fewer cholera deaths at Evergreen than on neighboring plantations. A medical doctor in residence at Evergreen also contributed to the saving of Rachel's slaves. Devastating epidemics among slaves slowed antebellum plantation operation, but as the supply of slaves was always adequate, plantation profits continued.

Although agriculture was the most important economic undertaking in antebellum Louisiana, manufacturing was becoming important as early as 1810. In that year the Louisiana territory boasted of seven tanneries, twelve shoemakers, fourteen hatteries, three saddlers' shops, two soap and candle makers, and twenty-eight distilleries. There also were thirty-three blacksmith shops, four gunsmiths, and three wagan makers. Most of these activities were located in New Orleans. Louisiana households in 1810 had 1,777 spinning wheels and 601 looms. The value of manufactured goods in the Louisiana territory that year has been estimated at $2000,000.[20]

By the time Louisiana was admitted to statehood, New Orleans had become the manufacturing and commercial center for the entire South. Cotton and sugarcane had become Louisiana's money crops. Cotton and sugar factors and other commission merchants engaged in business ventures advantageous to themselves as well as to the planters. Planters relied heavily on New Orleans banks to finance their loans for the purchase of land and slaves, and for the fire carriages, clothes, furniture, and other expensive items that characterized their life-style. The banks were sound, agriculture was flourishing, and industries were becoming profitable. Agriculture, manufacturing, and commerce reached a peak of prosperity in Louisiana during the 1820s and early 1830s.

The birth of Rachel O'Connor antedated this prosperous period by more than a generation. She was a child of the frontier who lived to see great changes. On March 13, 1774 (two years before the thirteen colonies on the Atlantic coast declared their independence and became the United States), she was born to Rachel Hopkins Swayze and her husband, Stephen Swayze. She was named after her mother. At the time of her birth, Rachel's parents lived in the Attakapa country near Bayou Teche. She had an older brother named William Swayze. Her father

20. Coxe, "Tabular Statements of the Several Branches of American Manufacturers by States, Territories, and Districts, 1810." *A Statement*, p. 38.

died when she was a very young child, and when she was four years old, her widowed mother married William Weeks, an Englishman who had migrated to Louisiana and became a sugar planter in the Teche country. In 1778, the Weeks family left Attakapa and came to live in the Feliciana district. William Weeks acquired a grant in Feliciana from the Spanish government, bought slaves, and established a home there for his wife, her two children (Rachel and William Swayze) and their three children (Pamela, Caleb, and David Weeks).

All evidence indicates that William Weeks loved dearly and provided as well for his two stepchildren as for his own three. When grown, Rachel and William Swayze acquired property in Feliciana, married, and reared families there. William Swayze first married Melissa Smith and they became the parents of Julia Ann; Charlotte; Clarissa; and William, Junior. By his second wife, Maria Jefferson, William had two children, Stephen Courtland and Love. (Love later became the wife of Charles Hoffman.) At the time of William Swayze's death in 1820, all his children were minors. His property was divided among the several children of his two marriages. His oldest daugher, Julia Ann, was married to James Scott. They lived at the Rapide settlement on Red River and made periodic visits to Feliciana to administer Julia Ann's property. The property belonging to the younger heirs of William's first marriage was administered for them by their aunt Rachel O'Connor with whom they made their home. Rachel Swayze, twice married and twice widowed in early adulthood, later became the mistress of Evergreen Plantation and the writer of these letters.

The three children born to William Weeks and Rachel Swayze Weeks became influential in Feliciana and figured prominently in Rachel's letters. Rachel's half sister, Pamela Weeks, married Henry Flower. Five sons and three daughters were born of that union. The oldest son, James, studied law in New Orleans and practiced his profession in St. Francisville. William, the second son, attended the newly established (1826) College of Louisiana at Jackson, Louisiana. Even as a child, little Louisa Flower was sent to a boarding school at Jackson conducted by a Miss Anders. Pamela and Henry Flower hired a tutor to teach young Sidney and David at home until they were also old enough to enter the College of Louisiana. Two of the Flower daughters, Maria and Louisa, married men named Collins. The second daughter Harriet, to the displeasure of several relatives, married a Mr. Handy, farm and storekeeper in the St. Francisville area. Stephen Flower died in early childhood.

Caleb Weeks, the second child of the Weeks-Swayze union, married and fathered two children, William David and Anne. Little is known about Caleb Weeks except that at his death about 1798, he left a landed estate to his children.

Of the three children of William and Rachel Swayze Weeks, it was their youngest son, David Weeks, who was to acquire the most property, to make the most money, and to own the most slaves. On the last day of December in 1818, he married Mary Clara Conrad. Eight children were born of that union, two of whom died in infancy. It was David who created a landed empire in the south Louisiana bayou country. His lands were obtained by inheritance and by purchase. His holdings included Parc Perdu, Rickahoe, Cypermort, Town Farm, Grand Cote Island and Weeks Island. He grew sugarcane, manufactured sugar, owned his own vessel, and transported his sugar to markets in New Orleans and along the eastern coast. It was he whom Rachel addressed in her letters as "my best of brothers".

Although William Weeks, the patriarch of that family, remained in Feliciana until his death in 1819, he maintained the land grants in Attakapa, which he had received from the Spanish government. These consisted of 800 arpents in the vicinity of Bayou Teche and 2,080 arpents further south at Grand Cote Island. His largest tract was located along Louisiana's coast and came to be known as Weeks Island. While William Weeks was living at Feliciana, sugarcane was cultivated on his Attakapa properties by overseers and slaves. Weeks Island and Grand Cote Island are not islands in the true sense. They are raised hilllike areas rising above the surrounding flat marshlands. The immediate lands sloping away from these raised areas contain fresh lakes and very rich soil. Indians of the area told tales of castrophic events that caused these "islands" to emerge. The topography of the area is unique to Louisiana's coastal lands. Even today whenever storms drive the tide inland, deer, snakes, birds, and numerous species of crawling animals rush from their swamp habitat to these elevated spots and huddle together until the water recedes.

Many aspects of the life of Rachel O'Connor remain a mystery. There is no extant record of her childhood or her formal education. However, the 157 letters she wrote to her relatives tell much of her life story. Rachel was an intelligent, hardworking, deeply religious woman. She was an interested participant in the life around her, and she was educated enought to put her thoughts into intelligent correspondence. In her time letter writing was the primary means of communication, and her letters reveal an interesting period of Louisiana's past. She described the busy life of a plantation mistress when the grand manner life-style was emerging. While in her early teens, Rachel married Richard Bell, who had received a Spanish land grant in Attakapa. In 1790 a son was born to Rachel and Richard Bell and was christened Stephen in memory of her father, Stephen Swayze. Richard died in 1792 leaving eighteen-year-old Rachel a widow with an infant son. For five years Rachel and her child lived with her stepfather William Weeks and her younger half sister and her two half brothers. Rachel's mother had died about 1790, but Rachel and her baby were welcomed by William, and she soon assumed the role of a mother to his young family. The closely knit family structure so apparent in Rachel's letters was cemented during those early years. Rachel developed a particularly deep and abiding affection for her youngest half brother, David Weeks, which was to last throughout their lives.

After five years of widowhood, Rachel Swayze Bell, aged twenty-three, married Hercules O'Connor, lately arrived from Ireland. The wedding took place in the spring of 1797. In 1798 Rachel was granted in her own name 276 arpents of land in Feliciana by the Spanish governor, Manuel Gayoso.[21] On this land the newlyweds built a log cabin and set up housekeeping. A letter from James Corrie, a friend from Hercules' native Ireland, dated May 22, 1797, congratulates "Friend O'Connor" on his marriage, inquires whether or not there were any more pretty widows in Feliciana, and seeks advice on the possibility of securing for himself a tract of land there. Rachel's land and that which she and Hercules acquired was located in what later became West Feliciana Parish. It was adjacent to Oakley Plantation, where Audubon painted many of his famous bird pictures. Rachel and Hercules purchased more land. Eventually their holdings amounted to more than a thousand acres. They purchased slaves, cultivated cotton, and shipped it to New Orleans markets. The crop at Evergreen Plantation averaged 120 bales per year. In 1807 a son was born to Rachel and Hercules and was given the name *James*. As their fortunes prospered, Rachel and Hercules built a dwelling, set up a cotton gin, and built a loom house. An indication of his parents' prosperity is the fact that James O'Connor as a young boy possessed in his own name six lots in the town of St.

21. U. S., Works Progress Administration of Louisiana, Survey of Federal Archives in Louisiana, *Greenburg Land Claims*, U. S. Land Office, Baton Rouge, La., bk. 1, pt. 2, pp. 403–407.

Francisville and more than two hundred acres of farm land. The O'Connor's comfortable home was built of cypress lumber in the frontier style of the day. A porch extended across the front and several fireplaces provided heat for warmth and for cooking. This cypress residence antedated by a generation the Greek revival styles of plantation architecture. Along the Mississippi the classic southern mansion with its stately white columns became commonplace only after the immense wealth from cotton and sugarcane crops made possible the employment of professional architects. As the numbers of slaves increased at Evergreen Plantation, slave quarters were laid out and cabins were built. Eventually an overseer's house was built.

Like many frontier settlers of his time, Hercules overindulged in corn whiskey. This addiction led to his death in 1820. Audubon, his neighbor, was called to his deathbed; but Hercules had already died before Audubon arrived. He remained all night with the corpse. Audubon stated that Hercules had literally drunk himself to death.[22]

Unfortunately the son James also became an habitual drinker. His mother suffered great trauma in her efforts to cope with his problem. Finally, because of his addiction, she was compelled to bar him from any control of his property.[23] Jame's drunkenness was general knowledge. Letters between relatives reveal concern for the recently widowed Rachel as she tries to keep her son "steady and sober." However, old John Barleycorn had a fatal grip on young James. He died on July 30, 1822, at the age of fifteen years.

A strong affection had early developed between Stephen Bell, Rachel's older son, and her youngest half brother, David Weeks, who were only four years apart. Their friendship flourished since both were reared in William Weeks's home during their early years. In 1814, when his Spanish grant was confirmed by the United States government, William Weeks deeded to his son David the 2,080 arpents of land at Grant Cote Island that he had received from the Spanish government. While still young David Weeks and Stephen Bell went to live on Grand Cote Island with high hopes of making fortunes by raising sugarcane. Rachel provided Stephen with two slaves and money for the venture. But young Stephen was unsuited tempermentally for life there. He had been courting a girl and considering marriage, but his Grand Cote residence precluded

---

22. Avery O. Craven, *Rachel of Old Louisiana* (Baton Rouge: Louisiana State University Press, 1975), p. 14.
23. Ibid.

both those plesant projects. He hated the heat and humidity and longed for more social life. Surrounded by wide expanses of marsh land, squawking water birds, croaking frogs, and buzzing mosquitoes, Stephen decided to leave Grand Cote Island. He sold his interest in the venture to David Weeks. He took his mother's two slaves back to Evergreen Plantation. He then went to New Orleans and undertook to establish a mercantile firm. After a brief stay at New Orleans, he returned to Feliciana and opened a general store at St. Francisville. The conveyance records at the West Feliciana Parish courthouse for the year 1820 reveal that Rachel owned three lots in the town and (since Stephen had no appreciable resources) it may be assumed that his store was located on his mother's town lots. But he was as unskilled at storekeeping as he was at raising sugarcane. He very soon was deeply indebted to his suppliers. It appeared he was born to fail. He died in 1821, young and debt ridden.

The most obnoxious claim against Stephen's estate was held by a New Orleans merchant, William Flower. It amounted to several thousand dollars. Alone and struggling to manage her plantation and provide for her slaves, forty-seven-year-old Rachel was faced with a law suit by Flower for payment of her deceased son's debt. This claim was particularly embarassing because William Flower's brother Henry Flower was married to Rachel's half sister, Pamela Weeks. In addition to Rachel's other cares, she suffered the loss by death of her husband Hercules O'Connor, in 1820, her older son, Stephen Bell, in 1821, and her younger son, James O'Connor, in 1822. She was almost overwhelmed by her bereavement, her debts, and harassment from the Flower law suit. Meanwhile Rachel's brother David Weeks had become wealthy from his Attakapa sugar plantation. To relieve Rachel of her cares, this sympathetic brother arranged for her to sell her plantation and slaves to him with the understanding that she remain there and manage the plantation and slaves as long as she lived. On March 16, 1830, Rachel deeded the bulk of her land to him for which she received a promissory note for $14,175. One week later, on March 23, 1830, she deeded nineteen slaves to him for which she received a promissory note for $9,500. Rachel held these notes and he assumed payment of her debts. Following David's death in 1834, the notes were given to Mary Weeks for the Week's heirs. Rachel's original deeds are among the records in the courthouse of West Feliciana Parish. The provisions that Rachel should manage Evergreen plantation and slaves during her lifetime and that she and her slaves should receive an adequate livelihood from the proceeds of the plantation are clearly stated in the original documents.

David's purchases did somewhat relieve Rachel's financial worries. But because she retained some property and some slaves in her own name, Rachel was plagued by William Flower's threats and accusations that her sales were tricks to deceive him and that titles to her property actually remained in her own hands. David asserted his ownership of the property and his intention of defending it. Eventually the threats and accusations ended. But by David's assumption of her son's debts, she obligated herself to spend the rest of her life managing a plantation and slaves legally owned by her brother and his family.

The 157 letters transcribed here constitute a significant part of the Weeks family papers. This collection consists of more than ten thousand items, which cover a period of 112 years. The collection is made up of land deeds, slave sales, copies of land surveys, promissory notes, invoices, steamboat and mercantile accounts, plantation inventories, wills, and family letters. In this work all persons, dates, places and events mentioned in the introduction, annotations, and afterword (unless otherwise indicated) are found in the Weeks family papers, the records contained in the West Feliciana Parish courthouse, and the United States census records.

On reading her letters, one wonders how Rachel received her schooling. It was far in advance of most persons of her day. Her penmanship is clear and legible. In editing the letters for modern readers, spelling and capitalization has been modernized. Punctuation has been modernized in places. The letters were written on very durable paper. Each was carefully folded to form and envelop and sealed with a dab of wax. The name and address of the recipient was written on the outside of the sealed letter. Often the means by which it was to be sent was also written on the outside. Many letters were hand carried, in which case the name of the bearer appeared in lower left corner of the face of the letter. Letters sent by steamboat sometimes included the name of the captain who was charged with delivering them.

Rachel's letters lay undisturbed in a trunk in the attic of the Weeks residence for approximately one hundred years until the middle of the twentieth century. The letters and other family papers reveal unusually affectionate family ties among the Weeks, Conrad, Towles, and Palfrey families, all of whom Rachel loved dearly. The letters show Rachel's abiding love for her family, friends, and slaves. They bring out the closeness of slave family ties and the sincere affection existing between the slaves and their mistresses. The feelings Rachel expressed in her letters indicate no sense of guilt for the inst…tition of slavery. She felt a maternal duty to care for her slaves. Though she was legally the absoulte owner of many, in actual practice her slaves owned her as much as she owned them.

Rachel's letters reveal her strength—physical, spiritual, moral, and creative. Such correspondence forms not only an account of an individual life, but also a firsthand historical record, for a period of twenty-two years, not influenced by retrospective thinking. In an age during which women had no "causes" to promote, and those of Rachel's social standing usually lived a life of ease in the grand manner characteristic of the antebellum South, Rachel O'Connor faced and overcame such obstacles as epidemics, lawsuits, hazards of travel, inclement weather, arrogance of overseers, and threatened slave uprisings. Surrounded by a thousand acres of land and seventy-seven slaves, she could have enjoyed the same life-style as her rich neighbors, but rather she chose to spend her life in fulfilling what she considered to be her duty to others. Among the dominant forces of her life were her Christian faith, her love for David and his family, and her unselfish concern for the welfare of her slaves. Detailed and unique expression, Rachel's letters provide an immediate and vivid insight into antebellum plantation life in Louisiana.

LETTERS

Doubtless, Rachel wrote earlier letters to relatives, but this one to David Weeks is the earliest known one in the collection.

Yellow fever rages throughout the Felicianas and the attending physician for one of John Swift's store clerks has made the mistake of performing an unauthorized autopsy.

br
West Parish, Feliciana, Nov--16, 1823

My dear brother,

I am alone, and the night's too long to venture to bed early knowing it is but seldom that I can sleep so long, and to be awake the latter part of the night causes me to feel unwell the day following. My mind has taken a ramble and has settled itself in the midst of your family where I heartily wish the rest of me could accompany it for a few days until it would be necessary to return home again. I have had a slight attack of rheumatism of late which is in my back where it occasions some pain in walking about, but with all, it is so favorable to what it has been in times past that I conclude it ungenerous, even, to complain.

My neighbor, Mrs. Pirrie, has been dangerously ill, not expected to recover. This evening word has come that she is better. I do not know her disease. She was on her way home from her Bayou Tunica Plantation and had to stop at Captain Mullford's where she is yet confined to her bed. Her children are all with her.

In my last I mentioned that Mr. Swift had been absent for some days. He had gone to get some land surveyed near Baton Rouge. During his absence his clerk took the yellow fever and died, whose death he lamented extremely. Dr. Barton attended this young man

3

during his illness, and after his death, he unfortunately took the liberty of opening him, *both body and head*, and took out his *stomach* which he carried home, and left the bed (with all belonging to it) besmeared with blood. How it may end, Heaven only knows. Mr. Swift's anger appears to be without bounds. He is determined to sue the Dr. and give him all the trouble in his power, and Mr. McVey, equally as full of revenge as Mr. Swift—both against the Dr. They were both here together and very friendly with each other, which appears to have been the case since their last settlement took place, and I am truly glad of it.

The yellow fever has carried off a great many for so small a place as St. Francis Ville, but they were chiefly strangers to me. A Mrs. Marks died on the 13 instant, since which I have not heard of any new cases. Mr. James Doyle, Dr. Slaughter, one of Mr. Handy's clerks, and the young man at Mr. Swift's is all that I knew anything about. Dr. Edward Chew caught it in town and died at home near Mrs. Percy's. I am very thankful the steamboats cannot get near you at this season of the year to spread yellow fever. It was them that brought it here.

Mr. Swift had some conversation with lawyer Watts relative to the suit in N. Orleans, which, if Mr. S—— judges right, the lawyer has very little hopes of gaining it for his employers. But don't mention it. Perhaps they may come out best yet.

Mr. McVey stayed several days with me last week, as he did not like to go to town. He is in fine spirits and talks strong of becoming a sugar planter. I have seventy bales of cotton pressed and hauling them as fast as possible to the river to ship for N. Orleans.

I answered my dear little niece's last letter on Saturday, which I am afraid she cannot read easily. It rained and they were pressing cotton and I had to stop very often to get whatever they wanted, which put me a little out of sorts and caused me not to write as large and plain as I had ought to have done. But she must not let it discourage her. I will try to do better hereafter. If she could only know how well I love her letters, she would write one every month at least.

Little Dr. Huff called here a few days ago, who lives in Washington, near Natchez, and says he is acquainted with Mrs. Dangerfield and her daughter and that they were both in good health.

My best respects to Mrs. Conrad, Mrs. Palfrey, Mrs. Harding, and their husbands, and my friend Mr. Alfred likewise, and all other friends. I have nearly lost hopes of ever receiving a letter from my sister, but this is loaded with love to her and yourself and the little children.

> I remain your affectionate sister,
> *R. O'Connor*

Rachel's extraordinary knowledge of horticulture aids her materially in her role as a planter. In this letter she advises her sister-in-law, Mary Weeks, on planting of leeks.

> Wednesday night, 15th June, 1824

My dear sister,

Agreeable to your request in your letter to Charlotte, I send you a recipe for planting leeks. The best way that I ever discovered is to take the roots out of the ground whenever the tops get ripe and plant them immediately again. Have your ground spaded up pretty deep and lay of your trenches about 11 or 12 inches apart, and dig them as deep as you conveniently can, and drop the roots about two inches apart in the trenches and cover them up. They will not come up before the last of August or the first of September, unless the weather sets in very wet, but you can have cucumber or watermellon seed in the same ground, or beans, or anything you choose, planted at the same time you do the leeks, only be careful not to let them hoe too deep, or they will disturb the leek roots before they sprout. Anything you plant will be done bearing before the leeks will be above the ground. After they get 4 or 5 inches in height, hill them occasionally as they grow high. All that is under the ground will be white and fit for use.

My dear sister, I can think of many things that I should be glad to write, but it is late and you say you intend writing to me by the next mail, which I will answer immediately. I received one from my brother this day, dated 11th of June, and I will answer it the next mail. Kiss little Frances at least a hundred times for me and remember me to my brother and the rest of your family.

> I remain your affectionate sister,
> *Rachel O'Connor*

The deluge of autumn rain has taken its toll on Rachel's cotton crop. The women and children are finishing the picking while the male slaves clear new ground. Rachel relates a conversation with William Flower while visiting her relatives, Pamela and Henry Flower.

Thursday, 14th October, 1824

My dear brother,

I received your letter of the 1st instant on the 12th. I don't know the cause of its being so long on the way, but indeed I can assure you it was very welcome, for I have been greatly distressed from the time I expected you to arrive until your letter relieved me. Sometimes I was afraid some misfortune had happened to you crossing the lake, and at other times I though probably you were all very sick and not able to write. But I'm truly thankful that times are no worse with you, your ague and fever did not continue long, and I hope your cold and cough is entirely well before this. And I am now glad that you did not come at the time you appointed, for you would have been gone by this time, and my hopes are raised anew with the hope of seeing you in December, if we should live unitl that time.

I have been very unwell 9 or 10 days with a cold and cough and some fever, but I begin to feel much better yesterday and today and I expect to be quite well again. From the way H. Flower wrote to me at the time his son James was so sick, I concluded they did not expect him to live until the next morning, and I started from home at dark and went up there in the night and found poor James as I expected, nearly gone, and his parents in great distress and without much hopes of his recovering again. But at length his disease took a favorable turn and he is now getting well. Dr. Duer said he was out of danger 5 or 6 days ago. But after I returned home, I had the worst cold I ever had. But still I am very glad I went when I did, for I think it was some comfort to his poor mother. She has not as much fortitude as we all think she has in such severe trials, which I discovered when she lost her little Stephen.

Since I have been so poorly, I have hired an overseer at 25 dollars pr. month for two months, if he behaves well, not otherwise. He was overseer for me one month about three years ago and behaved well. His name is Dickson. He has oversed one year since that for Luther Smith and two for Judge Rhea. He offers to stay next year for four hundred and fifty dollars, but that I shall leave to your better judgment when you come.

I am sorry to tell you that those late rains has nearly rotted all the cotton bolls. I have done boasting of my great crop of cotton. I am afraid I shall not have more than I had last year. I have seventy-five thousand weight on my book, and but very little more to pick. But I am not the only one that is served so. It is a general complaint over our settlement. I have set a part of the men to clear ground and shall set the rest of them as soon as I can get their axes fixed for them and let the women and children finish the cotton. I have only seventeen bales pressed. The press broke and I had to get it repaired, and since that time, the merchants said the gin cut the cotton so that it would not sell for half price, and I had to stop ginning to get some alterations made on the gin. But I have got it started at last. They say the cotton is much improved since the last work. Mr. Milladon wrote me last winter that Grover's work done more harm than good to the gin, and sent me some of the cotton and requested me to get some person that was a judge to examine it.

I have my two yoke of young oxen at work and they do very well. I have received four letters from my friend Swift since he has been in New York, and in every one of them he desires to be remembered to you. The last one was dated the 14th of Sep-tr and, at the time, he expected to start home by land in a few days. He said he hoped to get here in time to see you before you returned home. He said he had quite recovered his health and had begun to feel as well as ever again. Poor fellow, I begin to wish him at home very much. Mr. McVey has been extremely kind to me, but still I cannot take the same liberty in asking favors of him as I can with Swift. He has sent a great many goods to McVey that has arrived, and more on the way. He shipped some for N. Orleans the 12th of Sept-br which has not come yet. They have a full store now and so has Messrs. Collins and Cash, and Mr. Hull and his partner likewise.

Julia Ann and Clarissa went from here this morning quite well. The rain detained them ever since Sunday. Charlotte went from here on Monday week. They have to stay a great part of their time up there on account of their Negroes being so sickly and Lastley's cruelty together.

I wrote you on the 4th of this month and enclosed a copy of a letter that I received from H. Crawford, which I hope you have received before this. He says he must have a settlement, and payment

7

likewise. If you have not received my letter of the 4th instant, please to let me know and I will send you another copy of H. Crawford's letter to me.

Give my love to my dear sister. I hope she enjoys good health. I wish I could see her and her sweet little daughter. I am sorry Miss Elizabeth keeps so poorly. I think you had better bring her over with you. Perhaps the sight of some of these Bayou Sara beaux will cure her, and kill them, for when the get in *love*, they can't get over it until they take a trip to New York for their health. Maria Collins has a fine babe, but she says it is very cross. Pamela's youngest daughter is a fine child, but can't say one word yet.

I had the honor of seeing Wm. Flower, Esq. at Harry's. He appeared very friendly and said that he had heard that I was going to out crop them all. I told him I have been trying; he then gave his whiskers a pull and laughed heartily. How glad I should be if I could get clear of that man. I am always afraid to go to Harry's for fear of seeing him or Dave. I wish they were living in Orleans again, but they never say anything to me about money.

My dear brother, you say you wish I could see little Frances. You can't wish it more than I do. I think of her so often that I fancy I should know her, if I could see her, but I still live on hope.

I remain your affectionate sister,
Rachel O'Connor

Give my love to William Swayze. I wrote him some time ago, but he has not answered it yet.

Accounts of marriages, births, and children predominate in this letter to Rachel's sister-in-law Mary Weeks. She laments the unmarried state of her nieces, whose properties she manages.

July 11th, 1825

My dear sister,

After so long a silence, it will be a little awkward in the commencement, to renew correspondence, but I hope after you receive this, that you will feel yourself so much in my debt, that you will immediately answer it and tell me about that lovely little daughter and son of yours, who they look like, and repeat some of my dear little Frances' stories, and send me a small lock of each of their hair that I may enjoy the pleasure of seeing that much of them, let my fate be as it will.

You must excuse my childish way of writing to you. There's something that causes me to feel uncommonly serious whenever I attempt to write to you which I cannot account for unless it's being far advanced in years and in my dotage. I have been very poorly this summer, but fortunately it did not continue long, and at present I should enjoy as good health as ever I did if it were not for the way that I have been tortured with one of the worst boils for ten days past and very little appearance of its getting well yet, but I will bear it patiently and live on hope.

I have given you a history of our sister Flower's afflictions in my letter to my brother, which I have this moment sealed. There has been a number of births in our settlement of late. Dr. Chinn has had a son born lately and named Thomas Bolling Robertson Chinn; Dr. Pope, a daughter; and Dr. Isaac Smith, a daughter; and several others that are strangers to you. Mrs. Cash and Mrs. Semple will both enlarge their families shortly. Cash makes quite a fatherly appearance already and I expect Mrs. Skillman will have one in a few hours. The doctors and all hands are with her on that business. One of Richardson's sons was lately married to a Miss Kelly and they had a child in six weeks after marriage. And a young man by the name of Barris and Miss Ambrose, a niece of Mr. Thomas Ambrose, were married about the middle of March last and had a fine son 9 or 10 days ago. Old Mr. Jewel, the tailor, and Mrs. Hughes were married the last of June, but I don't expect they will be so smart, but there is no knowing; the old man has been almost crazy for a wife ever since he lost his first one.

There is not the least appearance of any of my girls changing their situation in life. I should rejoice greatly if one of the two eldest were married. They are at present in a very helpless situation without parents or brother that is old enough to take charge of their property, and their uncle being so far from them. I am truly thankful for your sake, and Sidney's also, that she is so happily married. I hope they may be a blessing to each other during life. I expect my Clarissa is as large, or perhaps larger, than you are. She is a fine healthy child, but I don't see her often, only once every three or four weeks.

Harriet Flower is as high as her sister Maria, but very slender, and I think her very handsome, but perhaps I am partial and should not judge. Little Louisa is a smart prattling child and swears like a sailor, and can dance and play the piano on every table or window that she sets near, and in the kitchen makes a large bench do, and sets the biscuit board up before her for a music book.

James is very fat and nearly as large as his father. Their children are all well. Maria and her daughter were well not long since. I am informed that William D. Weeks is at school at West Point, near New York.

Sometimes when your little son is asleep, be good enough to write me a few lines. If I should be alone, it will be company; if unwell, it will raise my spirits.

All happiness attend you and yours,
Rachel O'Connor

Good news and bad news characterize this letter. Rachel journeyed to the land office at the St. Helena courthouse and presented credentials proving the claim of her deceased son James O'Connor to 240 acres of land. But creditors are threatening Rachel and she desires the presence of her brother to alleviate her problems.

December 2, 1825

My dear brother,

Yesterday I had the pleasure of receiving a letter from you, written the 17th of November, which is the same time I wrote my last previous to this. I am sorry that you continue poorly, but I hope this cold weather will be of service to you. Be sure to let me know how you are every time you write.

I wish you would inquire of my sister Mary her reason for being so silent. I have not received one word from her this three months past. I am surprised that she ventures to let so much time pass without writing when she knows how well I can scold you for neglecting to write. But I will forgive her if she will begin to write me again and not scold her at this time—only give a few hints.

I am truly thankful to learn, by your last, that she and her little children are in good health and I hope in your next to be informed of your recovery. I am at present very well and I expect much smarter than you would think until after I have told you of a journey that I have lately taken out to St. Helena Court House, where the land office is kept, for the purpose of securing the 240 acres of land that formerly belonged to my poor James. I wrote to Thompson (who lives out there) several times to examine the records and let me know the real situation of the claim, and his answers always informed me that James' had never been recorded and that I would have to petition Congress, or otherwise purchase the land at one dollar and twenty-five cents pr. acre.

David Bradford is the interpreter that translates the Spanish in the Land Office at St. Helena, and from him I received a letter on the 23rd of last month informing me that they had at last found James' land on record and that it was highly necessary for me to send all the papers that I held respecting that land to the St. Helena Court House to the land office by the last of Nov-r, as the land commissioners would leave there by the first of Dec-br; and that this 240 acres would be returned as vacant land, as it was recorded on the list of rejected claims (granted 1804).

I considered on it one hour of time and wished for you to be here, and then finally concluded to go myself if I lived to do so, and started with no other than Arthur on Saturday last at 9 o'clock in the morning and arrived at my journey's end before sundown on Sunday—and got my business fixed so that they assured me that I would have not further trouble respecting it. My papers convinced them that the land was granted in 1803, and that it had been surveyed the second time in 1804, and improved in 1807 and 8.

I received a letter from Mr. Millandon yesterday advising me to send my cotton as soon as possible, that good cotton was selling at 17 cents, and that, he thought, would be the highest price this year. I have answered his letter and informed him that it would be impossible to send it as soon as he wished, as I had been late in getting the gin started. Please to give me your advice on the subject. You will find it better attended to. I want to do for the best, if I knew how. I am tired of being in debt.

I have all the crop gathered except some scattering cotton that Milly and Leak and the children will finish in a few days. I have fifty-seven bales pressed, and some ginned ready to press, and some to gin, and I still hope that the cotton crop will be larger than it was last year, but can't be sure until I get it ginned and pressed. I allow myself to have a faint hope of having corn enough to do until I have some ripe next year, but I may be mistaken. But if I am, I must peddle up money to buy more.

Give my love to my dear sister and babes and accept a large share yourself,

Your affectionate sister,

Rachel O'Connor

Judge Rhea has this moment left here. He says that he is in great need of *money*, and all I could do was to promise to do the best I could, and thank him for his past indulgences in my distresses, and the poor old man went away apparently satisfied. Garrald keeps constantly tormenting Swift for his money which he tells Gerrald not to be uneasy, that I am very industrious, and that you are rich and and will be over soon and that his money can be got out of the bank immediately on your arrival. Report says that there is some trouble about the land on Bayou Sara, that there is another claim to it, and I am afraid it is too true. Mr. Collins is to move up here again or perhaps has already come and J. Finly is to return. Henry Flower has lately been to N. Oreleans on that business, and come home, but I don't know what he done.

I like to forget to tell you of the marriage that has of late taken place between Mr. James Flower and Miss Sarah Mullallen. They were married on the 24th of Nov-r. Mrs. Eliza Barrow arrived home yesterday, but I have not seen her yet. I wish there was not water between here and where you live. I would surprise you with a little unexpected visit before long, now I find I can stand to ride so well. But I am afraid of deep water.

I have started the hands to burn and chop in the log ground and they're doing very well. I hope to get some more chopped down after the logs are rolled.

Do pray come over here next month. If you can only stay one week, it will convince the people that you are not tired out with my troubles, which I am sure there is many praying for. Do write to Swift to encourage him. My troubles are near, and he is my best friend. McVey is also good.

LETTERS

Rachel makes an abject apology to Mary Weeks for a "scold" administered in a former letter.

West Feliciana
January 23, 1826

My dear sister,

With the greatest of pleasure I received your last letter written the 1st of this month which I considered a precious New Years gift. But at the same time, must acknowledge that I fear that I am unworthy of such kind attention from you. In my last I must have surprised you, but I hope to be excused, after I inform you that I inconsiderately wrote my fears without taking time to reflect a moment, or once thinking that I ought to hope for the best, which has of late become my nature and appears unavoidable.

The boy that informed me of what he had heard, I believe to be innocent of wishing to do harm, and told me of what he had heard, from being alarmed himself, and as his duty, let me know of it. I am truly sorry that you have been afflicted with the cramp, and bad health otherwise. This summer past, I have known cotton strings tied on near where the cramp is worst, to be of service in that disease, particularly so if a little sulphur was tied in a cloth and sewed to the cord and worn constantly. I beg you to be very careful of yourself and not let the cares of the world lead you to expose your health. Your present situation makes such a caution requisite.

My sister's family are all in good health. Harriet is, as you observe, a most charming girl, and very dutiful to her parents. Her mother has great reason to be thankful, for her children are all good. I have been disappointed in getting to go up and see them for a long time by one thing or other. But of late I could not think of leaving home on account of my Negro woman being near having a young one, which was born on the 19th instant, and is this evening dying. I sincerely lament its poor mother's distresses.

I hope that you are happily fixed in New Town and your lovely little children in good health. One of my greatest pleasures is to receive a letter from you. You always tell so much about your darling babies.

My dear sister, I am afraid that you will find this a simple and unconnected piece, as my mind has been entirely employed on one subject ever since I had your last, on that part you call a scold, which I beg for mercy's sake to explain *unworthily* as I know my

13

treacherous pen could commit to paper, that I considered you selfish, is more than I am able to comprehend or account to you for a thought that has never once entered my mind, but far, far to the contrary. I can with safety and truth declare to you, and to the world, that I have ever considered you too generous to me and mine. My good friend, you must not think that I intend to insult you, as it appears I have done. It happened by some mistake or misplacing my words, and folding up my now hateful scroll, with a full heart, as I have often done without rereading it or examining it over, after I had finished writing. Please to copy it and enclose it to me so that I may have an opportunity of saying what I intended if I had done you and myself justice. I have not, nor ever shall, forget your kindness to my dear James during his stay at your house. Although his mind had become weak, he still had gratitude enough to remember the kind attention that he received from you and his uncle while he lived in your family. I certainly have made some great mistake in my letter, or what may justly be called a slip of the pen. But indeed my heart is innocent of ever once thinking that you had done wrong and this mistake of mine serves to convince me that I did not know your worth until the arrival of your letter, for I have been afraid that you would be blind to my faults, or let them pass unnoticed out of pity, as I had been unfortunate; but in that you would be doing wrong not to let me have an opportunity of speaking for myself, which shows your better judgment, *in all.*

My dear sister, I can say no more at present on a subject that is so painful the very thought makes me despise myself, but I still plead innocence. I shall pray for your answer to this and that you and yours may be forever blessed.

Rachel O'Connor

P.S. My little Negro babe is dead.

Racchel writes David on behalf of their sister, Pamela Weeks Flower, whose property (occupied by her son-in-law and daughter, Maria Collins) is in jeopardy.

May 3, 1826

My dear brother,

This is the third letter I have written to you since last night, all on the same subject. I came home last night from visiting your dear sister Pamela who sent for me the day before, for the purpose of telling me her distresses, and to get me to write you to come to her assistance immediately. A plantation about 12 miles from where Mr. Collins and Mr. Joseph Finley settled on Henry Flower's land is the place that Mr. Collins put his Negroes to make a crop this year. I believe it is H. F.'s old sugar plantation, and it is advertised for sale and will be sold on the 17th of this May, which will ruin Collins, and if that don't sell for the amount due, H. F.'s property on Bayou Sara must go next and very soon. They want her to mortgage her plantation to borrow money from bank to discharge the debt, but she will not without your advice. She wants you to come to secure her property before it is sold at public sale, which she says will certainly be the case if you don't come. Do, do, dear Brother, come. She is almost crazy. It is useless for me to say more, only that times is as bad, or worse, than it has ever been with them. Pray come for mercy's sake.

Your affectionate sister,

R. O'Connor

Three days later Rachel writes congratulating Mary on the birth of a son. Amid accounts of family members and friends, Rachel again emphasizes the urgency of David's attention to their sister's property that is threatened with public sale.

Near St. Francis Ville
May 7th, 1826

My dear sister,

I shall now commence my letter with wishing you much joy with your young son, and at the same time, pray that the three lovely babes may continue a blessing to their dear parents during life. Poor little William, I am sorry for him; he is so young, and to loose the name of being the youngest at one year and three months and six

15

days old. But on the other consideration, what is that small difficulty, a mere nothing when compared to the blessings of having a
brother. I hope, my dear sister, to hear of your entire recovery, and
the health of your family shortly. I received a letter from my brother
a few days since, dated the 27th of April last, which contained the
welcome news of a second son being added to his family and that
you were recovering very fast. Your own feeling may convey to you
the pleasure I felt at hearing of your safe delivery, but indeed I have
not words to express it.

I expect Arthur has arrived and delivered my letter before this to
my brother. I started him on Wednesday last over to your house on
my sister Pamela's business. She is in great trouble, but I hope my
brother will get over here to assist her with his advice before the
17th of this month, which is the day that their plantation is to be
sold at public sale; and if that should not bring the amount due,
their property on the Bayou Sara will be seized. (It is their plantation
on the coast that is already seized and advertised for sale.) This late
misfortune of my sister and her family's I mention for fear my letter
to my brother may be some unfortunate accident miscarry.

I enjoy very good health at present, and the girls likewise. Clarissa
is at school and doing well. Maria Collins expects to be confined
sometime this month. Her little daughter is a fine child. Our sister
looks poorly, but her babe is a middling large boy.

My garden has been extremely good, but it begins to appear rusty
now. We have very dull times. Almost every person appears distressed at the sudden fall in the price of cotton.

Dr. Ira Smith and his Lady and Mrs. Pirrie starts this morning for
New Orleans, and expects to start from there to New York on
Wednesday or Thursday next, to spend the summer and return in
Nov-br. They are the only people that don't appear to have some
distress or other to sink their spirits.

Eliza Barrow is to start up the Mississippi with her mother-in-law
(Old Mrs. Barrow) on their trip of pleasure, to the same parts, but
she don't expect to meet with her mother again until she returns
home. Mr. Hall and Miss Chisum are to be married the 9th or 10th
of this month. Mrs. McDermit's second son, John, has been at the
point of death for 2 or 3 weeks, caused by getting into a quarrel at
the river with a man that shot him and stabbed him shockingly—he
is some better and is expected to recover.

Please to remember me to Mrs. Palfrey and when you write, inform me the name of her *son* and how they are. I also send much love to Miss E. Conrad, and have a large store for another to send, but I believe it is best not to meddle with the business of others, and only request her to accept mine.

Do pray, my beloved sister, make my dear Frances talk of her unfortunate aunt so that she may remember that she once had such a relation, if fate is so that I am never to see her. Mr. Robbins and family has returned to the Bayou Sara. Mrs. Robbins is in bad health, but I am sorry to say that I have not as yet seen my dear nephew, Wm. D. Weeks. When I called he was not at home. His Aunt Pamela is much pleased with him.

May you ever by happy, now and forever, is the sincere prayer of your sister,

Rachel O'Connor

Rachel has had a fainting spell and writes David carefully outlining her wishes for the disposition of her property. Happily, she was to survive for another twenty years following that hot July day.

State of Louisiana, Parish of West Feliciana
July 12, 1826

My dear brother,

I have not had the pleasure of receiving a letter from you since the one from New Orleans during your last stay in that place. I have been favored with one from my dear sister Mary since your arrival home which informed me you had all been sick but the little babe. I hope it is not the case yet, and as this is Thursday, perhaps Daniel may bring me a letter from the post office which will set my mind at ease in that respect if I find that you are all recovered.

I must acknowledge I should not have commenced writing this until evening if a curious circumstance had not taken place yesterday at one o'clock, which has caused me to feel a little serious for fear of being taken off suddenly, and without ever naming to you some arrangements that I wish you to make, in case of such an accident.

At one o'clock I had returned home from the fields, after taking a long ride all through them, in as good health as I ever was, only very warm, set in the gallery (at least a quarter of an hour), to have some water drawn out of the well, and then took a drink, and in a few moments fell senseless on the floor, for a short time, but did not get hurt much. One of my feet pains me some, and a small bruise on one of my temples, is all that can be seen, but my breast feels very sore inside, and is painful on drawing a long breath. But I hope soon to recover what has happened, but for fear of another attack, more fatal, I concluded to write this.

I have already told you that I wish the property belonging to me, after my just debts were paid, equally divided in four parts—one fourth for yourself, one fourth for the heirs of Stephen Swayze (deceased), and one fourth for my poor sister Pamela; and as my poor brother Caleb (Weeks) has but one child living, I have concluded to request his son's fourth part, to be equally divided between my dear Mary Clarissa Swayze, and his son William James D. Weeks, which will be giving her a little more than she would otherwise get, and putting him nearer on a footing with the rest of my nephews and nieces, as the other families are larger, and nature appears to bind me to give her a little to herself, as she has ever claimed me for her mother. She always has wanted me to give her a girl by the name of Caroline, a daughter of Patience and Young Sam's which I should be glad for her to own, as so much of Wm. James D. Week's fourth, which is the greatest part of my arrangements that I have to make, or leave to be made. I think it would be best to sell the plantation, and stock of horses and cattle, and everything else except the poor Negroes, to assist in discharging the debts against the estate; but the Negroes I wish you to keep amongst the heirs of my dear mother.

Patience has been a faithful slave to *me* and mine in all my distresses for twenty-two years, for which I should be glad you would let her stay with any part of her family that she chooses, and not considered a slave any longer than I live. And Pless has been a great relief in my late troubles both in *sickness* and health for which I should be glad for her to be indulged in like manner, which is all that I have to say on the present melancholy subject.

Now, my dear brother, I have not written the above with an idea of impressing on your mind that I apprehend any danger from what has happened, for I expect to be well in a few days—but for fear of something of the kind, and probably more unfavorable, has caused me to think it my duty to write to you on the subject, and feeling convinced of of it being a relief to yourself to hold something to authorize to act as I know you will, when need requires.

Remember me to my dear sister Mary, and little Frances, and kiss the two little boys for me. May the blessings of God forever attend you and yours is the sincere prayer of your affectionate sister.

Rachel O'Connor

I just thought of my riding horse *Ball*. Should he be alive, please to take him home to your house and keep him while he lives. He must be yours.

R. O'Connor

Rachel compliments her niece Frances Weeks on her "pretty letter" and expresses the hope that Frances will visit her Feliciana relatives.

August 23, 1827

My dear and darling Frances,

I received your pretty letter two or three days ago, and felt so well pleased I made an attempt to answer it immediately, but when I compared it to yours and found that mine looked so ugly by the side of yours, I felt ashamed of my writing and threw it away. For you may know that I could not wish to let my sweet babe write a prettier letter than myself if I could help it; but after all, yours will look the best. My dear little Frances must not call her pretty writing *scribbling* any more; for indeed I think it the prettiest letter I have ever seen from so small a child. And I can assure you I was surprised when I found it to be your own writing, but never better pleased than when I came to the dear name of my sweet little Frances Weeks. But if your dear papa had not informed me that it was written by your own hand, I should have thought it to have been written by your teacher, the writing is so pretty. I intend to show it to all your little cousins, and the large ones too; for I scarcely think any of them can write so well.

Your cousins Charlotte and Clarissa is away from home, but as soon as they come, I will show them your letter and let them see how good you are to write to your old aunt. Your cousin Harriet has a fine little son. You must coax your good papa and mama to bring you and your little brothers and sister over to see us all. We should be overjoyed to see you coming.

I am sorry to hear of your dear mama being so long afflicted with sickness. But as she has begun to mend, I hope she may be quite well by this time, which will add much to the happiness of her lovely babes. You must write to me again very soon, for if you wait to learn to write prettier, I shall be ashamed to answer your letters because your writing will be so much better than mine. But I will be sure to answer every one just to let you see how much smarter you are than your aunt is, who is nearly eight times your age.

Give my kindest love to your dear papa and mama and your brothers William and Alfred, and sister Harriet. Kiss them all round for me. In your next you must let me know the name of your Aunt Elizabeth's babe and how she is and how your Aunt Sidney and her little children are. Ask your papa to be careful of the little dog that he so kindly saved for me. I am afraid the rats will carry me off they are so bad. I have lately made a little flower garden and got a very small hoe. I wish you could come and see how you like them. I expect you and Clarissa could plant all the pretties yourselves if you were here.

At present I am in very good health and hope this may find you enjoying the same blessing. Farewell, my charming, lovely, innocent babe. I remain your grateful and affectionate aunt,

Rachel O'Connor

William Flower had received an annonymous letter criticizing his lawsuit against Rachel. Henry Flower suspects that Rachel's friend the merchant John Swift is the sender. In a letter to David, Rachel relates this news and her lawyer's optimism as to the outcome of the suit.

December 8, 1827

My dear brother and sister,

I hope this may find you all enjoying health and happiness. At present my own health is very good and the girls and Mr. Conrad are likewise very well. We were landed at the Bayou Sara landing on Wednesday night about 9 o'clock, and came home the next morning. Found most of the slaves pretty well and everything else as much so as would be reasonable to expect. Mr. Stokes was laid up with the pleurisy, which I was afraid had been brought on by some frolic, but I believe I was mistaken. He is about again, but far from being well. I have not discovered anything amiss, but very little done to the house. George, unfortunately, cut his thumb nearly off shortly after I left home and has been laid up ever since, and Daniel's work don't show to much advantage. My old Daniel has saved a little over 25 dollars for me from the time I left home until I returned again; and the Dr. has attended very well to the garden.

Mr. Swift came out to see us last night. He was not at home when we passed through St. F. V., and this morning we had the big talk. He appeared very sorry that he had been displeased with us, and said that he thought we had acted right after he knew our reasons; and said he had written to yourself and me after he received our letters. I wish you would enclose mine in one from yourself. I should like to see it. You can read it before it is returned.

Henry Flower carried your letter and mine to Mr. Swift, and he showed ours to H.F., which alarmed him very much as he asked pardon, took all the blame on himself; declared that he was the only person that ever suspected Mr. Swift to be the writer of that letter; that his brother never had any such ideas, and acknowledged that the only reason he had to accuse him was his kindness to me, which I think a very poor excuse. If Henry Flower had any friendship for me, he would like Mr. Swift better.

Mr. Swift appears as anxious to serve me as ever. He has gone to Mr. Turner's this morning to assist him to take an inventory of poor Stephen's books, or at least of his estate from his books.

I went to see Mr. Turner before I came home and asked him how he was likely to come out with the Flowers. He said very well, that he still thought he should settle that debt for me very easy, but that it was necessary for me to petition the Probate Court to allow an inventory of the property to be taken; which he said would according to law clear me of being accountable for the debt, as I had never disposed of any part of the estate. I then requested him to lay in a petition for me which I suppose he has done and obtained if from his asking Mr. Swift to assist him today.

I asked Mr. Turner very particularly about the estate of William D. Weeks, whether the *will* could be broken or not. He said it could not be done by any other excepting his grandmother, that it was in her power to break it and obtain one fifth of the whole estate, and that the rest would belong to his widow; that neither yourself, nor Pamela, or Dr. Duer, or any other could claim one cent, which he said was hard, but so stated his will in law.

Ann Weeks has gone to the convent to finish her education. Mrs. Johnson, that bought your plantation, died on Wednesday last, and Wm. G. Johnson (the father of Richard and Mrs. Pleasant Harbour) lost another daughter the same day. She was burned to death by her clothes getting all on fire on her. Poor old people, how miserable they must be to loose three children in one fall.

Mr. Swift says it will not do for me to attempt to move until I am entirely clear of debt, and have some before hand; that if I should, I will have all my troubles to go over again. He says that if I will stay a few years longer, he will insure all debts settled, and with very little more trouble to myself; if no misfortune should happen to prevent. When you come over, you can be a better judge of all.

William Flower has appealed his case against Rachel. The suit causes embarassment for Rachel's half sister, Pamela Weeks Flower, and her family.

March 7, 1828

My dear brother,

I am afraid you will conclude, before this reaches you, that I have become very neglectful. I certainly feel bad myself when I think of its being so long since I have written you, but I hope you will excuse me this time. I intend to do better in the future. I had to go up to see Mr. Swayze after he came home and stay a few days with them. He is getting well quite fast. They all came home with me and stayed ever since, which has caused my silence to last so long, for I knew it would be impossible to write until they would be absent a short time.

I am at present in good health, entirely clear of the backache, and being employed in my garden all the time I can get. The plantation is in fine order and all doing very well, only this late frost has made my corn look extremely bad. I think we shall be ready to plant cotton seed early enough; the greatest part of the ground is now ready to plant. I made one hundred and eleven bales of cotton last year, which is all sold, but I cannot inform you the amount it brought, as the account sales are with Mr. Swift. I have much trouble in getting corn hauled home from the river, the roads are so muddy. Mr. Swift buys the corn (as yet) at three bits and a half pr. barrel.

The Flowers has appealed and the suit is to be tried again this month in New Orleans. I wish I may fare as well this time as I did last. I have not seen Henry Flower since I left your house, or any of his family excepting James. He comes very often. I expect the others are not pleased with me for writing to Pamela, but I think it saved him from being sued for scandal, and that they should be very thankful to get off without paying cost. James is at school at Jackson, and is much beloved. I think he is a good boy and very smart.

Mr. Clark, the surveyor of this parish, informed me that he has found the papers to the tract of land that once belonged to me in the parish judge's office in St. F. V., and that Henry Flower has sold the land to Joseph E. Johnson at eight dollars per acre. I don't want you to let H. F. know that I wrote to you about it. He might think me very busy. He don't know that I know anything of his either finding the papers or selling the land.

I have received two letters from you since I came home. I am glad your sugar crop done so well. I hope you will soon come over. I want to see you. Indeed I want to see you all more than I did before I went over to your house. Your little ones were strangers, but now I can recollect all their faces and little talk, which makes me want to see them and their dear mother. I wish she could only know how much I love her since I came home. I often think of my poor James. He said no person could think that his Aunt Mary had such an uncommon good heart until they lived with her awhile. Do remember me most affectionately to her and her sisters. The girls are all gone a visiting today and Wm. has gone with them. He intends to visit you shortly. Do write soon.

> I remain your affectionate sister,
> *R. O'Connor*

I had like to forget to tell you of Tom Chaney's killing old Mrs. Coursey's son with a club. He slipped up behind him where he was eating his supper and struck him dead, and then took all his own Negroes and run off. Tom was drunk at the time. Old Mr. Coursey formerly overseed for H.F. It all happened at Chaney's own house. I believe the boy lived with him. I never heard any cause for killing him, only that of Tom's being drunk.

Lest her presence embarass her relatives Henry and Pamela Flower, Rachel does not attend the wedding of her niece Harriet Flower to a Mr. Handy. William Flower had written Rachel an angry and insulting letter, a copy of which Rachel sends to David, with excerpts quoted after the letter to David.

June 9th 1828

My dear brother,

I have not received any letter from you or any of your family for nearly a month past. Yet I entertain a hope of you all being well. But I begin to be afraid you have given out the idea of coming over to see us this summer. William Swayze said it was doubtful; and from your silence on the subject of late I expect he guesses right.

I believe our sister is mending slowly. I have not seen her since she went from here, but I hear from her often. She never returned any answer to me nor even mentioned that she received my letter, with yours enclosed; still I feel convinced of Mark's delivering them into her hands secretly. Charlotte was at the wedding and says that they had a merry time of it. Harry, Wm., James, and David Flower all danced towards the breaking up time. I was cautious enough not to go, for fear of meeting my enemies, which I conclude quite charitable in me, not to wish to prevent their enjoyng themselves, as it certainly would if I had appeared among them. I have discovered very lately, that my friend Wm. Flower is more angry with me than usual. He threatens publishing the whole affair between him and myself, which he says will disgrace me in the eyes of the world, more than I can form an idea of; and that if I am not very, very cautious, *blood* will be *spilt* before all is settled. I expect this spite is arrived at Mr. Turner who appears quite at his ease, and as firm as ever in his friendship towards me.

I wish it was in my power to inform you all about this endless lawsuit, that is likely to give so much trouble. But it is so jumbled up together that it's hard to understand. Still Mr. Turner will have it that I have but little to fear. I did a few days since recieve a long epistle from Mr. F. wherein he expressed the indignation that he felt towards my self and friends. I expect you have some leisure hours to spare and would like something new to read to pass off the time pleasantly, from which I have concluded to enclose for your perusal a true copy of his letter to me. The original I have sent to Mr. Turner to answer; that is, if he thinks proper to do so. I feel too small to undertake to answer a letter to a person so high-standing in life as Mr. F., although I suppose he wished me to do so, and to commit myself too. But he scarcely will ever catch me napping again as long as I keep my senses.

I have quite regained my former good health, which is more than I expected, I kept ailing so long. The weather is so dry at present is all that I have to complain of. My crop is very clean and only needs rain to make it look beautiful. I feel thankful that my early corn was killed by the frost, since every other person's is destroyed by the drought and not worth a cent. Mine is young and may be good yet. Mr. Scott informs us that his whole plantation is under water and crop lost. Poor man, I sincerely pity him.

I hope the high water may not injure you; do let me know whether of not. Charlotte S. is with me. She copied the long letter for you. Give my kindest love to my dear sister and my sweet little Frances, and William, and my little Alfred. I hope he is a good boy yet. And kiss my little Harriet for me. No words can express my desire of seeing you all again.

I remain your affectionate sister,
R. O'Connor

(Excerpts from the enclosed letter of William Flower to Rachel O'Connor)

St. Francisville May 29, 1828

Mrs. Rachel O'Connor

Madam:

The indignation which I have felt towards you, or those of your friends whom you have managed to manage and conduct the matters in the controversy between us in relation to the debt due us by the estate of S. Bell, would have prevented me from having any further communication with you of my own accord, but the entreaties of my brother Henry, and enforced as he says, by his wife, your sister, has determined me otherwise.

Henry contends that the tricks, shifts, evasions and quibbles of the law which have been practiced on me for six years last on this subject have been entirely without your knowledge or consent, and that you have always been desirous and anxious to have a correct and fair settlement of our accounts with the estate of Bell made and would have been willing to have entered into any reasonable engagement for their liquidation and payment. . . . But since 1821, a system of deceit, intimidation, quibbling, and defamation has been practiced to injure and defraud us out of our just rights.

The plea that you were a married woman at the time of entering into the agreement with me in December, 1820, and not having the consent of your husband, is not binding on you now. This plea convinced me that a system of deceit and treachery had been practiced on us for years to defraud us of our just claims on you.—That such had been your intention as far back as 1820 when you were entering into engagements which you know you never had any intention of filling. . . .

(I submit) the following proposition: The debt against the estate of Stephen Bell be submitted to any three or five just and intelligent men, and that the verdict of these referees be made the judgment of the court at next session.

William Flower

Rachel recalls the pleasure of her visit with Mary Weeks and her family. Harriet Handy and her husband, newly weds, have visited Rachel. The estate of Rachel's deceased brother William Swayze is soon to be settled and she again worries that her nieces have no husbands to care for their property.

June 24, 1828

My dear sister,

I have been waiting a long time for something interesting to communicate to you, and have to commence without, at last, or never write again. I so seldom hear from you of late that I'm afraid of being forgotten unless I quicken your memory, even if it should be a letter filled with nonsense.

I must confess that I have not written so often as I wished to, for some time past, owing to my health being a little bad, of which I have quite recovered and feel very well again—and most sincerely do pray that this may find you and yours enjoying the same blessing. I am sorry to say that I, in a manner, repent visiting you last fall. It has caused me to feel a greater desire to see you all again. Your children were strangers; I had only heard of them, but now their little faces are in my mind. I think I could know them all (excepting little Harriet) if I were to meet them amongst strangers. When I parted with your sister Elizabeth, I had a hope of seeing her again this spring, but I scarcely expect to be so much favored now, although I still think she ought to come, and that her opportunity is better, as she could now be accompanied by her better half. I have every hope of her being happily married, but not more so than she deserves. That would be impossible in my opinion. How fortunate you have been to get your sisters married to such worthy men as Mr. Palfrey and Mr. Hardin. I believe Charlotte has no idea of marrying at all, from every appearance. Clarissa is still in Rapide and I know but little about her, and why I should feel troubled on her account, I know not, for indeed I do not know of any reason. Harriet and her good man has been to see me since their marriage. They are very loving. I never saw two more so. Mr. Handy inquired very particularly of his Uncle David and wanted to know of me when I expected him over to see me. He called me Aunt Rachel.

The only good news that I have worth relating is the appearance of a promising crop. It all looks very well. But withal, I don't like my overseer near as much as I formerly did. He thinks himself a much greater man since his marriage. I shall be glad, when his time is out, to get clear of him.

I believe our sister Pamela enjoys tolerable health again. She rides some which I hope will be of service to her. Your brother told Mr. Swift (who was in N. Oreleans last week) that he intended to visit his friend on Bayou Sara in next August. I sincerely hope that he may.

Please to inform my good brother that I have received the hogshead of sugar and five barrels of molasses, for which I return many thanks. The sugar, Mr. Handy and myself divided; I sent for H. F. to come himself, but he would not. He sent his son-in-law.

I feel afraid my brother will be displeased with me when he received the packet that I sent him, with Wm. Flower's long letter enclosed. I would have paid the postage if I had not been fearful of its being the cause of the bundle being lost by the way.

Remember me to my dear brother, and the darling babes, not forgetting Mr. and Mrs. Palfrey and Mr. and Mrs. Harding. Heaven grant you all health and happiness.

I remain your affectionate sister,
Rachel O'Connor

Rachel writes Mary Weeks relating family news. In a postscript she asks her sister-in-law to burn the letter, which obviously Mary did no do.

September 15, 1828

My dear sister,

This morning I feel a satisfaction that is seldom felt by me of late years. At this moment it appears as if all my luck had turned to good. Not more than an hour ago your kind letter was delivered to me, which has received more than forty welcomes already, and every breath is still adding more. You may not apprehend the smallest danger of not being pardoned; I do not know of its being possible for you to commit an error that one letter could not cure. But as yet I have never known of any to accuse you of. I am always happy to get a letter from you. I know your little family must keep you very busy. I'm sorry to learn the suffering of my dear little Harriet. Her little troubles begin young, but I pity you the most. I never can

forget a mother's distress over a sick child. Tell my dear little
Frances and Wm. to be very smart. Their little cousin Louisa
Flower wrote me a letter herself yesterday, and that I shall think
hard of them if they don't soon do so too. What charming sweet
babes they are, for getting to school so pretty. I have received a
letter from Charlotte this morning likewise. They are all well. I believe Mr. Scott and Julia Ann is still trying to get the property divided. I don't know what Wm. Swayze wishes on the subject, or
whether he knows himself, or not, I am at a loss to say. He is very
busy courting at present, and thinks of nothing but a wife, and indeed I do not know but he is in a fair way to obtain his wishes, he
stays so constantly where his heart appears to have taken abode. She
is a daughter of the late John Harbour. Her mother is a widow. I
expect she is a fine little girl, but I am afraid Wm. will fim himself
at a loss to provide for a family. I wish he could be back at school
again. His expenses would be less.

Charlotte and Clarissa would rather let it remain as it is until
their debts were paid, that is, the debts against their father's estate.
The girls are much more saving than Wm. He dashes about, dresses
fine, fears no expenses, agrees to follow every friend's advice, and
goes his own way at last.

Now, my dear sister, I have told you of receiving your letter and
one from Charlotte, which is a part of my pleasing luck today—and
must tell you the rest. Just before they were brought from the post
office, I rode all over my cotton fields, which I had not done for
three months before owing to my horse's having a sore back, and to
an unfriendly feeling towards my overseer. We have not agreed well
for several months, and I know his to be too obstinate to do any
better for my looking after him. So I concluded to let him have his
own way, only mind that he did not abuse the Negroes and the
horses, which was the only cause of our quarrels. But today I have
freely forgiven *all* within my own breast, my cotton crop appears so
uncommonly promising. Indeed I do think that I may expect 150
bales if no accident should prevent. There is great complaints in our
parish amongst the planters of their cotton crops. They all say that
they don't expect one half a crop from their cotton bushes dropping
the forms and rot together. And Mr. Luther Smith came through
four weeks ago and said that it was like his own—scarcely worth
calling a cotton field; that the bushes were there, but no bolls, which

discouraged me so much that I had no heart to write and have been silently grieving ever since until this day.

On Sunday week, my dear Pamela came to see me and stayed four days with me. I could scarcely know how to feel greatful enough for so much goodness. She has better health than I ever expected to see her have and has fattened very much. But she is very uneasy about brother David's not being pleased with Harriet's marriage. Says that it was too late to prevent it when his letter came. Do coax him to mention Harriet and Mr. Handy friendly in his letters to her. They are married now and it is useless to make her sorrowful. She asked me to write to him which I will do in a few days.

As you observed, our parish has been very healthy. November is drawing near; how glad I should be to start over to see you all again, but dare not leave home. My best respects to your sisters and brothers-in-law and brother and sister-in-law when you see them. Much love to my dear brother David and to your good self and the babies.

I remain your affectionate sister,

Rachel O'Connor

I have just been reading your letter over again and noticing Louisa and Patty being in a thriving way, caused me to recollect our sister's fine luck. They had five little Negroes born in less than two months; one of the women had twins. The children are all alive and well. Charlotte, Patty's sister, is the mother of one; they have two more women that she expects to be confined hourly. They have named them Caroline, Emoline, Eveline, and Adoline; the boy, Harry talks of calling Jackson.

I often hear from your worthy brother from Mr. Swift's letters, or the letters that Mr. Swift receives from him. I would write him myself if I had any pleasing news to inform him of. I shall ever esteem him as one of the best of friends.

Please to burn my letter shortly.

This letter to David details the settlement of the estate of Rachel's deceased brother William Swayze. The disposition of the property and slaves belonging to his minor heirs presents problems. Rachel

requests David to purchase the slaves and property of those heirs.
Plantation affairs and community news conclude the letter.

Jan-y 11th, 1829

My dear brother,

I have just received yours of the 7th instant which causes me to feel both glad and sorry. I am truly glad to find that my dear little Frances is once more restored to health and that she and her little brother learn so fast at school. I hope that they can soon be far enough advanced to write to me. But indeed I shall be continually uneasy if you do not write often while your health is so bad. In your next, do let me know what is the matter with you and the cause of your being sick for such a length of time, and how my sister's health is and her reasons for not writing. I have written three to her since I received any answer. I know she has a lovely little family—four kids to attend to—but that should not prevent her from writing, as it is one of the most pleasing subjects that she could commence her letter with, and fully as pleasant to me to read the news of her beloved family.

Mr. Scott and the girls arrived here on Christmas eve. He has since that time been over to see Mrs. Lyons and returned here again. Yesterday they all started up to their plantation. Tomorrow they expect to commence dividing their property. They all were in great hopes of getting it done without any dispute and I sincerely pray that they may.

Mrs. Lyons expects you to take Caleb' and David's part of the property, and poor Clarissa wishes you to take hers and allow her what you think would be right. I wish that you could make it convenient to yourself to do so I amy sorry to see her so distressed. She requested of me to mention it to you some time ago. If I had land enough, I would take her slaves myself. I have no more cleared than my own slaves can work and very little to clear. Do, my brother and sister, consider on it. She is a poor little orphan girl and it is our duty to take care of her, at least for a while.

Charlotte intends to put her slaves with Mr. Scott, and perhaps William may try to go to farming with his. I wish that he may do well, still I much fear it is doubtful. He may do better after he finds that he has but little to do with. If he don't change, it will take all his to wait on him. They expect to sell the land and divide the Negroes.

I have not heard whehter Wm and H. F. has appeared or not. Mr. Harraldson told Mr. Howell that they intend suing you for that debt, if they could not recover it from me. I have asked Mr. Scott respecting it, and he says that they cannot recover anything from you. Should either of the Mr. Conrads be with you, talk to them on the subject and learn their opinion.

I have got my crop gathered. The cotton has turned out pretty well considering all things. I have 90 bales pressed and I think there will be cotton enough to make 30 more after I get it ginned. My corn is, as usual, very small. Dr. Duer has got possession of poor brother Caleb's plantation and eighteen or twenty of the Negroes and all the stock. The rest of the Negroes belonging to the estate, Dr. Chinn has taken to his sugar plantation near Baton Rouge. I suppose Dr. Duer is to divide the crop between himself and Mr. Weathers, the husband of Ann Weeks, formerly.

Our sister Pamela is only middling. She keeps up and that is all. Mr. Handy and Harriet has moved to town. They are living in the house where the bank was formerly kept.

Judge Rhea's lady has lately been delivered of twins, a son and daughter. They have at this period fifteen children alive and one dead, and two sons-in-law and very soon expect a grandchild. They say that the old man is highly pleased at his good luck. Mrs. Rhea is not more than 37 years of age. Her family may yet be much larger.

I shall think the time very long to have to wait until the 15th of next month before I expect to see you, but I will be contented, hoping that I may be spared to see you at that time.

Mr. Swift saw Mr. Alfred Conrad in New Orleans last week. He was in very good health and talked of coming to see us shortly. You have not mentioned Mr. Palfrey's or Mr. Hardin's family for a long time. I hope they are all well also.

I remain your affectionate sister,
Rachel O'Connor

P.S. It is reported in our parish that Dr. Towle's sugar crop will bring at least thirty thousand dollars, which is more than he can know what to do with. I wish that he would bestow all that he don't need to poor me.

The high price of corn, the flourishing crops, the marriage of William Swayze, the jailing of a woman accused of murdering her hus-

band, and the recovery of a lost shirt take precedence over the Wil-liam Flower lawsuit in this letter. However, marital trouble is brewing in the household of Henry Flower and Pamela Weeks Flower. The bit was a part of the Spanish dollar worth twelve and one-half cents.

June 22nd, 1829

My dear brother,

I received your letter written during your stay in New Orleans. I was truly glad to hear of your continuing so well and that you had received letters from home giving accounts of your family being in good health and all concerns doing well. I hope soon to hear of your safe arrival home and that you found all well, your family in particular.

I scarcely think that I am entirely well this morning from the way I feel. I believe that I have taken a cold, but there is great reason to lay my present disagreeable feelings to the effects of the mind. I shall hope it may speedily wear away as it generally does in similar cases. My troubles at this time is owing to the scarcity of *corn* and the high price it bears. They will not sell one barrel under two dollars and a half. I have not had to pay over fourteen bits as yet, but I am trembling about the price of what is yet to buy. Mr. Swift did not buy it, as you advised him to do; he would not give up the idea of getting it on better terms, and I feel convinced of his wishing to do for the best; I am contented and thankful for his sincere friendship.

Patrick is in high spirits about the crop. He wishes you could see it now in its flourishing state, knowing that it would afford you great pleasure to see both cotton and corn look so well. He has been very industrious indeed. He has conquered the grass which few of my neighbors can say of theirs as yet. He made driver of Arthur four days and then put him to the hoe and drove him with the rest of the hands. The crop has never suffered for rain so far, and it is in better order than Stokes ever had his at this time of the year. The Negroes continue healthy. Bridget's hand is getting much better. She hoes pretty smartly.

I have not seen any of H. Flower's family since you left here. Mr. Handy told Daniel that they were all well and that Harriet had quite recovered, but very weak. I don't know whether Mr. Turner has done anything in their business or not. I have been very particular to examine every newspaper since he undertook their business, but noth-

33

ing has appeared yet to show a commencement, and if I were to see him, I should dislike to mention it to him. If Mrs. T. knew of it, I could find all she knows in an hour.

Wm. Swayze and his wife expects to move home sometime this week. They visited me once since their marriage together. Wm. has been to see us three times since. Mr. Smith is much pleased with you and says that you must go and see him again when you come over.

They have Mrs. Higginbotham in jail in Clinton and the man that shot her husband likewise. The sheriff did not venture to carry her to jail as they generally do, fearing that she might be tempted to take the does that she had threatened doing, if in case they came to take her to jail. He went to her house in a friendly manner and informed her that it was necessary for her to go to Clinton and lay in her claim to the property, or else she might not be allowed any part that belonged to her late husband, on which information she immediately started and went there where she was taken and confined.

The Negro woman belonging to Mr. Chaney that had been murdered on the road is layed to their mulatto man by the name of *Will*, but nothing has been done to him yet, and perhaps they may hush it up to save their Negro from being hung.

I have found one of your shirts that was lost at the time you went away. It had been rolled up in the blanket that they ironed on, but I cannot find the other. In your next, do let me know how many my sister put up for you. Since I found this one, I thought perhaps you forgot to count the one that you had on, but you can recall all about it. I blame myself very much for not taking more care of your clothes. I always done it before and shall hereafter. The bad news I heard of the suit in N. Orleans troubled me and must have caused me to neglect what I should not otherwise have done.

Remember my kind love to my dear sister and the children. I remain your affectionate sister,

R. O'Connor

Clarissa sends her love to you all. The enclosed copy of Mr. W's letter you will please to destroy as it might do harm by its being known. The fifty dollars is his fee. I think he must be *harried* for money.

LETTERS

The panic of 1829 reaches the Felicianas and Rachel worries that her slaves will starve. She writes David a lengthy letter relating the purchase of corn. While hauling the corn to her plantation, two of her slaves were caught selling some of it in the town of Jackson in the hope of pocketing a bit of money. The purchaser was caught by local citizens and punished in a unique manner. Old Daniel sulks for being relegated to the status of a field Negro. Runaway slaves are rampant in the Felicianas and Rachel recounts a particularly gruesome atrocity.

July 11, 1829

My dear brother,

I received two letters of the 1st instant several days ago. I do not know the reason for its raising my spirits more than common. I am always rejoiced to get letters from you and my sister Mary, but this last came at a time when corn had raised to three dollars a bushel and very little to be got even at that price, which had kept me grieving and lamenting my sad fate, until I scarcely knew whether I was living or not. Sometimes I would conclude that we must all starve, as soon as my potatoes were all eaten, and a number of other fears of the same kind harrassed my mind until your letter came, which acted like a charm and completely cured all my distresses. My hopes of doing better, sometimes or other raised again, since which I have done wonderfully. I had to pay fourteen bits a barrel for two cart loads, and then got two more loads, five miles the other side of Jackson, at one dollar and a half pr. barrel, which we are using now, and Mr. James Scott sent me word that he could spare me one cart load at one dollar pr. barrel, which I hope will keep us alive until my new corn will do to grind. Mr. Swift has been extremely good to search for corn. Whenever he heard of any to be sold that was not too high, he would immediately come out and let me know. I showed him your letter so that he might be on the lookout for his scolding. He laughed and said the corn traders had out generaled him this spring, but that he hoped to have satisfaction yet. He said he had written to you from N. Orleans and expected an answer, which, if it did not come soon, he would write to you again, from which I concluded his letter must be on business.

I have not seen Pamela since you left here nor Mr. F. since the day you sailed for N. Orleans. The news of her claiming her own property has got out; Mrs. Pirrie asked me about it several days ago.

I told her that there had been some such talk a year or two ago, but at that time she would not agree to have it done, to which she said that it was done now and that she expected that I knew of it as soon as any other. I then asked her what they had done. She said that Pamela had laid in her claims and that she would hold her own property and not leave Henry a cent to pay his debts. But she would not tell me who it was that informed her, only said it was known publicly.

I suppose it must have been Mr. Courtney that let her into the secret from his being one, with H. F., that endorsed for Jo Finley, to the amount of fourteen hundred dollars. Mrs. Pirrie said that Courney would have to pay that amount, which he would lose by Jo's estate being insolvent. Mr. Bowman informed me that H. F. had endorsed for J. Finley in favor of McMicklen to the amount of twelve thousand dollars, but I rather expect James Flower was one of the endorsers to that note, *which, if he is, John Mulhollen will begin to look sharp.* J. Finley applied to him to endorse for himself, for fifteen thousand, which he refused to do. Not one of H. F.'s family has been to see me since you were over, and I have not had time to visit them, since I have been so busily employed in search of corn, and money too.

Old Daniel has disgraced himself and become a field Negro again which has sunk his spirits very low. Him and big Sam was caught selling corn in Jackson as they passed through with a load home. The Jackson people gathered the man that received the corn from Daniel and Sam and made him ride a pine pole all through Jackson. His wife made a fuss about it, and they put her on the same pole and gave them a ride together.

Necessity obliges me to send some of the slaves to market to get money to help with hard times. I don't know how I could make out for fresh beef if I did not send to market for it. I send *Mark* now, who has done very well since he commenced.

Mr. Patrick appeared greatly pleased when he found that I had written you the fine order his crop was in. He says that he wants you to come very soon again, to hear you say that the crop is one of the best, for that it looks so well to him, that he can hardly credit his own eyes. He got Mr. Bowman to come over to see it yesterday, who said that he had seen many of the crops this year, but that none of them near as good, nor nothing like in as good order, and we are duty bound to believe the preacher.

I think I informed you of some runaway Negroes robbing Mrs. Pirrie's house, even her bedroom while she lay asleep in the night. Two of them were taken a few days after and a part of her things returned. Since that time, a man that lives in the Plains shot at some more runaways belonging to the same company, which offended them so highly that they watched until they caught a young Negro man belonging to him and cut his legs and arms off and then pulled out his eyes, and left him to die. When he was found, all he could say was that the runaway Negroes done it because his master had shot at them. The poor fellow soon bled to death. Since that, it has been discovered that there were twenty-five runaways in the swamp, all armed men. Yesterday John Dawson (with a hundred men) was to go in search of them, and report says that he found them and killed eight or ten of them, and indeed I wish it may be true.

I have heard that Harriet has got pretty well, all excepting her breasts. They are sore yet and her child disliked to suck her sugar-tit. In your next, do let me know how Elizabeth is, and all the rest of the family that lives near you.

William Swayze and his wife has moved home. Clarissa is at their house on a visit. Wm. writes me that he is very much in the grass. Charlotte is very sorry that she left Mrs. Lyons, since Mr. Scott told her that you intended to go there for her if she did not leave there previous to your going home.

What is the cause of my sister's not writing of late? I can make allowances and find excuses for her when she writes seldom, but none when entirely silent. My dear little Frances and William must soon write to me. I expect Frances might now if she would. And my sweet little Alfred is a good boy, I know, and my dear little Harriet is good, too, I hope. She is the only one of the four that I think I should not recollect their features even amongst strangers, and she is said to resemble myself. I believe I love her the better for it, and at the same time pity her more than all the rest, because she has not her share of beauty amongst them. Poor little darling, she must study to be good. My kindest love to my dear sister. Kiss all my sweet little darlings for me.

I remain your affectionate sister,

R. O'Connor

N.B. I cannot avoid telling you that Briget has a fine boy, born the 5th of this month, and that her hand is nearly well, much stronger than when you were here. Dr. Denny says that I must not not forget to send his best respects to you and tell you to make haste and come over again to see the crop while it is good.

The 4th of July was a day much noticed in St. Francisville, and I suppose there would have been many more there if it had not rained so severely. Mr. Bowman preached and John Dawson made a long speech, much to the purpose from accounts. Every person speaks highly in favor of both. But unfortunately, in the evening of the same day, Mrs. Gaitree, a merchant's wife, ran off with one of their clerks, left four poor little children worse off than being motherless, and carried one with her. Mr. Gaitree was expected to return home that night from N. Oreleans on board one steamboat, and Mrs. Gaitree and her clerk started in another to the same place, about three or four hours before she expected her husband to arrive home in St. F. V. But he has not come yet. I am very sorry for their poor little children to be so disgraced by their mother. Mrs. Gaitree was considered to be a beautiful woman, but not admired otherwise, although there has been very little said against her until since she ran off with their clerk and left her husband and children.

Old Mrs. Dunn has the measles very bad since you saw her last. She is better.

I expect my friend will think I had very little to do when I wrote this long epistle. I think I might claim three or four of your short ones for all *this*.

Yellow fever takes its toll in the St. Francisville area; the woman accused of murdering her husband is cleared of the charge but ostracized by the women of the town.

Note on outside of letter: "Please forward this with care and speed."

November 28, 1829

My dear brother,

It appears long since I received a letter from you, which must have occasioned me to feel greatly alarmed, if I were not in hopes of your silence being caused by your being on your island with your family attending to the making up of your crop of sugar.

It has been so sickly in St. Francis Ville since the yellow fever commenced that I am afraid to hear from there. Two young men died near the river below town, this week, from that dreadful disease, one of which was clerk in Mr. Handy's store. Two of his clerks died this fall. Mr. Swift stayed here last night. He says he is well; which, if he is, he deceives his looks. However I hope that he may escape being severely attacked, as the weather has become so cold. He had just returned from N. Oreleans. The yellow fever continued in some parts of the city. He saw Judge Workman and had a conversation with him respecting those everlasting law suits, in which the judge pledged his word he entertained great hopes of gaining. But I have not forgotten your good advice. I will not let myself get raised too high, to cause a fall, to occasion a wound the greater. My trust is in my God who orders all right. It is my duty that His will should be my pleasure, and I sincerely pray that fortitude may be granted me to obey.

In my last I mentioned being troubled with the rheumatism in my back again. It continued until the night before last, since which I have not felt it, and am at a loss to account for its sudden disappearance.

I expect our sister Pamela and family are well as I have not heard to the contrary. I have not seen any of them since I parted from her at Mr. Howell's about three weeks ago.

Arthur Adams has had the misfortune of having his gin house and forty bales of cotton burned to ashes, and Daniel Turnbull has met with his misfortunes likewise. He has lost a gin house and seventy bales of cotton, which by some accident caught fire and burned down. The place where the house got burned is up in the Barrow settlement, one that belonged to his wife. Mrs. Pirrie has got home. She looks worse than I ever saw her. She must have been very ill indeed. I seen her yesterday and was heartily sorry to see her so changed.

Mrs. Higginbotham has stood her trial and come off clear, by some means not well understood by her neighbors, who are greately displeased at her good luck. Some says it was owing to the judge being a Frenchman, not properly acquainted with the English language so as to understand the charge against her. Not a woman in Clinton would let her enter their doors. She was ordered from several where she expected to be received kindly. Mrs. Eadie's daughter, now Mrs. Airs, drove her from her doors, too, uncommonly spirited. The man that is accused of shooting Mr. Higginbotham was set at liberty, also, and immediately declared his determination was to kill another *man* before he died, who they concluded must be the *jailer*, and had him taken and sent to his old place of confinement again. How he will fare next is unknown.

Mr. Swift took 64 bales of my cotton down with him and *thinks* it was sold at ten cents, but not quite sure, as the news came just as he was going on board the boat and he had not time to know the particulars. I had six more bales pressed, but could not get them to the river soon enough to go with the others.

How does my little rat dog come on? I often think of him, the rats are so bad. I don't wish you to send him before you come yourself fearing he might get lost on the way over. I expect Julia Ann will visit us about Christmas. At that time Mr. Scott goes to N. Orleans on his business. Charlotte is at Mr. Howell's trying to get her plantation attended to. Wm. Swayze and Melinda are living with their father. Clarissa is at home with me and joins me in love to you all. I hope this may find my dear little Harriet quite restored to her health, and the rest of you enjoying the same blessing. I'm afraid that my patience are nearly worn out, and that I shall think hard of my sister Mary's not writing to me occasionally as she formerly did. I know my sweet little Frances will soon write to me again.

Adieu, my best of brothers. Do answer this as soon as possible for the sake of my little girl. Your most affectionate sister,

R. O'Connor

Mrs. Ben Smith and Mr. Montgomery are to be married this day.

Rachel's beloved niece Clarissa is now married to Lewis Davis. In a letter to David, Rachel encloses a newspaper clipping concerning the outcome of the suit separating Pamela's land and slaves from those of her husband. (Pamela's property amount to $14,973.64½).

Feb-ry 2nd, 1830

My dear brother,

Yours of the 26 of Dec-br only arrived a few days ago. What could have detained it so it so long, I know not. However it met a hearty welcome after its arrival. I had suffered much uneasiness, fearing your family were sick. I hope my dear sister Mary will soon be restored to her former good health and enjoy all the blessings of life with yourself and children. This is my third attempt at writing to you. I hope I may be permitted to finish it before anything should happen to prevent me doing so.

Our little Louisa has been for a long time at the point of death. Her first attack was the croup with continual fever. Her throat was so dreadfully affected that she could not swallow water, or scarcely breathe. I never seen any person so low to recover, after being sick so long. But her disease has taken a favorable turn and great hopes are entertained for her recovery. The rest of the family are well. Our sister is thin in flesh, but enjoys better health than she has for many years past, and quite clear of all her old pains; walks better than I ever seen her before. I stayed with her five days during which my heart did really ache. Poor little Louisa suffered so severely. After I returned home I was very sick for a few days. I had a severe cold and fevers, but I am nearly well again.

My little Clarissa and Lewis Davis were married the evening previous to New Year's Day; and the Saturday following, she returned to her old home where her father and mother lived and died, where they expect to live and try to do for the best. But my dear brother and sister must not think they were forgotten. She requested me to let you know the time and to ask you to come and see her married, which I done, and sent the letter to the post office as soon as the day was appointed, which was very soon after your letter came. Clarissa behaved so cleverly that I should be sorry that anything should appear against her. She would not consent to marry him until your letter came, nor then until I said she had better do so. Lewis Davis is under a good character; and I firmly believe, one amongst the best of young men. He is entirely clear of *debt* and has a very good beginning to commence with. He has nine Negroes, seven of them able to work; the other two are small boys; and three thousand dollars in cash, and a little yet due him out of his mother's estate—one tract of land fifteen miles below Baton Rouge, which he intends to sell.

Mr. Swift is very well, just returned from N. Orleans, where he left his three sisters at a boarding school. The old law suit remains, as it was, in the Supreme Court.

Mrs. McVea and her little son Cabot, ten years old, has just very lately arrived from Ireland. They come quite unexpectedly to Mr. McVea. He had never seen his little son. He left Ireland before the child was born. I have not seen them yet. Report says Mrs. McVea is pretty, and that little John Cabot is beautiful. I am to receive a visit from them shortly. Mr. McVea has put his son to school in Jackson. His lady is on a visit at Gen-rl McCausland's.

On Sunday last, a man came on shore, out of one of the up-country boats, and walking near the river, was shot through the head and died instantly without speaking one word. The boat moved off immediately and who shot the poor man is unknown.

On the 3rd of March a man is to be hung in St. Francis Ville, for killing another man, much in the same way, by stabbing to the heart.

Our poor sister wishes you could be with her when their property is to be valued and sold. If you can come, I will let you know the time.

Remember me most affectionately to my dear sister and the little ones. May every blessing attend you and yours, my best of brothers,

R. O'Connor

P.S. Clarissa was married in my old house. Mr. Scott called for Julia Ann on his way home from New Orleans and has taken her home. I am afraid he is in a bad way and that he never will be otherwise. He did not wait to see Lewis and Clarissa before he left here. I shall be shockingly disappointed if Clarissa's choice don't turn out to be much the best. Charlotte lives with me. Please to obsesrve the small enclosed paper.

Editor's Note: A copy of the enclosed newspaper clipping follows:

THE STATE OF LOUISIANA
Third District Court—Parish of West Feliciana
PAMELA WEEKS, wife of Henry Weeks
HENRY FLOWER, her husband—No. 753

DECEMBER 19, 1829.

It is ordered, adjudged, and decreed by the Court that Pamela Weeks, wife of Henry Flower, be separated in property from her said husband—see article 2399 and 2401 of the civil code—It is further ordered, adjudged, and decreed, that the tract of land upon which the parties reside containing six hundred and forty arpents more or less, is the separate property of the plaintiff, and that the slaves Ede, Esther, Sylla, Frank, Rose, Mary, Henry, Ann, Caroline, Bob, Comfort, Saul, Sarah, Bill, Charlotte, Adeline, and Harriet are also her separate property, and that she be put into immediate possession of the aforesaid property.

It is further ordered, adjudged and decreed, that the plaintiff recover of the defendant the sum of fourteen thousand nine hundred and seventy three dollars sixty four and a half cents with interest from the 5th day of June, 1829.—and that she is entitled to the right of a mortgage creditor upon all his land and slaves, taking date the 5th of April 1823.

It is further ordered, adjudged and decreed, that the defendant indemnify the plaintiff against the payment of her securityship to the Bank of St. Francisville, which is ascertained to be two thousand dollars, and in default thereof that his property be sold for that purpose and the money paid over to her to be appropriated to the discharge of the said debt of two thousand dollars, and that she have a lien on the defendants property for the same.

It is further ordered, adjudged and decreed, that the plaintiff is not in this action entitled to the crop or any part thereof as separate property, the same in the opinion of the Court enters into the community, and not having made a demand for any share in the community she cannot now be entitled to a decree in her favor for the crop.

December 30, 1829
L. ESNEAULT

Judge 4th District, sitting in the 3d District.
Truly extracted from the Judgment.
Clerk's office, Jan. 5, 1830.
Test—B. COLLINS, Clerk of said Court

Rachel again asked that a letter be burned.

Feb-ry 17th, 1830

My dear brother,

Yours of the 30th of Jan-ry came to hand Tuesday last. I am thankful to learn the good health you all enjoy, my sister in particular, as she has been poorly for sometime past. I hope she will be able to write again. I should be glad to receive a letter from her once more.

I am sorry you have to stay on the Island so much. It must be unpleasant to you both. But we often have to do as we can, not as we wish. I sincerely wish you great luck in the present crop of this year and all else. All the sugar planters fell short in their crops; some has not made half as much as they did the year before last. However the price is better, which will be in their favor, and in which I hope you may benefit much.

I feel very glad that you are pleased with the crop that I raised last year. I believe Mr. Patrick done the best he could both in raising and gathering the crop. He behaved so well that I was glad to

43

get him engaged on the same terms for another year. He is now preparing for another crop and is very forward in every part of his work. The whole plantation is under good fence and every part of the work managed with ease, so that I have no kind of uneasiness about either fields, or Negroes, only that of providing for them. He has had thirty acres cleared joining the little field that Stokes had cleared near Mrs. Pirrie's, which he is now bushing up and burning.

Dr. Denny is, as usual, very attentive to the sick ones and soon has them able to work again. Mr. Bowman has lost several slaves this fall and winter past; one fine young man died last night. Mrs. Pirrie and Dr. Ira Smith has some dangerously ill at this time.

My cotton is all sold but ten bales, and nearly all sold for ten cents. Mr. Swift says it has sold better than any other crop from this neighborhood. So, my dear brother, you can see I am still trying to creep along slowly with the help of good friends bestowed by a kind *God*. How glad I shall be if I should be spared to see you again. Your talk of coming to see us in the spring has raised new hopes of seeing you once more. When we parted last, I had such strong feelings on my way home from St. F. V. that I expected never to live to see you return here any more, but now I hope I was mistaken.

I have not seen our sister since my last letter to you. I expect she is well. Poor little Louisa is not able to walk yet. She has had such a sorrowful time of it. I sincerely pray that she may recover. She is a charming child. Charlotte has gone to see Clarissa at this time, but I expect she will be very glad to go home with you. I scarcely think she is contented with me, or indeed, with any of us over here. She appears dissatisfied at times and gives no reasons why she is so. Perhaps it might wear away if she were to go home with you. The change would be pleasant, and I think, add greatly to her happiness.

I have very good health and am doing all I can to make a garden. I have the ground in good order and some of it planted, but the rabbits eats all that comes up.

Mr. Swift has received a letter from you a few days ago which he intends answering soon. His three sisters has returned from N. Orleans and is at school with the Miss Coltders. They now have possession of Mr. James Flower's house about 2 or 3 miles from here. Mr. and Mrs. McVea are very happy. I seen him once since her arrival and wished him much joy. I have not seen her. I am informed their little son is beautiful.

Do, my beloved brother, write as often as possible no matter how short, so if I can know you are all well, I am contented. My kindest love to my dear sister and her babes.

Your affectionate sister,
R. O'Connor

Lewis Davis and Clarissa are well. They come to see me every two or three weeks. I love them both.

Burn this.

The debts of her deceased loved ones continue to plague Rachel. Eleven days following the previous letter, she writes an urgent appeal to David to assist her in a suit instituted by Henry Flower against the estate of her deceased brother William Stephen Swayze.

February 28th, 1830

My dear brother,

I hope, ere this, you have received my last; and, if so, you are no stranger to my distresses nor the anxious desire I have of seeing you. Do, pray, my dear brother, make every haste to get here that is in your power. Harry has behaved so meanly towards myself and those orphan children of our brother Stephen, that I look on him as as great an enemy as his brothers. They know I have written to you, but they cannot know that I had any other reasons, only that of Harry's suing me. Mr. Handy was here the day before yesterday and asked me if I expected you. I answered him (in a very serious manner) yes, that I should look for you to come in ten or twelve days. He asked me if I had written for you; I said yes. He asked what hurried, to which I carelessly answered nothing only the suit that H. F. had (of late) entered against me.

If you can come, we can secure *all* out of their power, with the greatest safety. I know you will feel afraid of their having a claim against you for the debts, but indeed they cannot. I would not ask you to come to bring you into trouble. Mr. Swift stayed here last night and we had a long talk on the subject of those two suits and the danger of their going against me. But he said if you come in time, it could be easily secured out of their power, or any other's whatever; and then they would be glad to compromise and settle on easy terms; take what we were willing to give. If you should be afraid to let me make it over to you, and take my receipt in full, I will not insist on your doing so, only come and see it done. The other will not undertake it if you are present.

When you come, should you see H. F. or Handy, don't let them know that you had heard of the suits being returned, or anything about it, but I hope to see you before them and have our talk first. I cannot bear the idea of H. F. and his friends enjoying the pleasure of breaking me up, which I am convinced is their mutual wish. What a fool Harry is to bite his nose off to spite his face!

The plantation is in good order and under good form—all doing well. Caroline had a young child the day before yesterday, and I expect Harriet to have one hourly, and Bridget's only eight months old the 6th of next month, which has the appearance of doing well.

O, dear me, how I want to see you. I am writing, but cannot half explain my desires. However, if you can save the property together, and I should be spared and have my health, I hope to convince you that my views were not selfish.

Give my love to my dear Frances. Tell her that I am so troubled that I have not written to her for some time, but that I will soon. She must kiss her little brothers and sister for me. Remember me very affectionately to my dear sister Mary whose health, I hope, continues to mend.

I remain your affectionate sister,
R. O'Connor

The domestic squabble between Henry and Pamela Weeks Flower results in Pamela's holding a mortgage against him. His property is to be sold and Rachel greatly desires David's presence to look after interests of his relatives.

Note on outside of envelope: "Please forward this with all possible speed."

March 6th, 1830

My dear brother,

Yours of the 20th of last month has just come to hand. I expect it arrived in St. Francis Ville on Thursday last. Daniel met the mail on his way that day, in a dreadful rain, which continued until the waters were so high that it was impossible to get to town before this morning.

I am sorry that I did not inform you before this that H.F.'s property is to be sold on the 22nd day of this month which enclosed paper will show. Mr. Handy told me that Harry had written to you on the subject and requested you to come over at that time, to assist them at the sale, which were my only reasons for not writing and informing you all. However, I hope and trust you will be over in time, for indeed I am watching the road constantly to see if you are not coming, although I know that I had not ought to expect you yet. But I must request you to come as soon as possible. My two letters previous to this will explain all and let you know how necessary it is for you to come immediately. Do, my dear brother, come and help me to save all we can. It is thought that a short time will make it forever too late for use to do anything towards securing the property out of the power of Harry and Wm. Flower. Mr. Swift has written to you on the same subject and appears as anxious for your arrival as myself. If you should see Mr. Handy or H.F. before you see me, be very cautious not to mention to them either Mr. Swift or the suits. They do not know that I have heard one word of its being returned to St. F.V. nor the danger I am in of being cost by adversaries. I think hard of H. F. for suing me the moment the joyful news came. He don't care how much cost I am run to. He is so secure himself that he has lost all feelings for others. They know that I have written for you to come, but do not know of any other business only that of H.F.'s suing me. How Mr. Handy will manage for our sister Pamela is hard to say. He has managed badly for himself. He expects to break in May; the debts of the old firm of Handy and Waddle has come against him and takes more than all to pay it up. Mr. Scillman, the present partner of Mr. Handy, refuses to have anything to do with the debts of Handy and Waddle. Don't let any of Harry's family know that I wrote this to you. Perhaps they would not like it. I never think they have much love for me since this long lawsuit has been between their brothers and myself. I don't think it should have effect on my sister, but I much fear it has. Whenever I am there, I cannot help feeling myself in the way, and sometimes mean into the bargain. I wish I may be wrong in my conjectures. I don't feel well today. I am surprised at myself, how I keep about as I have since this bad news came. I am so troubled. I still have great reason to hope that Clarissa has married a good man, which is a great comfort to me to think they can provide for themselves. Poor little girl, how my heart would ache for her if she lived with me yet.

I am very glad that you and your family enjoys good health. I sincerely wish it may last long. What can be the reason of my sister's not writing occasionally as she formerly did? Surely she is not angry with me. I am so apt to make blunders not intended, that I feel an uneasy dread on my mind whenever I think of her, but I can say with safety that it is far from my wishes to commit such an act; and if I have, I did not intend it. I want to see her very much. I want to see all. The moment I sink into trouble, my whole soul is seated in your family. It even leaves my dear Clarissa for a while, the only being that is left to call me mother. Much love to you all.

I remain your affectionate sister,
R. O'Connor

A few days earlier, David had purchased Evergreen and its slaves. Rachel expresses her deep gratitude to him for coming to her aid.

April 10, 1830

My dear brother,

I received your letter with great pleasure. I am truly thankful to find you arrived home safe, and found your family in good health, and heartily rejoice in the happy meeting of you all. I should have written long since if I had been alone. Clarissa and Mr. Davis came to see me shortly after you left here and stayed several days, and then Mr. and Mrs. Howell came, after which, the Miss Swifts, and now I have to stay every night with Mrs. Bowman who expects hourly to be confined and her mother has not been at home for a week. She stays constantly at Dr. Ira Smith's, fearing he might get sick. I do sincerely pity Eliza. She appears so sensible to her mother's neglect. However I ought not to mention it in my present humour. I feel vexed at the old lady's unkindness towards her youngest daughter and partiality to others. They are all her children and should be treated as such.

I went to St. Francis Ville to see Mr. Turner on the business you directed, but did not see him. He has gone to Clinton. I intend to go again when he returns home.

The work of the plantation goes very smoothly, nothing amiss since you were over. We are nearly done planting cotton seed and corn. Mr. Patrick has a very sore throat and looks bad, but continues very attentive to his business. I sincerely hope he may raise a good crop. The Negroes are all well and the teams in fine order.

I should indeed be very glad to go over to see your lovely family, and hope that the time may come that I can be spared without feeling as much uneasiness as at present if I should leave home. There is several small children, two of them sucking babes, and Harriet will soon have her young one if no misfortune should befall her, Henry and Sarah, theirs, in five or six months more, which will require my attention for some time, if I should live. And I feel a greater desire to take care of them, since I know they are yours, than I have done for several years past. I enjoy such perfect contentment of mind, so unusual to me, that at times I scarcely believe I am the same being. Should my health continue as good as it is at present, I shall hope to show the gratitude I feel in taking care, and managing, so as to add to what there now is, and make it as much better as lays in my power. But after I have done all I can, it will poorly reward so good a brother for the kindnesses bestowed on me in my distresses.

I have not heard from H. F.'s family since you saw them, nor Wm. Swayze either.

The enclosed seed is the small cucumber seed that my sister Mary sent for. I had it before you went away, but forgot to give it to you. I am afraid you forgot the little knives that my little boys sent to me for. Mr. Swift talks of visiting you, and if he does, I will send them by him and something for my little daughters too.

Give my kindest love to my dear sister and the little children. I must bid you farewell. Eliza Bowman has a messenger on its way for me. I will write again shortly.

I remain your affectionate sister,
R. O'Connor

The news of David's and Rachel's property transactions has become known. Rachel hears that she is being accused of cheating her nephew William Swayze. She writes to David of her fear that she is unwelcome at the home of their sister, Pamela Weeks Flower.

April 18th, 1830

My dear brother,

Since I received your last, I have written one, and now commenced the second, which I hope may find you all in good health. Our friends are all well; and, as for myself, I never enjoyed better than at present. How thankful I feel for so great a blessing.

I have not seen Mr. Turner since you left here. I went once, but did not see him. He has gone to Clinton and has remained there ever since.

Mr. Patrick has the plantation in fine order; forwarder than any of the planters in our neighborhood, which appears to cause some distress amongst them. However that may be wrong. We are ordered to love our neighbors as well as ourselves. The horses that you brought are very good and stand the work well. Indeed all the horses look extremely well. Big Buck's shoulder became very lame and swelled greatly. I got the Dr. to rowel him, which has cured his lameness, but his shoulder appears weak. Otherwise he is in fine health and spirits.

Your grass seed has not come up and am afraid will not as it has been so long in the ground. I will not disturb the ground for a long time yet to see if it will come or not. I wish you could get some more seed and let me try again. Perhaps I would have better luck the next time.

I wish you would inquire whether Mr. Dunkins came up or not and let me know. The news of our trades are creeping about. Mr. Courtney Smith says that I sold out to keep Wm. Swayze out of his part, because I must know that I could not live forever and thought proper to fix the business in time. Wm. has not been to see me since, but I don't intend to let that trouble me. Charlotte and Clarissa and Mr. Davis are kinder to me than before, and Mr. Swift continues the same. He could not be better. How my sister feels, I don't pretend to know. I have not either seen or heard from one of them since I seen you, and indeed, my dear brother, I cannot go to see them until Pamela comes to see me. I should be afraid they did not want me and think that I pushed my assurance too far, which is more than I can do. I should be glad to see any or all of them. They are near and dear to my heart, and will be during life. But with all, I should like to know whether they wished me to visit them now or not before I ventured there. I did not like Harry's suing me at first, which probably caused me some angry feelings towards myself. I have forgiven him and am no longer angry, but still think that I could not have served him so. I met David Flower when last in St. Francis Ville, who passed me wonderful cool, scarcely nodded his head, which appeared strong. He never would pass me before without shaking hands and inquiring after my health.

My love to my sister Mary and the little children, not forgetting yourself. I remain your ever affectionate and grateful sister,

R. O'Connor

Rachel is pleased that her sister Pamela plans to visit her.

May 22nd, 1830

My dear sister,

Your thrice welcome letter arrived yesterday, which I must acknowledge came unexpected, as you seldom write in your present situation, and had not written for some time previous, which at times gives some uneasiness. However I would always conclude that the cares of your family was sufficient employment and that you seldom had time to spare to write to those that feels so anxious to hear from you. And I can truly say that I was overjoyed to receive this, but when I came to the part that gave an account of the great loss that my dear Sidney has met in the *death of her little son*, I could truly say that all joys were of a short duration, for most sincerely do I lament the loss of their charming little boy, and the sorrows his death must occasion his father and mother and friends. I hope that they may soon become reconciled to their sad misfortune. It is our duty to submit to the will of Providence, which ought to be considered as soon as possible. Otherwise we may draw on ourselves double sorrows, the latter I accuse myself of. In times past, had I been more resigned at first, I don't think my misfortunes would have been so severe, which too late I do lament. But still hope to be forgiven what I so inconsiderately done.

Mr. Davis and Clarissa is here with me which will prevent my letter being very long. But I will soon write to you again when I am alone. I would have written to Harriet this morning for a receipt for to preserve the prickly cucumber, if her Uncle Wm. Flower had not been at her house pretty constant of late. He attends court hourly and I expect a message from me would be unpleasant while he is considered one of her family. As soon as he leaves the neighborhood, I will get it and enclose it to you. Charlotte and Clarissa are very well. They both send their love to you and family, also to Sidney and Elizabeth. They are extremely sorry for poor Mrs. Palfrey. Eliza Boman has a fine little daughter a month old tomorrow. She is very well indeed and Mr. Bowman is more delighted than I ever seen a man with a young child.

I have received a letter from my brother dated the 12th which I intend answering shortly. The crop is uncommonly promising at present and I sincerely hope may continue so. We have had very wet weather which assists the old land greatly.

I have enjoyed good health for a long time, for which I am very thankful. I hope this may find your health quite restored. I am sorry to hear of your being so poorly. I received the enclosed paper, sent by my dear little Frances. Poor little darling. I am sorry indeed for her loss. He was a sweet little cousin. She must not forget her promises. I am always glad to receive her letters. My sister talks of coming to see me, but I scarcely expect her before William Flower leaves those parts, and I shall not venture from home during his stay unless I am obliged. I received a letter from Julia Ann a few days ago. She was well at the time she wrote which I am afraid is all she has to boast of. Mr. Scott has to sail to N. Orleans often enough to spend all he can make. Clarissa has got a fine saving young man, and I shall be much deceived if they do not do well. I have not seen Wm. Swayze since my brother left me. They expect an heir shortly; and if I am not mistaken, Clarissa may look out, seven or eight months from this, but don't mention it should you write shortly; I may be mistaken.

Harriet Handy seen your brother in N. Orleans lately. She said they were all well and desired to be remembered to me. Give my love to Mr. and Mrs. Palfrey, Mr. and Mrs. Harding, and your eldest brother and his lady should they be with you, not forgetting my dear brother and his sweet babes. My dear sister, I must conclude after wishing you health and happiness, now and forever. I remain your affectionate sister.

R. O'Connor

The last two of the "orphans" Rachel reared have been wed. William Swayze is married to Melinda Harbour, and Charlotte Swayze has chosen Anthony Doherty. Rachel's after-Christmas letter reflects her optimism for the new year.

Jan-ry 16, 1831

My dear sister,

I am afraid you have all forgotten me. I have not received one line from you or my brother for five or six weeks past which occasioned me much uneasiness until Mr. Handy came to see me a few days ago and informed me of your troubles. He said that a Mr. Robert Davis (lately from Attakapas) had informed him that ten of your Negro men had undertaken to run away and that some peddlers happened to come acrost them, and decoyed them back to the island before they discovered their intention of returning them to their owners again. I am surprised they were not all drown. Surely they will never venture such a trip a second time. I hope my brother will not give out coming over here this winter or spring, but I know he will do for the best and I must not add to his troubles.

All appears to go on very well here. Mr. Patrick has commenced the new year as usual very industriously and I entertain every hope of his raising another good crop. He has one hundred and twenty-nine bales of cotton pressed, and I expect there is enough for thirty or forty more, but it is not ginned yet. We started the gin very soon after we commenced picking cotton, but it could not keep up with the pickers. I wish my brother could spare time to come and see how we manage his affairs in his absence. I will do as well as I know how, but perhaps he could learn me how to do much better. Clarissa's long illness and the drought together prevented me from making much by my garden, but I hope to do better this year if I live.

Charlotte and her husband are in good health and wonderful happy. She considers her choice one amongst the best, and I believe William and his wife are doing very well. Her father assists them very much. Clarissa and her husband makes out better than I expected them to do for some time. He is so young and inexperienced in cropping. She remains a pitiful looking object since her sickness. Poor Julia Ann lives far from me. I know very little about them or how they are doing, only that they had enjoyed good health all last year.

Mr. Handy and Harriet and their little son are all very well. She lives with her father and mother and he has become clerk for Maxwell and Hudson near the river for 50 dollars pr. month. Our sister and family are quite well, and my own health at present is very good.

Mr. Swift and sisters are all well and happy at last. His eldest sister stayed with me all last week and appears to be happy to see her friends once more. Your brother Alfred has been in St. Francis Ville very lately and did not come out to see me. I am afraid he is angry with me about something. I hope not. He would be one amongst the last that I would offend willingly. If I had heard of his being in town before he left there, I should have sent for him. Clarissa and Mr. Davis met him on his way to Howell's and he promised them to visit me the next day, which is the last I have heard of him.

Do, my dear sister, write to me and let me know how you all are and what you have named my little nephew. I long to hear his name and how all his little sisters and brothers are. My little Frances has not written to me for a long time. I think I have wrote twice to her since I received her last. Kiss all them for me. Please to mention in your next how both your sisters are. I hope poor Sidney has become reconciled to the loss of her son. She still has some children and may be happy. I sincerely wish Elizabeth's little son may prove a blessing to her. My love to my dear brother and his little ones, and much to yourself.

> I remain your affectionate sister,
> *R. O'Connor*

Rachel reports to David the bumper cotton crop of the previous fall, the first crop since his purchase of her estate. She inquires about the legality of an heir's demanding an additional payment for serving as an executrix of an estate.

March 17th, 1831

My dear brother,

This is only the second time I've written since you left me. The first part of the time there were company here; and since, I have been quite busy with my garden and nursing my little chickens. I have between 50 and 60 hatched and 13 hens setting. Surely I shall do a little at last. Mr. Patrick bought one thousand weight of pork today, at three and a half cents per lb. which amounts to thirty-five dollars and Mr. Swift paid for it. The last of your crop is pressed. It made forty more bales, one hundred and eighty bales the whole crop of cotton, and they commenced hauling it to the river this morning. if the weather holds fair, you may soon expect to hear of its arrival in N. Orleans, where I hope you may receive a good price for it.

The work of the plantation is going on very well. Your new horses plough charmingly and as gentle as dogs. The one that I bought for 25$ behaves quite well since the time he run off. The calves are all marked and branded. William Flower has recovered and returned to college. His little sister is with Mrs. Andrews at Jackson. The rest of your sister's family are well. They have received Sidney's letter and are much pleased with it. He must continue to be a good boy and write often to his dear mama.

Our old neighbor, Mrs. Percy, is no more. She *died* on Saturday night last. She had sold out to her son Robert, and had intended to move to Natchez to live with her daughter Jane, since the death of Mr. William, but she died at home. Her daughter came down to see her ere her death.

It is still thought that Mr. Browder has *drown himself.* I think it strange that he should apply to Green Davis to endorse for him, in the Woodville Bank, for six thousand dollars, and drew it only two days previous to his committing the act. Poor Davis is in a peck of *troubles,* about the *six thousand dollars.*

When you see Mr. Conrad, do please ask him if an heir who may have been appointed executor or executrix, or perhaps gurdian, can make a charge of ten percent against the estate, when they had to employ an attorney and other friends (to assist them in the business they should do themselves) at the expense of the estate. I have been told that an heir cannot claim anything for their services, agreeable to our laws, and I wish it may be the case. A. Doherty has made his brags of gaining twenty-three or four hundred dollars for what Charlotte done, which is no better than robbing the rest of her father's children, if they get it. She had Mr. Turner and Mr. Swift to assist her. She only had the name of it and they done the business. Mrs. Pirrie says that Lewis Stirling made a similar charge against the estate of his Uncle Solomon Alstone and had received his pay. When the other heirs discovered it to be unlawful, they made him return the money to them. I don't like to inquire of our lawyers for fear they might mention it.

Your hound slut was brought to St. F. V. again, but had left there before I heard of her being returned. If I should hear of her, I will send her home.

I hope this may find you and yours well and happy. My love to my dear sister and the children. Your affectionate sister,

R. O'Connor

How does the Negro boys behave? I hope they are satisfied and married. The Negroes here are all in fine health. Old Sampson has not been to the house since you left here, but he appears very pleasant when I see him.

Rachel writes a friendly letter to her niece Frances Weeks.

May 2nd, 1831

My dear Frances,

I have put off writing from time to time until I feel ashamed to commence a letter to my beloved little darling. I cannot lay it to forgetfulness. I often read your pretty letters over and over again and show them to your cousins, and tell them how smart you are and that they must try to follow your good example, otherwise they cannot expect to overtake you in learning. Mr. Handy and your Cousin Louisa Flower stayed with me last night on their way home to see Mr. Collins and your Cousin Maria and their little children who arrived two days ago. Poor little Louisa appeared overjoyed with the hope of seeing her eldest sister and family once more. Your Uncle H. Flower and family were in good health yesterday. James and William

Flower are to visit their sister on Saturday and return to their studies on Monday morning.

I have so many little chickens and turkeys to take care of that I scarcely have time to write, which I hope may apologize for the length of time I have neglected answering my sweet little darling's letter, and will venture to promise that unless some new grievous misfortune should overtake me, I shall not, in health, be guilty of the same fault again during life.

Your Cousin Charlotte returned home yesterday after spending a week with me. I had to promise to visit her in two or three weeks if my health should continue good.

Inform your papa that Mr. Charley has commenced working at his press this morning. It has been uncommonly dry for some time past.

Give my love to your Cousin Sidney and your little brothers and sister, not forgetting your uncles and aunts. I hope your next may bring news of their all being in good health.

Please remember me most affectionately to your dear papa and mama and kiss my little F. W. for me. I think you all could afford to give him to me and let him be my babe. Could not my dear Frances prevail on her dear parents to bring her over to see her relations the next visit her papa bestows on us? Adieu, my sweet child. May every blessing attend you here and hereafter, now and forever, are the prayers of your affectionate aunt,

Rachel O'Connor

P.S. I have seen Mr. Bowman and mentioned the land, but he would not agree to sell any part of it. He said that he would endeavour to bring the white clover seed.

The unfortunate litigation is soon to be settled, three referees having been appointed. Rachel tells David that William Flower seems confident of victory.

August 4th, 1831

My dear brother,

I believe it to be fully a month since I received a letter from you, the last said that you were all well, that your own health was much better than it had been for a long time. I hope it may be the case yet. But I am exteremely anxious to hear from you again. This week has been so wet and all the creeks are so very high that I have not sent to the post office to inquire for letters. Perhaps good luck may send me one tomorrow. I wrote to you last week which more than likely may be lost owing to the dreadful rains and high waters.

I mentioned the death of Mr. McVey in my last, which I lament so greatly that I must speak of him a second time and remember during life the many kindnesses he bestowed on me in all my troubles.

Clarissa has returned home. Her health don't appear to improve. Dr. Stone attends her and will certainly do for the best, but I much fear she has already suffered too severely ever to regain her health as it once was. She despairs of it herself, but appears resigned to her fate. Her situation distresses me much. I had not the smallest idea that I loved her so dearly. Harriet Handy has named her daughter Emily Pamela. Mr. Swift has taken his sisters up to Cincinnati and left them with their brother-in-law and sister, and returned home himself, and is laying very sick at his plantation every since his arrival.

I have enjoyed my health for some time. I wish it may continue. Some of the Negroes are sick; poor little Isaac has been very sick three or four days. I think he is better tonight. His fever is not so high as it has been. He has passed three worms today. I keep him and his mother in my room with me at night.

Phillis is one of the most industrious animals I ever saw. She and the Dr. has killed seven rats today. When they run up between the house logs out of her reach, he chases them down to her. She has six fine puppies. I shall keep one pair of them and give the others to our friends.

Mr. Patrick has saved a part of the fodder and thinks he will get the rest saved in a few days. He has about 30 acres of land cut down. He keeps very industrious, but I think less work might do the crop. He never lays it by until he has to commence picking cotton. However I never say a word about it to him. I know him to be a good farmer and I must not cause him to act wrong. All my neighbors follow his plan of planting. The wind has injured Dr. Ira Smith's crop very much, and many others, *but not yours.*

My love to my sister and the little children. It is past midnight, so my dear, I will bid you farewell and pray God bless you and yours.

R. O'Connor

P.S. 6th of August: I retained my letter with a hope of getting one from you yesterday, but was disappointed which occasioned me much uneasiness respecting the health of your family. I hope my sister may be well. Do write soon.

I received a letter from Mr. Nubling (one of the referees in the Flower suit) saying that Joseph Bernard had declined serving as agreeful to the appointment heretofore, and wishing another appointed in his place. I believe the settlement is to take place soon and whatever is to be, relative to that unfortunate affair, will shortly be known. I have written to Mr. Turner and enclosed Nubling's letter, with all other papers that I can find. Mr. Swift stayed here the night before last and appeared extremely clever as usual. He left his sisters at school in Cincinnati. When you write, let it be so that he may see your letter, as he has long been accustomed to see them and might feel neglected otherwise. Should you have anything to say that would be improper for him to read, write it on a small paper and enclose it in your letter. He inquired after you and family and appeared anxious to hear from you all. Since the death of Dr. Isaac Smith, his eldest daughter has died with two days sickness.

Thompson's Creek and the Bayou Sara has been higher of late than they have for many years past, which has injured those that live near them greatly. Their banks has fell in dreadfully from accounts. Lewis Davis lost two or three acres of corn and cotton, with all his ploughs, by the freshes. Perhaps he may find his ploughs when the waters fall. The horse that I paid twenty-five dollars for dropped dead in the plough a few days ago without any signs of sickness. I had him opened and the Dr. said one part of his insides was bursted. He was a good work animal, but always wild, trying to run off with the plough. The other horses are all well and in fine order—two pretty little horse colts this year, and nineteen calves, and seven little lambs, not a month old. I hope I shall have better luck with them than I had last winter. Should this troublesome settlement prove any ways easy, I think I shall be able to do better. I cannot help being distressed and now I can scarcely describe my feelings bad enough, which makes me hate myself for being so simple. If I could hear from you, I should feel better.

Our poor sister's children are all well. I saw James and William Flower a few days ago. Mr. Handy talks of visiting you soon and next spring taking a trip with his family to see his parents which he says will only cost him 4 or 5 hundred dollars, which he considers trifling. I want to go up to see Harriet, but old Wm. F. is in the neighborhood, and I suppose there, and I don't like to venture on that account. Mr. Swift says he is wonderful smiling, his expectations are so flattering. Poor animal, I believe I wish every other living thing better than I do him. The boy that I sent this morning to Mr. Turner with the papers has returned and brought his answer, which I will enclose to you.

Your affectionate sister,
R. O'Connor

Sickness and death are subjects of this letter. Alarmed by the news of David's stiff thumb, Rachel proposes a cure for it. (This letter was obviously misdated. Its conents prove that it belongs in this sequence.)

August 24, 1831

My dear brother,

I hope ere this your thumb is well, but not receiving any letter of late makes me fear not, and I must not expect my sister to write often at present from knowing her distress occasions her more fatigue than she is able to undergo. But a sick family will cause any good wife and mother (such as she has proved herself to be) to exert while their strength lasts and very often longer than they are really able. I feel quite uneasy about her. I'm afraid she may be sick at the moment. How is the poor little babe's arm? I pray it may not prove to be anything serious or hurtful hereafter to his dear little arm. Do some of you write soon and let me know how you all are. I have been very sick five or six days with the ague and fever. My eyes are so weak that it is troublesome for me to see sufficient to write. Tomorrow is my sick day and every day getting weaker, which causes me to be afraid to put off writing, as a short time may put it out of my power.

We have had many deaths very lately. Old Mrs. Hail, Mrs. Robert Percy, and one of her sisters, both lately married, a son of Mr. Wetherstran's who was a young man grown, and a son of Mr.

Leak's all died very near each other. I am told that Mr. Swift is still laying at the point of death. Mr. Crenon, who lives in Jackson, is laying very ill. Mr. Flower and Louisa went from here today. Harry's family are all well. Mrs. Pirrie has the ague and fever and I am informed lays very sick.

Do let me know how you intend to get your bagging and cordage. Had you not better have it sent from N. Orleans? Perhaps it may not come as high as it will to buy it here. I shall have to get one piece to make picking bags; the rest can be done as you think best. I still hope you may have a good crop. The rains has made it rot some. I was over every part of it some time ago. It promised fair then.

Friday 26—I found myself too weak to finish my letter and yesterday my chill and fever was very bad. Today I scarcely set up any, I am so very weak. I received your letter dated the 17th yesterday, but I was too sick to read it until this morning. I am sorry your thumb remains stiff. I have known the oil of earthworms to relieve that much. Gather them and put them into a vial and cork it close and then put the vial in the middle of a loaf and bake it until done, as other bread is baked, and let it remain until cold which will turn the earthworms to oil, and rub your thumb. It can do no harm, if no good.

Miss Ann Cattner came and stayed last night with me and was very kind indeed. Lewis Davis came to see me last night, but had not heard of my being sick until he came here. He has gone home for Clarissa. They will be down by the time I take the ague if possible. Mrs. Robert Percy is yet alive and some hopes of her recovery. How it came to be reported that she was dead, I know not. Mr. Handy told me. Mr. Swift is laying as sick as ever. Mr. Isaac Johnson desired Mr. A. Doherty to give his compliments to me and tell me if I wished the settlement between William Flower and myself to be put off, that it might be kept unsettled for ten years to come, which is all I have heard about it since I wrote you. Mr. A. Doherty stayed with me the night before last. Charlotte is middling well, but too clumsy to come this far.

Now my dear, dear brother and sister, should we never be permitted to see each other again on earth, my blessing will remain with you. Farewell.

R. O'Connor

The Negroes are all well, but let me know how the Negro shoes are to be got. I expect they will commence picking cotton tomorrow morning. Patrick is in a hurry to get some pressed the moment he can. I don't know his reason, but I rather expect he has some bet on it.

An unfounded rumor of a Negro rebellion in the Felicianas causes Rachel to leave Clarissa's sick bed and hurry home. Rachel immediately writes Davis so that he will not fear for her safety.

October 13, 1831

My dear brother,

I returned home from Mr. Davis' on Monday last and found all as well as I could expect. The Negroes that I left sick had got some better. The Dr. had been very attentive and done all in his power for them. During my absence I found Clarissa very low, not able to set up a moment, nor to stand alone after being raised on her feet. I had very little hopes of ever seeing her walk again; but after I had been with her a few days, her spirits revived, and the fevers became lighter until they were gone. The three last days that I was with her she had no sign of fever—only very weak.

I felt so uneasy about home the last two days that I stayed with her (owing to the dreadful talk about the Negroes rebelling) that I had no rest and dare not mention a word of it to her, which made it worse. At length, I ventured to tell her how sick I left some of them and persuaded her to let me come home to see how they were, but I had to promise her to return again the last of this week, which I shall have to do, and perhaps have to stay a few days until she can come home with me.

Before I came home Mrs. Pirrie had been told that all the Negroes on little Robert Barrow's plantation had armed themselves and claimed their liberty. She instantly started screaming and crying as loud as she could for Patrick to start and see about them, which he refused to do, and said that if there was anything of that, his place was at home and must do all he could to take care of those under his charge. General Dawson raised his men and went there where he found the overseer and the Negroes very busy at gathering the crops, as peaceable as lambs, and not one word of truth in the report; neither do I see any reason to be afraid. They all behave well, but shockingly frightened at the patrols being ordered out. Poor little Fan is afraid to go after the geese without a pass. I have been afraid that you would hear that something dreadful had happened to us and cause you uneasiness, which makes me write sooner than I should otherwise do to let you know all is peace so far.

I have received a letter from my dear Frances very lately and will answer it soon. I am anxious to hear about the races. I had written her shortly before the arrival of her last.

My best respects to Mr. Charles Conrad, Mr. and Mrs. Palfrey, Mr. and Mrs. Harding, and kindest love to my dear sister Mary and all the little ones.

> I remain your affectionate sister,
> *R. O'Connor*

Do let me know when you wish cotton sent to New Orleans. I can send fifty bales at any time you think proper. One o'clock at night. My dear brother, adieu at present.

One month later death claims the infant son of David and Mary Weeks. Rachel writes a condolence letter.

> November 13th, 1831

My dear sister,

I wish that this may find you restored to health and that the dear little babe may be doing well, with the rest of your family. Pray do not let your sorrows overcome your strength. Consider the dear little ones with you and their father who could feel no happiness without you. A world of earthly riches could make no amends for the loss of such a wife and mother.

In all our severe trials we must pray to God to strengthen us both in body and mind that we give not up to despair; otherwise we sink before we consider our disobedience to the will of the *Blessed* who giveth and taketh at pleasure. I am sorry, very sorry, for our late loss. But, dear children, you are wrong. The little angel is happy.

What more can we wish for? The same God that gave him has taken him to himself where all is happiness. A few days since, in looking over some papers, I observed some lines written on the death of an infant son which caused me to think of you both, and with a hope of its being a comfort, I immediately copied it for the purpose of sending it to you. Do consider it well. It appears to me to be truth itself.

Sidney Flower came here on Monday last, this far, on his way home. He looked better than I ever saw him before; spoke most affectionately of you all and lamented parting with his cousins. His eyes filled with tears when he mentioned where he parted with his uncle on the road.

Charlotte has a son born the 3rd of this month and doing well, I have not seen her since, only heard the news. I will try to go there soon. Clarissa's illness prevented me from getting the Negro clothing fixed as early in the year as I commonly do for them. However I am pretty well through with them at last. Clarissa went from here on Sunday last, in better health than I have seen her for a long time. I wish it may continue, but I dare not raise one hope. Most sincerely do I pray that I have the power to resign *all* as I had ought to, knowing the *will* of God to be just.

Julia Ann writes they are well. William and Melinda are getting over their sickness, but poor Melinda had a severe attack, was even despaired of two days and nights. Harriet Handy has the fattest babe I ever saw. Its head and hair resembles its grandmother's beyond describing.

My love to my dear brother and the children. With many prayers for the happiness of you all, I remain,

Your ever affectionate sister,
R. O'Connor

Mr. Dunn, who formerly kept a boarding house in St. Francis Ville, shot his own brains out with a pistol on Monday last. I have not heard the cause of his doing so yet.

Editor's note: The lines on the death of an infant son, mentioned in Rachel's letter, were not found in the collection.

Sickness and death take their toll of both blacks and whites. Rachel congratulates David and Mary on the birth of another son. She wor-

*ries about the heedlessness of Harriet Handy and her husband. But
Rachel is cheered by visits from young relatives.*

Jan-ry 11, 1832

My dear brother,

Since I received yours of the 30th of Dec-br, I have commenced
two letters which sickeness prevented me from finishing. I had to
expose myself a little when the hogs were killed, and perhaps *eat too
freely* of the good fresh meat which caused me to be very sick for a
few days. However I hope the worst is over at present. This morning I feel pretty well again.

William and Louisa Flower stayed with me last night and started
this morning to Jackson to their schools. They were at home during
Christmas holidays. The family are all well excepting Harriet Handy
and she had begun to recover from a severe cold. Their old cook
woman, Liddy, died of the same disease on Thursday last, and Charlotte has been dangerously ill, but was some better yesterday before
Wm. left home. Dr. Keep said he had a hope she might recover.
They had nine Negroes sick when the children came from home yesterday morning. James Flower is at home studying law. He has just
returned from New Orleans. I believe he had just arrived home from
the North in Nov-br. He came to see me once. He certainly is a
most charming youth. I really think that James and William are all
their friends could wish them to be. I do not know of their being
guilty of one fault of any kind whatever. Harry has hired a teacher
for Sidney and David at home. The boys says he is a very smart
man. They appear much pleased with him.

Harriet's girl is still here. Her child was born the 13th of Dec-br.
I expect Handy guessed right from every appearance, but it is a poor
little starved looking thing. I would scarcely give four bits for it. I
rather think Harriet has carried a pretty high hand since she has had
sale management. Poor thoughtless girl—it is hard to know how she
and Handy will make out. They hold their heads as high and appear
unconcerned as tho' they had wherewith to support every extravang-
ance. I believe it would be best to give her all she is to get and let
them try themselves. They are preparing to visit Mr. Handy's relations this spring. They speak of starting in May. From what Harriet
said to Clarissa, she must expect the old people will settle something
on her and her children if she goes for it. Don't mention that I

65

wrote this to you. When I see you, I will tell you all I know and let you judge for yourself.

I expect Mr. Patrick will soon want his money and I don't know where to get it for him. Mr. Swift is either pushed or not willing to part with his money, I don't know which. I gave orders on him to the Negroes for the amount of their crops of corn and pumpkins and he only pays them a little now and then and keeps them running to town every Sunday for what they get. He is in N. Orleans at present. The have never made any settlement between the Swayze estate and Harry Flower yet. Old Wm. F. told A. Doherty that he had ought to oblige me to make up all that was missing, and not his brother Henry, and to allow him his account against the estate, which you may be sure did not make me feel very loving towards him for a short time after I heard of it. Old Dr. Flower's mean set of sons; they covet all that every other family has worked for; and after they get it, they fool it all away without becoming one cent the richer. I don't think Harry has more sense than a gander or he would conduct better. That wedding they made for Jane Marburg must have cost them $100 at least. They had Dr. Beverly Smith and his wife nearly two months last spring, and three young ladies until Bell's marriage, and much other company. I have heard that several has observed how different they manage to that of old times.

The Bower horse belongs to a Mr. Duplantier near Baton Rouge. There is to be a race near St. Francis Ville this week, where the Dr. and Patrick thinks they can find out every particular, after which I shall let you know all about him.

I am sorry the bales do not weigh more. I said so much to the pressers that I thought they would tramp the cotton well. There has been one hundred and twenty-five bales pressed, which is all the crop of cotton. Seventeen of them are here yet. The roads are so bad I am afraid to let them undertake to haul them to the river. Several fine woods oxen has mired in the mud and died there in the road.

Clarissa is very well. Julia Ann is on a visit amongst us for a month past; Charlotte and her son, Robert Hail, are well, but I have not seen her since the birth of her child.

I am very glad your little babe is doing so well. I hope you will name him David. You have had better luck than any of us. Perhaps the name may prove fortunate to your son. I hope my dear sister Mary enjoys good health with yourself and little children, and bears up against such misfortunes as Providence thinks proper to send. It is the common lot of all, and we are in duty bound to submit.

Young McQueen died a few days ago and left a wife and 2 small children in low circumstances. Dr. Keasby died lately also, and a number of Negroes through the Bayou Sara settlements all with severe colds. Jessy Davit who was overseer for Mr. Bowman last year lost his wife in June and was married again in [*Editor's note:* Rest of letter missing.]

Clarissa has accidentally poisoned herself, but her life is saved. Although no extant letter relates it, Pamela Weeks Flower has died during the year 1831 (prior to the time her daughter, Harriet Handy, was given the "sales management" mentioned in Rachel's last letter), and Henry Flower is trying to get married again. In this letter to David, Rachel expresses her fear concerning the upcoming trial.

April 25, 1832

My dear brother,

We appear to be forgetting each other quite fast. You have not written for a long time and I am sorry to acknowledge that of late I have committed the same fault. Shortly after I wrote last to you, Lewis Davis came for me to go and see Clarissa who lay very sick. She had made a great mistake in taking some medicine. She thought she felt a little unwell and concluded it best to take some magnesia, and after she had taken the dose, found that she had swallowed (at least) an ounce and a half of tartar emetic. How her life has been saved I cannot tell. God is merciful and done all. They got a great deal up before it had time to dissolve in her stomach. The Drs. are all surprised at her being yet alive and pretty well again. Wm. Swayze has been layed up with a swelled leg. When I saw it, I was afraid it would be a long time before he could walk. He did not know the cause; it came without any hurt. I have since heard he was better. My own health is very good at present. Old Mrs. Turnbull died about two weeks ago. I shall look for you over shortly. The weather will soon be very warm and unpleasant to travel.

H. F. is trying his best to get married. He parted with Miss Terry with tears in his eyes. Harriet and Handy speaks of starting on their journey soon, and then I expect the old man will get married without fail. They have called a family meeting since you saw them, and put too much power in their father's power for the good of his children. He can now sell or mortgage land at pleasure, and borrow money out of bank, which he intends doing to draw money for Handy's trip, I have been told. He says he will sell a part of the old plantation that he lives on, and all the swamp land that he owns. He will certainly ruin his children if there cannot be a stop put to his having the management of the estate. I am sorry for his family. What will become of them after all is gone?

The first Monday in May is the beginning of court here. You know my heart trembles at the thought. Patrtick is going on very well with his new crop. I am certain he is doing his best with it. I wish it would rain. The ground is very dry. He has every part of his crop planted and working it over.

My garden begins to look pretty well. I have gathered a smart little bag of *money* since you left me. I have made out better than I had done for a long time before. I have sixteen young calves on my book for this year and my guinea hogs grow finely.

Black Sam's eldest daughter (Ginney) had a little daughter the 14th of April (this month), It was the smallest child I ever saw. I had no hopes of its living for several days. but it begins to grow some and keeps well. Perhaps it may live. That makes three mulattoes born this year and living yet.

Corn keeps very high. Sometimes they ask ten bits pr. barrel. It is a dollar now. I wish you could be here to judge for the best. I do not know how to act. Little *cash* (on hand) keeps sending me word corn will be very high this year.

Sunday night: It commenced raining as I finished the above and rained ever since, so I had not any opportunity of sending my letter to the post office. Perhaps Daniel may get there this morning. I feel very uneasy to hear from you as it has been so long since I received a letter. Genney and her little child keeps quite well. I hope it may live. We are well. I have not heard how corn sells since I wrote the above.

My love to my dear sister Mary and all the children. Tell Frances to write soon. I remain your ever affectionate sister,

Rachel O'Connor

You must excuse the badness of my letter. I wrote in a hurry, pretty near night when my little chickens were to be put away. Perhaps you can make it out. Patrick and Dr. Denny are very anxious to hear how your race ended. I heard the Dr. say he had dreamed about it, but I don't recollect what his dream was.

In a news filled letter to Mary, Rachel encloses a letter from Mr. Turner to be shown to David. Mr. Turner has informed Rachel that the Flower brothers are most displeased with the verdict of the trial.

June 4th, 1832

My dear sister,

I received your kind and affectionate letter of the 9th of May long since, and should have answered it much sooner if I had not been too unwell to write. This is the first day that I have been able to set up for two weeks past, and quite unwell previous to that. I have mended very much today and hope soon to be able to attend my garden and other little affairs as usual. Your letter raised my spirits greatly. I had long wished to prevail on you to write, but scarcely expected you to undertake the task. I consider myself under many obligations to you for your continual goodness, and particularly so for your last letter. I know it was written with a sore heart, *from woeful experience*; but you are young and have so lovely a family with you that I hope and pray for your former happiness to be restored, and that kind fortune may smile on your future days so that the time may shortly come your blessings may be filled to the brim and sweet contentment ever yours.

I sincerely wish I could have confidence enough in an overseer to leave all under his care and visit you again. Nothing on earth could give me greater pleasure than once more to see you all together and to be with my dear little darling children and become acquainted with them again. Mr. Davis and Clarissa were very anxious to accompany me to your house shortly after my brother returned home; but I felt so afraid that my brother might be injured through some neglect of the overseer, or that he might become too great a man in my absence to do well, that I concluded it my duty to remain at home, which I now think I happened to do right.

The little Negroes proved sickly in the spring. I never saw such a number of worms pass from children in my life. I have been doctoring them ever since March. I hope they are pretty clear of worms now, as they begin to look so healthy and fat. *Stokes* behaved so bad when I left him in charge of the plantation the time I went to see you, that I am afraid to venture that far off a second time. I felt sorry to fill a letter with complaints after I returned home, and remained silent. I was glad I had been to see you, which made amends for all. Patrick is one of the best of farmers; he will raise a good crop if possible, but don't think of anything else. He is careful of his work horses. I rather suppose he would like to treat a few of the Negroes better than the others, if he dare. I talked to him this morning on that very subject, but he pleaded off pretty well and appears in a fine humor. He is really well behaved toward myself. He never has given any impudence yet.

I am very glad you are pleased with the gardening. I shall save and procure all the seed and plants I possibly can for you. The two small vines you mentioned are called corncockle. They bear a beautiful bluish purple flower in large clusters. They bloom in May. Should you want more, I can send plenty when I send the others.

H. Flower and the children are all well; the old man is not married yet. Our friends enjoy good health at present. I have been expecting my brother all last month. I hope he has not given out the trip. Old Mrs. Legendre died on Friday last. My dear sister will excuse all mistakes. My head is weak. Should I get well again, I will try to do better. Enclosed you will find a letter from Mr. Turner to me; please show it to my brother. My love to him and the children with many prayers for your health and happiness. Farewell, my beloved sister.

R. O'Connor

Editor's note: In a letter from John Turner (lawyer) to Rachel, dated July 8, 1832, about the verdict in the suit of Messrs. Flower, Turner advised Rachel to continue her usual action of stating that she had "no title" to property about her. If the sheriff, acting on orders from the Flower brothers, should attempt to seize property, he would be liable to a suit for damages by David Weeks.

Mr. Turner also stated that Mr. A Doherty had told him that Clarissa had been salivated by a dose of calomel.

LETTERS

Rachel writes to David of the sheriff's attempt to execute writs of seizure. She also writes about the new overseer. Simpson Patrick had been fired for immorality with female slaves.

July 8th, 1832

My dear brother,

I received your letter written in N. Orleans, where I learned the stiffness of my *friends*. Yesterday the sheriff visited me again, authorized to seize property to satisfy the claims against me. He said his first orders were to demand my money of me. I told him he might do so, but that would be all he had any right to expect; for it was well known that necessity had obliged me to sell all and every part of property that I owned on earth to pay my just debts and had paid the money away as far as it would go to those who I justly owed. He appeared to study very seriously for some time and then went away.

Mr. Swift stayed here the night before last and told me of a long search he and Judge Dawson, Mr. Witherstrand, and several others had before they could find where the sales of the land and the rest of the property had been recorded, that you bought last of me, and at last found it in the Mortgage Book, where all were mortgaged until paid. Very early yesterday morning, I went to the Clerk's office (with Mr. Swift) and released the mortgage, and acknowledged the notes paid, and come home before the sheriff came to perform his duty by levying an execution on all he could find belonging to me. In your next, I wish you to say whether I have done right or not. I have written to Mr. Turner and informed him in that manner the sheriff acted yesterday and requested his advice on the subject.

I am much better in health, but keep weak yet. Clarissa is sick and I feel afraid to undertake to ride that distance to see her. Mr. Swift speaks of starting up the Mississippi on Tuesday next. Mulkey, your new overseer, behaves very well. I think he will do well for a year or two at least. He pleased Mr. M. Caleb four years and would have been there yet, had not Courtland Smith got angry with the overseer on some trifling occasion. Mr. M. Caleb speaks well of him. Mulkey and his wife are both sick with a fever, but I hope it may not last long. Patrick behaves too mean to be a white man. His tracks are often found where he has been sneaking about after those Negro girls. He pesters Mr. Bowman's in the same way. Mrs. Pirrie

71

stays so much at Dr. Ira Smith's that she knows very little about home or how it is managed.

H. F. has told Mr. Swift that he intends to get married this fall; that he feels too active and smart to live a single life; and that Miss Terry will make and excellent poor man's wife—she can milk and wash and do anything.

We had a fine rain on Friday last, the first that wet the land since you were here. I got my potato vines planted on Friday evening. I hope they may do well. The corn has suffered greatly for rain. I never saw the ground so parched before. It made me sick to look at the corn. The cotton did not look so bad. Mr. Swift has been nearly drown out for three weeks. The grass has nearly overrun his crop owing to the wet weather. He says his corn stalks are so loaded with corn that they bend to the ground.

I hope this may find you all well and enjoying every earthly blessing. My love to my sister Mary and the little ones. I intend writing her soon. I remain your affectionate sister,

Rachel O'Connor

July 9th: I have received a letter from Mr. Turner and enclose it to you. Clarissa is on the mend.

Rachel writes to David of a cholera epidemic and of the accusations of fraud by the Flower brothers.

August 26th, 1832

My dear brother,

I have just received your kind letter dated the 10 instant. I am truly sorry to learn from it that my dear sister Mary, yourself, and poor little Harriet had been sick. We have so much sickness about here that I tremble at the idea of your family being in danger of sharing the same distresses. Our neighborhood for a great distance round about has suffered much from sickness and deaths of late, many of whom were strangers to me. Mrs. Jane Bell, a daughter of Wm. Marburg, died last week and left a young child a few hours old. Another lady who lived in St. Francis Ville, a mantua-maker, died only two days before Mrs. Bell; and a number of men, a part of which were boatmen. One man and child died in less than an hour after they were landed out of one of the steamboats.

We have been greatly favored on this plantation so far; no uncommon disease has taken place, nor has any of the Negroes been confined more than two or three days at once, only Bridget's child that I mentioned being sick in my last, which I am sorry to say continues very poorly still. It has fevers every day and looks bad, but I hope the poor little thing will get well after she gets her teeth cut through. Dr. Denny does not consider it dangerously ill; otherwise I should have but little hopes.

I have received a letter, dated the 28th of July, from Harriet Handy. They were well and at his father's in Snow Hill. She appears to be in high spirits and much pleased with the treatment she received from her new relations. Their only trouble was the fear of the cholera overtaking them, which is, at the present moment, the dread of *all* I know or hear of. Sometimes we get word of its being very near us and again not so near. I have received the medicine with the bagging cord that I wrote to Mr. Linton for.

August 27th, 1832

Yesterday evening Julia Ann came from Alexandria with her brother William, who had went up for her after he had heard of Mr. Scott's death. She looks miserable indeed and appears broken hearted—very seldom speaks unless spoken to.

I have not heard anything how the suit went, but I am rather inclined to think there will not be any trial this court. Mr. Turner delayed taking, or applying for, an appeal for the purpose of putting off the trial until next August. He said it was in his power to appeal anytime within a year after they gained the suit last. Mr. Turner informed me that it was your wish to keep it in law as long as possible.

Mr. Mulkey behaves very well and manages with much ease. I believe no white person troubles the quarters now. I am very particular to deliver your orders as soon as they come. And, so far, Mr. Mulkey has done his duty in every respect, and I yet think him a smart man on a plantation. He has about twenty thousand weight of cotton picked, and the gin running from the start. He has got up a part of the little wild mares and broke them to the gin. He is careful of the horses and the stock. A distemper has got amongst Mrs. Pirrie's and Mr. Bowman's cattle. They die fast, but none of yours has taken it yet. I have been doctoring them ever since. I mix something with their salt constantly.

I wish I had it in my power to convey my real feelings to you. Your last kind letter makes my heart overflow with the truest kind of gratitude. *I hope in God* you may hold all, and that it may prosper with you and yours during time. All that I can do towards taking care of it is my greatest happiness. Sometimes I really long to start and end my days with you and my best of sisters, amongst your little children; but Clarissa cannot bear the idea of my leaving her. She declares she will go with me, let me go when I will. She is a poor weakly little girl that could not bear much sorrow, and the dread of throwing her into a spell of sickness keeps me silent on the subject.

I have bought three barrels of lime to have the Negro houses white-washed, as all the people near here are doing to try to keep the cholera away. I have their bedding and houses aired often, which is said to be very necessary. Their wearing clothes are kept clean and victuals cooked done. I have all the milk churned every morning to have it sweet for them, which is said to be the best for them to eat.

I have not heard from Harrie's family lately, but I expect they are well, or I should have heard it. Mrs. Pirrie has been complaining for a month. She looks bad. Little Robert Barrow continues quite sick. His mother is most worsted from fatigue. Charlotte looks pretty well now. She really has a fine son. They were down to see me 8 or 10 days ago. Clarissa is only middling well. Her health will scarcely ever be as good as it formerly was, but they are doing very well. Lewis has a good crop and is comfortably fixed. He has his house finished off quite snug.

My love to my dear sister and the children. Do write soon and let me know how you all are. I am so very uneasy about your healths. Times are so sickly with us in many parts, but worse in the East Parish than here. A great number has died with bowel complaints. Mr. Carter, in the Plains, has lost one of his daughters.

Heaven preserve my best of brothers are the prayers of your unfortunate sister,

Rachel O'Connor

I came near forgetting to inform you that the old well caved in so that no person would venture to mend it. I have had another one dug. They came to water in 48 feet and it is good. I have paid for

the digging of it with my market money and we are now fixed
again.
Editor's note: In a letter to David Weeks, September 1, 1832, John
Turner advises him to deny William Flower's charge of fraud in the
acquisition of Rachel's property and to look upon William's letter
containing the charge as a "scarecrow."

*Rachel sends a desperate appeal to David to come at once to forstall
the seizure of his property.*

Saturday night, Sept-br 29, 1832

My dear brother,

   I am obliged to send Arthur to let you know the unfortunate
situation of your affairs over here. The sheriff has levied an execution
on the cotton at the landing and intends to come out to the plantation to do the same with all on it. I expect him every moment of
my life. I have just returned home from Mr. Turner's. He says he is
not authorized to act for you in every respect, particularly in giving
his bond agreeable to law, but I cannot explain it to you as I wish.
Perhaps you may be lawyer enough to know more of their forms
than I do. Mr. Turner told me today that he would do all in his
power to save the property for you, that he should be extremely glad
to see you on business, that he had a hope of making them repent
the steps they had taken, and still I am afraid he is very uneasy. Do
pray, my dear brother, come over with Arthur if you possibly can
leave home. I much fear you will lose greatly if you do not. They
are determined to seize all, if it should only be to injure you. Pray
don't let one trip over give any advantage to them over you. Mr.
Turner wrote to lawyer Downs early this morning on your business,
but had not received his answer when I came away. He appeared to
be in deep study all day. He is certainly a good friend and wishes to
have everything fixed according to law when he commences. If you
cannot come over yourself, you had better have the advice of a lawyer and authorize Mr. Turner agreeable to law respecting the bond,
and to act for yourself also. But I hope you can come and see to it
yourself, which will be much the best. And if you do come, be in a

hurry, for my sake. I shall write by the first mail for fear of something happening to Arthur on his way to detain him. I sent Arthur up to Mr. Turner with a letter last night after sundown to let him know of their levying an execution on the cotton and he returned before day with an answer from Mr. T. to myself, which I enclose to you. Please make *Arthur* return as soon as possible so that I may hear from you. Should my brother be from home, my dear sister will please send for him instantly and forever oblige a sister in distress. God bless you both is the prayer of your unfortunate sister,

R. O'Connor

The next day Rachel writes an urgent appeal to Mary in case her letter to David did not reach him.

Sunday, 30th Sept-br, 1832

My dear sister,

I am sorry to say that it is necessary to relate *news* so unpleasant to hear, which I should not trouble you with, if it were not dangerous to delay time. On Friday evening about 4 o'clock, I received a letter from Mr. C. Cash saying that the Messrs. Flower had levied an execution on the cotton bales at the river and intended to do the same on the plantation. I immediately wrote a few lines to Mr. Turner and enclosed Cash's letter and started Arthur off in the rain to carry it to him, and about 11 o'clock he returned home with Mr. Turner's answer to me, expressing his sorrows for the vexation they continually give me, and desired I would visit him very early next morning, which I done, and heard all he had to say on the unfortunate subject; returned home in the evening and concluded to start Arthur on horseback to my brother to let him know the state of his affairs on Bayou Sara and request him to come as soon as possible to try to check their proceedings.

Mr. Turner said that he was not sufficiently authorized to proceed in the business against them for my brother—that he must either see, or hear from by letter, giving him power to act. He said something about a bond that had to be given in some way, but I cannot recollect the particulars, and must not undertake it. I hope Arthur may arrive at your house safe and my brother can come with him; if so, they can be here by this day week, which will answer every purpose. Mr. T. appeared uneasy, but said he had hopes of making them repent their rashness. Mrs. Turner informed me of a secret that relieved my mind much, but I am not at liberty to mention it at present, and it would take me too long to write it, and I do not know whether Mr. T. allowed her to tell me or not.

Do, my dear sister, write to me occasionally. You cannot form an idea what satisfaction it affords me, and I really need something to help me to bear up against misfortunes. If anything should happen to Arthur so that he should not get to your house *before this*, do start my brother as soon as possible. He has no time to lose and I hope he may save much by his trip. I expect you will scarcely understand my letter, but will have to guess it out as near as you can. I am frightened out of my wits. Tomorrow I shall look for the sheriff to seize all they can. I have given orders to those about the house to take the children and run if they have the smallest opportunity.

Heaven bless you, my dear sister. Farewell,
R. O'Connor

Editor's note: Three days after this letter was written, the sheriff notifies Rachel that all the cotton and twenty-six slaves are to be sold at a sheriff's sale thirty days later.

Rachel again pleads for David's attention to his property.

Saturday night, 9 o'clock
Octo-br 6th, 1832

My dear brother,

Arthur arrived home this morning at 8 o'clock with two letters for me, one from Mr. Turner and one from Mr. Downs. As soon as I read them I started to St. Francis Ville, where I expected to find Mr. Turner in his office, but was disappointed. I then continued my journey towards his house with a hope of meeting him on his way to his office, in which I was disappointed again. Even when I reached his house, he had gone to Jackson on some business, but I waited until he came home, to deliver your letter to him, with the one directed to Mr. Downs. He read them both, then observed that you had not received his letter written on Monday last. I told him that it took five days for a letter to reach you, and that of course, it had not time to get there before Arthur came away. He said he would hand your letter to Mr. Downs, and that they both would write to you on Monday next.

This is the third time that I have been to see Mr. Turner since this day week, on the business that I wrote to you per Arthur in all my difficulties. I never had so great a fright; my heart almost failed. On Tuesday, the sheriff came and seized all the cotton on the plantation, and a part of the Negroes, which he left in charge of Mr. Mulkey. Twenty-five bales were hauled to the landing. They have taken them to N. Orleans, and God only knows what will become of them. If you do not attend the business, *all will be lost.* Mr. Turner says I must not speak on the subject; that if I do, it will weaken your claim to the property, which is what they are trying for. He says that your claim is good in law, but that you must attend to it—either come yourself, or impower some person to act for you. You will have to be advised and directed by your lawyers, or you may depend, all will be lost, which indeed I cannot bear to think of. If you could only know how I feel, you would try to take care for yourself. It is not for myself that I plead so hard; it is for yourself and family. I must own that I sincerely pity the Negroes. They all flew to the woods like wild hogs and carried their little ones with them and returned after he went away. *Poor little Isaac is one that is seized.* I wish I had sent him to you by Arthur, or that I had never loved him as I do. He is the smartest little boy on the place by far. If you will save them from being sold to strangers, I will ask no more. If you wish to move them to your island, I shall not say one word against your doing so. And if you think proper to let them remain here, I shall be happy in doing the best I can for you and them. I believe it is 16 or 18 that are seized, and perhaps the rest of them may be in like manner ere this reaches you. I dare not mention the business to one living, only Mr. Turner, fearing it might injure you. But, indeed, I have pleaded hard to him to save it for you. I am sensible of being wrong to write to you as I now do, but you must forgive me. My heart is so sore that I really cannot help it *this* night. Mr. Turner says their proceedings are illegal and that he hopes all is for the best if rightly managed, I have to appear as indifferent as a fool to every person, and even to the sheriff, while he is making every use of his low authority. Poor me, I dare not say one word. Harraldson is all the lawyer they have employed. Acey Brown and James Flower has gone security for all damages brought against Wm. F. There are three securities, but one goes by the name of *secret*, who is yet unknown.

My love to my dear sister and the little ones. I remain your affectionate sister,

R. O'Connor

Editor's note: True to his promise to Rachel, John Turner wrote to David on the following Monday, October 8, 1832, relating the seizure of her property and advising him to send an injunction or a special power of attorney. Three days later, October 11, 1832, Turner sends David a blank petition for claiming the seized property and for obtaining an injunction against its sale. David must sign it before a justice or a judge, and he must get an affidavit at the foot of the petition signed by a justice or a judge. Turner requests David to get someone to serve as security for damages.

Rachel sends Arthur with another urgent appeal to David and notifies him of his lawyer's suit for damages.

October 12, 1832

My dear brother,

Mr. Lewis Davis started early this morning, through the rain, expecting to go on board the *Telegraph*, until he met the steamboat at Plaquemine, that passes where you live every Monday, but got disappointed, as the *Telegraph* stayed a day and night longer than usual; and as Clarissa is very sick, I'm afraid to let him leave her at present—which obliges me to start Arthur over to you again on horseback with papers that Mr. Davis had started with to you. Mr. Davis will meet him at Iberville where Mr. Turner wishes to have the papers signed by Judge Bushnell. You have no time to lose; all is hurry and bustle. I scarcely sleep any, my mind is, and has been, so tormented about your business. Arthur must be at Iberville by Friday or Saturday next at the fartherest, be the weather rain or shine. Can you not come that far with him for your own satisfaction and safety?

I would willingly do so myself if it would be of any service to you. The papers that Arthur carries to you must be returned by him. You will know what to do, or what is necessary to be done, when you see the papers.

Mr. Turner and Major Downs has sued the securities, sheriff, and all concerned for damages; and from what I can learn, they are much frightened. Courtney sent me word yesterday that he should come to see me on the business—which he may as well let alone for all I shall do or say. Do pray, my dear brother, make all possible haste. I believe all is in your favor if you only attend to your business, as you had ought to.

Heaven bless you and yours are the prayers of your faithful sister,

R. O'Connor

The dreaded cholera comes to St. Francisville via the steamboats on the Mississippi River and Rachel promises her brother a "receipt" for its treatment.

Nov-br 6th, 1832

My dear brother,

I have not heard from you since Arthur came home and then you had been very sick. He said you did not look well. I hope you are quite restored to health again, and that my dear sister and the children are all in good health also. We are dreadfully alarmed about the cholera. One man died in St. Francis Ville with it today. He was only sick three hours from the moment he felt it. All the boats are stopped from passing up and down the river between New Orleans and here. We are informed that they die very fast in N. Orleans, often two hundred in a day. Pray don't remain in New Town with your family. Either take them to the country or the island where you will be much safer. But do continue to write to me and let me know how you are. Don't let us neglect each other the short time we have to live. Direct your letters to Jackson, East Feliciana, La. Perhaps it will not be so dangerous to send there as to St. Francis Ville, near the Mississippi. You cannot know how bad I feel. I am so distressed about you and your family. You have not heard what a shocking disease it is, yet there is hope if attended to instantly. I will enclose you a receipt, that is said to be the best and most to be depended on. It's the one that Mr. Swift used for his sisters and is recommended to Dr. Ira Smith by a brother of his who is a Dr. in New York and who only lost four patients out of 72. I pray you both not to think lightly of it, but to make it known to your friends and relations so that they all may profit by it.

I have engaged Mr. Mulkey to oversee for you next year at six hundred dollars, and to keep his family in meal, and feed his riding horse. He is a sober man and understands planting as well as any other I know of. But if you think I have done wrong in any way, let me know soon. I can make such alterations as you direct. He knows that I am acting for you and not for myself. I do not know any other that would do as well as he does. Mr. Swift says that one man will answer as well as another, but you know better than that. There is many an overseer that cannot get near the work done by the hands that Mulkey can, and he don't appear to wish to abuse the Negroes, nor to have wives amongst them so far.

Clarissa is better. She can set up and walk about a little. Her mouth and tongue keeps very sore. Julia Ann is here with her. The last I heard of Handy and Harriet there were to come home by sea; which, if they have started, I do not know what will become of them. I have not seen any of Henry Flower's family for some time. I believe James and William is still at Mr. Collin's. I dare not send Old Daniel to market, nor let one leave home. I will do all in my power to take care of them.

Should my brother be on the island, and my sister at home, I pray her to write to me and let me know how they are. I consider you both as one and the same. My letters are intended for you both no matter which they may be directed to. God grant that you all may escape the *cholera* and enjoy perfect health. I remain your affectionate sister,

R. O'Connor

I had forgotten to tell you that your bales of cotton is still at home. The sheriff won't let them be sent to market. Mr. Turner will not let me mention anything about your busines whatever. He says I must not show the least interest on any account if I wish you well. He can inform you all.

It is so late tonight that I cannot copy the receipt which I promised in my letter. I must write it off soon for you.

The next day Rachel sends a letter to Mary enclosing the promised "receipt" for cholera. A note on the outside of the letter directs the postmaster to forward it with all possible care and speed.

Nov-br 7, 1832

My dear sister,

The opposite page is the receipt that I mentioned in my last letter to my brother in which I have great hopes from its being spoken to highly of by Mr. Swift who saw its effect on his sisters and others on board the same boat. We are all well at present, but I almost fear that every day may be our last. We have so much news of cholera from New Orleans up the Mississippi. As far as I can hear of, it is raging. Do not remain in town with your family. It will surely get there. You will be more safe on the island, or out in the country. Do for mercy's sake write me soon. The uneasiness I endure will kill me unless I can hear from you and how you are. The report of the man dying yesterday in 3 hours of cholera is false. He was only drunk; he is getting well today. There is no cholera in St. Francis Ville now. Clarissa will soon be well if she is not frightened to death in hearing how bad the cholera is, and has been.

Please to inform my brother of there being taxes on 520 acres of land not paid in 1829, which is charged $10.80 cents, advertised in the *Phenix*, which says if not paid with other costs due on said land in thirty days after the third publication, said list of taxes shall be forwarded to the collector of said Parish of West Feliciana to collect the same in the manner printed out by law. It is in a long list of other lands in the same situation belonging to a number of different people. I do not know where my brother's land lays, unless in the Plains. He had better write to Mr. Swift and have it settled. My love to my dear brother. Kiss all my sweet babes for me. Tell them to be good children and remember they are born to die. Heaven grant you all escape from the disease I so sincerely dread. Farewell, my dear brother and sister,

Rachel O'Connor

Editor's note: Rachel's "receipt" for cure of cholera:

Premonitory symptoms of cholera and a mode of treatment recommended by a gentleman who practiced amongst it: — A diarrhea, or looseness in the bowels, copious discharges, with little or no pain except a slight griping after the discharge, are the first symptoms of the disease. Therefore all persons residing in the cholera region, are sincerely solicited not to suffer the symptoms, above described, to steal upon them without alarm, or to allow more than two or three discharges from the bowels to take place, ere they use the necessary remedy to retard its progress. The following medicines will without doubt stop its progress if taken in time. Viz: Take a dose of calomel (your habitual quantity), in three hours after, take a dose of castor oil to work it off, which is all that is necessary, if taken in the first stage of premonitory symptoms.

If the patient is taken with vomiting, and followed with cramps or spasms, which is the first indication of cholera, then there is no time to be lost. Copious bleeding from the arm should be immediately resorted to (ere the pulse sinks, which occurs very soon), then cup the abdomen over with as many cups, say fifteen to thirty, as the patient can bear; when the cups are taken off, apply a large blister plaster all over the place. If the extremities become cold, put mustard plasters on the ankles, inside the calves of the legs, and also on the wrists. Rub the parts that are cramped with your naked hand, or a piece of warm flannel. In order to keep up a correspondent heat, use a blanket steeped in hot brandy and laudanum, which wrap around the patient and remove and repeat the same whenever it loses the necessary heat.

Apply hot bricks to the feet; give ingestions made of one quart of warm soap suds, mixed with one tablespoonful of table salt, with two spoonfulls of brown sugar and two of castor oil. Repeat the same as often as may appear necessary. Drinks may be composed of brandy toddy and hot tea, and indulge occasionally with such drinks as the patient may desire. In case of constant vomiting, ten drops of laudanum, five drops of ether, mixed with a little loaf of sugar and water ought to be given every ten minutes. The pulse is the criterion to judge of the necessity of bleeding, but heed the pulse; if entirely gone, bleed and that very copiously.

A week later Rachel, fearing the cholera may have reached the At-takapa area, writes appealing for news. She includes accounts of family and plantation affairs.

November 14, 1832

My dear brother,

I received your letter of the 6th instant this day, as you expected. I am afraid some has been lost. I have written often and enclosed many receipts to cure cholera. I expect the last is the surest and best. There has several died of cholera at the landing, but they were landed from steamboats either from N. Orleans or from above, and died in a few hours and were buried instantly. Some market Negroes from Point Coupe that were sent on board the boats with their marketing caught the disease and died, but no others has taken it yet. St. Francis Ville is perfectly healthy at this time, but I do not let the Negroes go there or any other place. I am very afraid of it. The boats are all stopped running. They cannot get men to work on board. They have refused six dollars per day, owing to their dying so fast.

James Flower is here tonight on his way home from Mr. Collins'. He is in fine health and left his sister and family all well. I am glad your sugar cane is so fine. It will be a great pity to lose any of it. James Flower says that Mr. Collins cuts the cane so that it falls on each other and serves to cover itself so that it is secured from the frost until he gets the rest made into sugar. I shall take care of your draft in favor of Mr. Swift until the man comes with your mares and colts, and do as you direct. Mr. Mulkey had seventy-eight bales pressed, which I hope are heavy, but they will not let them be sent off yet. If the cholera continues bad, you had better not come. I don't think they will have any court in Dec-br unless it is gone before that time.

I don't feel very well today myself, but I hope there is not much the matter. This cholera is a great trouble to me. I have ordered the Negroes to let me know the moment they feel unwell, but not pretend to be so when they are not. Dr. Denny thinks he can cure it, if it should come. *But if I live* and find it necessary, I shall send for another to assist him and do all I can to save them. Mr. Swift says he will come in case it should come amongst us. I expect he knows more than any of the Doctors, as he has been amongst it and attended his sisters through the whole disease.

Clarissa has gone home. She was mending. I hope she may recover her health again. Mr. Courtland Smith has fenced up his lane to his house and wrote on a paper and posted it on a post at the end of his land saying friends and foes pass by

Mulkey is very industrious so far. I hope he will do well. If you have any orders to give, you should let me know. I can tell him. Perhaps he would do better to be directed by you. He appears anxious to please you and for you to come over.

My dear brother and sister, I will bid you a good night. It is late and I am a little unwell. I remain your affectionate sister,

R. O'Connor

Editor's note: A letter of John Turner to David Weeks, November 23, 1832, about the case of William Flower versus Rachel O'Connor states that David Weeks's injunction against seizure of her cotton and slaves was filed and the case was postponed—the cotton is to remain in Mr. Swift's possession pending settlement of case.

The Weeks family escapes the cholera. In her joy over their safety, Rachel pens a lengthy letter filled with news of family and neighbors.

Nov-br 27, 1832

My dear sister,

Yours of the 14th instant arrived last evening with one from my brother written on the 16th. No earthly news could have relieved my mind more than to hear you were all alive and well. I am constantly thinking and wishing to hear from you; and when I receive a letter, I am afraid to open it fearing it may bring something dreadful. You could scarcely imagine how light my heart felt after I had read your letters. I am overjoyed to find you intend to take your family to the island where I hope you will be safe. All large water courses are said to be dangerous particularly where boats pass up and down, as few are without some on board that has, or has had, the cholera, let it come from where it will. That is what causes it to be so often in St. Francis Ville. Several had died at the river and a few in town with it. Two young men lay very low yesterday. I scarcely expect they are alive now. Mr. Dater died four days ago. I don't let any peson go there and the overseer is equally careful and as much afraid as myself. He has a family of his own and behaves very well so far. I don't feel much alarmed now. I hope to escape it by being careful.

85

The way you mention of clothing your family in flannel is said to be of great use in keeping the cholera away. I hope in God it may prove a blessing to you and yours. Clarissa has gone home two weeks ago yesterday. I went to see her on Sunday and returned the next day. She still appears miserable. She mends slowly. I don't expect her to live long owing to her own imprudence. She wants to be smart, and her health will not admit of her being exposed. If there was the smallest need of her acting as she does, I could forgive it. Mr. Davis is all goodness and will not say a word to her, let her act as she will, which causes much trouble. The cause of her last illness was the fear of the cholera. His cotton was very open, and she took a small girl and white-washed their Negro houses to keep it away, not having the smallest idea of her situation, as she never expected to be in that way again after what she had suffered in losing her first child, and now has lost her second. Charlotte and Julia Ann were with her yesterday where I parted with them in the evening. Charlotte looks very well indeed. Mr. Handy and his family has reached home safe and well. They brought eleven Negroes with them, eight that is grown and three children. He has been to see me and appears delighted with their trip. He says his relations all say he will soon get rich and that he, himself, can see nothing to prevent it.

My dearest and kind sister, pray don't think that I ever let the thoughts of want trouble me when such a sister and brother as I have are alive. I have to much confidence in you both to think of that. I should think meanly of myself to have any such fears after all the kindnesses you both have bestowed me. Let me need it or not, you have never failed. But with all, I must not let your kindnesses cause me to forget or neglect my own duty, and sit at ease while Wm. Flower and the sheriff carries all your property on this side of the Mississippi off. That I must not do. Any and every means in my power to prevent it is a pleasure to me, so much so, that I could ride Big Black 30 miles a day with all ease one day with another, while I am frightened. But as soon as that is over, *old age* returns and I could not undergo more than one half.

Julia Ann Scott has been to see Mr. and Mrs. Turner since I saw them, and Mrs. Turner told her that Harraldson, who is W. F.'s lawyer, told Mr. Turner they had made a great mistake in levying on the Negroes; that Wm. F. only ordered the cotton seized, and had written to Harraldson and scolded him so much in his letter that he had almost made up his mind to throw up the business. W. F.

said they had overreached themselves and that he did not know what the consquences might be. From what Mrs. Turner said, Mr. Turner was delighted to hear of the mistake and declared nothing could have happened better. Don't mention it out of your family. Perhaps Mr. Turner would be displeased with her for telling J.A.S.

I never enjoyed better health than at present. I have quite re-covered from my sickness that I had last summer. If Mr. Turner had consented, I should have went over to see you the last time that I had to send Arthur; but after he said it would operate much against your concerns, I gave out the trip.

Mrs. Eliza Bowman expects to be confined hourly and her mother lays at the point of death at Dr. Ira Smith's. She has been sick neraly five months. She will be 59 years of age the 2nd of Dec-br, which is a great age to have her monthly discharges return and to last 4 or 5 months without intermission, which has been the case with her. She is much reduced.

I heard Mr. Palfrey has taken his family to his plantation, but I am truly sorry that he intends to return to Franklin so soon himself. He will be in danger and make Mrs. Palfrey so unhappy about his being there. I hope Mr. Harding will be safe on his plantation. Surely he would not remain there if he thought otherwise. I have saved you some seeds and expect to get some from Harriet Handy which I will send the first opportunity. The *arbor vitae* did not bear any seeds this year. We had so much wet weather just as the seeds began to ripen that they did not do well.

I am sorry about your brother Alfred remaining in New Orleans through all the sickly season. It may induce him to risk it again. The city is now said to be healthy. I sincerely hope your brothers may return home safe. If they find it is dangerous to come on board a boat, they will return by land. Many has come that way to avoid the cholera.

I have heard of the death of Mr. Towles. I am sorry for his family. I never seen Mrs. Towles, but I love her for your sake. My love to your brothers and sisters. How much I want to see you all. Kiss my dear and darling babes, Frances, William, Alfred, Harriet, and Charles; and then make them kiss their dear father and mother for me. Heaven preserve your precious lives and guard you from all harm are the prayers of your truly grateful and affectionate sister,

R. O'Connor

Once again Rachel is disappointed in an overseer. She tells Mary of her disillusionment.

Dec-br 16th, 1832

My dear sister,

I received your letter dated the 2nd of this present month which I acknowledge came rather unexpectedly, from receiving one from you shortly before, and from knowing you are not fond of writing, and that your family cares are sufficient employment, all of which causes me to be tenfold thankful to you and to my great and kind Creator for giving me such good and kind friends that never tires, even when I am almost tired of myself, were I not afraid to die. I did not neglect answering your letters previous to this last, and enclosed it in one to my brother for you and sent it to the post office in Jackson. I was afraid to send it to St. Francis Ville while the cholera reamined there at the landing. Surely they would not neglect forwarding my letter from Jackson, but I begin to think St. Francis Ville is the safest post office.

I have been quite sick since I wrote last. I was taken the first night of this month and have not been able to write until now since. I requested Dr. Denny to write to my brother, which he done, but I did not see his letter. He was uncommonly attentive to me during my illness which caused me to believe he thought me dangerously ill, but I never once asked his opinion on the subject. I am still very weak—not able to set up all day, but much better than I was a few days ago and hope soon to recover my health once more.

Mr. Davis left here yesterday. He says Clarissa begins to look pretty again and he appeared overjoyed to tell me the news so dear to his heart. Certainly Clarissa cannot be sensible of the blessings kind heaven has bestowed her in a husband or she would be more careful of her health.

Charlotte and her son are in good health. She has, for some time past, indulged a hope of getting to live on the old plantation where her father and mother formerly lived, but Mr. Doherty has given out the idea of moving there, which is a sad disappointment to her, as her whole heart was set on getting there. I am sorry for her. That appeared to be her last and only hope of a comfortable home. Julia Ann lives with Charlotte. She and Mr. Doherty are going to Alexandria shortly. I believe Mr. Scott's estate is to be sold the first of next month. Mr. Handy and family are at her father's. I have not heard from them for some time. Mrs. Eliza Bowman had a fine son born on the 10th instant to the great joy of both its parents. They have named him James Pirrie. Mrs. Pirrie continues in very low health. She has lived at Dr. Ira Smith's for a month past, and is not able to return home yet. She has not seen her young grandson. Poor old Mrs. Chaney died the 5th of this month.

I delivered the enclosed letter from my brother to Mr. Mulkey. He appears much raised and I am afraid wants to be a great man, but I shall know better what to think of him by the time my brother comes. We had some words the day I took sick, at night, about some corn I found left in the field, but I think he has done very well since, after I told him he could go whenever he pleased. He is getting the logs ready to roll where Patrick cleared. He understands farming very well. His greatest fault is untruth. He will seldom tell the truth if he can avoid it. He will even tell stories on the Negroes when angry with them. But I still hope he will manage to raise one good crop at least. He is taking good care of the race mares. They really look pretty. I would not trust them to his care until I got sick, but I think they look better now. The oldest mare is the craziest animal I ever seen. They have to be kept apart, or she would ruin the young mare, and she looks like she might fly. Several has called to see my race horses and praised them greatly.

We had no court this month owing to the cholera being in town. Mr. Turner attended court at Point Coupe which I think was the cause of his not answering my brother's letters. When he returned home he was very sick, and thought it to be the cholera. However he has got well.

I long to see my dear Frances' letter. My love to her and my dear brother and the other dear little ones, not forgetting my dear and best of sisters. I remain your ever affectionate sister,

R. O'Connor

Rachel writes a Christmas Eve letter to her brother.

Dec-br 24, 1832

My dear brother,

I have just received your letter dated the 14th instant. I am very thankful to learn from it that your healths continue so good. We ought to return thanks hourly for the many blessings we receive, particularly from the lucky escape from the *cholera*, so far. The people appears to have lost all dread at present. I seldom hear it mentioned unless I ask about it myself. Jackson and St. Francis Ville are clear of it, and quite healthy. I was very sick when Dr. Denny wrote to you. I requested him to write as I could not at that time, but I am now quite well again, and hope to see you soon over here. Your mares are doing very well indeed. They look better than they did at first. Mr. Mulkey has them well attended to. Every person that calls asks to see my race horses. They all praise the oldest mare greatly and says the young one looks like she might run fast.

I have visited Mrs. Pirrie twice since I got better. She is at Dr. Smith's. I am afraid her case is doubtful. She has four doctors attending her: Dr. Smith, Dr. Harriford, Mr. McKeloy, and Dr. Durer. The latter has come down the river and brought a wife. He has married a sister of his other wife. I wrote two long letters some time in the last month, as near as I can recollect; one to my sister Mary, and enclosed in it one to yourself, which Dr. Denny directed, as I was tired writing, and I sent them to the post office in Jackson, since which I have received a letter from my sister and understood that they had not arrived at the time she wrote last. I hope the post master did not neglect sending them. I have written since to my sister.

I have seen Mr. Swift and requested of him to get the oats to sow, and told the overseer to have the ground ready for an early oat patch as you direct. I don't think there will be any chance to buy corn until the corn boats arrive. Some say the price of corn will be high this next spring and others say not. I hope we can make out until March. We have thirty hogs to kill for meat, which will help some. My little stumply hogs will soon increase. I don't let them run out. I have thirteen young lambs, and I am getting my garden in good order. If I can only have good health, I will try to make it bring something in the spring.

Mr. Handy and Harriet has been to see me. They both look very well. They are going to live at Beach Hill. Judge Mathews let them have land to work of the best quality, they say. Sidney and David

Flower left here this morning. They are in fine health. Clarissa is mending fast. Mr. Doherty, Charlotte, and Julia Ann has gone to Alexandria. Mr. Scott's estate is to be sold soon.

Henry Flower has sued the heirs of Stephen Swayze again for six thousand dollars and myself for one thousand and six hundred on my Stephen's account. Mr. Lobdell is his lawyer.

I am truly glad your sugar cane turns out so well. I hope you can save it all and that it may bring a good price. I shall have enough to do me next year out of what you sent me last. It was of the best quality, and I have been careful of it. James Flower is here tonight. He is in good health and speaks of going to N. Orleans to study law.

Mulkey is getting on with his work rolling logs. He has the women cutting briars and clearing them away. They finished pressing the cotton today, which held out to make 120 bales and I hope heavy ones.

My love to my dear sister and the children. I wish you all a pleasant Christmas and a happy New Year, and that you all may live to enjoy many more. Christmas Eve, 10 o'clock at night. I remain your affectionate sister,

R. O'Connor

P.S. Please let me know whether you received my double letter, one to each of you. Perhaps they were written in this month. I have forgotten the date. I do not wish them to fall into the hands of strangers.

Editor's note: On December 26, 1822, J. Downs advises David that his injunction against the Flower brothers was executed and the advertised sheriff's sale was stopped.

Rachel's affectionate letter to David relates that plantation operations are progressing well.

January 19, 1833

My dear brother,

I received yours of the 8th instant this morning. I shall start Arthur on Monday morning with your mares to Mr. Duncan's plantation below Baton Rouge if the weather continues fair so that he can travel. I hope you get them home safe. They are beautiful and in fine order. I really like to look at them and see the young mare play. You will have to keep them separate owing to the oldest being so cross to the other, and may perhaps cripple her by either being in a stable or pasture together. I wish the old mare's colt may do well. Young Douglass said she would have it in April.

Lewis Davis left here this morning. He requested of me to ask you the first time I wrote to bring one hogshead of your best sugar over for himself and Mr. A. Doherty. Charlotte and Clarissa will not agree to let them buy any other. They are great hands for preserves which require good sugar to make them nice, and they have set their hearts on getting some of yours. The girls has often threw out hints to me since you sent this last sugar to me, but I let them hint away and took care of my sugar in the meantime.

Old Mrs. Chaney's property was sold yesterday, and I got Mr. Davis to come down to buy corn for you, if it sold reasonable. He bought eighty barrels at one dollar pr. barrel and got afraid to bid for any more. They say it is good corn. We shall commence hauling it on Monday and soon finish as the distance is so short.

They finished rolling logs last evening. Mr. Mulkey is wishing for you to come. I believe he wants to get some new fashion ploughs and I do not know what else; but he knows it to be useless to apply to me unless you direct me to get them for him. I have no cause to complain of him now. He is very industrious and behaves well and appears to confine himself more to the truth than usual. I have great hopes of his making you a good crop. The news of cholera has died away again which makes me anxious to see you come. I am really glad your sugar crop proves to be so good. You will get a high price for it this year. I understood that the most of the sugar planters have done badly. You had another young Negro born this morning. Charity has a fine daughter, just like Patrick.

I have, of late, discovered that cotton seed will make cows give much more milk when boiled. I have tried it for sometime past, and boiled seed are better for my guinea hogs also. I wish you could buy one of them large kettles at Plaquemine for me to cook cotton seed in. I can soon make butter to pay for it.

My guinea sows will soon have pigs and I must feed them with something. I have eighteen pretty lambs and nine young calves not more than a month old; so you see all is doing wonderful well, and I am really thankful for it. I have been very fortunate in saving the meat that we killed. So far, all is safe and sound, and you would be surprised to see so much raised here.

Clarissa is getting quite healthy. She says you must go to see them when you come, and then she will come and stay with you until you start home. They are doing very well, and I expect she wants to show you how smart they are. Mr. Howell has bought the middle place, that formerly belonged to Brother Caleb, and 24 Negroes from Mr. Barrow, and is to pay twenty-five thousand and five hundred dollars in four years for it. He sold his plantation to old Mr. Roberts for 4000$.

I have heard that Mr. Courtney often inquires for you and appears anxious to see you, and that Wm. F. has written to Harraldson to try to have the cotton sold. I hope they are paying up in mind a little for the trouble they caused me last fall.

I am sorry my sister has a sore finger, but I hope it may not keep sore long. I shall be glad to receive another letter when she is able to write, but I do not complain. She has been very good to write. The last came quite unexpected. Her family is large and keeps her busy of course, and I take it truly kind in her to write occasionally; that is, whenever she can spare the time, I shall be thankful.

George has been very low this winter. I nearly lost hope for a while. At length, I concluded to send to Dr. Bell for some of Dr. Chapman's cough drops, which relieved him very soon and he enjoys better health at present than he has for a long time.

My love to my dear and good sister and the little ones. It is now midnight and middling cold and my fire getting low. I will conclude and wish my beloved and best of brothers a goodnight. I remain your affectionate sister,

R. O'Connor

Editor's note: In the first paragraph of this letter, Rachel is referring to Ashland Plantation, home of Duncan F. Kenner. A fine private race track surrounded his mansion and extended beyond the gardens at the rear. Traces of this track are evident today in the placement of the century-old liveoak trees that bordered it. Duncan Kenner was famous for his beautiful race horses and horse lovers attended many races at his track.

David has visited Rachel and her happiness is evident in this letter to Mary.

March 3rd, 1833

My dear sister,

I had no idea of letting as much time pass off before I answered the letter that my brother delivered to me as I have done. You will certainly consider yourself neglected by my long silence. During my brother's short stay, I felt too happy to even spare time to write to my best of sisters; but intended to write to you the next day after he left me, which a visit from Mr. Swift and two of his sisters prevented, who stayed several days before they returned home, during which Mrs. Pirrie became worse, and was considered dangerously ill, and sent for me, where I had to stay a day or two, until Mr. Doherty and Charlotte came to see me and remained until two o'clock this evening, at which time they started homeward. Mrs. Pirrie has gone to New Orleans to see Dr. Boam, with a hope of finding relief. Dr. Smith and his wife has gone down with her. I am now alone, and my first thoughts were to write to you. I hope and trust my brother is with you and his dear little ones ere this, where this may find you all enjoying health and happiness.

I put all flowers, bushes, and evergreens that I could collect in a box for you and sent them by him. I had none of the yellow rose, but Charlotte has since sent to Natchez and procured a little, which if it should live, and I am spared, I will send you some the first opportunity.

Last night and the one previous has been dreadfully cold and almost ruined my garden. My early peas appear to be killed and all in the garden looks bad. I feel discouraged, but will do the best I can. We have the corn all hauled home that my brother brought before he left here, and the plantation business going on very well. Please inform my brother that the large kettle has come safe and that I

have had it hauled home today. It is a fine one indeed and I am
really truly thankful to him for it. I will be very industrious and try
to make it pay for itself by boiling cotton seed for the cows.

My love to my dear and good brother and all his dear little children. Please to remember me very affectionately to your sisters and
brothers should any of them be with you. My health and happiness
be yours, attended by every other blessing now and forever, are the
sincere wishes of your truly grateful sister,

R. O'Connor

Spring planting progresses despite unusually heavy rains.

March 21, 1833

My dear brother,

I received your letter written the 2nd instant and should have answered ere this if there had been any way of conveying it to the post
office. This is the first fair day we have had for ten days past and I
don't expect Alexander's Creek has been crossed during the whole
rain. Daniel is going to try in the morning. I am glad you arrived
home safe and found your family well. Yesterday I felt poorly, but
today I am quite well again. Mr. Mulkey has just finished planting
the field next to Mrs. Pirrie's in corn as the rain commenced, which
is now up and growing. He would have had all the corn planted if it
had been possible; the several and constant rains put it out of his
power. I expect he will get all the corn planted this week. I sent to
Mr. A. Doherty for seed corn and got of the best kind, which I
hope may do well. I sent Mulkey to the river the next day after I
received your letter to see about corn. He could have bargained for
three hundred barrels at five bits and a half pr. barrel at that time;
how it is now, I do not know, as no person has been there since,
not even one has been seen passing that way. I have received the fine
large kettle that you sent me from N. Orleans, and have it pretty
well fixed with brick and cooking full of cotton seed at present,
which answers the purpose extremely well.

The Negroes are all well excepting Bridget, who I expect is in the
family way. There has not been any cotton seed brought to the land-

ing worth buying yet. Mr. Mulkey had no work for the children today and I took them to carry manure in the garden, and to have to watch them that they do no harm, which will cause many blunders in my letter, but you will have to make it out as well as you can. I will try to do better next time I write. In your next, let me know how my sister is and whether you got your little boxes over safe or not. The little crabapple trees that I planted are growing; I hope yours are too. Those late rains have almost ruined my garden. It makes me sorry to look at it.

My love to my dear sister and the children, not forgetting yourself. I remain your most affectionate sister,

Rachel O'Connor

Having those children to mind keeps my mind so employed that I can think of but little else. After I looked over my letter, I really felt ashamed of it. However you must excuse *all* for this time. I must acknowledge I am troubled. Yesterday at 12 o'clock, Isaac swallowed a middling large metal button, which has not yet passed off; but, as he continues well, I hope it may.

Editor's note: The litigation continues as William Flower petitions the court on March 22, 1833, to void the sales of Rachel's property to David and David's injunction against his seizures of property.

David has hired James Bedell, a master builder, to construct his beautiful home, which was later called Shadows-on-the-Teche. Begun in 1831 and completed in 1834, this house is built of brick from Teche clay and of cypress from nearby swamps. It is located in New Town (New Iberia) on a four-acre site fronted by the Old Spanish Trail to Texas, with Bayou Teche behind it. In this letter Rachel expresses happiness as the house nears completion and advises Mary about shrubs and flowers for her garden. She still worries about the renewal of the Flower lawsuit.

LETTERS

April 9th, 1833

My dear sister,

Yours of the 23rd of March came to hand four days ago. I tried
to answer it immediately, but really could not. My feelings were
overcome between hope and fear. I put your letter in my bosom and
walked about several minutes before I ventured to open it. The
thoughts of cholera first struck my mind and my heart failed me. At
length I looked it over, without reading half, skipping a part and
reading a few words until I came to the end, which encouraged me,
and I commenced at the beginning and read all. After I found that
yourself and your family were all alive and no misfortune happened,
my greatful feelings towards my *Creator* were so sensible that I had
not power to write. The idea of cholera being near you and that a
part of your Negroes had already had it distresses me extremely.

My own health continues quite good, and I could pass off my time
very comfortable were it not for the continual dread of losing my
nearest and dearest friends. Pray let me hear from you often, once a
week at least, by some of your family. I mustn't ask so great a favor
of yourself. I am aware of your having sufficient employment in your
family, and I still recollect the cares of a mother and wife. I do most
sincerely wish it had been in my power to have left home and moved
to be one of your family the day I lost my youngest son (which care
of my three nieces prevented at the time). My distresses were so
great that I could have abandoned and forsaken all freely, and have
been happy in your family nursing the little children. If an overseer
could be procured that would conduct as he had ought to do, and be
honest, I should be more than happy to spend a part of my time
with you and yours.

I had a hope that Patrick would answer every purpose, but soon
discovered my mistake. The man that is here at present behaves very
well, and I verily believe will make a good crop of corn, cotton, and
potatoes. He has 6 or 7 acres of the latter planted, and is now
planting cotton seed and appears to be going on with his work as
well as possible. But after all, if he was left to himself, he would
soon become a great man and think of very little else except to play
and eat, and spoil the Negroes into the bargain. Mayo Grey oversees
for Mr. Henderson on the place that formerly belonged to John Mulhollen. You would be surprised at his conduct towards his employer
who places every confidence in his honesty.

97

Yet I hope to see you all comfortably fixed in your new house. I should be miserable without that hope. I am very glad to hear of my dear and good brother's being in better health. I pray it may continue so, and that you both may be spared to see your children happily settled and doing well. You, my dear sister, should not despair. You are yong and I hope may spend fifty years in your new house and that my brother may live to protect you and yours.

I think the two leaves that you enclosed are both one kind from their being so much alike; and that the bush is *periwinkle.* I do not see that they resemble any other leaf in the garden. The periwinkle is a small evergreen vine that bears blue flowers, very pretty near the pickets where they can run up them and small flower bushes. The syringa grows 11 or 12 feet high, looks more like a vine than a bush, and needs something to support it to keep it from bending and growing crooked. I have several planted in the same place with crape myrtle and twisted together which keeps the syringa straight. The syringa bears white flowers and are in bloom at this time. The crape myrtle blooms in June or July, which nearly prevents a person from observing that there is two kinds planted in one place. They both stand the cold weather without shading. The Jerusalem cherry is a small green bush that bears berries resembling plums only full of seeds like the red peppers. Sometimes the leaves gets killed in very cold winters, but they come from the root again. The scarlet lights grow like pinks and bear seed in the same manner and often live all winter. The butter-and-eggs never gives out; the seed falls and comes up again something like the larkspur. The plants will have to be thinned like the larkspurs. The flower in the box is tender and needs to set in a shady place where the sun shines but little during the summer and covered from frost in winter. The flower first appears a greenish white and in several days becomes a beautiful pink colour, which lasts some days. Sometimes the flowers are blue. A part of mine were blue last summer. They are beautiful when they do well. The dirt must be worked a little with a fork in the box. I always heard them called autancha, but Dr. Denny says the proper name is hortancha. That is a Latin name. I have a small cutting of the yellow rose that Charlotte sent down for you which I will send if it lives until next winter. Have you any of the flowering almond? I can send you some next winter if you want it. It was rather late to move it when my brother was over last. If I *live* and have my *health,* I hope to send you some flower seed against another year. I was too sickly to save any last year for you.

The girls are all well. Their husbands are busy with their planting. I have not seen them lately. I'm sorry to say that my brother and myself are sued again. I have sent my papers to Mr. Turner. Mrs. Pirrie continues very unwell. William Shipp, a son of Lucy Benard, shot himself with a pistol and died instantly in N. Orleans.

My love to my dear brother and the children. I remain your ever affectionate sister,

Rachel O'Connor

I had like to forget to inform you of my late purchase. I mentioned it to my brother in my last, and the man had his spinning machine sent out in Daniel's cart, which done so well I bought it for 140$ and paid him this morning. I have been very industrious to raise that amount. I hope to save its price if it continues to do well. It spins beautiful thread. The man stayed two days to learn me how to spin on it.

The rains almost ruined my garden. I cannot get it to look right since, but I will keep trying. Perhaps it will change for the better at last.

11 o'clock at night. No person is awake but myself. My eyes are dim. My pen is bad. You will be puzzled to read this I am sure. Mrs. Pirrie's fine carpenter has given passes, or rather sold them out at five dollars apiece, to Negroes in the neighborhood. Some has run away. Mr. Bowman has one gone, and sent another to N. Orleans to be put to the ball and chain, and now the carpenter has run away himself since the affair has been discovered.

Twelve barrels of molasses has been sent up to Mr. Swift which is hauled home. The barrel of syrup has not been sent up, or at least we have not heard of its coming. The hogshead of sugar is at Mr. Swift's for A. Doherty and L. Davis. Mr. Mulkey bought three hundred barrels of corn from Mr. Samuel McAllister at six bits pr. barrel, which comes to two hundred and twenty-five dollars, for which I gave a draft, and the one I gave in favor of Mr. Swift for seventy-two dollars for the pork that I bought for the Negroes. The two drafts added together amounts to 297-$, which is all the drafts I shall need that I know of.

A few days later the sheriff again visits Rachel and presents "a bundle of papers," which she sends to her lawyer. Despite this, Rachel writes a happy letter to David telling of her new spinning machine. A new loom house is being built, which it appears, will make it simpler to clothe the Negroes.

April 20, 1833

My dear brother,

I received your letter several days ago and have intended answering it, but something would happen to prevent doing so. The day before yesterday Mrs. Lewis came from Woodville, and I had to go over with her to see Mrs. Pirrie, who continues in very low health. And yesterday Mrs. Turner came, which put a stop to my writing again. This morning I hope to let you see that I have not forgotten you yet. I am truly glad the cholera has left New Town without doing much harm. Some of your Negroes were down with it, but as they escaped *death*, I think you very lucky, and still more so, as yourself and family did not take it. Do write often (for a while at least) or I shall feel uneasy fearing the cholera has returned. I have not heard of its being nearer than N. Orleans. S.F.V. is quite healthy at present, and my own health is very good. I have nothing to complain of only the sheriff. One came sometime ago and handed me a bundle of paper which I sent to Mr. Turner, who is out at Clinton, and Mrs. Turner has not seen him since.

May is nearly here. I shall soon begin to look out for you to come, but you never mention it in your letters. Mr. Mulkey is doing extremely well so far. I hope you will find him the smartest overseer that ever had the management of this place and that he will raise the best crop for you of any that ever overseed here. I really think it is that hope that causes me to feel so well. His corn looks beautiful and he has a fine large piece of ground planted in sweet potatoes, and is nearly done planting cotton seed. The corn has been worked over once and will be again next week.

I expect you will be surprised at me for buying a spinning machine that cost one hundred and forty dollars. I really did refuse taking it and tried to keep myself from wanting it, but after I seen it set agoing, I lost my fortitude that I previously thought so firm and agreed to take it and paid the man for it and now I am so bad off as before. I cannot get any cotton in the seed to spin until we raise some, which I consider a great loss in the spinning way. Fran and

100

myself could spin some every day which would be a great help in clothing the Negroes. Mr. Mulkey has promised to build me a new loom house that will hold two looms after his crop is laid by, and George is making another loom now. Arthur can learn another how to weave, and weave himself at the same time, by having two looms.

I know you will laugh at my getting into such a working notion just now. Indeed it appears strange to myself and I feel afraid to let my mind have its own way too much for fear I'm counting chickens before they are hatched. My garden begins to look pretty well, and the new part joining is all planted and we are working in them every day. Old Daniel says he knows you will be pleased when you come.

I still have more good news. The mare that Daniel worked in his cart had a fine horse colt and the 11th day of this month, the most unexpected circumstance I ever knew. Not one of us had any idea of her being with foal. Her next will be a fine blooded animal, a nephew or niece to your young mare. Mr. Mulkey and Dr. Denny said they were certain you would be pleased to have her sent to that horse, which caused me to do so. It will cost 20$, which must be kept secret, as his price is 40$. The man that has the horse is very friendly towards Mulkey, and he made the bargain.

My love to my dear sister and the children. I know my dear Frances will write soon when her little brother Charles is taking a nap. Not one of H. F.'s children has been to see me since you were here. I am afraid they were not pleased at my not calling at their house with you.

No more at present from your ever affectionate sister,

Rachel O'Connor

The spring rains cause mud and mire and an influx of cotton worms. The Feliciana relatives are well, but David is ailing. In her letter to Mary, Rachel hopes that Dr. Denny can cure her brother's illness.

May 6th, 1833

My dear sister,

I received yours of the 17th of April more than a week ago and have been trying to find time to answer it every day since, but something continually put a stop to my doing so. Mrs. Pirrie is laying very low. I don't expect she can ever recover her health again, although she is better today than common and appears to raise hopes of herself. Mr. Davis and Clarissa left here this morning. They both are in good health. Charlotte is pretty far advanced in the family way. She expects to be confined in August. Her sister, Julia Ann, stays very constant with her. I am told they have a wonderful sight of chickens this spring to attend to. Wm. Swayze and his wife were here on Friday and Saturday last, with their children. Their son is a fine fat boy and in good health. Their little daughter is a fat babe, but very small and pretty. They were well.

I am overjoyed to find by your last that the cholera had left the neighborhood near you. I sincerely hope it may not return again. St. Francis Ville is clear of it yet. I wish it may continue. We are all in good health. The Negroes hold out wonderfully considering the weather. I scarcely ever seen so much rain at once. The ground is all mud and mire. Even the garden is dangerous, it is so muddy and slippery.

Mr. Mulkey has every appearance of a fine crop of corn and cotton and sweet potatoes, all of which is doing very well at present. But I am sorry to say that I am afraid of the worms doing harm. A part of the fields are covered with them, but as yet they have not destroyed any part of the crop. They are very bad in my little garden and pester me much, but the loss is not great. Mr. Swayze's cotton is ruined. He has to plant it over again. and A. Doherty likewise. Lewis Davis' is not so bad yet. Cotton seed is scarce, but not with us. We have to be very secret about it.

If my brother comes over here this month, he will be pleased with his crop unless the worms destroy it. Mulkey really behaves well and is very industrious in every respect. Mr. Bowman hired a man to oversee for him by the name of Carr (in Jan-ry last) who done very well for some time. At length he took to getting drunk so often that Mr. Bowman discharged him and paid him his money without any quarrel, and Carr continued to visit the place occasionally and sleep in the overseer's house where he formerly lived, and last Saturday night he started off with one of Mr. Bowman's Negro girls and was

taken, with her, near Lewis Stirling's by some men in search of runaway negroes. They returned the girl, but unfortunately let the thief
go because he begged so hard. Mr. Bowman has been quite unfortunate this year with his slaves. One of his men has been run away 2
or 3 months. He has a free pass that Mrs. Pirrie's carpenter wrote
for him, and another they discovered was preparing to go on the
same kind, and they sent him to the ball and chain in New Orleans
where they talk of keeping him. The carpenter has wrote a pass for
himself and gone also.

I wish the young mare had been in a situation to show how smart
she could run. I had a hope she would win the prize. A Mr. Bower
owns a beautiful young horse, which is said to be a brother of hers,
by the name of Son Albert, and is to be run this fall. It is the same
horse that I mentioned in my letter to my brother. If Dr. Denny has
been fortunate enough to cure my brother of a disease that appeared
to be lurking in his breast, I must never forget the favor and will
overlook many faults for his goodness. He is generally very lucky in
making cures and seldom loses a patient. I wish he knew how to
take care of himself.

My love to my dear brother and all the dear little children. I still
expect my dear Frances to write sometimes. Fare-well, my dear and
best of sisters. I pray that Heaven may reward your goodness.

R. O'Connor

Let me know whether the oldest mare has a colt or not and what
it is. I wish it may prove pretty.

*Rachel notifies David of the sheriff's ban on the sale of her cotton
and of Henry Flower's victory in a suit against the Swayze heirs.*

June 9th, 1833

My dear brother,

I expect you must think that I have forgotten you, or that I am
no more. I went home with Clarissa the Tuesday after you left us
and returned home again the Sunday following with Clarissa and Mr.
Davis; found all at home very well. Harriet had been delivered of a
little daughter the night previous (the 1st of June) to the great joy of

Old Sampson, which adds one more to the stock of Negroes and much to my comfort to see them doing well for the sake of you and yours.

Your letter written in N. Orleans had been brought home and handed me the moment I came. I was truly glad to find you had fixed it so that it would be safe to send your cotton to market. I started the cart the next morning and continued it until the sheriff forbid, and Mr. Swift wrote out to me not to send any more, at which time I lay very sick, not able to go and see Mr. Turner about it. Lawyer Smith (the bearer of Mr. Swift's letter) promised me to inquire into the business, of Mr. Turner, tomorrow and let me know what Mr. Turner said on the subject. 18 of your bales of cotton has been shipped to Mr. Linton and 12 at the landing which the sheriff took charge of, and then forbid any more being hauled.

I have been very sick 4 or 5 days with a bowel complaint. I took medicine instantly, but without having relief for several days. This is the first time I have felt able to set up to write since my sickness commenced. Mr. Davis is sick also. He is here and has taken medicine today. Dr. Denny lays in violent fever at this moment. I am afraid he will have a severe spell. Poor little Clarissa is well, but kept very busy nursing the sick. The cholera is bad at the landing. Several Negroes has died within a few days with it. I don't let Daniel go there now.

Mr. Mulkey says he has mastered the grass and can attend the crop very easy now. He appears in high spirits and can boast yet of the best crop in the parish, which I hope is so. I will go and see it myself when I get well enough.

The suit between H. Flower and the heirs to the Swayze estate has been decided some time and it appears, from what Mr. Hall told Mr. L. Davis, that H.F. has gain three hundred and fifty dollars to be paid him by the heirs. *But poor me has gone clear for once.* He recovered nothing from Stephen Bell, so I hope Harry has done sending his long papers to me during my lifetime.

Clarissa is in great trouble for fear H. F. will demand his 350$ before you can send her his note that you so kindly gave her when she saw you last. She says I must beg of you to send it soon, so that she may be ready to settle with him when called on.

My dear brother will excuse this letter. My head is weak from the pain I have suffered of late, but I have been better this evening. I hope soon to get about again. Clarissa will remain with me until I can spare her. She sends her love to her uncle and aunt and her little cousins. My love to my dear sister Mary and all my dear little children. Heaven bless and preserve you all here and hereafter are the prayers of your affectionate sister,

Rachel O'Connor

Dr. Denny continues very sick. His fever keeps extremely high with a severe vomiting.

Rachel advises David that the sheriff's ban on cotton sale is lifted. She wonders if David has departed on his proposed sea voyage in hope of a cure for his poor health. Hoping to help her brother care for the health of his family and slaves, she writes a note on the outside of her letter. "Vinegar, salt, and paregoric, mixed together, is almost a sure cure for diarrhea, taken in small doses as need requires."

June 16th, 1833

My dear brother,

I have not received any letters since the one written in N. Orleans. Sometimes I am induced to think you have taken a trip to sea, for your health, as you had an idea of doing so, if your health didn't improve shortly. It is so sickly almost everywhere that I feel uneasy indeed; I may say distressed continually, every moment expecting bad news to arrive from some quarter. Last week we were very sickly. I was quite sick myself for several days and about the same time, seven Negroes were taken very sick with bowel complaint. And to make the matter worse, the Dr. was taken down with a violent ague and severe fevers. Mr. Swift called in to see me and gave me a receipt showing how he made pills for the chloera and directed me to give them instantly. The Dr. observed the hurry and bustle in me, trying to get the pills made for the sick ones; he soon roused up, fever and all, and assisted to prepare the medicine for them, and I gave everyone that needed it their portion which operated pretty well so that in a few days, they were able to go to work. And I believe the fright cured me, so that we are all well at present expecting Pless who is confined to her bed with a sore foot caused by a stone bruise on the sole of her foot, and Harriet's child, two weeks old last night.

Mr. Swift prevailed on the sheriff to let your cotton bales be hauled to the landing and sent on as fast as possible. I have not found out how they continued to put a stop to their being sent to market as they did for several days. Perhaps I may when I see Mr. Swift again. I was not able to ride to Mr. Turner's at the time, or I should have done so. But Mr. Swift mentioned it to him in St. Francis Ville. He appeared surprised; said he had not heard of the arrangement being made, and of course, did not know how to advise on the subject. We have 54 bales to haul yet. Yesterday we had a fine rain, the first since you left us. Mr. Mulkey says one day's work will put him entirely out of the grass. I do really hope he may raise a good crop.

I have not heard of any person having the cholera in St. F. V. for several days past. I am told that it is dreadful bad in Rapids; that the planters are leaving their crops and camping out in the pine woods with what Negroes they have left alive. Judge Dawson has very lately returned from there and expects to visit the Attakapas in three weeks. James Flower has been to see me since his return from N. Orleans. He looks well and appears to be as good as usual, and we could not wish him better. He has an idea of buying the Spence place with fifteen Negroes on it at sixteen thousand dollars, to be paid in four years—four thousand each payment.

I really have a fine garden full of everything good to eat, which I dare not use, neither will it sell, so I fear my marketing will not amount to much this year after all.

I had a fine piece of ground planted with potato vines last evening after the rain. My vines are much longer than Mr. Mulkey's. His are not long enought to cut yet, but he says his will be the largest when digging time comes, although he dislikes to hear me boasting of my good luck.

A Negro man that belonged to the partnership of Swift and Crenon, where Mr. Swift still carries on the plantation, burned all the Negroes' houses down on Friday last, and then run away, to be revenged of Mr. Swift for having him whipped for some fault or other. I have not the particulars. The Negro was a preacher.

Remember me most affectionately to my dear sister and the children. Should my brother be from home, I must request it as a particular favor of my sister to write a few lines to let me know how you all are. Otherwise I shall not expect her to write owing to her present condition.

My letters are intended for you both *as one*, no matter which they are direct to. I remain your affectionate sister,

Rachel O'Connor

Rachel writes David of her continued concern for his health. She takes the liberty of ordering medicine for him from Baltimore.

June 23, 1833

My dear brother,

I received your letter of the 10th instant. Your health being no better than when I saw you last gave me so much uneasiness that I had not power to answer it. I tried to do so, but mind wandered on all subjects excepting the right one. At length I concluded to ask the favor of Dr. Bell to send for four dozen bottles of medicine that relieved you so much, which he readily agreed to undertake. Dr. Denny made out the bill for me and I sent it to Dr. Bell, which I expect is on its way ere this, and will be here in two months at least. You will have to direct me how to contrive it over to you, should I be fortunate enough to get it here. If you say the word, I can send Arthur who will carry all safe to you.

Dr. Denny thinks it will cure you if you take if for a length of time. You must not think hard of me for sending for the medicine. I was useless until I done so, even a trouble to myself; but now *hope* has become a *comfort* and I feel much better. Perhaps it may be all for the best that your dear family could not bear the idea of your venturing a sea voyage. Dr. Denny says I must ask you whether you got any of the medicine in N. Orleans or not; that you expected to find some there for you when you left here.

All your bales are hauled but four cart loads which will be taken down this week. The sheriff prevented me from sending any several days, and I do not know from what authority yet. I was sick at the time; not able to ride to inquire into the business. Mr. Swift saw Courtney and talked to him, after which he agreed to let Mr. Swift ship the cotton agreeable to the arrangements between yourself and

Wm. Flower. Courtney is one of the meanest beings on earth, and if I ever see you again, I can convince you of the same. But it will be made public before Mrs. Pirrie's estate is settled up. The old lady only gave her youngest daughter about one third of her Negroes, and them the meanest kind she had, and very little of her land. Dr. Ira Smith is to get all the rest, which is all owing to the lies our honorable sheriff made and told to her, which she found out before her death, but too late to make any changes in her will.

Mr. Mulkey requested of me to inform you that he had one of the most promising crops in the ground that he ever had of both corn and cotton, which I think is true. Those late rains make the crop look fine indeed. He has all in fine order, which few can say besides himself in our neighborhood. Mr. Bowman, Mr. Luther Smith, Mr. C. Smith, and Mr. Boone are yet dreadfully in the grass.

Very few has died with the cholera near here yet. The report of its being so bad in St. F. V. was false. None has been taken and died with it in that place this year. Some has been landed from steamboats sick with it and died, and some dead that had died on board. St. F. V. is very health at present and Jackson also. Several of your Negroes here appeared to be in that way, which were relieved by medicine very soon. Lyd is a little sick now, but no ways dangerous. The Dr. has got quite well again.

How is your sugar crop on the island and all other concerns? I hope all may do well this year. How must I manage with your bales this crop—send them to the landing when ready or not? The oats are all cut and put up, and now my little calves have a fine pasture and look well. I have 24; that is to say 24 this year. They are really pretty little things and grow fast.

My little waiting man, Isaac, came near to being badly hurt yesterday by his running up to one of the horses and catching his mane, which frightened the horse and caused him to jump on the child, but fortunately did not hurt him much. In your letter, please to mention my sister's health. I don't expect her to write at present. Should she feel well enough, I should be very glad to receive one. I am afraid my dear Frances has forgotten her old aunt. She don't write any of late. My love to my dear sister and her little ones. I hope soon to hear of my dear and only brother being in better health. I pray that the cholera may not visit New Town again.

Your affectionate sister,
Rachel O'Connor

The state of David's health is ever present in Rachel's thoughts.

June 30th, 1833

My dear brother,

I have not received any letter from you for some time. Your last said the cholera was in St. Martins Ville and that you much feared would soon reach N. Town, which causes me to suffer great uneasiness of mind. But I hope our troubles will not cause us to forget to write to each other while we do live.

I did not mention in my last that I had been, and still continue, quite unwell; not entirely layed up, though scarcely able to keep about, with a bowel complaint. I have been better for 2 or 3 days past and hope soon to feel well once more. At present I am very weak. Mulkey went to S. Francis Ville yesterday and returned in the evening with news of the cholera being at the river; that several lay dangerously ill, and that people were greatly alarmed. This morning *Clem*, the blacksmith, came out and says it is as healthy as common at this season of the year; that he had not heard of the cholera being at the river, which is all I know about it now. Judge Dawson would have been over in your neighborhood before this if he had not been afraid to travel while the cholera remains so bad in different parts. I sent Mr. Mulkey to see him yesterday and to ask the favor of him to carry a few of the bottles that has the medicine in them that you are taking. The Judge sent me word that he would carry some to you whenever he went. Dr. Bell was very fortunate in getting them sent to him soon. Dr. Denny says that you must take it constant, which he thinks will cure your disease.

James Flower was throw'd from a horse a few days ago and badly hurt in his head. If I had been able to ride that far, I would have went to see him; but as it was, I could not. His brother Wm. sent me word of his being hurt by Old Daniel. He was better at that time and Wm. said he would be down to see me soon.

Mr. Mulkey was wishing for you to be here to look at your crop last night as he had it in fine order and it looked so well; that all it needed at present was rain. Dr. Denny says the same. I have been too poorly to ride out to see it myself. I have got some seed cotton from Mr. McCaleb at last, and tomorow I shall commence spinning. Mr. Mulkey is to let me have Old Leah to assist in spinning and Old Milly to weave. He has not built my new loom house yet, but talks of doing so soon. He can really direct work well and manage to a good advantage. I wish he loved *truth* and *honour* better than he does. He would then be a useful being.

George has been very sick again. He is better today and can walk about some: I send him anything he wants, but could not walk that far to see him. The Dr. attended him and Charity was nurse.

Excuse my letter. I write to let you know that I am yet in the land of the living. My love to my dear sister and the children. Wishing you all health and happiness, I remain your affectionate sister,

R. O'Connor

Despite Rachel's anxiety about David's poor health, she writes Mary about plantation and family affairs and adds a bit of Feliciana gossip.

August 3rd, 1833

My dear sister,

I have not received a letter for some time, but I hope you and family are well. Should you not feel able to write yourself, do get some of your friends to write a few lines to let me know how you are. I know the distress of your mind unless you have been more fortunate than myself. I have not heard from my brother since he sailed for New York. I sent regularly to the post office with a hope of receiving a letter from him, but as yet none has arrived. If I could hear of his health being better, and likely to be restored once more, how very comfortable and easy my mind would be to what it is at present, hanging between hope and despair, which causes me not to sleep well and constantly dreaming confused and unpleasant dreams, which I seldom escape during any distress of mind. Sometimes I think I am sick, I feel so very bad. Yet I believe that one letter from either of you would prove a cure at present.

We had a fine rain at last which has done much good. The crops and gardens had heretofore suffered greatly in different parts of both East and West Feliciana. All plantation business goes on pretty well. The overseer still appears anxious to please my brother in his management on the plantation; and, to him, I appear confident of my brother's return sometime in next month. Charlotte was still about a few days ago and quite well. I expect Mr. Davis and Clarissa down this evening if all are well at home. Julia Ann is with Charlotte, where she expected to remain during her confinment.

Mr. Handy and family are well. I rather expect Harriet is in the family way, but her health is very good. Her brother James has had a severe attack of the bilious fever, but got better ere I heard of his being sick. The rest of his family are well.

Since Mrs. Sterling's trip to Browns Ville, where her parents live, the *old man* has been quite silent. I have not once heard of his going courting or being in *love* with any lady whatever, which may be caused by his being already engaged and waiting for the lady's return with consent from her parents to their union. If so, I wish them great luck. Should you be with your sister, request her to write. I should be glad to receive letters from both of them. I certainly feel a great interest in their welfare, perhaps greater than they have an idea of. My *friendship was formed towards them* when little girls, and has never diminished.

In my last I mentioned what Dr. Denny said respecting cure of ringworms which was only to hold the part affected under water as long as possible. If the ringworm still continues on your child's face, I can (by applying to Dr. Bell) have a cure for tetter and ringworms sent from Baltimore prepared and sold by Dr. David Brown of that place. If you wish me to do so, let me know in your next. It will take two months to send and get it here, but better wait that long for a certain cure than to let the poor babe suffer for a medicine so easily procured.

Report says that a *young lawyer shot himself* in *Clinton, East Parish* on Sunday. He was a partner of Maj-r Downs. I have forgotten his name at this moment. We are entirely clear of the cholera throughout the neighborhood at present. I hope it has not visited New Town again as you much feared it would in your last.

My kindest respects to your sisters and all friends. Kiss my dear Frances, William, Alfred, Harriet, and Charles for me. *Greatly do I wish to see them and yourself.* Heaven guard and protect you through all difficulties and troubles of life are the sincere prayers of your affectionate sister,

Rachel O'Connor

P. S. I was so very sick when I received your letter mentioning the ringworm that I really forgot to mention it in my answer, at which time I was very sick also.

Two days later Rachel writes Mary of receiving a letter from David. Hope is revived.

August 5th, 1833

My dear sister,

I have just received a letter from my brother dated from New Haven, July 12, where he says he arrived on the 10th after a very pleasant passage without experiencing the least sickness at sea or any difficulty whatever, and that he thinks his health better than when he left home. He wishes me to write on the arrival of his letter, and direct to the care of Mr. A. H. Douglas, Gallatin, Tennessee, where he expects to call on his way home.

I have just finished a very long letter to him. I expect it will make him twice glad, for I am certain he must feel glad to come to the end of three pages closely written. I really feel so much relieved myself since I read his letter that I scarcely think myself the same being that existed an hour previous to the arrival of his letter. Surely my spirits are not so raised (as has often been the case) to experience a fall, that I may find it the more severe. I conclude that he had much hopes of returning health from his manner of writing. His spirits were good and his mind easy and contented.

I am in good health at present and all appears to be doing well. I am some alarmed about the stock of cattle and horses, from a distemper that has of late made its appearance (cheifly in the East Parish) that kills them very fast. From 10 to 12 has been found dead in one place where they drink water; and on old Mrs. Turnbull's place in the Plains where her stock has been kept for a length of time, a hundred died in one day. If hogs eat the flesh, they die also, but it has no effect on dogs.

I hope to hear from you soon. I hope the cholera did not spread in N. Town, although I am very uneasy and wish to hear more about you, and where you are. My dear sister must rest contented and make herself as happy as possible. Indeed we have great reason to return thanks to the great giver of all good for preserving and sparing a life so dear to us. How rejoiced will his dear babes be to hear of their father's being in a fair way to get well. How simple I am writing. You will doubtless receive a letter from him before you see this. However I will forward this, that you may see the effect of joy on a weak mind. Mine at present is quite like a child, scarcely can recollect a subject sufficient to make sense of it before it rambles to some other. I wrote to you on Saturday last which probably may reach you at the same time this will, which will surprise you to receive two letters from the same person, one dated the 3rd and the other the 5th.

My love to your sisters and the children. I remain your ever affectionate sister,

R. O'Connor

Along with Rachel's pleasant expectation of David's arrival is her grief over the deaths of slaves and friends and the prevalence of cholera.

September 1st, 1833

My dear sister,

I much fear you will (by the time this reaches you) consider me very ungrateful or neglectful towards yourself. I received your kind letter dated the 10th of July on the 23rd of August, but it had been in the house at home a week ere I saw it owing to my being from home at its arrival. I went up to see Charlotte on the 15th of August; found her unwell and delivered of a fine son at 5 o'clock the same evening. She appeared to be doing very well when I left her to return home. She spoke of naming her son Stephen Lewis which I expect will be its name, but I have not heard from her since I returned home. I had to stay several days longer there than I had any idea of when I left home. The day being so extremely warm, it caused me to feel bad before we reached Mr. Doherty's and in a few hours after, I became very sick and fever several days. They sent for a Dr. Varney who attended me until I got better. Mr. Doherty procured a fine carriage and two gentle horses, with the driver, to convey me home which he thought the only way it would be possible for me to be able to stand the journey. As we came near where you formerly lived, I met a Negro man coming for me. He said the Negroes lay very sick at home, which I found as he said when I came. Poor Old Daniel, the market man, was one, who has since died. He was upward of sixty years old, but I can safely say, I never lamented the death of a Negro as I do his. He had long been very useful and

113

more faithful than any other Negro will ever be to me. I never shall have the same confidence in another. Dr. Denny done all in his power to save the old man, day and night, until he died; and I nursed him as I would a child and kept his old wife constantly with him to wait on him. I feel satisfied with my conduct toward him. Still I lament his loss. The rest of the sick Negroes are alive, but a part very low. I never had so much sickness amongst the Negroes before since I lived on the plantation. There has several others been sick since I came home. I feel so discouraged that I am afraid I shall not be able to bear up against my misfortunes. But I will do the best I can while I do live. If I could have spared the time from nursing the sick, I certainly should have written to you before this, which I hope will excuse what may have appeared like neglect.

I was overjoyed to hear of the birth of your son and that you and your child were doing so well. My brother being from home caused me to pity your lonesome situation and I often felt great uneasiness about you and family. But I hope kind providence will permit you all to meet again and long enjoy each others company. I have received a second letter from my dear brother dated the 28th of July, New York, which says his health is much improved and he hoped soon to feel quite well, which has relieved my mind greatly.

Mr. John Swift died the 24th of August. I pity his three sisters very much indeed. They have lost a good brother. A number has died of late, both black and white, which were strangers to me. Both East and West Parish has been dreadfully sickly. Mulkey, our overseer, has been very low. His whole family has been sick. I am about myself, but not very well. My niece, Julia Ann, came home with me from Mrs. Doherty's and is still with me. She would not agree to let me come alone. She desires to be remembered to you and the children. I am sorry to see her so low spirited. Mrs. Meeker, formerly Mrs. J. Finley, lays at the point of death. Harriet Handy is well. Their Negroes has been very sickly. You would wonder (if you could see how often I am called for to the sick) how I write at all, bad as it is. They scarcely let me set half an hour at a time. Perhaps you may make it out and feel convinced of a willing mind.

I received a very friendly letter from my young friend, your brother Alfred, dated the 13th of August. He had received a letter from my brother and immediately informed me of the good news. How thankful I am to God for such good and true friends. I wish it may be ever in my power to convince him of the gratitude I feel.

Yesterday I stopped owing to one of the girls getting dangerously ill. This morning she is better. One small girl died belonging to Mr. Bowman last night.

God only knows what will become of us. I never knew it so sickly. Seven of Mr. Samuel McCaleb's white family were laying at the point of death yesterday. The whole neighborhood is distressed. I hope it may not be the case where you live. I don't hear of the cholera being anywhere near us, but bilious fevers are dreadful. Mr. Lewis Davis came here last night. He left several Negroes sick at home; himself and Clarissa are well, or were, at the time he came from home. I hope my dear brother may come home safe. I expect him shortly. Your last letter was dated July, but I have just observed the post mark to be August, which shows the mistake in you. I hope to hear from you very soon. God bless you and yours are the prayers of your affectionate sister,

R. O'Connor

Rachel writes Mary that her own health is miraculously restored since hearing of David's improved health.

Sept-br 15th, 1833

My dear sister,

I received one charming long letter from you since I wrote to you last which I should have answered ere this, if I had not written to you only two days previous to its arrival. I am truly thankful to you for the trouble you take in writing to me. It is a great comfort to me, much more so than a person would imagine that had never lived far from their relations. I often carry a letter in my bosom to read occasionally until another comes. I hope this may find yourself and the dear little ones enjoying good health. You have never mentioned the little babe's name or whether you have given it any or not; but I suppose you intend to wait for its father to give it a name, who I expect very soon. His last letter was dated the 2nd instant. He then expected to be with me in fifteen days, which is the day after tomorrow. From that time I shall expect him hourly. His health had improved very much, and I hope to see him pretty soon once more.

Since I heard of his being on the mend, I have got quite well myself. I feel surprised to find my strength return so fast. Clarissa would insist that my uneasiness caused me to keep so poorly.

It has been uncommonly sickly this year. There has been seventeen Negroes very sick on this place at one time. I was dreadfully alarmed for a while, but thanks be to kind providence, they are all in a fair way to recover. Some has gone to work. The loss of my old market man is great, but I am thankful that no more of them died. Dr. Ira Smith has lost five Negroes very lately; Mr. Bowman one.

I have sent twenty bales of cotton to Mr. Linton, which I hope will bring a good price (for all your sakes). I directed Mr. Linton to hold the money subject to my brother's order. I hope the cotton crop will be pretty good. The overseer would have had more cotton ready for market if the Negroes had not been so very sickly.

My garden looks bad. Sometimes I start out to have some work done in it and try to get it to look better again; but the moment I get in there, I think of Old *Daniel*, and of all his work, for such a long period of time, which makes me so sorry that I don't stay long. This day Charlotte's little son is a month old. I have not heard from any of them for two weeks. I am afraid they are detained by sickness or some of them would have been to see me before this. I heard that Mr. Handy's white family were well a few days ago, but that he had some Negroes sick.

My dear Frances don't write to me now. I really longed to receive a letter from my little darling once more. She could tell me so much about her dear little brothers and sister Harriet, and all her uncles and aunts and how many cousins she has and their names.

Mrs. Pirrie's fine house appears to be forsaken by all her family. An overseer and his family lives in it at present.

Heaven bless you, my dear and good sister, and guard you safe through life with your little family are the sincere prayers of your affectionate sister,

Rachel O'Connor

In a letter to David, Rachel relives the pleasure of his visit. She relates her anxiety over the conduct of her overseer.

October 13, 1833

My dear brother,

I have not received any letter from you since you started from here on your way homeward, where I hope and trust you arrived safe on Saturday following after you left me. I should suffer great uneasiness if I did not know the world of business you would have to attend to after you had rested yourself sufficient to undertake the task. I hope you continue to improve in health and that you found your beloved wife and children enjoying good health. I am thankful to have it in my power to inform you that my own health at present is very good and that I feel quite industrious and willing to do all the little good I can.

The Negroes are all quite well, excepting Bridget who about three hours ago was delivered of a fine son, and both mother and child doing very well, which is three boys and one girl born this year, and all alive and well. Mulkey is going on very well with his crop. He has a good parcel of hay pulled, and intends pulling more, and is very industrious. I think more so than he has been yet. No person could complain of his management since you left here. He once asked me if you were not angry with him while here. I told him no, but that you would have been better pleased to have seen the place better slicked up roundabout. He said that it was impossible at that time as the hands had nearly all been so very sick. I then told him if he wished to prove himself a true pentitent, he must do better hereafter. He said that he would do all in his power and made some excuse to get off. After he had gone, I turned to his wife and talked very serious concerning every part of his conduct, be it good or bad, and then observed how well he could manage and direct a farm if he would only do as well as he knew how; that he understood farming as well as anyone that I knew of, which if he would not act according to his knowledge, would cause people to say that he was like all overseers—could not bear good treatment, which I requested of her to tell him so that he might know what he had to depend on, which she says she did and that he made every fair promise necessary, which I believe, as he has done so well ever since in every respect.

The gin became so dull and out of order that I had to get a man to come and sharpen it. He began yesterday. Mulkey says he is doing the work very well. I am to pay him fifteen dollars. They have fifty-seven bales pressed, but only forty sent to N. Orleans yet.

James Flower is only middling well. Wm. has been very sick and scarcely able to set up yet. The rest of the family are well. Judge Rhea's family are very sickly yet. He has lost his two eldest daughters and one grandchild since you left here. Mr. McCaleb has lost one son about ten years old and one grandchild last week. One of Mr. Weatherstrand's sons died last week. He was 19 or 20 years old. A Mrs. Tigert also died who left four small children.

My love to my dear sister and her little ones. Heaven grant you all health and happiness. I remain your affectionate sister,

Rachel O'Connor

Rachel has become aware of the relations of overseer Mulkey and the slave women and reports his conduct to her ailing brother. She pens a note on the outside of her letter: "Postmaster will much oblige by forwarding this speedily."

Oct-br 23, 1833

My dear brother,

Since I wrote you last I have received two letters, one dated the 8th and the other the 12th of this month. They both came together. How that happened, I do not know, but I had constantly sent in search of letters every mail day. I felt so uneasy about your health that I could not avoid doing so. However I am now very glad that it happened as it did as I should have suffered so much uneasiness about my dear little Alfred. I lose all hopes so soon that I should never expected him to recover his health again. Your last gives every encouraging hope of his recovery, and I pray that your next may bring word of his being quite well once more. How thankful I feel that you had got home to comfort my best of sisters in her severe troubles. I am sorry for you both. I am no stranger to such distresses that I never can forget while I live. If he has recovered, we are happy. Heaven bless and preserve my darling son amongst the other sweet babes and grant that you may all be well and happy.

Our neighborhood continues very sickly in many places. In my last I informed you of the death of Judge Rhea's two eldest daughters (Mrs. Cooper and Mrs. Watts); since their mother has died, and the youngest child of Mrs. Watts also. Mr. McCaleb has lost a son and grandson. Many others has died that I don't expect you ever knew. Captain James Williams lays at the point of death. His wife is recovering slowly. One of their grandchildren died lately. Mrs. Bowman is very sick at this time—not able to walk she is so extremely weak. I stayed with her last night and returned home today and found all well.

The night before last we had a severe frost which I fear has ruined all the young bolls that were nearly ripe. Mulkey is gathering the corn. It holds out better than I expected. When I wrote last, I had raised a hope he would behave better, but I now think it is very doubtful. He is a shameless being—nearly as bad as Patrick—in the same way. If it was not for that, he could oversee very well; but as it is, he has too many ladies to please. He appears to have a desire of saying something about another year, but I have given him no opportunity. Neither will I encourage him in the least. You may judge of his conduct when you come.

A man by the name of Germany, who is said to be a good sober industrious man, applied to me for an overseer's birth. I told him I would write to you and that he would have to wait for your answer. He overseed for Mr. Bowman last year and behaved very well, which I had often heard them both say before he left there. Today I talked to Mr. and Mrs. Bowman particularly about Germany. They both spoke highly of him as a very sober industrious good man. He has a wife, but no children nor Negroes. His father and family lives three miles from Lewis Davis and are said to be industrious people. Mr. Bowman said there would be no danger of Germany's behaving as overseers commonly did amongst the Negroes; that he was too fond of his wife to behave in that way. So now, my dear brother, judge for yourself and do for the best. The terms that Germany wishes you to agree to is that you will find him and his wife in corn meal and 400 lbs. of good meat, 150 lbs. sugar, 50 lbs. coffee, one barrel of flour, and 25 lbs. of lard, and to pay him four hundred and seventy dollars for overseeing a year. He has no horse to feed.

My love to my dear sister and children. Past midnight, so my best of brothers, goodnight.

R. O'Connor

Excuse all mistakes. I was up very late last night with Mrs. Bowman and it is quite late now. My fire is out and I am pretty cold so that it is difficult to write, bad as I have.

119

Rachel decides to fire overseer Mulkey and seeks David's advice about hiring Jacob Germany for the job.
Editor's note: In 1833 there is a record of Jacob Germany (who was to become Rachel's overseer the next year) purchasing a "gentleman's whip" at a Plains, Louisiana, store in the area.

October 31, 1833

My dear brother,

I feel much uneasiness about my dear little Alfred. He was still sick when you wrote last, yet you entertained hopes of his being on the mend, and I pray that this may find him quite restored to health. In your last you did not mention your own health. I expect your anxiety about your little *son* caused you to forget all else. How is my dear sister and all her darling little ones?

My health at present is very good. I have great reason to be very thankful to kind providence for so great a favor. I can attend to every part of my little business with the greatest ease which affords me much pleasure. This evening I finished digging the sweet potatoes that I had raised in my garden. They proved extremely good. I am certain I have more than one hundred bushels. Mr. Mulkey's has not turned out so well as mine has, but still they are pretty good. He expects to finish digging his the day after tomorrow. His corn has done wonderful. He has filled one crib and has enough in another to last until Christmas. But I am afraid the cotton will not prove as good as I had a wish it should be. They have 66 bales pressed, and a good parcel picked, and some little to pick. But I am certain it cannot hold out to make a large crop of cotton. The severe frost ruined the late bolls. It is a very general complaint throughout the neighborhood.

Mulkey behaves well in every respect except one, and in that one I must say he is worse than Patrick ever was while he was overseer here, but I don't say anything to him now. I wish him to part in peace. Major Downs has engaged him for next year to oversee seventeen hands and gives the same that he gets here, *so Mulkey says.* I hope they may do well. He is a smart overseer, but a dirty beast after all.

In my last, I mentioned a Mr. Germany that wished to oversee here for you next year. He has a wife, but no children nor Negroes. Neither does he wish to keep a horse to ride, which I think much the best. It will save 30 or 40 barrels of corn, at least, in the course of a year. He offers to come for four hundred and seventy dollars and find him four hundred weight of meat and one hundred and fifty weight of sugar, fifty weight of coffee, twenty-five pounds of lard, and one barrel of flour, as near as I can recollect. But I expect you have received my letter ere this, which informed you all. I have had another talk with Mr. and Mrs. Bowman about Germany. They still recommend him highly as a good industrious overseer, and one that they believe to be entirely clear of the fault so common amongst overseers. They both told me that during the time he lived with them, he quarreled with a carpenter that they had hired and drove him away for bad behaviour of the same kind. I wish you to let me know as soon as you make up your mind so that I may let Germany know your answer. Several others has applied for a birth, but none worth naming.

The Negroes are all well. It keeps very sickly in many places. Mr. Kendrick has lost his youngest daughter, nearly grown. Harriet Handy has lost her Negro woman that had a child two years ago last Jan-ry. She died in four days sickness.

Mr. Dunbar's fine new gin house and forty bales of cotton was burned to ashes night before last. A Negro woman was burned to death amongst the cotton also. Wm. Flower has had a severe spell of sickness. He is some better, but not able to ride. Mr. and Mrs. Meeker has lost their little son. Mr. Turner sent here today to inquire about the horse that he is to get from you, which had not arrived yet. I promised to send him as soon as he come.

My love to my dear sister and the children. I hope to see you soon. God bless you and yours, my best of brothers. I remain your affectionate sister,

R. O'Connor

Judge Mathews lays very ill in Virginia. They don't expect him to return home this year.

All that you wrote to New Orleans for has come except the Dr.'s saddle. He appears sadly disappointed. He is afraid they have neglected delivering it from on board the St. Boat.

Three days later an event of unusual magnitude takes place. Upon David's request, Rachel permits five of her young slave men to travel

via steamboat to The Cottage Plantation, home of David's brother-in-law Frederick A. Conrad, to assist in harvesting his crop of sugar cane.

Nov-br 3rd, 1833

My dear brother,

I received your last on the 1st day of Nov. I am overjoyed to find that my dear little Alfred had recovered and that the rest of you were well.

Agreeable to your request, I have sent five young Negro men to Mr. F. A. Conrad to assist him in cutting his sugar cane. A Mr. Wm. Wicoff came for them. He lives near Baton Rouge. They started on board of a steamboat from St. Francis Ville. The young gentleman promised that Mr. Conrad would write to me instantly and let me know whether the boys arrived safe or not. There has so many accidents happened to steamboats of late that my heart trembled for their safety. They are all young and never been farther than where Mr. Lewis Davis lives, which caused the very idea of being sent amongst strangers to frighten them out of their senses almost. I really was so sorry for them that if I had not been afraid you would have been displeased with me, I should not have sent them. I am very uneasy, fearing they may take the cholera and die. They have all been very sick this season and might die with a slight attack. I sent Dave, Eben, Harry, Littleton, and Frank. Pray write to Mr. Conrad to be careful of them. They were born and raised here with me which causes me to love them better than I had ought, but my heart must remain as it pleased God to form it. I have no power to change it or make it otherwise. Dave will be 23 years old the last day of Dec-br next; the other four are younger.

Mr. Mulkey said it would be impossible to do you justice in saving the crop if more than five were taken away. You had better get Mr. Conrad to send them home the moment he can spare them. They had ought to make a large number of rails. The old ones are so rotton, and there is a plenty of rail timber on the log ground where the logs are to be rolled this winter.

Littleton proved too young and giddy for a market man. I had to take Arthur, who does better than his father ever did. In him I find poor Old Daniel's loss quite made up, which is a greater relief than you would imagine.

A Mr. Collier has brought your bay horse. He delivered him to Mr. Lewis Davis, who rode him down in company with Clarissa. This morning I sent Arthur to deliver your horse to Mr. Turner as you directed me to do. Mr. Turner being at Clinton attending court, Mrs. Turner did not receive him, fearing the horse might be neglected during Mr. Turner's absence. Arthur tells me that Mrs. Turner was delivered of a *son* and *daughter* yesterday evening and all doing well. Mr. Davis and Clarissa are in fine health. They send their love to you and family.

There has been six steamboats *lost* on the Mississippi within a short time. The St. Martin a few days ago was burned and forty passengers lost their lives. Craven Cash was burned to death. Ruffin Sterling had threw himself overboard and had nearly drown when some person brought him to land and used means to save his life; otherwise he would have been lost. Report says that another up-country steamboat was lost yesterday with 1000 bales of cotton on board and a number of people also. When the boys are to return, do let them walk. They can come home in two days without risking their lives on water and in fire.

Do excuse me. I feel so alarmed from so many misfortunes lately happened that I have no rest in my sleep. My dreams distress me continually. My love to my dear sister and the children. I remain your affectionate sister,

R. O'Connor

Rachel is more than ever displeased with Mulkey and longs for a new overseer. She relates the appearance of a great blaze in the heavens and falling stars.

November 16th, 1833

My dear brother,

I received yours of the 6th instant yesterday.

You appear sorry to find by my letters that Mulkey follows his old trade in *bad doings.* When I wrote to you I really had hopes, but soon found them groundless. His wife done all in her power to reclaim him and make him do better. Her heart appeared set on remaining another year. But I discovered he appeared indifferent and careless whether or not, and after a while found that he had been engaged to oversee for Major Downs shortly after you went from here (which his wife did not know). He reports that he is to get six hundred dollars, and meal to do his family, and corn for his horse, to oversee seventeen hands. You may recollect that I mentioned young McCaleb visiting Mulkey often while you was here. I expected then some of them wanted him to oversee, but I didn't think him any loss. He has been pretty drunk several times since he engaged to Downs and has a white Miss in St. Francisville which draws much of his attention and money also, which will soon cause him to neglect his business. Maj-r Downs will have to watch him or he will do more harm than good. Mulkey has six in family—himself and wife, three big sons, and his Negro woman, and a horse to feed. Germany has only himself and his wife, not even a horse to feed and wait on. He appears to be a smart young man about twenty-seven years of age. He raised the best crop that ever Mr. Bowman had, excepting the one that Handy raised. I really hope he will do better than Mulkey has done since he came here.

In my letter I expect I have made a mistake of five dollars. Dr. Denny says that Germany said four hundred and seventy-five dollars. I understood him four hundred and seventy. The other articles, I am sure is right. He gave it to me in writing and I have it yet; which after all is added together will not amount to more than 530-$, or there about, which will be seventy dollars less than Mulkey gets in cash. Germany's family being so small makes it much less, and less trouble. Mulkey's boys are ever in the way and so often sick and very troublesome. I would rather have an overseer with only a wife than one without. No woman is pleased to have straggling overseers visiting their house in search of their old sweethearts, and a single man don't care how many comes.

Mrs. Bowman says that Germany's wife is a very decent woman; and if so, none of those fellows will venture near their house. Both Mr. and Mrs. Bowman gives them a good character and think him clear of having any favorites, or even letting others have any on the place where he oversees. But I don't expect to get him for less than I first named to you. I requested him to say the lowest he could take. I think he appears like a good man and that he may do very well. I am afraid that I cannot tell him about keeping only one dog and no pups. I must leave that for you to do. If I was angry with him about something bad, I could tell him and think no trouble in doing so.

There has been three others applied for an overseer's birth. One of them said him name was Gay. His wife was a daughter of old Wm. Bell. He said his wife wished to get here on account of the relationship. I knew that would not do. I never could please them, but I told him he must wait and see you; that you would be here the first of December. Gay is very lame. he asked six hundred dollars and more provisions than Germany; another had a wife and two daughters. I forget his price. He is waiting on you also; and another high flyer, a single man, by the name of Brian. His price is 600 dollars and he is waiting to see you. Brian, the single man, was a smart looking young man, but he would soon be like the others—have six or seven ladies in tthe field that the rest dare not speak to, for fear of giving offense. He was dressed very fine and was quite a handsome young Carolina man.

Wm. Flower is in bad health. You would scarcely know him. He has been here with me for 8 or 10 days. He returned home yesterday.

Did you see the great lights, resembling stars, falling from the heavens on Tuesday, long before daylight, the 12th instant? Some say they commenced falling at 4 o'clock in the morning. When I saw it first, it was later. Mrs. Mulkey observed it first here. She was dreadfully frightened and had all called up, white and black, and seat Joe down to waken Dr. Denny and he called Fan and made her call me. I had never seen anything like it before and felt bad. *Mrs. Mulkey says that she saw a great large blaze open, and a man come out of the blaze as large as Dr. Denny.* That last part I did not see. You have it as I have been informed.

I sent Dave, Eben, Harry, Littleton, and Frank on the first of this month to Mr. Conrad, as you directed me to do. They are there yet, and I hope well. I feel uneasy for fear they may get sick and die. They were very low this year.

Mulkey is trying to build another corn house to put the new ground corn in, so that he may gather it in. He has some cotton to pick yet, and seventy-five bales pressed. I am afraid it will not make a hundred bales in all, but I am not sure yet. Twenty bales were on board the Columbia when the bottom fell out and were lost. Mr. Caskaden said that Mr. Linton had them insured at sixty dollars a bale.

My kindest love to my dear sister. I hope the little babe is well again ere this. Have you named it yet, or not? You had ought to call it David. I am middling well. I hope to live to see you all once more at least. You always forget to mention how your health is now. I remain your affectionate sister,

R. *O'Connor*

Editor's note: The pre-dawn disturbance in the sky witnessed by residents of Evergreen Plantation was the Leonid meteor shower, the most famous example of its kind in modern times. From a disintegrating comet, thousands of tiny objects were pulled down into the atmosphere between midnight and dawn, resulting in what astromomers call a meteor shower. Apparently diverging from the constellation of Leo, this event became known as the Leonid shower.

A distraught Rachel writes David of her anxiety for her absent slaves and the treatment they are receiving. She repeats her contempt for the overseer's conduct.

November 20, 1833

My dear brother,

I have written once since I received your last, but I did not mention the behavior of the Negro boys that I sent to Mr. Conrad. I had not made their new coats for them this fall. Their last winter ones were quite good, and the *warning* so short, that I had not time to prepare clothes for them as I should like to have done, but done as well as I could and started them the next morning after hearing of it at 12 o'clock the day previous. After they were gone, I became very uneasy about their being at the sugar works without their new coats. I concluded to make each of that five a good warm blanket coat and send them down by Arthur, which I done. Arthur returned home the next day with a letter from Mr. Conrad saying that Harry, Eben and Littleton had left him and undertaken to make their way home, which by some means were taken and lodged in jail at Baton Rouge, where he found them and took them back again to his plantation, where he says they behaved very well since.

I cannot help thinking that Mulkey gave them bad advice, or they never would have thought of acting so. Them boys are too young to undertake the likes, unless encouraged by some person. Dave, he loves; I expect he advised him to behave well; and Frank being only eighteen years of age, concluded to remain with Dave. The other three, Mulkey had a particular spite at. Eben caught him and Eliza together and told Mrs. Mulkey of it which caused a great fuss; but, as he was guilty, he could not whip Eben unless I said so, which I was very clear of doing. She and Eben were to go together as man and wife, but now I don't expect he will take her. The next day, the young madam was confined to her room where I found her and whipped her myself, and then cut her curls off, and then started her to field where she had been ever since without grumbling once. Mulkey knew all that I done and what it was for, but never mentioned it to me. He now enjoys the company of his ladies undisturbed, and from what I can hear, rejoiced on hearing the boys had to be whipped. If I did not think his talking to them had been the cause of their acting as they have, of course, I could blame none but themselves. But as it is, I hate the wretch on earth. He has long since reported that money would not tempt him to oversee here another year, which I know is a lie, as he never tells the truth anytime. But I hope you may find that he is no loss. I must acknowledge he is a first rate hand to raise and work a crop, but a trifling *whelp* at gathering it in as ever was. He wants to make fun of Germany, who I am sure cannot be as mean as he is. I don't expect he will make one hundred bales of cotton this crop. If you could come over before the first of Dec-br and turn him away, you would save the corn very much by it. Germany could come at any time and would be better than this fellow is doing now.

However, perhaps, my dear brother should make some allowances for my present humour. I know I am vexed at his conduct and could see him well whipped willingly. Bad as Patrick acted, he was not one half as bad as this villain; and his sons are as mean as himself.

Pray forgive my cross letter. Thanks be to kind providence, I am in a good humour with you and yours. And I hope soon to be clear of those that I am angry with. His time is nearly out. My love to my dear sister and the children. I remain your affectionate sister,

R. O'Connor

Do let the boys return again after Mr. Conrad has done with them. I promised them that you would let them come home again and Mulkey would rejoice at my disappointment and theirs.

Rachel spends a cold December night writing to David about her fears for the absent slaves.

Dec-br 6th, 1833

My dear brother,

Yours of the 23rd of last month has arrived some time since, which I had ought to have answered ere this, but did not do so owing to my writing two letters nearly of the same date shortly before.

I hope your family continues in good health and that your little children are learning fast, particularly as William intends writing to me soon. I shall have a constant look out for letters until theirs come. Your own health continuing in the same state gives me great uneasiness. I am afraid you will let so much time pass off without doing anything to strengthen you, to assist nature, that in time you may find your disease hard to cure. Pray consider the loss you must be to your family. When I think of you being in low health, my very heart trembles. I scarcely dare entertain a hope of seeing you this winter, since the cholera has commenced again. Report says it is raging in New Orleans and on each side of the Mississippi all along the coast, and of course on board the steamboats. I suffer so much distress of mind that my time passes off miserably. I don't think I sleep one hour in the twenty-four for a week or ten days. If I had piles of money that would reach the moon, I would give it all freely for peace of mind. I am tormented with frightful dreams the little time that I do sleep, so that I dread to see night approaching. I try to bear it patiently, but the fear of some great misfortune being near destroys all fortitude.

I have discharged Mulkey, or rather advised him to quit the last day of Nov-br, which he done peaceably. We are still on friendly terms. He has commenced with Ma-jr Downs. His family is to move tomorrow, bitterly against his wife's will. Germany is to come with his wife on Sunday or Monday. I hope in God he may do well for you.

Mrs. Carpenter, a daughter of Mrs. Marbury, died about ten days ago. She left a large family to grieve her loss. Mr. Samuel Dunbar of Natchez died a month or six weeks before Mrs. Carpenter. Mr. Howell has been laying at the point of death for a long time. I am told that his family is much distressed. Charlotte and her youngest son are with me this week. They are all well at present.

Court has commenced which is all I know about it yet. I have a very unpleasant subject to undertake, which grieves me to the heart to commence, but I will confess *all* and tell the truth on myself. If I have acted wrong, I can safely declare that I thought otherwise and my intentions were innocent.

In the first instance, Harry and Frank came home on the first of this month. Frank looked so much worsted that I was sorry for him. Harry did not look so bad. They told me they left Eben sick, which alarmed me, and I fixed Arthur immediately and started him down to see about him, and to bring him home by some means or other. I also wrote to Mr. Conrad to let Dave and Littleton come at the same time, without the smallest idea of giving offense or being refused. He ordered Arthur home without either saying or writing an answer to my letter. So I do not know whether he ever intends to let me hear from the boys again or not. They may be *dead* by this time. A number died on that plantation with cholera, or something else, very lately. The overseer and driver are the cruelest beings I ever heard of. If the boys are alive, I wish you would send them home. It is high time they were all malling rails, and preparing for another crop. All the plantations near here are at such work.

I sent your horse to Mr. Turner on the last day of Nov-br and have not heard from him since. My poor old Ball horse died last Sunday. Big Black is in fine order.

My love to my dear sister Mary and the children. It is past one o'clock at night; all asleep but myself. My dear brother, goodnight. I remain your affectionate sister,

R. O'Connor

The Dr. has received the new saddle and bridle since I wrote to you.

The welfare of her slaves ranked second only to Rachel's love for David and his family. At this Christmas season, she writes a brief letter about plantation affairs.

Dec-br 22nd, 1833

My dear brother,

I have not received any letter from you for a length of time, but I hope and trust in *God* you are all *well*. Perhaps your new regulations on your island has kept you busily employed. While I heard of the cholera being so dreadfully bad, I did not wish you to venture the journey over, but now if you are not afraid to come, I should be very glad to see you. I was taken quite sick one night and day since I wrote you last, and not very well yet, though some better.

Poor Old Sampson died early this morning. He was only sick a few days and I really had every attention paid to the old man. I had no idea that his death could distress me and cause my heart to feel so sore as I find by experience it does. I should have been much happier at this time if I had never owned any living thing. Old Ball died this day two weeks ago and I could not help being sorry about him. Old Milly and George and four little children are very sick, but not so bad as the others. Clarissa is still with me to assist me in nursing them until they get better. Dr. Denny is very sick today. I am afraid he may have a severe spell.

I think you will be pleased with Mr. Germany as an overseer. He has behaved very well so far.

Do let me know how you all are. My love to my dear sister and the children. Excuse my short letter. My very heart is sorrowful. I remain your affectionate sister,

R. O'Connor

In this letter to David, Rachel rejoices in the safe return of the three remaining Negros from Frederick Conrad's plantation.

Jan-ry 2nd, 1834

My dear brother,

Your letter dated the 16th of Dec-br did not arrive until Tuesday last and I had it brought out on Wednsday, which was yesterday. It had been in Franklin on its way here which I expect detained it so long. I am extremely glad to learn from your last that you were all well and that you intend to come over here this month.

I mentioned in one of my last letters to you the number of bales when all was pressed. There was only eighty-four bales of cotton. I never felt more hurt at a small crop before. Mulkey had kept my hopes up to the very last and still said there would be a middling crop. When I found how much it fell short, I could not bear to see him. Should he come for a draft of five hundred and fifty dollars, I will give it as you direct; otherwise he may wait until you come over. I have been informed that Mr. Benjamin Kendrick and several other gentlemen who sent their cotton to Mr. Linton for years past, were dissatisfied with his sales this crop and never before. They think it has been caused by Mr. Linton's being from home of late.

Mr. Germany continues very industrious and I really hope may do well for you. I like him very much so far. He is careful of the corn and horses, and sees to every part of his business and stays all the time at home. But when you come, you can judge for yourself. We have twenty-two hogs to kill this winter. We shall kill a part tomorrow as the weather is so cold. I have seventeen fine little lambs and expect more. I hope I may save them all. I have got over my fright about the cholera once more. People were constantly passing to and from court and everyone had some bad news of cholera being every place they heard from, which nearly turned my brains at that time.

Harriet Handy has been dangerously ill and came near losing her little one. She is about seven months gone. She has got better when I heard from her last, and I hope the worst is over and that she may recover. Mr. Luther Smith died on the 22nd of last month, and Mrs. Kendrick died the 25th. Mr. Howell has been very sick for a long time. One of his sisters had come down the river to take charge of his family.

You wish me to say much sugar I shall need. I think that two barrels will be plenty for my use and for the overseer also. He is to have one hundred weight. I have let him have ten pounds of coffee and ten of sugar since he commenced.

I am very glad to hear of Mr. Charles Conrad being in such good spirits respecting the suit against me. God only knows how thankful I should feel for your sake. My whole heart is set on doing for you and your family; that is, if I could do anything at all. Yet I know I have not the power to do much. But the only happiness I enjoy is in trying to make some returns for all your goodness to me. I write this to you that you may know that I still have a grateful heart that never forgets one act of kindness bestowed on me, but I have not the fortitude to say these words to you when we are together. I have long wished to do so, but cannot command my feelings sufficiently to express myself as I would wish.

I have not heard the girls say anything about sugar this year. They are not here at this time. Tell my dear little Wm. to write as soon as possible and I will make choice of some warm day to answer it. My hand cramps so in cold weather that I scarcely can make out to write any. I answered my dear little Frances' letter. I hope it reached her safe.

The Negro boys are all at home. Harry and Frank ran away and came home first, and in ten or twelve days after, Dave and Littleton came without leave from Mr. Conrad. I was sorry that they all came away as they did, but I thought it useless to send them back. I was afraid they might start home again and perhaps get shot (as runaways) on their way home, and die in the woods, which would be a great loss to you. They are all fine boys to work at home. No overseer ever complained of them here. They still brought me word of Eben being sick and I got Mr. A. Doherty to take a trip down on board of the steamboat for him, which he done. The boy looked bad, but is now well. If I was in your place, I would not charge Mr. Conrad for the time they were with him. He is a young man just beginning in the world, and should be encouraged by his friends. I am very glad to find that you were not displeased with me for sending Arthur down for them. I felt as if I was doing right until all was past, and then got afraid I had acted wrong, although I had considered the affair *well* before I sent him.

I hope the little babe may have a name before you leave it to come here. I long to know what its name is to be. Has my dear sister forgotten me? She hever writes of late. I feel anxious to receive a letter from her. My kindest love to her and the dear little ones. James Flower came up to see us during the Christmas holidays, but intends to return to New Orleans shortly. James is as usual, one of the best of young men. It does my heart good to see him turn out so well. It is quite late at night and very cold. My dear and best of brothers, farewell. I remain your affectionate sister,

R. O'Connor

This letter to David is the first of the several letters that Rachel heads "Evergreen," the name by which she called her home.

Evergreen Feb-ry 19th, 1834

My dear brother,

I have been quite unwell for ten or twelve days past. I never has a cold to affect my breast in the same way before. In the first part of the night, I could sleep some, but I had to set up the latter part of every night, my cough was so uncommonly severe. I am some better, but far from being well. Every day appears to bring something new to complain of. Perhaps I may get to feel well again, *God* only knows.

Clarissa has been very sick. Mr. Davis got frightened and sent for me, but I dare not undertake to go. I felt certain that I must give out before I reach their house, and even if I made out to stand the journey, I could not be of any service to them and should only be in their way. I prevailed on Dr. Denny to go up and see her on Friday last, where he is yet. Mr. Davis came to see me yesterday. Clarissa had begun to mend and to talk of coming down to see me. Hannah's son, by the name of Sam, the boy that worked with Clem, the black-smith, took a violent cold and died in twenty-four hours. He was a fine boy and a favorite with both Clarissa and Mr. Davis. His death being so sudden and unexpected caused Clarissa so great a shock that she came near to going also. The rest of the girls are well. Caleb Swayze is either at Mr. Doherty's or Mr. Davis' and will be to see me shortly.

Mr. Germany has good health ever since you went from here and is very industrious. He is out with the hands every morning before day light and stays constantly with them; comes home when they come, and returns to the field with them. He is very careful of the horses. I really like both him and his wife very much. They could

133

not be more attentive and kind than they both have been to me; and particularly so since I have been sick. I have great reason to feel much gratitude to the little woman for her goodness to me.

You will be disappointed in getting the cotton seed that you expected Robert Davis to send down. When he got there, he found that the Girtleys had let all their seed be lost through neglect. Do let me know how you wish me to act—whether you will venture to plant the same seed again or not. I had to give a draft (on the 15th instant) for eighteen dollars in favor of F. H. Cocoran, the man that made three jumping shovel ploughs in Jackson. Mulkey called them bull tongue ploughs. He had them made to break up the new ground last spring. Please to mention the draft to Mr. Linton when you write to him.

I have not received one line from any of you since we parted. I hope and pray that nothing may be the matter with any of you. Mr. Swift's two youngest sisters were here yesterday. They were dressed in deep mourning and appear heartbroken with grief. My heart bleeds for the poor unfortunate girls.

My garden begins to look pretty well since warm weather commenced. Arthur really behaves well *so far*. He does better than his father ever did. He is a great help to me. I hope he may continue good. Mr. Germany is much pleased with your new horses. He says they work very well. My little colt begins to look pretty again. His sore is well now and I hope he may keep so.

When I set down to write I did not expect to make out ten lines, but you find my letter long enough. I hope my dear little Wm. received my letter long since. My sister has not written for a long time. I should be glad to see one from her if she could spare that much time for her little David. My love to her and the children. I remain your affectionate sister,

R. O'Connor

I begin to feel sorry for Lid. The iron is rather tight on her neck.

Editor's note: The female slave "Lid," who had been caught with the overseer, Mulkey, is being punished by means of an iron collar around her neck.

L E T T E R S

Rachel writes an affectionate letter to her younger nephew William Weeks. A message evidently intended mainly for the boy's parents relates the vengeful actions of a slave girl.

March 9th, 1834

My dear nephew,

I am afraid you will think you are neglected as I have not answered your kind letter before this, which I certainly should have done if I had been able to write since I received it. I have been quite sick for three weeks with a bad cold which caused me to suffer so much pain in my breast that I could not set to write. My cough would be worse at that time than any other. I am some better, but not very well yet, which I hope will excuse my long delay. I am so thankful to you for writing to me that I shall always answer your pretty letters (instantly) if I am well enough to write.

I have just received a letter from your dear mama and little sister, Frances, and will answer in a few days. Tell your mama that I think she had better let her little tree stand where it is until it blooms and bears seed. She may lose it by transplanting. I do not know anything about them. I have never seen one. Mine died very soon.

Your cousin William Flower is here tonight. They are all well at Your Uncle Harry's. Your cousin Harriet Handy has a young son and has named him *George*. When I see Sidney, I shall deliver your message.

A Negro girl contrived some way of putting *poison* in a sugar dish amongst some sugar that came near killing Mr. A. Doherty, and your Cousin Charlotte, and their two little sons, and 3 or 4 Negroes. They all eat of it and drank of it in coffee before the poison was discovered. They are all better but their oldest son and one Negro woman. The girl that mixed the poison with the sugar is one that Mr. Doherty had lately bought. She is about fourteen years old. She acknowledged the act and said she done it to kill the cook woman.

My dear little son, my writing is so bad that you will not be able to read it without help. I am so poorly that I cannot do any better. My love to your dear papa and mama, and all your dear little brothers and sisters. *God* bless you, my sweet son, and grant that you may ever be a good child are the sincere prayers of your truly affectionate aunt,

R. O'Connor

In a letter to Mary, Rachel tells of her pleasure at the completion of David's new home.
Editor's note: This house was built under David's supervision as a residence for his family. It was occupied by David himself for the few remaining weeks before his departure for the North in search of health. His death occurred while he was absent from home. Today this house is a property of the National Trust for Historic Preservation, willed to that agency by David's great-grandson, Weeks Hall. A researcher for the National Trust has stated that Rachel's letters about the plants and shrubs she shared with Mary provided valuable assistance in the restoration of the gardens surrounding the house to their original beauty.

Evergreen March 14, 1834

My dear sister,

I return you many thanks for your kind letter. Your little David being young and (of course) requires much nursing, from which I did not expect you to write. I am truly thankful to learn from your last that my dear brother's health is no worse and that he continues in good spirits. I hope in *God* he may yet be restored and live to see his dear children happily settled. I should have answered your letter long since if it had been possible. I have been much afflicted of late. At first, I had a severe cold which settled in my breast and occasioned so much pain that I could not write. After I began to mend, something got the matter with my right hand and caused my fingers to swell so that I could not write which I suppose to be the rheumatism that fell in my hand. It is some better, but not well yet. I have had rheumatism in my arms often, but never in my hands before.

I answered my dear little William's letter as soon as I could. He will find it badly done, but I could not do any better. When my hand gets well, I will write to him again.

Three of the little Negro children has been very sick. Today they appear better and I hope the worst is over at present. Clarissa has been sick, but has recovered again. Caleb Swayze is over on a visit amongst us. He is a fine looking young man. The wet weather and high water has detained him for a length of time at Mr. Doherty's. The last I heard from them, they were pretty well. They all made a lucky escape considering the dreadful attempt their girl made of poisoning the whole family. She is one that Mr. Doherty lately bought and given to Charlotte for a house girl, about fourteen years old. She stole the keys and slipped into their store house, where they had set the poison, mixed with corn meal, to kill rats and brought out some and mixed it with sugar in the sugar dish, which they used of until discovered, by their being so sick.

Mrs. Courtney died on the 4th instant.

The root you mentioned finding in the box is called *virginia rose*. The top dies after the first severe frost, but the root remains alive in the ground and grows again in the spring. The seed will grow also. The roots become larger every year and yield more sprouts. If it is not too late, you may move the root with safety. I think you might venture it any time this month.

The pride of India is a tree that I know nothing about. Mine all died very young. You had better let it remain where it is until it bears seed. I have been informed they are beautiful when in bloom.

I put a few plants amongst the green onions that my brother carried over last that bears pretty white flowers in the last of October or first of November. They are called *October roses*.

If my dear sister could only know the pleasure it affords me to serve her, she would never hesitate, or feel the least backward, in asking any information that is in my power to give during life. I will write to my dear Frances soon. I feel myself under obligation to the sweet children for their kind attention to me. I am well pleased to hear of their new house as they are to tell me of it and I hope it may prove a blessing to them and their parents and that you all may long enjoy the comforts that earth can bestow. My love to my dear brother and his children.

Mr. Germany is doing as welll as the weather will permit of. I never knew so much wet weather as has been this year. It has been one continual rain. I have my garden all planted, but I don't think it will grow as it had ought from the pains I have taken. I love the garden and cannot be content out of it. I have my house yard covered with *evergreens*, and now call it by that *name*.

I remain your ever grateful and affectionate sister,

R. O'Connor

Please to inform my brother that I made a mistake when I wrote to him regarding Mr. Germany's provisions. He had given it to me in writing, which Dr. Denny saw, but I lost it for some time and really thought that I recollected and was right, excepting the sugar. That is 150, and I said one hundred. I have the paper safe now.

Rachel writes a friendly letter to her niece Frances Weeks.

Evergreen March 19th, 1834

My dear niece,

I received your kind letter of the 8th of last month some time ago, which sickness prevented answering until now. My hand and fingers are nearly well again. There being so much wet weather, it caused my old troublesome complaint (the rheumatism) to return which for the first time affected my hand and fingers. Previous to that I had taken a cold that caused me to be very sick and to suffer severe pain in my breast which I feel pretty well recovered of at present. But like all old people, something must be the matter. All day for two days past, my head has been dreadfully out of order and tormented with a giddiness. Tonight I feel better. I wish it may stay away.

The flowers that I sent by your dear papa last are called October roses. They are beautiful in the last of October or the first of November. Those that I sent over bear white flowers. Sometimes they bloom in the spring, but are much prettier in the fall. Since I sent them I have procured three other colours—a dark red, a yellow, and pink; which if they live, I will send you a part the first opportunity. They never bear any seed. I have a pretty little flower garden. I wish you had a part of the small collection that I have. Your cousins always brings me something to plant in it.

Your cousins Wm. and Caleb Swayze stayed with me last night. They were well. Your Cousin Charlotte and family has got over being poisoned. I had a great desire to go to and see them, but did not venture. I am so apt to get sick if I go from home that I think it not prudent to undertake it.

Tell your papa that his shirts will be made for him by the time he comes. I have two at home now and the others nearly finished.

Your Cousin Harriet Handy has a fine young son and named him George. Please to inform your papa that the letter has arrived after taking a trip to Alabama through some mismanagement in placing the letter from Baton Rouge that your uncle wrote to me. Mr. Conrad said it would confer a great favor by answering it, which I should have done had it arrived as he expected, but I think it unnecessary now.

I hope your brother Wm. has received my letter which I think I wrote on the 9th instant. It was badly written, but would show a willing mind to do right. I also wrote your dear mama on the 14th and to your dear papa the 16th. On the 17th I received a letter from your Cousin Charlotte Doherty wishing me to write to your papa and request the favor of him to send her one barrel of his good sugar and that Mr. Doherty would pay for it when he paid for the other.

Kiss all your little brothers and sister for me. Remember me most affectionately to your dear and good parents. I remain your ever loving aunt,

Rachel O'Connor

In this letter to David, Rachel requests him to permit the removal of the iron collar from the neck of a female slave.

April 2, 1834

My dear brother,

I received your last several days ago, but Clarissa being here (rather low spirited), I concluded it prudent to wait until she returned home before I answered your letter. Mr. Doherty's family has recovered from being poisoned. It is wonderful how they escaped *death*. Mr. Germany is doing very well. He cannot do otherwise, he is so attentive, stays constantly with the hands while they are at work and at home nights and Sundays constantly. If they continue to behave, as they have so far, I shall ever respect both himself and his wife as good people. He has all his corn planted and nearly worked over and commenced planting cotton seed on Monday, the last day of March. The weather being so dreadfully wet was much against his work and kept him very uneasy in mind.

Some of the Negroes has been very sick. Three of the children were taken first—two of Bridget's, Isaac and Little Sam, and one of Charity's little girls. They were very sick indeed, but are now well. After they began to recover, Joe, Eben, Dave, Littleton, and Amos were all taken very ill in the course of a few days. Joe and Eben were dreadfully swelled—first in their feet and then their whole body; and shortly after Amos was worse than either of the other two. I had to keep him in the room with me for several days and nights and have him rubbed. His feet and legs were perfectly cold, and as I thought, the signs of death appeared plain for some time; but I am thankful to say that I was very agreeable disappointed. The poor boy is much better and is able to work some. Joe lost the use of his arm during the time he was so swelled, which lasted 8 or 10 days, and Eben became extremely stiff also. The Dr. never seen any in the same way before. Dave and Littleton had severe fevers, which only lasted a few days before they were able to return to their work again. Joe and Eben and Amos were sick indeed. I little expected them ever to recover. They had every attention or they must have died.

Mr. Germany has all the ground planted in sweet potatoes that you had laid off for him. The slips held out to plant the ground over. My garden looks prettier than it ever did before. Every foot of the ground is planted, and I work it nicely. I have the upper part planted (mostly) with sweet potatoes as usual, and what I have left, Arthur is selling at a dollar a bushel.

Mr. Germany makes no complaints of the Negroes and all appears to go on smoothly. I *should be glad* if you let the iron be taken of Lid's neck. I begin to feel sorry for her. She was a good girl before that villain came here, and I scarcely think there is one Negro woman in existence that is not guilty of the same *wickedness*. They are poor ignorant beings, born to serve out their days, and are led astray by such vile wretches as Mulkey, who will, no doubt, have to account ere long for the sin they commit and are the cause of being committed.

Mr. Doherty's girl caused me to think seriously. None of those poor Negroes should have any desire to take any person's life, as she has done. Bain, Mr. Young's son-in-law, has forbid Mulkey coming or visiting his Negro quarter at night—told him (in the presence of two or three others) that if he did, he would certainly whip him. Mulkey said he never had but one fist fight, and said at the same time that he never would fight another— that he would use a musket to defend himself. His answer was, "Very well, use it."

I am pretty well all day, but I think a little feverish at night. I can't rest much and am troubled with uneasy dreams. I am overjoyed to see daylight appear. I have the cramp so bad. I hope in God your health may continued to improve. The loss of a parent is great. You are worth at least one hundred thousand dollars to your little children. How many families are brought low by the loss of their parents. A widowed mother cannot manage her affairs as a father can; they are afraid to speak for themselves.

Mr. Davis has just returned from New Orleans and has brought a new gig up. He says he bought it for me to ride in and wanted me to go home with them today. But I pled off and remained at home. Dr. Denny is very well, but don't say anything about the races. He is dodging about as usual—as happy as a prince. Liveret and Capt. Jack found a boatman drunk, near the river, and wet his head with spirits of turpentine and set it on fire and came near burning the man to death. They both had to run to the swamp where they are yet.

My love to my dear sister and the children. I remain your affectionate sister,

Rachel O'Connor

I have procured the cotton seed that you wanted. Old David Thomas was married a month ago, whose wife was buried the day that you arrived here from the north. You may recollect the Negro boy that you saw on the road who informed you of his mistress' death.

David has requested that Rachel send to him some of the slaves he had purchased from her. In this letter Rachel acknowledges David's

ownership of the slaves, but the grieving of the old slave parents and Rachel's own love for the slaves cause her to hesitate.

April 21, 1834

My dear brother,

I received your last three or four days ago, but could not get time to answer it, as Charlotte and Clarissa were here. Every night I intended to write; but when night would come, I would feel tired by the time I would get them to bed. This morning they all started home, and I immediately set myself to write to one of the best of brothers.

I do not know what should cause you to think that you had hurt my feelings in the least. I must have made some mistake that I was not aware of when I wrote, for indeed, I knew that I made very free in requesting the favor of you to let them remain together this year, for which I considered it my duty to consent to your moving them all together whenever you thought proper. The old Negro women would grieve so much to part with their boys that I really could not undertake to send a part, which was the only cause of my writing as I did. Old Black Sam and John was very unruly. I was glad when you took them away. Sampson had always been a good boy, but as I had a hope that his leg would be cured by bathing it in the sea, I was glad to get him started for your sake. He would be a valuable boy if his leg could be got well. After they were gone, the old ones made such long sorrowful faces that I made up my mind to let all go at once, rather than see them as they were. I am perfectly happy in their being yours. All I ever meant by the requested favor that the slaves remain together at Evergreen Plantation this year, is that otherwise I could not make out to clear the estate from all embar-rassments and have the pleasure of bestowing it to you, as I had long intended, (which you would have found by my *will* at my death, had not my enemies proved too severe for me to venture it any longer). In my younger days I have often wished to know whether I could hold out true to another's interest, *and so far*, I am pleased with myself, for I never felt happier in trying to do the best when my sons were alive, than I now do for you. Which I hope will prove to you that I had no thoughts when I wrote you on the subject, wherein you concluded my feelings had been hurt. I am so sensible of all your goodness to me to suffer a hard thought of you. If I had not been sure of your granting any reasonable request, I

should not have undertaken to ask you to let them stay out this
year. I know my own weakness. I wish I could command myself as
many can, but that is out of my power to say that I can do right at
all times. If I could, I had ought to have sent the two that you
wanted instantly. But you will soon be over, I hope, and conclude on
what is to be done.

What I wrote to you frightened Clarissa out of her wits. She declared that she would go with me and never return unless I did, and
Charlotte made great lamentation also. I had not the smallest idea of
making such a fuss, or I should not have told them anything about
it. However your last letter pleased them very much and caused them
to bestow many blessings on you as one of the best brothers that
ever was. Charlotte and Julia now has finished your seven handsome
shirts and brought them down. You need not bring many with you
as they are here.

Mr. Germany is doing very well—has all land planted and continues very industrious—never goes from home and behaves well. All
really like him and his wife. They are so clever and make little
trouble. He is very saving and attends to his business better than any
other ever did here. One of your horses died suddenly. Mr. Germany
had him opened and found him eaten through his maw with botts. I
gave him all we knew, but could not save him. Daniel's mare is not
with foal. I was really sorry to discover that. Thomas Dorch has a
fine large dun horse that he has agreed to let three mares go to, at
twelve dollars each, and insure them. If they have no colt, he gets
no pay.

Our corn begins to get low. I am afraid it will not last out the
month, and it keeps high. Every person has to buy, which keeps up
the price. I have got eighty dollars laid up to buy pork, and spoke to
Mr. Caskadin to be on the look out for a bargain. Arthur behaves
very well. My potatoes comes in good play now. He gets a dollar a
bushel and my garden is really fine. The Irish potatoes are all in
blossom. Mr. Germany has planted all the ground in sweet potatoes
that you laid off, and I have a fine patch of my own in the new
garden for market next spring.

The scarlet fever has been in Jackson a long time which is much
against my marketing, as I dare not let Arthur go there. Mr. Hambleton's family had it; one child died.

You took your little son to New Orleans. Can't you bring some
of them with you over here? I should be very glad to see them.

Perhaps my sister will take a trip also. We should be very glad to see her. Since I have heard of your health being better, I have not quite well again. I had almost despaired for some time. My dreadful cough lasted so long, and the rheumatism returned and affected my hand and fingers. The doctor is very well and as fat as usual.

My love to my dear sister and your little ones. I remain (as usual) your ever affectionate sister.

Rachel O'Connor

As Rachel writes David of plantation affairs, she reiterates their good fortune in having the overseer Germany.

May 12, 1834

My dear brother,

It appears long since I receive a letter from any of you. Even the children has not written of late. I hope nothing has happened to any of the family to have occasioned the long silence. I have not written myself as often as I had ought owing to my garden being very good; and as I expected you on the first of the month, I had a wish to make it still better by that time, so as to surprise you on your arrival, which caused me to spend the whole of my time attending it. And after all I'm afraid you are not coming to see it, as court has adjourned without even commencing business through some management of the sheriff, which has disappointed me in my great hopes of making money during the time of court; but I must do as well as I can with it now. My health is pretty good at present, and I feel as anxious as I ever did in younger days.

I have got meat bought and paid for sufficient to do us all until killing time comes again, but I am frightened about corn. We are nearly out, and very little at the landing, which is selling at a dollar and a half per. barrel, and from 10 to 25 carts and wagons passing every day for corn and flour. I sent some time ago and bought seven barrels of coarse flour at three dollars, two bits pr. barrel, which was all that was there at the price. Mr. Germany gave the last of it to the Negroes this morning. We have some corn yet, but precious little. Mr. Lewis David bought 300 bushels of oats at forty cents pr.

bushel and let me have one half to feed the horses. I have a fine Irish potato patch, which will help to feed the Negroes until corn comes. I have taken the liberty of writing Mr. Linton for eight barrels of rice and one bag of coffee this day. I could not think of paying a dollar and a half pr. barrel for corn. I sent to Mr. Caskaden some time ago for advice respecting corn. He sent me word not to be uneasy, that it would soon be very low—that there was 600 boats on the river loaded with corn, which fact ended all my fears at that period, particularly as I expected you over soon. But if I get the rice, I can make out without giving all you have for corn. I sent Mr. Germany to town yesterday to inquire the price of rice in the city. Mr. Caskaden had just received the prices from N. Orleans, which said rice sold at six dollars a barrel, which made me conclude it the cheapest plan. If I have done wrong, I shall be truly sorry but I still hope not so far.

Mr. Germany is doing very well. He is really an industrious little man, and I have great hope of seeing you perfectly satisfied with his management. He is careful of the teams and everything in his charge. He will finish scraping the cotton tomorrow. There has been two dreadful hail storms in the settlement, the last one four days ago. They were all around us and ruined many crops, but fortunately we have escaped as yet. Mr. Boat Barrow's whole crop was beat into the earth by the last. He speaks of planting over in corn—that he thinks it too late for cotton. Mr. Germany heard yesterday that poor Lewis Davis' crop is ruined by the hail. I expect A Doherty's is equally bad off. I feel truly sorry for them. The storm was very bad out through the redwood settlement.

I hope you come over yet. The place is quite healthy. In your next, do let me know how your health is. When you wrote last, you were on the mend. God grant that you may be quite restored to your former good health.

Old Mr. Hambleton's eldest son—about 21 years of age—lays at Mr. Germany's house dreadfully hurt by his horse rolling over him in our lane. I am afraid he will not live until tomorrow.

Since Caleb Swayze returned home, I have received a letter from him saying that he found his relations, and Negroes, very sick—that a daughter of Old Joe's was not expected to live through the night.

Can you recollect of seeing a young man, for a short time, on board the steamboat Vermillion, from the Attakapas, where it loaded for some minutes? Caleb says he went on board, walked through the cabin and saw every passenger on board, but recognized no one except Mr. Baker, and the passengers who came up on board the packet, who had since told him that you were on board the Vermillion at the same time that he was on board. He says you must be greatly changed in appearance or he should have known you.

I believe our relations are all well. I have not heard of any being sick for some time. The Dr. continues well as ever and lives perfectly at his ease—not the least bit uneasy at the high price of corn or anything else. I make out very well at spinning. Old Leigh spins nineteen skeins every week, which will make 13 yards of cloth, good measure, which is the work of three good spinners, and one skein over.

My love to my dear sister and the little ones. I hope soon to hear of your all being well. Little William has not given me a history of his journey to the city. He must have seen something new worth relating. I hope the hail has not reached your island and that you are doing well on it. Mr. Bowman's merchant has failed in New Orleans, and Mr. B. has lost six thousand and nine hundred dollars by him, a very great loss indeed.

Much love to my dear and good brother. I remain, as usual, your ever grateful and affectionate sister,

R. O'Connor

Rachel is distraught at learning that David's health has taken a turn for the worse. She rises from her sick bed to write a brief letter to Mary asking for details.

June 12, 1834

My dear sister,

I have not heard from any of you since my brother's letter from Franklin, who said he was that far on his journey towards the north. From his melancholy way of writing, I much feared he felt doubtful. He said he was very weak, but I still entertained hopes until this morning. It appears that Mrs. Mathews should have seen a lady from the Attakapa in N. Orleans, who should have painted his case extremely doubtful that he had wasted away to skin and bone. Pray, my dear sister, inform me your opinion on which I can depend. Report says that he became worse and returned home again from Franklin; but, as bad news generally gets worse the farther it goes, I will try to hope that all is not so bad until I hear from you.

I have been quite sick 6 or 8 days. I could not sit up any yesterday. This morning I am stunned to the very heart. I scarcely know whether I have feelings or not. Kiss all my dear little children for me. Could they know my distressed feelings, they would pity me that loves you all so dear. My dear and beloved sister will excuse my short letter. I am not able to write more. Merciful Father, assist us all through misfortunes and grant that we may bear them as we had ought are the prayers of your unfortunate sister,

Rachel O'Connor

A broken-hearted Rachel writes to Mary seeking comfort instead of giving it.

June 18, 1934

My dearest and best of sisters,

I received your kind letter dated 7th of this month, on the same evening that I had directed a few lines to you, early the morning previous, which I had sent to the office. Every line appears to be printed on my heart, yet have no power to express the gratitude I feel towards so kind a sister. You have ever been all and everything to me, which appears plainer and plainer every moment. I hope kind providence will shortly ease your sorrows. I have ever considered it our duty to submit patiently, but I fear I shall fail in this last trial. I have lost all my near relations, all my brothers and sisters, and bore it with fortitude until this last, and only, brother. Should he be taken before me, surely my days will end; and you, may beloved sister, must guard against grief. Pray don't let your sorrows rob your little ones of a mother. I wish I had it in my power to reward your good brother, Alfred, for his goodness to my brother in his distressed situation. I could be happy to wait on him all the days of my life, let them be more or less. Pray encourage your sweet little children.

Their dear father is sick, but we must trust in God who is able to restore his health and permit his return to his distressed friends.

I have this moment received a letter from my brother dated the first of June after he had started and was at sea. He says that he feels stronger than he did when he left home and that he hopes to return to us soon, mentions the many obligations he is under to your kind brother. His whole life is filled with so much goodness that I scarcely know whether I am in existence or not. I will try to take care of all and do as well as I can if my health will permit. I am still unwell owing to the unhappy state of my mind. O, my dear sister, what am I to do? My sorrows are too great for old age to bear. Pray forgive me. I know I am doing wrong. I had ought to comfort you. Your sorrows are already too great.

The crop is progressing and all is doing well. Mr. Germany and his wife continues very clever and attentive. My garden has become uncommonly good and would be so still if I had any heart to pay attention to it.

My love to my dear and darling babes. My tears flow freely for them. You, my beloved sister, can know the feelings of a broken heart; our little ones are too young. My beloved brother says I may expect another letter about the 10th of July. I shall try to live on hope until that time. I feel ashamed of my letter, after looking it over, but the situation of my mind will not admit of my doing any better at the present.

Charlotte and Julia Ann and Clarissa and Harriet Handy has all been to see me very lately and tried to comfort me all in their power; but I had rather be alone where I can sit and cry to myself without troubling any other. God forever bless you and yours are the daily prayers of your unfortunate and affectionate sister,

Rachel O'Connor

In her anguish Rachel turns to religion for comfort as she pens this letter to Mary.

July 6th, 1834

My dear sister,

I have received your letter written the 15th of June and am sorry
to say that my health is no better. I suffer severely with less hopes
of recovery every attack. Now and then I am better for a day or
two, but that don't last long. If I could sleep at night, it would rest
me greatly, but amongst other distresses, that blessing is denied me.
When I get worried out and fall into a sleep, in a few moments I
am awakened by some dreadful dream that frightens me so greatly
that I recollect very little of all that I have been dreaming about,
which leaves me in a most shocking way. The palpitation of my
heart is so violent that at times I have to cry out for mercy in deep
distress. Poor Julia Ann remained with me until a few days ago, but
I kept my distressed feelings a secret from her. I knew it to be out
of her power to relieve me and her uneasiness would only add to my
misery. I take my sorrow to my God and pray for mercy and deliver-
ance from guilt through faith in the atoning sacrifice of Christ, my
Saviour. My afflictions on earth has become habitual, but to think of
an endless eternity distracts my brains, when one disobedient act is
sufficient to condemn a sinner and banish them from all the precious
promises of the gospel. O, that I had always felt as I now feel; if
they had wanted my coat, they might have taken my cloak also
rather than suffer in mind as I now do. I can pray for all fervently.
If all creation could be worthy of heaven and of the blessings of
God, it would meet my most earnest prayers. But my ever dear sister, don't let me cause you any sorrow. I hope and trust that you
are happy and that your dear and dutiful babes may cause you to be
more so. They were so good while I was with you and them that I
cannot feel afraid of any change for the worse, and their amiable
teacher will still continue to explain much to them and lead them in
the paths of their duty to God and you.

I have once heard that Clarissa appears to be on the mend, but I
have not seen Mr. Davis nor Mr. Doherty since she has been so
sick. They stay constantly with her, which alarms me much.

I hope my beloved sister may not suffer any uneasiness about my
earthly supplies. I have all that I could wish for. Your brother sent
much more than I should have thought of or asked for. The crop is
doing very well. The constant rain makes it grow fast and the grass
also, but the hands are doing very well.

I'm glad to hear of your house girls behaving so well. I have no doubt of your judging mean low white men being the chief cause of their disobedience. It is always the case where they are. They cause more punishment to be inflicted amongst the poor ignorant slaves than all else they commit. Otherwise any white man that encourages the likes are next to the old evil one in badness.

My best to Mr. Heaton and much love to your brother and the dear good children. With sincere wishes for your health and happiness, I remain your ever affectionate sister.

Rachel O'Connor

In this letter to David's fourteen-year-old daughter, Frances, Rachel preaches acceptance of death, whether it be human or animal, as the will of Providence.

July 24, 1834

My dear niece,

I received your kind letter of the 12th instant last evening. Words cannot express the joy I felt, and yet feel, on receiving a letter from you once more. I had been afraid that you were all sick or so broken-hearted about your dear papa leaving home in low health that I had lost hopes of your having any time to think of poor me. But I am truly thankful to find my mistake and will daily pray to be forgiven and that endless blessings may be bestowed on you for your goodness to me.

I am very sorry to learn that our dear Alfred has been so sick. Poor little boy; this is his second attack and both severe ones. I pity your dear mama. Her distresses are great. I know her sorrows, but I hope kind providence will assist her through and turn all her troubles into joy at last.

I have been very sick myself ever since I wrote your mama last. A part of the time I could not raise my head nor let it be raised without fainting. I do not recollect of ever being so weak before, during which a letter arrived from your amiable Uncle Alfred Conrad saying they had landed safe in New Haven and that your dear papa improved much at sea, but that the weather being colder caused his disease to return a little, which he thought would only last a few days and then I would receive a letter from himself. I shall never forget the many favors that your best of uncles has bestowed me, and this last the greatest of all. Who would have followed a brother as he did, to take care of him?

In a few hours after the arrival of your uncle's letter, the fever disappeared and only returned once more. This is the first time I have attempted to write since my sickness. Your cousin, Julia Ann Scott, has been constantly with me. She has been extremely good. I do not know how I could have done without her. Clarissa stayed a part of the time with me, but some of their Negroes were sick at home. The cholera has been on two plantations within six miles of me; one lost six Negroes and the other two. But I still hope to escape. We are very careful about their victuals and otherwise in every respect.

I have lost the big black horse that your papa brought over and left for me to ride. He died while I lay so sick. I never lamented the loss of a horse as I did him. He was in good order and died so. Two others died with the same disease and a number of our hogs died with a swelled throat, but I hope the worst is over. All are well now. Tell your mama that Mr. Germany continues to be very *industrious* and that he has every appearance of a fine crop of both corn and cotton, and that both himself and his wife were truly kind to me while I was sick.

Should you hear from your papa, do let me know of it. I am so distressed about him that I have no rest. In my sleep my dreams are about him. My kindest love to your dear and good mama and little brothers and sister Harriet. I begin to feel tired. I am weak yet and will conclude for the present.

I wish you all health and fortitude, but I hope all is for the best and that we may be happy. Heaven bless you, my dear and darling child. I remain your affectionate aunt,

R. O'Connor

In this morbid letter to Mary, Rachel includes brief hopeful phrases, but her overriding preoccupation is with the health of herself and others and with death.

July 30, 1834

My dear sister,

Yours of the 20th instant arrived four days ago; and at the same time, I received one from your brother Alfred, written in New Haven, which is the second letter your good brother has written me from that place since they landed. The date of the first was the 21st of June and the second the 4th of July. The first afforded much relief which I greatly needed as I lay in a high fever at the time his letter arrived, and had done for eight or ten days previous with but little intermission during that length of time, only now and then a severe chill which generally increased the fever. But the good news your brother's letter contained raised my hopes instantly and the fever soon abated to the surprise of all around me. Mrs. Bowman had stayed much with me and intended to remain that night; but when she saw me so much better, she concluded that she might venture home to see some sick Negroes. Clarissa and Mr. Davis were here and Julia Ann came the same evening. I am quite clear of fever, but reamin weak. Poor Julia Ann has been very sick and looks very bad yet, but hope she will recover by degrees. Her fevers are broke.

Your brother's letter of the 4th instant appears more discouraging. He says my poor brother's health is in the same state that it was when he left home owing to the sudden change in the weather which has caused him to take cold and his disease to return, but that he had no doubt of his soon being on the mend again from the kind attention of the good lady you mentioned and from the comfortable situation that kind providence had placed him in with so amiable and charitable a family. He had received one letter from me which was all I had written until yesterday, as I did not know where to direct my letters. I did not expect they would remain long in one place until they reached their journey's end. I answered my dear Frances' letter a few days since. I hope my dear little Alfred is quite recovered and that yourself and the rest of your family are in good health.

My dear sister, we must trust and hope in God and not give way to despair—perhaps he will grant our prayers by trusting in His mercy.

The crop is very promising at present. Should no misfortune overtake it, I shall be sadly disappointed if it should not prove good. The overseer is very attentive to his business and continues to be a good man. Both himself and is wife paid every attention to me during my sickness, for which I feel much indebtedness to them for their kindness. The Negroes are all well excepting one child who is not dangerously ill yet—. The cholera has made its appearance on a few plantations. One man has lost eight Negroes by the cholera and six by fevers. The former commenced from eating tainted meat. The owner's name is Wade Richardson, son-in-law to Mrs. Harbour. She has lost two of cholera. I have been very careful to have the Negro's provisions sound and cooked good, and hope to continue so. Mr. Germany had all the mellon vines destroyed and watched the green corn closely from them. Five of the most valuable horses has died lately with a disease unknown to us all, amongst which the big brown horse that my poor brother left me for a riding horse died. I never lamented a horse as I do him. I never rode so gentle and so safe one before.

The note you mentioned being sent for collection came before my brother left home, or very shortly after. I immediately answered his letter and enclosed the two receipts as he directed me to do and sent the note to Mr. Turner by Julia Ann Scott, by whom Mr. T. returned his receipt for the same. I hope my letter may not be lost. Perhaps you have one not opened, or forwarded it to my brother after he had left home. I am at a loss how to write other receipts, as I have not the dates, the notes being at Mr. Turner's, and I should not like to explain the affair to him unless my brother said so. I hope three or four months will bring my brother home to direct us how to arrange right.

The dear little children never mention the new house that they once were so delighted with. I am sorry for them, but I hope you are yet to see much happiness in it. Should kind providence restore their father to health again, they will be better judges of the blessings bestowed them and enjoy his company with greater pleasure. We seldom form an idea of how dear we are to each other until we find that we are in danger of being separated forever. I must request it of you, my dear and best of sisters, not to let our present distresses injure your health. Consider your little children. The loss of a mother is as great as that of a father. It is a heart-breaking subject to mention, and freely does my tears flow in penning those lines, but could not avoid begging of you to be careful of your health. In my next to my brother I shall request of him to wear flannel and to be on his guard for the sake of those that love him so dearly.

My best respects to your sisters and their husbands and kindest love to my dear babes. Tell Wm. to write. I am afraid of being forgotten. Their letters are precious to me.

My paper is nearly written over and it is nearly night. I will pray to God to bless my dearly beloved sister and bid her goodnight. Do write occasionally, and if I am well enough, I shall do the same. I remain your affectionate and unfortunate sister,

Rachel O'Connor

Rachel finds relief in writing to Mary.

August 12th, 1834

My dear sister,

I received your thrice welcome letter of the twentieth of July a few days since, which I should have answered instantly if I had not written to you only a short time previous to its arrival, which I hope you have since received as I informed you very particularly respecting the note you mentioned in your two last letters.

The letter with the enclosed note from my brother came before he left home, which I answered immediately with a hope of its reaching him before he started on his journey. I wrote the two receipts as he directed and enclosed them (at the same time) to him. The note is in Mr. Turner's hands and I cannot recollect the dates of the two different payment from Mr. Swift, otherwise I could forward the receipts, and I do not know whether I had ought to explain the affair to Mr. Turner or not. So I have concluded to let it remain as it is until further advised. I shall be sorry if my letter to my brother should be lost, with the enclosed receipts. It was a very long one, and no doubt of its appearing uncommonly simple to any other excepting yourselves, who are so accustomed to receive the likes from me that nothing more is expected.

I still remain very weak and often poorly. I feel ashamed to have to complain as often as I do. Sometimes I am a little feverish, then again the backache, or a pain in my head; but I much fear all is caused by the *heart ache*. If I could hear that my poor brother's health had begun to mend, I should feel well; but as it is, I cannot rest from disturb'd dreams. I have not received any letter since the one from your good brother dated the 4th of July, at which time my dear brother was quite poorly from a cold taken by the sudden change in the weather. I have been expecting a letter and shall be uneasy until it comes.

I have just discovered my mistake. Your last letter is dated the 2nd of August, but I had the previous one laying before me. Surely you would not be surprised to hear that I had gone crazy. Sometimes I conclude it is really the case, my head is so weak. But my dear sister must not think anything troublesome to me that is in my power to do for her. That is my greatest satisfaction and only study; but I do so little, you would scarcely think so.

I hope your next will bring news of your health being good, and of my dear little *David Weeks* being well also. The name is dear to me, but to write it causes tears to flow freely. I set and think about you and your children and the distresses of you all until my heart is almost broken. I am thankful to kind Providence to know that you have a plenty (should it be attended with a blessing); but with all, you could not be happy. Forgive me, my best of sisters, I had forgotten myself. *We must be resigned*, and trust, and hope in the mercy of God. Pray don't let your sorrows overcome you or forget your little ones. Talk much to them; often tell them that all is born to die, and that they must be good little children and *Pray to God to Save their Precious Souls for Christ's Sake.*

Our relations are all well. It is generally healthy at present—no talk of cholera being in the neighborhood. None of the horses has died since I wrote you last, and only a few of the cattle. Two of the horses had the disease since. Mr. Germany gave a quart of castor oil to each, and bled them freely, and they got well again. He really behaves well, continues very careful, and has a promising crop on the plantation. Both himself and his wife were extremely kind to me during my sickness. My own children could not have been more so. They had a little son born on the second of this month and doing very well.

I hope to receive a letter from my dear Frances shortly, and that it may bring good news. My dear little William must write also. They can have no idea how much I love their letters. I feel myself troublesome, but it cannot last long. They must bear with old age.

You forget to mention your sisters. How are Sidney and Elizabeth and their little families? I have ever since our first acquaintance felt much friendship for them both. I have not forgotten their kind attention when I was over to see you. I had not the pleasure of seeing Mrs. Towles, but she is your sister and has experienced much sorrow of late which causes me often to think of her and wish her happy with her little ones, and sincerely hope that she may be doing well. Should I get a letter from your brother, or mine, I will let you know of it instantly, and I must beg of you to do the same by me. My dear sister, I wish you much happiness. My love to your sisters and your children. I remain your affectionate sister,

R. O'Connor

Julia Ann Scott stays most of her time with me. Since I have been sick, the children has formed an idea that my days are nearly spent on earth. They are very attentive indeed. Charlotte wishes me to go and stay a while with her, but I cannot bear to go so far from home. I have lived on this place thirty-seven years and now it appears like a part of myself. Even the girls love their old home yet, and have become quite sensible of my doing all that ever was in my power to make them comfortable and happy during their stay with me. I am very glad they are satisfied with my former treatment. Charlotte is very comfortable fixed. Her house is far from a fine one, but enough so to enjoy life. Mr. Doherty provides well for his family and makes them happy. Julia Ann has lived the most of her time with them since the death of Mr. Scott. She appears satisfied and loves him as a brother. They have two fine sons. They send the oldest down here often and let him stay two or three weeks. He has been here three weeks this time. His Aunt Julia Ann went to see her brother, William Swayze, yesterday evening and took Robert with her. They are to return in a few days. I think him the wildest child I ever knew.

Wm. Swayze has a son and daughter. They are quite well now. I think Wm. will do very well. He has become very steady and behaves extremely well and industrious.

Mr. Handy and Harriet has three children, two sons and a daughter. I hope they will do very well. He is industrious and Harriet smart. I really do not know one more so.

My dear sister, after I had fill'd the other two pages and concluded my letter finished, you see I could not stop my pen. I find relief in writing to you, although I have nothing worth relating nor even worth taking the time to read. Farewell, my beloved sister. Heaven forever bless you and yours.

R. O'C.

On September 9, Rachel received a letter from Alfred Conrad dated August 16. The letter tells of David's critical condition. In an agony of grief, Rachel writes an answer to him, not knowing that David had died sixteen days earlier.

Sept-br 10, 1834

Mr. A. J. Conrad
My dear friend,
Miserable as I am I must write you a few lines. I received your letter dated the 16th of August last evening. A more distressed unhappy being never was, and I hope never may be while the world lasts, than my poor unfortunate self.

From your letter dated the 28th of July, I had raised my hopes, my beloved brother had mended so much from the 22nd which was the date of your letter to Mr. Doherty. My God is able to raise him again. I must hope and trust in his mercy. Should your next bring the fatal news of his being no more, this bruised heart of mine must break. I have bore up against many trials, knowing it to be my duty to submit to the will of providence, but I am now too weak and advanced in life to stand the loss of so dear and only a brother. I shall be left too much alone in the world to bear so great a loss. I have been sick nearly all the time since he started from home. As soon as I got able to write, I wrote often. I am much grieved at your not getting my letters. I directed them to the care of A. Heaton, Esq. as you requested. My best of friends, pray to God for me. Ask all the good to pray for me. My heart and head burns. I am a distressed object indeed. Do write and let me know all. Unless I gain strength fast, I shall scarcely be in a situation to leave home. I wish I may, but do for mercy's sake, call and see me. Don't return by sea. Storms are very often at this season of the year. The river is the safest.

I received a letter from my sister Mary a few days ago. The children were well, but she sadly distressed herself. Mrs. Palfrey was with her, and Mrs. Harding had only left there a few days previous. They were all well.

My dear friend, I sincerely pray that you may never feel as I do at this period. I never felt as I do now. God only knows what is becoming of me. Most willingly could I lay at the feet of all those kind friends that has attended on my beloved and kind brother and wash them with my tears, and I could find a plenty. They flow freely, but could I shed rivers of them, they would not be too much.

Heaven guard and protect you from harm, my best of friends. I remain your most unhappy, yet faithful friend,

Rachel O'Connor

Two months pass following the news of David's death before Rachel undertakes this letter to Mary. Although she thinks she will die of grief, she does, in fact, survive her brother by twelve years. She takes hold bravely of harvesting the crop in order to benefit David's survivors.

October 27, 1834

My dear sister,

I once more undertake to write you a few lines. I wish it was in my power to comfort you. I know your sorrows are great and that no earthly being can ease your heart. But I hope you will consider your little children and live for their sakes. No person can do by them like yourself. Your affectionate brothers and sisters will kindly assist you. I am too far advanced in life to expect comfort in this world. The kindnesses of yourself and that of my dearest and best of brothers has kept me alive, and happier than any other could have been after meeting the many afflictions that had fallen my lot. But I much fear that his death will be too severe a loss for me ever to get over. His past kindnesses almost breaks my heart. Had he ever crossed me, I could have borne it better. I can set for hours and think of his many and never ending kindnesses to me. I am very thankful that I had sense enough to see and know his goodness during his life. I had long thought I had no reason to complain of my lot while so good a brother has left to comfort me. Now that he is taken away, I can scarcely forbear complaining. He was the last and I loved him better than all that had gone before. I had set my whole heart on him and seldom grieved for those that had been taken long since. But now I can think of them all. I hope they are happier than myself and that we may be permitted to meet hereafter.

I expect your brother Alfred hourly. His last letter informed me that he expected to be here by the first of next month. I am anxious to see him. He has been very attentive and kind to me. He has written constantly, and continue to do so yet. And his kind attention to my beloved brother showed the truest friendship. Pray teach your dear children to love him for the kindness he bestowed their dear and best of fathers.

Since the death of my poor brother, I have received a letter from Mrs. Heaton. The kind lady writes uncommonly friendly; gives much good advice. I hope I may benefit by her goodness. Her very name is dear to me. She mentions your brother extremely friendly. He was with them at that time.

Julia Ann is with me. She has never left me since my severe distresses of late. She is a good companion in grief. She is naturally of a melancholy turn. Charlotte Doherty and Harriet Handy has been to see me. They look very well. Charlotte expects to be confined in Feb-ry next. Her youngest son was one year old the 15th of August last. Mr. Davis and Clarissa are well. I hope to receive a letter from you ere long. The children must write also. No heart ever felt a more sincere love than mine for you all. The interest I feel for yourself and your children keeps me alive. Should we meet hereafter you will find me faithful in every respect. Mr. B. Smith has written two letters to me and speaks very kindly. He wished to know the situation of the crop. The cotton that was picked during the severe rains is yellow and moldy owing to the leaves being beaten by the continual rains. The first picking, and what is being gathered now, is beautiful. We have sixty-five bales pressed and 10 or 12 more ginned ready to press. I expect there is nearly ninety bales picked all together and a plenty in the field to pick, I hope the crop may turn out pretty well after all. Previous to the wet weather, I never saw a finer prospect. The corn is all gathered and has turned out pretty well. When your brother Alfred comes, I will show him all the crop and tell him everything so that he may inform yu ever particular. We are hauling bales to the landing to be sent to N. Orleans. Mr. Smith may direct as he thinks proper. I will answer this second letter ere long. The first I answered long since.

Please to remember me most affectionately to your sisters and return many thanks to Mr. Palfrey for his kind letter. I intend to write to him, but my heart has been too full to do so as yet. My love to my darling children. May kind providence guard you and them, here and hereafter, in perfect happiness are the prayers of your unfortunate sister,

R. O'Connor

Excuse all mistakes. My eyes are sore. When I undertake to write to you, I must cry without ceasing. My dear sister, pray for me.

Mary's brother, Alfred Conrad, replaces David in the management of Evergreen Plantation. Rachel is greatly pleased with Alfred's guardianship and with the overseer.

Dec. 26, 1824

My dear sister,

It has been long since I received a line from yourself. I feel very anxious to know how you are. I hope you will write after this reaches you. I received a letter from your good brother Alfred after he arrived home. I was greatly rejoiced to hear of your being in tolerable health and that the dear children were all well. The morning that Mr. Conrad's letter was handed to me from the post office, I had just prepared to start on a visit to Charlotte. Mr. Doherty had come down the evening previous in his gig to take me home with him. Otherwise I should have answered his letter long since. The weather proved so wet that I could not get home again in less than eight days, and has rained, even, on every day since so that I could not attempt to send any person to St. Francis Ville with my letters or to inquire if any had arrived for me. And, as so much time has passed since the arrival of Mr. Conrad's last letter, I feel at a loss to know where to direct one to him at the present moment as he may be at this period in New Orleans or perhaps on his way home. He expected to be up sometime in this month. Should he be still with you, please to inform him how it happened that I did not write to him.

I was quite sick two days and nights at Mr. Doherty's, but feel pretty well recovered again, but seldom or ever enjoy as good health as I formerly did. Charlotte expects to be confined in Feb-ry. She enjoys fine health. I never seen her look better than at present. Julia Ann is well, but very thin in flesh and extremely weak. Mr. Davis and Clarissa are very well. Samuel Doherty and Miss Ronklen (a granddaughter of Gen'l Robert McCausland) were married on the 12th of Nov-br, and he became a widower on the seventeenth of Dec-br. Her horse threw her on their way to old Mr. Doherty's, which accompanied by a severe cold, occasioned her death.

I have a great desire to go over to see you, and when I feel well, fully conclude I am going sometime this winter, which a few hours of sickness discourages instantly. How it may turn out, *God* only knows. Yourself and children are ever uppermost in my mind, and I sincerely pray that it may continue while I live. Indeed, my dear sister, the hope of seeing the beloved heirs of my dear brother do well is the greatest comfort that I now enjoy. And your best of brothers spoke so kindly to me that I almost concluded him my guardian angel in whom the care of my declining years has been placed. Often, very often, do I return thanks to God for bestowing me such kind friends on earth. An inexperienced person knows little how to value sincere friendship, which severe afflictions has long since taught me to prize beyond all other earthly blessings. Do, my dear sister, write me a few lines. It is a duty we owe each other during life. My love to my dear little ones. I hope through the mercy and assistance of kind providence to hear of your becoming calm and resigned to the will of heaven. Dear sister, remember the dear and helpless little ones that so much need your care. May every blessing be yours, my best of sisters, are the daily prayers of your unfortunate sister,

Rachel O'Connor

P.S. A Mr. Black called to see me yesterday who said he had formerly lived in the Attakapas and the was acquainted with yourself and family. Mr. Conrad mentioned some disturbance amongst your Negroes on the island that he was going to silence very soon. Mr. Black says that he understood two of the men had been shot and dangerously wounded by the overseers. He thinks one was Harry Little. The name of the other he could not recollect. Do let me know all about it and how it happened. I am afraid the overseer is to blame. So many turns out bad.

The crop of cotton has not turned out as large as I expected owing to the first frost being so severe. It killed young bolls so dead that they rotted, which has caused it to be much less. I have sent one hundred and one bales to New Orleans. There will be a few more to send yet, but not many. The corn crop is very good. Mr. Germany done all he could, for the best, and continues to behave very well. I think him the best overseer I ever knew.

Rachel writes her neice Frances her pleasant expectations of a visit with David's family.

Jan-ry 7, 1835

My dear niece,

I have received your kind and affectionate letter which afforded me much satisfaction. I am very thankful to find that your dear mama is in tolerable health. I sincerely hope that she may be resigned to the *will* of Providence and yet may enjoy many comfortable days in the company of her good children. I long to see you all, and if sickness should not prevent it, or some other unforeseen misfortune, I shall soon be with you. I intend to go with your Uncle Alfred whenever he is ready to start home. I have received letters from him very lately. He was in good health and expected to be here from N. Orleans as soon as he could settle his business so that he could leave the city. He has some business to attend to here which may detain him a few days, I can't say how long, after which he intends visiting your cousins all around, before we leave this for your house. At first I felt afraid to undertake to visit you, where I should see your once happy mother with her darling children all around her, fearing the little fortitude that remained might fail and that I might do more harm than good. I am well aware of my own weakness and will endeavor to guard myself as much as possible. I am very thankful to you, my dear and beloved child, for the many kind offers you make of doing so much for me. I wish that I may ever deserve so much kindness, but I will do all in my power, and *He* that giveth all good will reward you bountifully. I have lived through much sorrow, yet I dare not complain. My God is kinder to me than I can deserve. How wretched should I be if it were not His good will to bestow me such true and good friends. Scarcely an hour passes without my calling all this to mind and offering thanks for his mercies. Forgive me, my sweet and charitable child, I ought not to distress you with the melancholy feelings of my mind that will intrude at times. I hope your good little brothers and sister may continue as dutiful as they now are. Your Uncle Alfred says that he never knew so charming a family of children as you all are. I want part, but must wait your dear mama's pleasure. I must not occasion her one moment's grief. I have seen yourself and William and Alfred and Harriet, and imagine I should know all but Harriet. She was only a few weeks old. I don't expecct that I recollect her features. Poor little Charles and David, I have not seen yet.

Your Cousin David Swayze was taken with a violent fever, which continued so severe that it carried him off in a few days. Mrs. Lyons has no grandchild left but Caleb Swayze. Mrs. Boatwright has lost all her children. The last one died six weeks before David Swayze, and she is in a low state of health herself. Much do I pity poor Mrs. Lyons and her daughter.

My kindest love to your dear mama and brothers and sister Harriet. I remain your affectionate and grateful aunt,

Rachel O'Connor

Old Mrs. Doherty died the 27th of Dec-br, just ten days after her young daughter-in-law died.

Seemingly without even realizing it, Rachel has again revived her pleasure in friends and plantation activities.

March 30, 1835

My dear sister,

I promised to write as soon as I became able. I now undertake to do so, but much fear you may find it poorly done. I am very weak and at times concede I am sick. I wish it may prove to be only my imagination. We were all landed safe at the Bayou Sara landing place on the Saturday following after we parted with you, about nine o'clock in the morning, but could not meet with an opportunity of being conveyed home until Mr. Davis, by mere accident, met with Mr. Fort who on hearing our difficulties instantly made an offer of his gig with his horse and driver and hurried home to fulfill his generous promise, but it proved too late before the gig arrived to venture the little journey home, as the roads were so bad in places that we had to walk in many parts of it. However late as the gig arrived, we could not command ourselves from venturing to make a start homeward and made our way as far as Judge Dawson's where we were kindly received and, I believe, with much joy. Indeed I had not an idea of still having so many sincere friends as I now believe I have. A report of my *death* had reached this neighborhood which appears to have revived their old feelings of friendship beyond my expectations. But to continue with the history of my journey home— on Sunday morning the Judge ordered his carriage and conveyed us safely home in high style.

The Iberia was detained in several places on the lake from being caught by stumps and mud owing to the low water; but the captain, being much of a gentleman, caused all on board to pity his distresses and wait the rise of water patiently.

I found all in good health at home excepting one child which is recovering fast. One of the men has been quite sick since I came, which is all the sickness that has been on the plantation from the time I left it to this date—only what George had, who is seldom well. Mr. Germany has conducted so well in every respect that I sincerely think his honest and honourable behavior deserves much praise, rather than otherwise. He has his corn up and growing charmingly and the plantation in fine order. I have had the black horse set to work. He ploughs elegantly. He can now help raise corn to feed him on, and as I scarcely ever expect to ride again, I have concluded it unnecessary for Mr. Conrad to be at the trouble and expense of bringing Baltimore over here, and no doubt his work may be needed at home and he would be doing nothing here. My feelings would put it out of question. I could not see him put in the plough—and from his being so poor in flesh and with a sore foot, I'm afraid he is not well and might die shortly which would distress me much.

I hope this may find yourself and family in good health, and that it may be long enjoyed. I feel all the gratitude that any being ever felt for the kindness bestowed by you all during my sickness. My best respects to your ever kind brother and Mr. B. Smith and much love to the dear children. I pray they may ever be attended with blessings from above and dutiful to the kindest of mothers.

My best of sisters, I have written a longer letter than I expected to do. It is the first attempt since I returned. It may puzzle you to read it and is of little consequence at best.

Do try to be happy. God has been kind to you. You enjoy every earthly blessing. Consider the many thousands that has not house or home, nor where to lay their head, and still the hope of finding a resting place in heaven affords them contentment and happiness. My spirits are low. I daily lament my many sad and grevious misfortunes. I can pray for every soul that lives and wish them never to experience the different sensations that falls to my lot. But it has been the will of my Heavenly Father to place me on earth. May it be His pleasure to guide me through them safely. I have ever wished to serve out my days faithfully—which remains my chiefest *study* yet. Farewell, my dear sister. Heaven bless you and yours,

Rachel O'Connor

In her bereavement Rachel's mind turns to past hardships, and yet she asks Alfred Conrad, to whom she wrote this letter, to purchase for her some gay calico so that she can make new dresses for the slave women.

April 12, 1835

Dear friend,

I received your kind favor of the 3rd instant last evening. I am happy to learn from it that yourself and family enjoy good health. I hope soon to hear that my sister has been reconciled. I am truly sorry for her. I have experienced all kinds of troubles myself which has learned me to lament the sorrows of others. I have written to her once since I reached home. My hand has become so unsteady that it is seldom in my power to write. This evening it behaves better. I can guide my pen with ease.

Mr. Germany has the plantation in good order and full as forward with planting as any other in the neighborhood. I feel perfectly satisfied with his management and can see no reason to complain. He is far from putting himself on a footing with those under his charge. He has no favorite misses to fight and abuse the boys about, and all goes on as it should do. He is the only man that ever overseed on this place that I could say with truth, that I thought him clear of that meanness.

I hope to make out without buying any corn this year, and to raise enough to do next (*should I live to need it*). I cannot guard against misfortunes. Much depends on the season, and more on a blessing from Him than bestowest all good. I dare not say how large the crop may turn out. My will is good and I do all in my power. The Negroes has been quite healthy and do their work cheerfully. Should they be sick, I'll do as I ever have done—take care of them for their own sakes, and for charity's sake, and for the sake of those I love. A penny saved is as good as a penny earned, which is the advice I received from my good old parents, who by their industry collected a large property and bestowed it to their younger children.

I feel more in debt to Dr. Denny than I ever did before. His attention to my family (as a physician) has been attended with a blessing. Several has been sick, a few days at a time, since I came home; but are soon able to return to their work again as usual. The loss of so many lives on the island in so short a time, and on hearing that Mr. Charles Mulhollen had lost twenty-five Negroes by severe colds near Bayou Beef where he lives—and that Mr. Buck has also lost several in like manner, near Port Gibson, has alarmed me and opened my eyes to the many favors bestowed me and caused me to feel much gratitude both at home and abroad. I shall ever remember the kindness I received from my sister and yourself and Dr. Smith with unfeigned thanks and with most grateful feelings.

I shall send the corn as you direct on board the Bayou Sara. The Huntsville don't run at present. I have set the black horse to plough. He understands it well. He has eat much corn and must help raise more. He looks well indeed. Levin is very glad to hear from his old father and promises to obey all his orders. I can wait until May for the articles you mentioned. Should my coffee run out, I can borrow. My neighbors are more than kind since my return.

I long to see you all. If I can get a pony for Charley, he shall surely have one. How is Harriet's head? Can my little David fight the people as usual? I hope this may find you all enjoying good health. My hand begins to shake. I remain your affectionate friend,

R. O'Connor

I must request the favor of you to add twenty-eight yards of cheap calico in your memorandum for me. Please let it be gay. I have always given a dress of such to every woman after having a young child. I am now in debt to four that has young babes, *and fine ones too.* They do much better by being encouraged a little and I have ever thought they deserved it. Should bed blankets be cheaper in the spring than they are in the fall, I should be glad to have fifteen pairs sent up to divide amongst the Negroes. I bought that many last summer from Mr. K. Dunbar and pay'd for them myself, but they will need some more to keep their children warm next winter. I have got behind in my little business by being from home so long. Otherwise I could have bought the calico for them at home without troubling you with my nonsense.

My garden is late. Nothing in it yet, and I get but little milk. I have to let the calves run with the cows until the pasture gets better, which will be some time yet. The winter being so very cold, they had to feed the cotton seed away to save the cattle, which throws my business very much out of sorts until we commence ginning the new crop.

I concluded that my letter was finished last night, but this morning I have made a new start and filled the other page. When you come, I hope you may find us very industrious people and all doing well. I wish the crop may prove *more* than good; but should it please *God* not to grant my wishes, I will try to make it up in taking care of what is here, which had been the way that the greatest part of this property has been collected together. We began the world very poor when we came to this place the 5th of June, 1797. We had only provisions to last us two days and had to trust in Providence for the next. Our meals had to be very scant and handled carefully which learned me to be thankful for a little, and value it much. And I leave it to yourself to judge whether I have a right to feel as I do.

In this letter to Frances, among routine plantation news, Rachel expresses her continuing confidence and pleasure in Jacob Germany as he begins overseeing his second crop on her plantation.

April 17, 1835

My dear niece,

I have received two letters from you since I came from your house. I should have written before this had it not been nearly out of my power to do so owing to my hand trembling ever since my late illness. I feel quite well, but my strength don't return. I try to attend my garden and household affairs as usual, which appears to be as much as I am able to do. Mr. Germany is doing very well. I think he will raise corn enough to last next year if some great misfortune should not happen to prevent it. Corn is selling at a dollar and a half pr. barrel. What would become of poor me if I had to buy now? I had to buy a little to plant amongst the cotton, as it suits better for that purpose than flint corn, but I have paid for it out of my little marketing.

Your Cousin Charlotte has not named her babe yet. They are waiting for Julia Ann to come. She has not returned from Alexandria yet, neither have they any idea when, or how long, it may be before she comes. Mr. Davis has been to see me three times since we arrived home, but your Cousin Clarissa found so much to do in her garden that she could not spare the time to leave home. I expect her next week. They are all in good health. I am sorry to hear of your dear mama having sore eyes. I fear she reads too much by candle light. She ought to be very cautious as it might injury her sight greatly. How is my dear little Harriet's head? Do let me know in your next.

I saw Mr. Clark on board the boat that we came up in from Plaquemine. He said that one third of the old plantation on Bayou Sara belongs to the estate of your papa. Milly says that Clarissa put the shawl you mentioned on top of the curtain over the bed where she and Mr. Davis sleep. I had the corn put on board the Bayou Sara as your Uncle Alfred directed, and got Dr. Denny to write to the gentleman at Plaquemine to forward it to him by the first opportunity. The bag was well filled with shelled corn, which the Doctor marked as your uncle requested in his letter to me. I wrote to your mama pretty soon after I came home. It was my first attempt and badly done, but I concluded it would show that the will was good if I only had power to guide my pen.

Please to remember me very affectionately to your uncles and aunts and kiss your dear mama and little David for me and tell all your little brothers and sister Harriet to write—that I shall ever be glad to receive their letters. I shall expect your Uncle Alfred in May. I remain your affectionate aunt,

Rachel O'Connor

Editor's note: In this letter Rachel mentions the one-third interest of David's heirs in his father's estate. The estate of the late William Weeks was divided equally among his three children. David Weeks had been the last surviving child of William Weeks.

In this letter Rachel preaches preparedness for the hereafter, but her interests are obviously on worldly things as well.

May 18, 1835

My dear sister,

I received your letter long since, but have not been able to answer it. I was very sick when it first came and remained so for several days after, and after my health began to mend, I gained strength slow. I attempted to write to you, but found it out of my power. Clarissa wrote to you last week. I am sorry to learn from your letter that you could not guard against grief. I had indulged a hope of your becoming more composed for the sake of your dear children. They need all your attention to prepare them to meet their creator in a future day when I most sincerely pray we may enjoy a resting place amongst the blessed through the mercy of God. My low state of health causes me to reflect much on the nothingness of this world. It is better to suffer during this life which soon passes off than to be forever in torment hereafter.

The plantation affairs are doing very well—a fine large crop planted and using every means to work it. The Negroes are often sick a few days, but soon recover and return to their work. One little babe lays very sick at present. My garden is late. I don't expect much from it this spring, and I am afraid to try for much poultry as the corn is getting scarce. I hope to make it hold out. If not, we must put ourselves on short allowance for a while.

I expect Charlotte and Clarissa here today. They have been at their brother William's for several days past. The girls are very kind to me. They both came and stayed with me until I began to get better. Julia Ann has returned from Rapids, but I have not seen her since, so I cannot inform you anything respecting her visit to you, but I hope she may conclude to go. Mr. Doherty and Charlotte speaks of naming their son Caleb. He is a fine large child. I don't think that I ever seen three finer boys than theirs. Mr. Doherty bought an excellent cook when last in New Orleans, which he paid seven hundred and fifty dollars for, so that Charlotte is comfortable in that respect.

James Flower stayed with me last night. He says their family are all in fine health—his father particularly so. James is a fine interesting youth. No parent could wish a more charming son.

I have not heard from your brother Alfred of late. Perhaps he may be in the city at this time. My meat is getting low. I hope he will forward the eight barrels of *pork* before this is gone. I would buy some here if I could make anything out of my garden, but that is out of my power this year.

Please remember me most affectionately to Dr. Smith and Mr. B. Smith and Mr. Stinson, and much love to your brother and all my dear little children. I hope God may grant you much happiness. I remain your affectionate and truly grateful sister,

Rachel O'Connor

Poor little Issac is much pleased with the present you sent him. He says they make prettier trousers in the Attakapas than over here. Patience sends many thanks for her frock and for the babies' also. The old woman really conducted well during my absence.

Rachel is a woman of property and is always interested in acquiring and cultivating more land. She writes Alfred Conrad an urgent letter asking him to purchase four hundred acres offered for sale near her plantation.

June 2, 1835

My dear friend,

I feel disappointed in not having the pleasure of seeing you today. Arthur has just returned from St. Francis Ville. He saw James

Flower who directed him to inform me that you had found it out of your power to leave the city until the next trip of the Bayou Sara steamboat for this place.

Mr. Weems has offered his plantation for sale. His price is four thousand dollars to be paid if four payments—one, two, three, and four years. There is four hundred acres of land with some improvements made since Mr. W. settled on the place. I wish you could agree with him for it, as it would add much to this plantation and could be paid for easily without missing the amount in that length of time. There is several trying to buy it. Land sells soon in this neighborhood. I am afraid it will be sold before I can hear from you.

I am still poorly—sometimes not able to leave my bed. I feel better today. We have had some rain today—the first that has been here in five weeks. The crop is in good order and all going very well. My meat begins to get low. I think you had better bring some with you when you come. The articles that you sent last came safe. I return you many thanks for your kind attention. I pray that kind Heaven may reward you for your goodness.

I had to ask the favor of Dr. Denny to write you a few lines a few days ago. I was very sick at the time and could not write myself. My sister has not written for some time. I am afraid she or some of her family are sick. I am seldom able to write to them myself. Should my health ever be restored, I shall write to them as usual.

The pigs looks very well. I keep them in the lower part of my garden. I hope to see you soon and tell you all the little news I have without writing it. My nieces are gone home and I am alone at present. My little Issac helps me in talk, otherwise I should forget how. I remain, my dear young friend, your affectionate and grateful friend,

R. O'Connor

Rachel's thoughts increasingly dwell upon death, as revealed in this letter to fifteen-year-old Frances Weeks.

June 29, 1835

My dear niece,

I had the happiness of receiving a kind and affectionate letter from you previous to your uncle's leaving here. It afforded me much comfort to hear of you all being in good health, excepting your kind mama who continued sorrowful. I hope and pray that time may restore her to contentment (at least), if not to happiness. We must submit to the will of providence and had ought to do so without a murmur knowing all is just and right that is done by him that cannot err. But I hope God will forgive us. We grieve at being parted from our dear relations, which is out of our power to avoid.

I am sorry to inform you of my present trials. My dear Clarissa is laying extremely low at Mr. Doherty's. They entertained no hopes of her being spared all last week. Yesterday Dr. Harriford thought her a little better. They sent for me, but I was very sick and could not go. I sent them word that if she should be taken from this world of sorrow at this time, I should soon be with her in all probability. This morning I feel some better, from which I concluded to write you a few lines, fearing you might think my sickness had caused me to forget you. You must often talk to your dear little brothers and sister. Tell them how greatly I love you all, and in particular, how very grateful they must ever continue to their good and kind mother, whose only happiness is to serve them. Your good and pious teacher (no doubt) will often explain to you all the duty that children owe their parents; and you, being good children, will benefit by his advice. Your kindness to your dear mother will be remembered by him who rewards all goodness.

I hope your good Uncle Alfred has arrived home long since, and that his former good health may be quite restored. Tell him that I have not seen Mr. Davis since he went from here some days before your uncle's arrival. Owing to your Cousin Clarissa's being so sick of late, your Cousin Julia Ann don't speak of visiting you at this time; yet I think she would be happy in doing so if she was not afraid to leave me, knowing from the weak state of my health, I am not long for this world unless a great change should take place.

I received a letter from your dear mama a few days ago which I will answer as soon as I feel well enough. Tell her that I feel truly thankful for all her kindnesses and that there is nothing I could desire on earth that she and her brother has not sent me—much more than I expected, or should have thought of had I made out a memorandum for myself.

My dear child, excuse all mistakes. I am in great trouble about my dear Clarissa and very weak and broken-hearted. Your Cousin Charlotte has named her son Caleb. Remember me most affectionately to your Uncle Alfred. My best respects to Dr. Smith, Mr. Stinson, Mr. B. Smith, and Mr. Walch, and much love to your dear mama, and my dear William, and Alfred, and Harriet, and Charles, and David, not forgetting yourself. Often do I pray that blessings may be bestowed on you through the mercy of God. I remain your affectionate aunt,

R. O'Connor

In a despondent letter to Alfred Conrad, Rachel tells of the neighborhood's fear of a slave insurrection agitated by John A. Murrell's outlaw gang.

August 3, 1835

Dear friend,

I was too unwell to write last mail and poorly yet. I do not know what is the matter with me. I sincerely hope that no other person ever had, or may have, such feelings as torture me hourly. In my dreams I call out for my mother to come to me; but alas, I have no parents to comfort me in my sorrow; and if I had, perhaps they would be tired of me. I am tired of myself. But I hope and pray that the world may bear with me a little longer. My time must soon end and I shall be no longer a trouble to anyone.

The people has become greatly alarmed from some reports in circulation. I will enclose a piece to you from which you can form an idea of their fears, but I have not suffered one moment's uneasiness. I feel perfectly contented in that respect. I hope I have raised them better than to have such wicked principles. It is the mean white men that is the sole cause of all. The country if full of Murrell's men and I fear they may yet do harm. It is supposed they are determined on it. The gentlemen in this parish has concluded to raise money by subscription to hire a company of men to ride day and night as a

guard over all the parish. Dr. Ira Smith and Mrs. Bowman sub-
scribed $100 each. Mr. C. Smith, $50, and William S. Swayze, $20.
They came to me, but I told them they must apply to you; that I
could not undertake anything of the kind unless authorized by you to
do so. They agree to pay twenty-five cents for every slave they own.
So you can direct me as you think proper.

Britton, the gin wright, has not come for his money yet, but I
expect him soon, after which I shall enclose to you his receipt for
same. My house leaks so bad that it is wet constantly in many parts.
I have applied to Mr. Doherty to agree with a man to get cypress
shingles to cover it over anew. I thought at the time I could make
enough by marketing to pay for the shingles, but I find it out of my
power owing to my bad health. I have not stopped Arthur one day
since you left here, and George but very seldom. What little I have
made, I have paid away towards expenses of the plantation. Mr. Germany has every appearance of a good crop, and I expect the price of
shingles will have to come out of it. Every little expense causes my
heart to tremble, yet all cannot be avoided. I hope through the mercy
of God that the plantation will bring corn sufficient to last next
year. It has been dreadful in the East Parish.

I have received your letter per last mail and was glad to learn
from it all were well and that my best of sisters has become more
reconciled to her fate. Sometimes ere long, I will write to her. I am
in debt one letter to my dear Frances and little Charles which I
must not forget. My love to my dear sister and the children. Every
happiness attend you all,

R. O'Connor

Clarissa is better and returned home, but I have not seen her
since.

Poor old Dr. Powell (the father-in-law of Dr. Williams) has ended
his earthly troubles at last by shooting himself through the head with
a pistol. God help his unnatural sons-in-law. Will his little property
reward them for what they have caused to obtain it? His spirit was
above bearing what they were willing to inflict.

Editor's Note: John A. Murrell ranks among Louisiana's most noto-
rious outlaws. Son of a fanatical frontier preacher, he could recite
reams of the Old Testament to someone then murder him in cold
blood. His hideout was for many years called *no man's land*. It was
located in the Kitsatchie forest between the Spanish fort of Los

Adaes and the western frontier of the United States. It was owned
by no country and had no government. It became a part of the state
of Louisiana in 1821. The area is characterized by many hills, caves,
rivers, and lakes. This terrain afforded Murrell and his gang hiding
places for their loot. The Spanish El Camino Real (which originated
at Mexico City and extended north and east to the fort of Los
Adaes) ran through no man's land. It was the route used by gold-
laden travellers and stage passengers. The Murrell gang raided travellers, murdered them, slit the abdomens, took out the organs, filled
the corpses with sand, then sunk the bodies into rivers or lakes.
Murrell's success in adding local persons of low character to his gang
contributed much to his raids. Besides gold, Murrell stole horses, cattle and slaves. The caves of no man's land were large enough to
accommodate large amounts of plunder. Murrell stole slaves with
promises of freedom to them, then sold them and pocketed the
money. His Feliciana raid in 1835 was a slave-stealing venture,
which resulted in the forming of local vigilantes and punishment of
gang members who were apprehended. John A. Murrell, born about
the year 1800, continued his activities until 1844, when he is believed to have been murdered and buried beside Kitsatchie Creek.

*As anxiety continues over John A Murrell's activity among the Ne-
groes, Rachel expressed to Alfred Conrad her complete confidence in
her own slaves and overseer and blames the present unrest among
slaves upon the sins of white overseers.*

August 24, 1835
Dear friend,
Your last brought word of your being unwell, which occasions me
some uneasiness. It is very sickly over her and many die. Mr. Bowman is laying extemely low. He has three doctors attending on him.
They were greatly alarmed this morning and nearly despaired. I sent
over this evening to know how he was. They sent me word he
continued much the same. I am truly sorry and shall mourn his
death sincerely, should he not recover. They are like affectionate children to me. No son could have showed more kindness than he has

175

ever done since our first acquaintance and his lovely little wife is all goodness. She had a severe attack of fever only a few days before he was take so ill. My poor Clarissa has recovered her health again, but I have not seen her since you left here. Their Negroes are very sickly and they have to stay at home to nurse them. We have had some very sick Negroes on this place of late, but they are all alive yet and I hope may recover. Mr. Bowman has lost seven black children since March last.

Mr. Germany has been poorly a few days, but did not lay up. I never knew an overseer as attentive to his business as he continues to be. He is the first overseer that I ever liked in every respect. He is an honest man and his word can be depended on. He has every appearance of a fine crop of corn and cotton.

The people are afraid of all strangers and will not employ them, particularly as overseers, fearing they might belong to the party that has caused so much trouble in many parts. They are taken up on all occasions and whipped like dogs and confined until they stand their trial. It is thought there is a great number of that Murrell company yet and some are very much alarmed. I expect I should not feel as easy in mind if Mr. Germany was like the most of overseers, sneaking after the Negro woman (meaner than mean itself) which is the sole cause of all that has happened amongst the Negroes.

I wish you would let me know in your next how to manage respecting the Negro crops. I have always bought it, rather than let any get if from them, as it comes much cheaper than can be got elsewhere. But whatever you say shall be done. I am so afraid of acting wrong and bringing blame on myself that I am at a great loss how to do in small matters of that kind. I am well enough to keep about the most of my time, but don't feel as I formerly did. However I am resigned to my fate and will do as near right as I know how. My love to my dear sister and the children. I should write oftener if my hand would become steady again, but that will scarcely ever be case in this world. Much happiness attend you all is the sincere wish of your friend,

R. O'Connor

In this letter to Frances Weeks, Rachel obviously does not approve of the inhumane punishment meted to the white agitators.

Sept. 7, 1835

My dear niece,

I received your kind letter pr. last mail, which I should have answered ere this had not misfortunes happened to prevent. My good friend Mr. Bowman lay very sick about two weeks, and on Sunday, the 30th of August, he *died.* I hope and trust in God that he may be happy, but indeed he knew nothing but happiness in his beloved little family. On earth he was blessed with a lovely wife and three darling children. It is out of my power to describe the distress and grief his poor widow has underwent and continues in the same way, if not worse. How thankful should I feel could she become resigned to her fate. Your Cousin Julia Ann is with her from whom I hope she may receive comfort. I dare not venture to visit her more than a few hours at a time; her grief would break my heart; that is, if I had a heart to break. I saw Mr. B. in his last moments, which never can be forgotten during life.

It has been uncommonly sickly of late. A great number has died both white and black, and some are laying at the point of death at present. The Negroes on this plantation are all alive yet, but some has been very sick. Two are sick now. Two of the women has had little babies in the last month and are doing very well.

All the papers are fill'd with bad news. If they continue hanging, as they have done for sometime past, we should be careful of our children, otherwise the world might be left without people. Our neighborhood continues very quiet, particularly the blacks—not one being found guilty of any bad act yet, but the white men are taken on all occasions. They have one in jail that they expect to hang, which is more merciful than is common, for they generally whip them nearly to death. They call it Lynch's Law, giving from two to three hundred lashes and then let them go with orders to be out of the state in eight hours.

Your Cousin Clarissa has recovered her health pretty well again. Mr. Davis has sold his plantation and talks of going to Madison County to live. He expects to start in search of a place to settle in a few days from this date. Mr. A. Doherty and family were well not long since. Some of their Negroes were sick. Wm. Swayze lost one fine man by death. Your Cousin James Flower is sick, but I hope not dangerously ill.

I am sorry to learn by your last that your dear mama continues so poorly. Your uncle mentioned in his last that she had been very sick.

177

My dear and darling children, you must use every means to comfort her and make her happy. My own health is a little better than usual.

Tell your uncle that sickness at home and abroad has prevented me from answering his letter as yet. I shall enclose Britton's receipt for 40-$. Please to hand it to him. I forgot to send it before as I had ought to have done. Mr. Germany is doing very well and I hope he may surprise you all in making so good a crop. Tell your brothers and sister that I never pass a day without thinking of you all and praying that blessings may attend you and yours. My best respects to your kind teacher and much love to your mama and Uncle Alfred and all your little brothers and sisters. I remain your affectionate aunt,

Rachel O'Connor

Grief and trouble are the subjects of this letter to Frances Weeks.

Oct. 12, 1835

My dear niece,

I received your kind letter sometime since, but could not answer it owing to a rising on my hand which is really sore yet. I have had my hand wrapped up for ten days, and it had become very painful before I began to nurse it, which perhaps caused it to be worse than it might have otherwise been had I attended it sooner. My health has become quite good, much more so than I ever expected in my long spell of sickness—about fifteen months.

Mr. Davis has gone to Madison County in search of land where he expects to settle should the country suit him after he sees it. I am sorry to part from them, but have not said one discouraging word.

Your Cousin Charlotte has lost her youngest son. It was truly a most lovely babe. Mr. Doherty sent his carriage for me and I went and stayed seven days with them. They were greatly distressed, and poor Julia Ann mourns as sincerely as its parents. If a house of mourning is good for me, I had ought to become good indeed, for I see enough, could I profit by it. Poor Mrs. Bowman is wasted away to a shadow. I much fear her time is short unless she becomes reconciled to the misfortune that has fallen to her lot. I hope this may find you all in good health and your dear mama doing the best she can for her beloved little ones.

Please inform your mama and uncle that I have sent thirty bales of cotton to New Orleans which has arrived safe and that I expect to send thirty more next week. We are doing very well at present. The weather is dry and the hands pick fast. The corn proves extremely good.

Excuse my short letter. My hand is too painful to write a long one. Remember me affectionately to your dear mama and Uncle Alfred and all your brothers and sister Harriet. I remain your affectionate aunt,

R. O'Connor

For two years following David's death, Alfred Conrad (who managed David's estate for his sister, Mary Conrad Weeks) was the most frequent recipient of Rachel's letters. Considering her great affection for Mary, it is not surprising that Rachel's letters to Alfred include information about family and friends as well as plantation business. The sickness among the slaves and the engaging of overseer Germany for another year are not as urgent to her as her request in this letter that Alfred purchase the property of the late John Swift that is adjacent to Rachel's own property.

1835, Oct. 21

My dear friend,

Your kind favor of the 7th instant arrived safe. I am truly thankful to find that yourself and family were in good health. Times are sickly. We have had much more on this plantation than usual, but I do not know of any that escaped this year. Mrs. Bowman has lost a fine little girl about seven years old since Mr. Bowman's death— which is eight since the first of March last that has died out of their slaves, all children which is to be wondered at, when they are so carefully attended to as she has ever done. She is a pious woman and considers that her duty.

Poor Mr. Doherty and Charlotte has lost their youngest son. It was a beautiful babe. They were well. Julia Ann and Clarissa were

well also. Mr. Davis has gone in search of land and has not returned
yet. His and Mr. Doherty's Negroes has been uncommonly sickly.
Their doctor's bill will be high this year.

I have engaged Mr. Germany to oversee another year, for which
he is to receive five hundred dollars out of the sales of the crop of
cotton—only twenty-five dollars more than he got last year and is to
get this year. He agreed to stay much cheaper than I expected. Had
I not considered it as much in favor of the heirs, as to my ease, I
should not have been so anxious to engage him again. If my brother
were alive, he would be pleased to know and see his management
and pay the 500-$, and 400 lbs. of good meat, 150 lbs. of sugar, 50
lbs. coffee, 25 lbs. lard, and one barrel of flour freely—which is
what I have promised him for next year and he well deserves it.

Patrick is an honest man and understands cropping as well as any
overseer needs to do, but the company that he delights in is low and
dark. How he retained his honest principles and has so many priva-
does of the blackest colour is wonderful; but not more so than true.
He gets 600-$ for overseeing little Robert Barrow's farm this year
and four in provisions and horse feed, and another gets the same
agreeable to poor Mrs. Bowman's bargain for overseeing the place
that formerly belonged to Mrs. Pirrie. And A. Davis is to get 700-$
for overseeing the plantation that Mrs. Bowman now lives on, and I
really believe Mr. Germany to be equal in knowledge, honour, and
honesty with the best and highest priced overseers amongst them. I
have taken the pains to write the above with a hope of convincing
yourself and my sister, and all concerned, that my views are not
selfish, but intended for the good of all which, if it affords the satisfaction I sincerely wish, I shall pass off the few days allotted me
contentedly and as I expected had my brother lived.

Now I have a particular favor to ask which I hope and pray may
be complied with, and one that will add greatly to the estate and to
the convenience of this plantation. Mr. Swift owned, or claimed, a
tract of land joining this place which will be sold at public sale at
some period not very distant. I want you to have it bought in. My
brother intended to place that power in me, fearing any other might
keep the land, should it sell cheap, but we forgot to have it done.
The Miss Swifts has come down, and as soon as I hear from you, I
will try to see them and mention the subject, and then inform you
instantly. At my death, it will pay well for the money paid, and
perhaps long before, in cropping. Mr. Hambleton could now get dou-

ble what he paid Lawyer Weems for his land if he would part with it. I was sadly disappointed in missing that bargain, and shall be again should you not get this of which I have been speaking.

There is 65 bales pressed and would have went down in the boat today. That is, if the roads were not so bad that it is not possible to haul them to the landing until dry weather comes once more.

Please to let my sister see this, as it is intended for you both. I have not written to her of late. I have not been able to write often. I am not quite so well now. This wet weather don't agree with me. I have got my old house nicely covered. Mr. Doherty agreed for the shingles at 4-$ pr. thousand. They will have to be paid for. Mr. Germany made George and Littleton cover the house.

My love to my dear sister and the darling children. Wishing all happiness to yourself and them, I remain your sincere friend,

R. O'Connor

This is the 21st of Oct-br, but I don't know when it will reach you. The mail is gone. It rained so I could not send it in time for the mail. I am sorry the children has lost their amiable teacher. I hope he may return to them as expected.

Yours, etc., *R. O'C.*

Rachel writes Mary of her interest in acquiring even more land. She is pleased at the promise of a visit from Frances Weeks, who is attending Miss B. Garnet's boarding school at Baton Rouge.

Dec-br 14, 1835

My dear sister,

Your kind letter of the 25th of last month arrived five or six days ago. Perhaps it lay in the office a day or two before they sent it out to me. I have nothing in my garden worth sending to market and only send once a week to inquire for letters. My health was so bad all the spring and summer that my garden became a wilderness. It nearly broke my heart to look at it. I really had no idea that my attention could be missed so much, as my long illness had proved to me. Even after I felt well, I remained so weak that a few moments walking tired and threw me into a fever instantly which distressed me beyond all the little patience I had left, which often caused me to hide myself and cry for hours; but thanks to kind providence, I am quite well again and if I can keep so, I will try to make a good garden by spring.

I am very glad that my dear little Harriet's head has got well. I hope in God it may continue so. Should your eyes continue weak, write short letters. I am thankful for a few lines from you. I have so many things since I came home that causes me to think of you. I am at this moment writing by light of one of the lamps that you gave me. I generally fix it every day to light me at night. This causes me to think on you. Then the two baskets will happen in my way, and every time I see my arms, all your goodness appears in a moment. The places that was blistered has not got white yet.

I received a letter a few days since from my dear Frances. She appears to be quite happy—everyone kind and attentive to her. Her only trouble is being absent from her beloved mama which shows the goodness of her heart. I am pleased with her in that. It shows her sincere love. Let her situation be ever so pleasant, her mind still wanders home to her dearest and best of friends. She continues to promise a visit of two or three weeks to me when the sugar making is over so that her Uncle Alfred can come with her and bring her brother Alfred with hm. Do let poor little Wm. come also, so that I may see the dear little boy once more, and why not come yourself and bring the other three children with you. I will do all in my power to make you comfortable.

We have been much favored this year. The crop of corn has turned wonderful. If no misfortune should befall it, there will be enough to do this year by buying the Negro crops at five bits pr. barrel, out of which they buy their summer clothing for themselves. I have sent ninety-nine bales of cotton to N. Orleans, and sixteen more are pressed which will be sent in a few days, and some to pick out of the field yet—perhaps ten or twelve bales, which I think an excellent crop considering the wet season. I am still as well pleased with Mr. Germany as ever, and I expect you will see that it is not without reason from the crop he has raised.

Two of the Miss Swifts has been to see me. They are to inquire respecting the tract of land and if they can make the claim good, they will let us have it. I wrote to your brother sometime ago and mentioned the terms that Dr. Pope's plantation was offered on. I wish he would come and buy if for the estate. The titles of that are good and would be a great advantage in raising crops and allow some for pasture.

I have a great desire to manage for the best the time I have to live, and by adding some more land to this place, would afford me a much fairer chance of doing so, and land will be higher every year anywhere near St. Francis Ville. Charlotte and Mr. Doherty will move to the plantation that formerly belonged to her parents by the first of Jan-ry next. I don't know where Mr. Davis will settle yet.

Poor Mrs. Bowman is really to be pitied. She came near to losing her little daughter the day before yesterday by getting a pin in her throat. She got it down, and I hope the worse is over.

My love to the children and best respects to your brother. I remain your affectionate sister,

R. O'Connor

Excuse all mistakes. It is very late at night. Mr. and Mrs. Germany's oldest babe is very sick. They had one born the 2nd of August, 1834, and another the 1st of August, 1835.

The prospect of acquiring the plantation of Robert Hail prompts Rachel to write a brief note to Alfred Conrad relating details for possible purchase.

January 4, 1836

My dear friend,

I am afraid my letters will become troublesome unless I could have something good to inform you of. However I am thankful that I have nothing bad. All are well and making a new start for another crop, should we be spared to do so. I have been expecting you to come for some time past and still on the lookout for you. Mr. Robert Hail sent me word, pr. Mr. Germany a few days ago, that he could not let you have his plantation this year as he had no other place for his hands to make a crop at present, but that he would sell it and deliver it to you next year; that if he could see you the agreement could be concluded to that effect. He is now in New Orleans. Should you see him, do try to get it. He will value it higher after next year and it will bring a good price at any time.

Several are trying to get it, but I hope you may disappoint them at present. Cotton brings a good price now and I don't think you should be afraid to venture the price of the land. It is near here and will be a great advantage, perhaps more so than you now think. I should prefer it to Mr. Swift's. The land is better and the titles good.

Excuse my short letter. It is late at night and I am very tired. I have been working all day in my garden trying to make ready for planting a spring crop once more. I can scarcely write my fingers are so stiff from working with the spade. I have good health at present and my greatest comfort is working in my old garden.

My love to my sister and the children. Much happiness to you all. Goodnight.

R. O'Connor

In a letter to Mary, Rachel rejoices that Mr. Stinson, the children's tutor, teaches them their duty toward God and man. A rumoured Christmas uprising of slaves is thwarted.

Jan-y 11, 1836

My dear sister,

Your kind and affectionate letter, dated the 30th of last month, did not arrive until the 8th of this month. I do not know the cause of its being so long on the way, but I assure you that it met a hearty welcome after a tedious journey. I had been afraid for several days that something had happened to you from some uneasy dreams, which I tried to not think of, as I am continually expecting some new misfortune, but I find by your letter that you were not in good health.

I expected to be quite alone on Christmas day, and should, if my poor little Clarissa had not come down the day previous and stayed until the day after Christmas. Mr. Davis did not like to be from home at that time and did not come. Clarissa and myself spoke of you several times that day. How sorry I should have been had I have known your situation—*laying in a fever.* I hope you may be able to collect fortitude to bear the absence of my dear little Frances for a short time. Most sincerely do I pray for you both, but pray don't indulge grief to the ruin of your health. I shall be truly glad to see her and her little brother with their Uncle Alfred and will try to make them happy. *Should I live*, I hope the children and yourself may spend a part of the time with me yet.

I have got a good cover on the house and find it very comfortable. My health has become so good that I have almost forgotten my age. I can attend to my affairs with ease and I hope to do some good for awhile. You write so loving and kind to me that my very heart overflows with gratitude, and I will assure you that the confidence you place in me shall not be abused, and promise to take the same care that I have ever done, and render a just account of every cent to yourself and your brother. The greatest earthly wish that I now entertain is to afford you satisfaction.

I have sixteen little Negroes a raising, the oldest of the sixteen, a little turned of six years old, all very healthy children, excepting my little favorite *Issac*. He is subject to a cough, but seldom sick enough to lay up. The poor little fellow is laying at my feet sound asleep. I wish I did not love him, as I do, *but it is so*, and I cannot help it.

Mr. Germany keeps the plantation and Negroes in good order, and all else according; and I am trying to fix my gardens, as they used to be, once more. Being sick so long, with little hopes of ever recovering, they got greatly out of order; but I have improved the looks much of late.

I have sent the crop of cotton to New Orleans—126 bales in all, and have corn enough at home to serve the plantation this season. Mr. Davis has moved over to Thompson's Creek, in the East Parish, about 20 miles from me. He rents the place this year. God only knows where they will go next. Charlotte has been at the point of death. About Christmas, or a few days after, when I heard from her last, they thought her rather on the mend. Poor Charlotte has been unfortunate. I have not seen her since she got sick last.

I am glad to find by your last, that you are willing to add more land to this. I think with good luck, the crop would be larger and soon pay the price of another tract. I have written last mail to your brother and requested of him to try to bargain Hail out of his. It is most excellent land for corn and cotton, and no way inconvenient to this plantation.

I am really glad to hear of Mr. Stinson's return. It would have been much against the children had he not returned to them again.

Where is there another so moral and who takes the pains to set good examples as he did in teaching them their duty to God and man?

Now, my best of sisters, I must inform you of this day sixteen years ago, being the day that my dear, dear Stephen was laid in earth, a loss that causes my heart to bleed and will during life. Kiss my little ones for me and tell them how much I want to see them all. I have never found a white colt for my dear little Charley yet, but I love them all alike and when I get for one, I must get for all. If your brother is at home, please remember me most affectionately to him. Tell him I am looking for him to come.

At a ball on the 8th in Saint Francis Ville, Dr. Hearn's lady, setting near a window, was stabbed in the back, but is living yet. It is not known who stabbed her. They had not been married long. She was formerly a Miss Jewel.

The Negroes over at Thompson's Creek had some idea of a raising about Christmas and had the business planned when a Negro woman informed on them and had a stop put to their wickedness, by hanging two Negroes, and a search was made for one or two white men which made their escape so far. Report says there were two more Negroes that ought to be hung if justice had taken place, but their masters were rich, which proved excuse enough to save them.

It is past midnight; excuse all mistakes. I remain your affectionate sister,

Rachel O'Connor

My dear sister:

It is now the 13th. I wrote the above on Monday, but could not get it sent to the post office it rained so constantly ever since. I hope to send it tomorrow morning. We are all well at present. Tell Al'fd that I shall expect him to help me work my flower garden.

Plans for operating the plantation for the new year must be attended to. Rachel requests Alfred Conrad's presence in making those plans.

Feb-ry 2nd, 1836

Dear sir,

I did not receive your kind favor with the enclosed letter to Mr. R. Hail until yesterday owing to no person (from this place) being in town for 8 to 10 days past. The waters has been very high, rather dangerous, crossing Alexander's Creek; and not knowing it to be necessary to send, I neglected doing so, which caused your letter to remain in the post office so long.

I will send your letter to Mr. Hail very soon. I am truly glad to find you are pleased with the cotton crop. For my own part, I am satisfied with Mr. Germany's conduct in every respect. If ever an overseer done his duty, he has done his since he commenced on this plantation and continues to do so, and I believe is equally as careful of the corn and horses, and all else, as he would be were they his own. I never knew one to behave so well before and scarcely ever expect to experience it in another, and what is still better, he is an honest man in every respect.

I was afraid you would think it extravagant in me to say more than eight barrels of pork, but I must own it gave out the first week in Nov-br, and I gave it all out every dinnertime myself with a sparing hand; but I have made out without buying, since the price of pork was from seventeen to twenty dollars per barrel and I did not venture to get any. I scarcely know how I managed to do without. I certainly could not if it had not been for some wild hogs of mine that has run in the range for years that Mr. Germany hunted up and shot which done until we could get some fattened to kill at home. But I think I cannot make out this year with less than twelve barrels at least, besides this raised at home—and do any justice to the Negroes. I had to send for a bag of coffee to give the overseer his 50 weight. His year commences the 9th of Dec-br.

I have not sugar to last this year. The overseer has to get a hundred and fifty weight. He had that much last year, and I have some for him this year, but not enough for the whole allowance.

You have really been fortunate in your sugar crop—405 hogsheads is doing well, but I see you still wish to do better and I hope every blessing may attend you and yours. I have the sheep at home that you directed me to send to your brother for. They are beautiful and doing well. I would rather you could come over and settle up at this time yourself. I don't like to ask for money. After this time you can arrange the business so that I may do all easily.

Should you go to New Orleans before you come here, I wish you would buy me a small box of fresh garden seed. I will try to make the price of it by marketing, if *no more*. I am very thankful to my sister and yourself for all your kindnesses and will accept of some money when you come to pay small demands that cannot be avoided, and keep an account of it for the satisfaction of all parties, which I think my duty.

I received a letter from my dear Frances at the same time I received yours. It was written on the 23rd of Jan-ry. She was well and perfectly happy. She mentioned you and her dear mama very affectionately. She expects you and her brother to accompany her up here. Pray don't disappoint us. It is so cold that I cannot write. You will have to guess it along as well as you can.

My best respects to Mr. Stinson and Dr. Smith and kindest love to my dear sister and the children. I remain your ever grateful friend,

R. O'Connor

Rachel apologizes for troubling Alfred Conrad but again urges his attention to the most pressing debts.

March 9th, 1836

My dear friend,

I have at this moment received your most esteemed favor of the 6th instant. I had heard of your being in the city pr. Mr. Davis and expecting you here hourly, but your letter destroys all my hopes of seeing you before April which I am truly sorry for. To come at this time would only detain you a few days and I must still beg of you to come if possible. My word is out to the people (where money is due for the plantation) that you will be here this month to settle and pay them which they are now in earnest expectation. I am sorry for poor Clem, the blacksmith. He is in need of his, and Mr. K. Dunbar has been kind and very obliging to me in every respect, and several others which I wish paid. The shingles that I had bought to cover the house remains unpaid. Do, my good friend, come this one time, after which perhaps the business may be arranged in a way that I could make out to trouble you less. You had ought to come and see how well we are doing. Kind providence appears to bless our undertakings *so far*. Mr. Germany continues to manage very well. His business goes on like clockwork. None ever done as well on this place before.

I feel so distressed at the idea of your not coming that I cannot think of anything that I may need this year—only a little *tea* and some lamp oil. The pork for the Negroes may be put off for a month or two should you wish it.

My health is pretty good—only a pain in my right shoulder in wet or cold weather proves very troublesome and nearly prevents me from writing at times, which is the case at present.

With hopes of seeing your shortly, I will bid you farewell. I remain your affectionate and troublesome friend,

R. O'Connor

In a letter to Alfred Conrad, Rachel is full of plans for the growing season and again begs him to acquire the Hail place.

March 18, 1836

My dear friend,

Your kind favor of the 16th instant has this evening arrived and is now laying before me. I feel a loss for words to express my gratitude towards yourself and sister for all the goodness *continually* bestowed me.

The 20 barrels of molasses and 2 barrels of sugar arrived several days ago and are nearly hauled home. And this evening the demijohn of lamp oil and a caddy of tea and a bundle of garden seed came out in the cart, forwarded by Mr. K. Dunbar, agreeable to your request for which I return many, many thanks. I hope to have a good garden when you come, or at least I shall try for it if my health permits. I have had a dreadful attack of rheumatism of late and am quite poorly yet. At times it is not possible for me to write occasioned by the pain in my arm. Julia Ann has come down in their carriage to see if it would not be of service to me to ride occasionally in it, which will be a good opportunity for me to get to St. Francis Ville to see Mr. Dunbar and receive the $200 you so kindly sent to me and at

189

the same time call for their accounts and examine, and do as you direct, which I shall deliver to you whenever I have the pleasure of seeing you, with a hope of every satisfaction. No earthly blessing could afford me more pleasure.

I am glad to see that you entertain hopes of pork being lower in price ere long. I shall continue very saving and make what I have last as long as possible. I have a fine chance of young hogs coming on for another year should no disease carry them off as it did last year. Mr. Germany is really very attentive to hogs and horses and sheep—indeed stock of all kinds—and manages the Negroes and the plantation affairs first rate with as much anxiety as he could possible do if it was for himself.

I still hope you may trade Mr. Hail out of his land yet. It brings good crops; and as cotton sells pretty well now, you would scarcely miss the price of it in a short time. There is a fine chance of little Negroes coming on (should a blessing continue to attend them). They may assist greatly in a few years. *My little favorite boy is worth a large amount.* He can work the garden (some) already and his little innocent talk is my greatest company. I hope you may find all well when you reach home. Don't forget to bring some of the children over with you. I should be glad to see you all. I made an attempt at writing a letter to my sister a day or two ago which will only show the will to remember her, for I continue poorly and my fingers are stiff.

Julia Ann joins me in love to you all. I remain your affectionate friend,

Rachel O'Connor

I am afraid the Miss Swifts cannot make sufficient titles to the land they claim. Mr. Hail's claim to his is good.

Rachel writes William Weeks asking for a visit from him and the other Weeks children. She suggests plans for their entertainment.

April 2, 1836

My dear nephew,

The pleasure that the arrival of your kind letter afforded me is beyond my power to express. It came unexpectedly and, of course, gave greater joy. I have read it over and over again and it still continues new. Your beloved hand held the pen and guided it well. It is written beautiful and I hope you will write often and tell me how you all are. I am sorry to hear of your dear mama having a rising on her hand so as to prevent her from writing. My dear son, you will be very kind and attentive to her. It will give you pleasure when you recollect how dutiful you was to your amiable mother when you become a man, and God will love and bless you forever.

When you get through your studies pretty well (and your mama can spare you) do come and stay some time with me. I will endeavor to make you comfortable and happy and perhaps Mr. Stinson would accompany you. I should be truly glad to see him.

The measles are in many places throughout the parish. Mrs. Bowman's two youngest children are just recovering. However I think they were much favored. They had it light. Tell your brother Alfred that the measles will soon be gone and then I shall expect him to come. Your little brothers, Charles and David, must come also. They can help me in my garden. I have two little hoes at their service and a larger one for myself. We can work together and if my dear little Harriet could come, we would amuse ourselves in feeding the little chickens.

I have become quite helpless within a short time from being so afflicted with rheumatism in my right shoulder. It is painful to move my arm, hand, or fingers. I often find it impossible to write a line; otherwise I should write much oftener to your mama and your Uncle Alfred. I have not received a letter from your sister Frances in a long time, but I hope to see her when your uncle comes. I had not heard of your Cousin Caleb Swayze being so near being married until your letter informed me. I wish him good luck in his undetakings.

I should be extremely glad to see your mama, but I fear I never shall. I hope to see your uncle ere long. I would try to write to him if I knew where to direct my letter. The last I received from him he was in New Orleans and expected to return home very soon and from there come over here in this month.

My dear son, you will (no doubt) find this difficult to read. I have written it in great pain. Indeed I can scarcely write any since the

191

reheumatism has returned again. Perhaps when the weather becomes warm and dry I may get better. My best respects to Mr. Stinson and kindest love to your dear mama and your brothers and sisters. Your ever affectionate aunt,

Rachel O'Connor

Rachel writes a long letter to Mary containing news of plantation affairs. She rejoices that her nephew James Flower has returned safely from the Indian war.

April 5, 1836

My dear sister,

Your kind favor of the 26th of March has come to hand. I expect it lay in the post office several days as I had received a letter dated the 23rd of March from my dear little William who informed me of your having a rising on your forefinger on your right hand which prevented you from writing from which I did not expect you to be able to undertake the task in so short a time and did not send to inquire for letters until yesterday at which time I received yours with great joy.

Your brother has not arrived here yet. He is still in the city no doubt. I am sorry the measles are so generally over the state as they are now. They are near me. I'm afraid they may get amongst the Negroes. None of them has had the measles excepting a few of the very old ones, and not all of them, but I trust in my God who will order all for the best. When they disappear, do let some of the children come and stay some time and if possible, come yourself. I am truly sorry for poor Mrs. Palfrey. Her trip to N. Orleans will be a source of trouble to her, but I hope they may reach home safe. I feel uneasy about my dear Frances' state. I hope and pray she may escape. I have not heard from her of late, from which I have been expecting her hourly. I have written very little since my hand and arm has become so stiff from rheumatism settling in my right shoulder. As the weather becomes warmer, I hope the pain may wear away. I had learned from my little William's letter that Caleb's marriage with Miss Ted was near. I wish them much happiness. I have not seen either of his sisters since I heard the news of marriage.

Mr. Doherty has moved to the old plantation where my brother Stephen had lived and cultivated land. Charlotte and Julia Ann are living in the house where they were born—in sight of the graveyard where their parents lay. Poor Julia Ann came down in their carriage for me. They had concluded amongst themselves that a little journey would be of service. We went to St. Francis Ville first where I received 200-$ from Mr. K. Dunbar which your brother sent and from there we continued our journey to Mr. Doherty's where we found all well and much more comfortable than I expected. I stayed four days. The house and all around reminded me of so many different scenes that it is hard even for myself to know what my feelings were. We went to the graveyard and looked over ground where their parents lay. I found it a melancholy relief, but still felt better satisfied with myself for doing so. Previously as we passed through St. Francis Ville, in sight of the church, I mentioned to Julia Ann that I had a desire to see graves where my own family lay, but she appeared so unwilling to let me go that I gave it out.

Mr. Davis and Clarissa has moved so far away (nearly thirty miles) that we are strangers to each other's concerns. He has to come in on business, but she seldom comes.

My dear sister, I return you many thanks for so kindly agreeing to have a new chimney put in my room. The brick that I had when this old one was built were broken and rotten and was built by two old Negroes, and each one continued the half that he commenced. One being more crafty than the other picked all the best brick for his own side of the chimney, which is pretty solid, but the other half is crumbling away fast, but *always smoked*. I should have mentioned it to you while I was with you, but I had a wish to make it do until your affairs could be settled up pretty well.

Poor Mrs. Bowman can still be truly called a child of sorrow. She appears to think of nothing excepting her losses and crosses and her only pleasure is in telling over and over the many kindnesses bestowed her by her dearly beloved husband. Her two younger children are just getting well of the measles. Little James has a bad cough yet. Mrs. Bowman has bestowed me a new armoire to remain mine during life, and returned to her, which she says she will keep for my sake. Her friendship towards myself is not like that of a neighbor's child, but like that of an affectionate daughter to her own mother. In naming over your kindnesses to me she will often say how good you are, or that you are surely a good woman, and then turn to me and say that I had ought to bless God for his goodness, that he never would leave me friendless, and much more on the same subject. She is quite a sensible and religious woman and little James one of the sweetest babes. Mrs. Bowman's misfortunes continues to follow. In the last month she has lost a fine house girl about ten years old by being badly burned. It was one that Mr. Bowman had bought and gave her for a house servant.

The good account you gave of dear little William causes me heartfelt joys. He will no doubt remain a good and dutiful son. His reward will be great both in heaven and on earth where all good children are rewarded.

Mr. Germany manages as usual extremely well. The plantation is in fine order and all doing well. If we should escape the measles, I hope with the blessing of providence, he may raise a good crop again. He is very attentive to the stock. The hogs are doing very well. I hope no distemper gets amongst them again. The male hog that your brother sent me got to fighting with a stronger one and died from the hurt. The other will soon have a young family. I have to let the calves run out mostly for want of a pasture. I have a small place of oats coming on.

I wish Patty and Louisa great luck with their little ones. The latter is really smart. Her other babe is a year old. Two has been born here since I came from your house. They are fine babies. One was a daughter of Plassis, who is now a grandmother and Patience a great grandmother. I have sixteen little ones, the oldest six years old the 6th of July last. All fine healthy little children. My greatest favorite, to all appearances, in healthy, but so lean and thin in flesh that I get uneasy about him very often. Bridget, the woman that had her child the 21st of February last while I was with you, will soon have another. She has four children—the oldest only six years last July. She has a dreadful rising on the thumb of her right hand. It is far from being well yet. I am afraid she may lose the first joint.

James Flowers has just returned from the war against the Indians, but I have not seen him yet. I had trouble enough about his being gone. How is my dear little Harriet making out with her little garden? She used to work much in it when I was at your house. Mine suffers much by my arm being lame. All gardens are late with us. I do not know the reason. Does my little Alfred ride the goat, or has he caused him to keep his distance? My love to all the little ones. Kiss them for me. Remember me most affectionately to Dr. Smith and Mr. Stinson. Heaven grant you many days of happiness and contentment in the company of your lovely family and the prayers of your ever affectionate sister,

Rachel O'Connor

Rachel is appalled at plantation expenses; but in this letter to Alfred Conrad, she again expressed her confindence in Germany as an excellent overseer.

April 13, 1836

Dear friend,

Agreeable to your request I have had the accounts that were owing the merchants in St. Francis Ville collected and settled pr. Mr. K. Dunbar and given a draft in favor of himself (this day) on Messrs Lambeth and Thompson for the amount of $488.48, which pays the different accounts due. I have all their papers ready in a bundle to show you when you come which I hope you may find correct.

John Stirling's account was $16.50 for 5 small axes and one broad ax; K. Dunbar's account, Jan-ry 15, 1834, for $5.38—articles that my brother got for himself which had not been settled until now; Dr. H. Bain's account for some blacksmith work done in his shop that could not be done at home pr. Clem, $11.75; Dr. S. B. Mc-Kelvy's bill for medicine, $54.38; John Morris for two small tables that I bought myself, $10; 17,750 shingles for $71.00; B. Marshall's for the storage, drayage, and freight of last year's sugar and molasses, $17.51.

The above mentioned accounts were settled by Mr. K. Dunbar (at my request) and entered in his own account against the estate which the draft pays. I received $200 from Mr. K. Dunbar forwarded to me by yourself, which I divided amongst the Negroes in part payment for their last year's crop. Clem's $28 was paid out of it also. Mr. Germany has an account of all the Negro crops and what is still due them to show you.

The gin became greatly out of order before the cotton was ginned last crop. Towards the last it would scarcely gin one bale a day. I have employed a first rate gin maker to work on it. He says he can make it gin three bales per day. His character is good. All the family of the Barrows has engaged him to prepare their gins for their next crops. Germany says the work is well done and has no doubt of its ginning three bales a day when the work is finished. I expect his charge will be seventy or eight dollars, for which I shall have to give a draft. *I hope I am doing right.* Someone would have to work on the gin, otherwise it could not gin the cotton.

I am frightened at the expenses of the plantation which I make as small as possible and cannot make less do. Mrs. Bowman's doctor's bill nearly amounts to the expenses of this plantation, and 10 or 12 of her Negroes has died since I came from the Attakapas. So all things considered, I think we should not complain. If I have done anything *wrong*, do let me know so that I may do better hereafter.

Mr. Germany is doing very well—nearly done planting his crop, has the whole place in fine order. The horses are in good working order and keep healthy as yet. The last horses that I bought proves very good. You will soon have to look out for some pork. It is getting very scarce with me. If you should wish it, I can get Mr. K. Dunbar to buy it for you, perhaps as cheap as any other, but do as you think right. You ought to be the best judge.

I am getting better of the rheumatism as the weather gets warmer. I can write a little again. My love to my best of sisters and all the dear babes. I remain your ever affectionate friend,

Rachel O'Connor

Rachel writes Alfred Conrad that she is being dunned for taxes. She relates a neighbor's trouble with a defiant slave woman.

May 26, 1836

My dear friend,

Your kind favor of the 11th instant is laying before me. I received it several days ago, but could not find time to write you an answer and even now have to write it in the night by lamp light. A few of the Negroes has been sick and my little *Isaac* very sick. For a short time I thought that my favorite little boy could not recover. But fortunately his distresses did not last long which I suppose was caused by worms. He was left very weak, but about again nearly as smart as ever.

After that trouble was over another come on instantly. I had great reason to fear that one of my best friends lay on her death bed. On Sunday night last, after supper, Mrs. Bowman found fault with one of her female servants and undertook to chastise her herself, but the girl returned the blows and proved too strong for her mistress, threw her down and beat her unmercifully on the head and face, which swelled greatly and turned so black that I could not have known her by seeing her. Poor little woman is confined to her bed yet, but she is not considered dangerously ill. The girl is confined, and I expect will be hung. She is an uncommonly smart yellow woman and a first rate house servant, one that Mrs. Pirrie bought in N. Orleans six or seven years ago. She was her waiter and nurse until her death. I have no doubt of some mean white man being the cause of the trouble; (if so) what a pity he had not been black.

I hope this may find you restored to health and on the brink of starting over to see us. May is nearly gone, but I am convinced you will come if you possibly can be spared from home. Your mentioning the sweet little children causes my heart to ache. Dearly do I love them and long to see them all again. I received a letter from my dear Frances of late. She is happy in her situation and has the same goodness that she ever had. I wish you could bring her to see me.

I am glad you are pleased with the drafts that I forwarded to N. Orleans. You will find all correct when you see the papers now in my hands for that purpose. They are dunning me for the taxes, but I have put them off a short time by telling them you are to be here this month. *Do say how I must act.* I had to write to N. Orleans for some pork. It has not had time to get here yet. I only wrote 3 or 4 days ago. Mr. Germany says that he hopes to need fifteen pieces of cotton bagging, ten coils of cordage, and fifteen pounds of sewing twine to bale up the cotton this year. He wishes it to be strong. It answers much better. The cordage was not strong last year. I am glad to find you have so promising a crop on the island. You really have good luck. God grant it may continue.

I hope that Mr. Stinson may continue long with the children. So good a man may be of much service to them. Why does my sister forget to write to me? She knows that her letters are prized by me. When she remains silent so long, I become alarmed and afraid she is sick. My kindest love to her and the children. Much happiness attend you all. Your most affectionate friend,

R. O'Connor

P.S. I had like to forgot to inform you that the crop looks very well, only the severe rains are against the cotton. Excuse all mistakes. It is two o'clock at night.

Rachel writes Mary of recent events, including the punishment of Mrs. Bowman's slave woman, while she muses on the thirty-nine years since she and Hercules founded Evergreen plantation.

June 5th, 1836

My dear sister,

I received your kind letter of the 13th of last month some time since and was much gratified. From you not writing of late, I became afraid something had befallen you and that you did not wish me to know of it. However I am happy now. Your thrice welcome letter has cured me of all my fears. Most sincerely do I return thanks to God for the safety of our beloved little Charles. Poor little boy might have been lost in an instant from so dangerous a fall had not kind providence protected him in time of danger. Your suffering on his account were as great as his. I have been a mother. I know their feelings and how to pity their distresses.

I should have written ere this had I not written shortly previous to its arrival to your brother and mentioned the unfortunate circumstance that had fallen to poor Mrs. Bowman's lot and wished the trial to be over so that I could inform you the rest. I expected the girl to be hung without a doubt and so did every other person that heard and saw how she had acted, but Mrs. Bowman pleaded so hard for the girl's life to be spared and to let her be punished in some other say, that in mercy to the poor woman's feelings, they done so, at least she thinks so, and shipped her for N. Orleans to be confined for life, either in the dungeon or put to the ball and chain. Mrs. Bowman looks bad yet.

I have not seen either of the girls for a long time. Clarissa sent word yesterday that she would be here on Wednesday next and stay some time. Charlotte and Julia Ann are so engaged in raising chickens that they think of little else. Robert goes to school to old Mr. Murray, the same teacher that taught his father and mother and his uncles and aunts on both sides of the house for two or three years while small. They are much attached to the poor old man and treat him as a father. I have just received a letter from Harriet Handy. They are highly pleased with their situation. Harriet says she never felt better satisfied and happy that at present. They are settled on the Washita near Monroe. It is said to be a fine country. James Flower has bought their old plantation at 22-$ pr. acre. My dear Frances writes often to me and never fails to mention being well satisfied and pleased with the good treatment she receives from her friends and teachers, which shows that she has a good heart and is very sensible.

The crop bids fair to be very good and I hope may. I am sorry that your brother could not come, or that he did not come when at Baton Rouge last. Mr. Hail now asks eight thousand dollars for his plantation, but I expected him to raise the price when he learned its value, and said so long since, but it will be all the same in less than a hundred years from this.

This day, thirty-nine years ago, we moved our *little all* to this place. I have been very serious all day trying to call to my memory every act, thought, word, and deed during the thirty-nine years past; and ask forgiveness for all faults; and pray for a blessing for the time to come and try by every means to deserve it in my power. We came to this place in 1797. It is wonderful to think over all the misfortunes that I have lived through since that date and still fear death.

The measles, mumps, and whooping cough continues in the neighborhood and has been for a length of time, but we have not had it yet. The Negroes are all well at this time and going on with work finely. Mr. Germany is a good manager and conducts well. I was so much afflicted during the winter and spring with the rheumatism that I could not attend to my garden as I had intended. I have very little more than will do the plantation *at home*, but I continue to hope to do better. My health is pretty good at present, and if I can only keep so, I shall endeavour to have a good fall garden. My neighbors laugh when they see my garden. They know that it is not long since they have had the chance—but in all my troubles, I have not neglected anything else, and feel as anxious to do for the best as I ever did, for which I am truly thankful (because I think it right to be so that all may prove just when time is no more). I am sorry for Dr. Smith. I hope in God he may yet be restored to good health and enjoy many happy years in his family. I love the man for his kindness to me and should be happy to have it in my power to serve him. I shall remember during life his kindnesses *to you all*. Often do I recollect the dear little children standing by him and sincerely did I pray for them. In your next please inform me how by dear little Harriet's head is—whether it keeps well or not.

It is needless to say how much I wish to see you all. Your own feelings are sufficient to let your know. I hope your brother may come soon. I should be glad to see him, but I am afraid of being too troublesome to him. I wish him to see my papers to convince all parties that all is just and right that I have done. If not, it is caused through some unknown mistake.

Mrs. Bowman's carriage is now in sight. I must conclude. May every blessing attend you and yours.

R. O'Connor

Rachel recollects with pleasure a visit from David's children and maintains her interest in plantation affairs, especially her gardening; but she dwells increasingly upon death. In this letter to Mary, she philosophizes on the death of her former overseer Simpson Patrick.

July 26th, 1836

My dear sister,

I have not written as soon as I intended. When your brother and the children left me here, Julia Ann came down shortly after, and brought Stephen Doherty (Charlotte's youngest son) which caused me to delay some time, and weather being so warm, I found it almost impossible to do anything.

In the first instance, I must return you my sincere and grateful thanks for letting the children come to see me. I had hoped for the favor, but scarcely expected you to venture the distance unless you could undertake the journey with them. I have not heard from anyone of you since Mr. Conrad left St. Francis Ville, but I hope all is well and soon to receive a letter.

In the next place, I must let you know how thankful I feel for the presents you so kindly sent by your little son, which I value for both your sakes. I felt sorry at the first that I had no way of carrying them about to see their relations. It appeared to me that I had never thought of needing such a convenience for anyone before. Perhaps if Mrs. Bowman had been at home, I could have done better; but still I do not know. I am so fearful of becoming a trouble to my friends that I scarcely dare ask favors that I feel convinced of being made welcome to.

My dear Francis continues the same good quiet well disposed person as ever. I could not observe the smallest change, only that of being a little larger and more experienced, and my dear Alfred in the same way. He is a fine light hearted little boy. I wish he may never see any trouble to lower his spirits, but live and die happy.

You have no idea how sorry I feel when I think of parting with them without having the smallest gift to bestow them and perhaps may not live to see them again. But I never go anywhere to see things that would please children, so that is out of my power. When they become older, they will consider that part. I hope and pray that it may not discourage the other children from coming and their dear mother also. If I could meet with a little white pony, I should nearly be tempted to steal it for my dear Charley, if I could not obtain it otherwise. Do please to let my dear William come when an opportunity offers. And if you should come this fall, as I hope you may, you will bring my dear little Harriet and David. I want to see you all. I don't know which I feel most anxious to see.

I have received two letters from Mrs. Bowman since she left home, the last written in Louisville. She appeared to be getting on very well. I hope she is at her journey's end ere this. Patrick oversaw one of her plantations and had managed very well. This was the second year. She will feel greatly at a loss when she hears of his death. He died on Thursday last, the 21st instant. I am sorry about him myself. He was a greater enemy to his own soul than to any other. I hope the all merciful God may forgive and pardon him.

Dr. Pope died the 2nd of this month and Mrs. Brau about the same time at Pointe Coupee, and Mr. B. House, our former postmaster, fell overboard on his way from New Orleans and was drown not long since.

Please to show this letter to your brother Alfred and request of him to look on it as written to you both. I will write to him ere long. I have received the rice and fish that I knew of his sending for to the city with a fine box of raisins and another of cordial that I had not thought of his sending for. I am truly thankful to him. I hope kind providence may reward his goodness.

Mr. Germany is doing very well. He will commence pulling fodder next week. The Negroes are middling healthy. Bridget, the woman that had a child the 21st of February, 1835, while I was at your house, was delivered of another on the 28th of June and both doing well. She has at this time five living children that were born in less than seven years—and herself only a few months over 22 years old. Poor body. I really pity her to have them so fast. I expect another one to be confined very soon, that never has had one born alive and only one born dead 2 or 3 years ago, that is nearly 27 years old.

If you could see the old house yard, you would be pleased with the appearance it makes at this time. The crape myrtle trees are in full bloom, perfectly red, and many other flowers, trees, and shrubs. I don't think it ever looked so pretty before. I pray that there may not come a storm of wind and blow down all the beauty that I so dearly love—as it happened once before when I admired it greatly. Indeed I must acknowledge that I blame my own vanity for the storm being sent to destroy my pride, or rather vain glory. But I hope I have better feelings on the present occasion. I know that I deserve no part of the praise. All belongs to my *God*, the bestower of all good.

My love to the children and best respects to Mr. Conrad, with many kind wishes to my best of sisters. I remain, and hope ever shall, your affectionate and grateful sister,

R. O'Connor

In your next, please to let me know how Dr. Smith is. I hope in God he may be recovered.

Sometime previous to this letter there had been a misunderstanding about plantation management contained in a letter from Alfred Conrad. Upon receipt of the letter, Rachel makes a soul-searching review

L E T T E R S

*of her conduct before penning this spirited reply in which she la-
ments the misunderstanding.*

July 30th, 1836

My dear friend,

Yours of the 20th instant has just been handed me. I am sorry to
learn the sickness amongst your Negroes which I hope may not last
long and that they may all be restored to their former good health. I
am thankful to learn the good health of the family which I pray may
continue.

I shall write to Mr. Hail as you direct, but I do not know
whether he is at home or not. However I don't expect he is far off.

The appearance of a renewal of old and grievous afflictions has
almost distracted me. Never did I feel more humbled than I do at
the present moment. God is my witness that I wish to act right.
Since the arrival of your letter I have walked the garden with
uplifted hands in fervent prayer to my God, laying my situation before him who knows all things, and on my knees with face to the
floor asked his assistance praying to be directed the way that is right;
and more, my dearly beloved friend, I must ask yourself and my
sister to consider my unfortunate disposition, which my dearly beloved brother was well aware of, and could have informed you that,
to separate me from this plantation and the slaves on it would cause
the remainder of my days to pass off in deep sorrow. If I could only
be as many others in the world are, I would willingly sign anything
you think proper; but as it is, and to change the affair from what it
was in the commencement, would be in a manner consenting to my
own misery and wretchedness. Not that I should either judge yourself
or my beloved sister of even having a desire to make the smallest
change. But in a short time my nieces may marry and perhaps their
husbands might not have that feeling for me, that they in justice
ought to have. I am at this period in my sixty-third year of age, and
according to the course of nature, shall not be a trouble to my
friends much longer and must pray to them to bear the will of providence patiently that blessings may follow in return. I am alone in the
world. My mother's children are all gone before me. I have none to
ask advice of. Neither have I ask any. At the time you mentioned
the signing of a new writing, and I gave my reasons for not wishing
to sign it, you asked me if I had seen Mr. Turner lately and I
answered truth in saying that I had not. The last time that I was at

203

his house, my brother David was with me, and I saw him at Mr. Bowman's burying, and once after that on business of Mrs. Bowman's, but I did not mention business or ask one question, nor was asked any by him whatever more than how do, and farewell.

I have several letters from my brother, one in particular written at sea, giving me very serious advice which I wish to follow as near as possible. My reasons for making the request some time ago of having the property returned into my hands again was owing to an idea formed by myself of your being discontented in some way with my management from which I concluded to make the offer, but applied to none but my sister and yourself on the business. I never thought any more on the subject since I received your answer. You should feel sensible of my wanting to act right. You know I retained no papers against the estate, but carried them with me and endorsed them; and anything I had, I bestowed it to him previously, which his letters could convince you if you doubt my word.

You will (no doubt) find yourself disgusted with the acknowledgment I make of the attachment I feel toward those Negroes on this place, but I do not see that I could be otherwise after the care that I have taken to raise them and the blessings the Lord of Heaven and earth bestowed in causing them to prosper under my care.

The Negroes has been quite sickly of late. Charity's three little yellow girls all lay sick at one time. Dr. Denny gave the youngest out, but it is better. The other two are sick still, but I hope not dangerous. Seven of the field hands were laid up the greater part of this week; a part are on the mend. Wm. S. Swayze sent here this morning for Dr. Denny. His wife lay extremely ill. The Dr. has not returned yet. I fear she may be very sick.

Several has died of late. Mr. B. House, Dr. Pope, Patrick that overseed for me, and Mrs. Brau died at Point Coupee, and others that were strangers to me living in St. Francis Ville.

Mr. Germany has been dreadfully tormented with the toothache. His face is much swelled and I fear it will break.

The corn is middling good. I suffered some time for rain, but nothing when compared with Mr. A. Doherty's unfortunate luck. I have not heard of his getting any rain yet. Cotton appears pretty promising so far.

My dear little Alfred forgot his walking cane and knife when he left here. I have laid them away for him. The millet that you ordered Mr. Doherty to buy for me answers an excellent purpose, for

which I return you many thanks and for a box of raisins and another
of sirup and a keg of salmon, one of rice and one of mackerel, all of
which I hope may assist to pave your way to Heaven amongst the
ever blessed. I had to give a draft in favor of Mr. K. Dunbar for 59
dollars to pay for 70 barrels of corn and one barrel of flour.

My love to my sister and the children. Your most affectionate
friend,

Rachel O'Connor

*The ever present topics of the weather, the crops, and the prevalence
of sickness dominate this letter to Mary.*

Oct-br 2nd, 1836

My dear sister,

I have not written for a long time. I have been sick and not able
to do anything until with a few days past I began to attend to my
business as usual.

The Negroes has been uncommonly sickly, 12 or 13 laid up at
once with severe fevers. Mrs. Germany and one of her children lay
very sick for a long time. The child is yet very low. The mother
begins to set up some.

Mrs. Bowman's people has suffered greatly from sickness. Seven
small ones has *died* since she went from home. I think she has lost
22 or 23 Negroes by death since the time I started over to see you
last. *I am sorry for my dear friend.* Her troubles are great. I pray
God may support her under the many severe trials that fall to her
lot. I received several letters from her, the last dated the 22nd of
August. She had arrived safe amongst her friends in Browns Ville,
Penn., where she and her little ones are yet. But as soon as the
water rises, I shall expect her home. I have not been able to write
to her as I expected or as I intended.

Mr. Davis had a severe spell of fever. Clarissa has escaped so far.
Mr. Doherty, Charlotte, and Julia Ann are well and their youngest
son has also been well, but poor little Robert has had the ague and
fever. Where is Frances? I have not heard from her since she left
here. Sometimes I conclude you have taken her home. James Flower

has been very sick. You have no idea how sickly it has been for a
month or six weeks past and many has died, particularly Negroes.
Dr. Denny has got a good practice. I hope he may yet do pretty
well.

In the next boat I shall send some bales of cotton to market. I
can't say the number. There is 23 pressed and some more to press. I
fear the crop will prove small this year owing to the continual rains.
Even the corn don't turn out as it did last year. I have got two new
chimneys built very lately which proves extremely good. I hope to
have a pleasanter time of it in that respect than I have had for years
back. I gave a draft to the brick layer for putting up the chimneys
for forty-two dollars, dated the 24th of Sept-br. One of the chimneys
is double. I had to get two thousand and five hundred new brick
from Mrs. Bowman before she left home which are to be paid for
yet. I do not know what her charge will be.

Please remember me most affectionately to your brother. I have
long expected him to come, but as Mr. Hail has changed his mind
respecting his farm, I suppose he scarcely will find the time to spare.
My love to the children and much to yourself. May you all enjoy
health and happiness are the prayers of your unfortunate sister,

Rachel O'Connor

*Rachel's illness and her other troubles cause a lapse of nine months
in her letter writing. A visit from Mary had comforted her. In this
letter to Frances Weeks, hard times (which in later years were
known as the "panic of 1837") strike a telling blow against Rachel,
now sixty-four years of age and in poor health.*

June 29, 1837

My dear niece,

Your kind favor of the 10th instant came to hand long since,
which would have been answered ere this if I had been able to
write. I have had the fever, but am now better and about again. I
have much to attend to. The little Negroes have the whooping
cough, and a part of them very sick. Dr. Denny gave medicine to

seven of them this morning. I hope they may all live and get well again.

Your Cousin Charlotte has a fine daughter and named her for its Aunt Julia Ann. Mr. Davis and Clarissa has gone to live on the plantation where their Negroes are making a crop and I see them but seldom. I am glad to find by your letter that you think of coming to see me. You are young and have nothing to prevent you. If it was possible for me to visit your dear and good mama and yourself, with your brothers and sister, it would afford me joy indeed. But I am far advanced in life and not able to travel. I ventured a trip to see your Cousin Charlotte while confined, which caused me a spell of the fever. I expected it, as I seldom fail if I go from home.

I have got some fringe nearly like the other which answers the purpose very well. Your uncle mentioned in his letter previous to yours, that none of the same pattern could be found. I am truly thankful to you (my dear child) for the trouble you have taken and for the two pretty baskets you sent me by your mama. I received a letter from your brother Alfred saying they were all well. I hope your mama may have good health and be long spared to her children whom she dotes on, and that they may all prove a blessing to her.

All the news we have is of the hard times. I never knew the complaint so general before. The rich appears to be as much distressed as the poor and *all* in want.

We have had a fine rain which was greatly needed. Many crops had begun to die from the long dry weather. I wish your Uncle Frank and his lady great joy. And I hope that their time may be long and happy and that their lifetime may prove a continual honeymoon with all blessings added.

In your next do let me know whether your mama found Charlotte or not. I am surprised at the ungrateful girl. Some of the little ones are coughing dreadfully. I must go to them. May kind providence forever bless you, my darling child, are the prayers of your affectionate aunt,

Rachel O'Connor

Rachel's grave illness causes another lapse of nine months in her letter writing. Duty compels her to render an account of plantation

affairs to Alfred Conrad, in which she relates the sad news that little Isaac has died, and that the overseer Jacob Germany had left her at the end of the previous year.

March 28th, 1838

Dear Sir,

I have this moment received and read your letter of the 25th instant. The molasses and armed chair came safe for which I return many thanks and will see that Charlotte gets a barrel of sugar out of the hogshead agreeable to my sister's request.

This is the third attempt that I have made to write for better than six months past and still my hand trembles like a leaf in the wind with weakness and can only write a few lines at a time.

On the 22nd of September last I lost my little Isaac, and I have not enjoyed a day of health since, though I am rather on the mend. I sincerely hope and pray that his little spirit is at rest, and that mine may join in like manner whenever it should be the will of providence to call me from this earth.

Germany left here at the end of last year. He did well, but became dissatisfied. I gave him a draft and sent him off. I am now doing very well.

The old gin house came near falling ere the last was ginned and I have two first rate carpenters building another. They have it raised and will commence covering it shortly. The gin is worn out also. I shall have to get another by the time the cotton is raised. Timber is very scarce. Mr. Hambleton gave me some, and the rest I had to buy, particularly the shingles and a part of the plank and some plank for my dwelling house which it needed to make it comfortable, all of which I employed Mr. K. Dunbar to buy for me. I am aware of the times being hard, and do not spend money, only for provisions and for the good of the plantation which I consider my duty for the short time I have to live.

Clarissa has written several times during my illness, the last to yourself about the first of this month, but I never received any answer which I thought very strange. She has a fine son born on Christmas Day.

Charlotte has been dangerously ill with liver complaint, but I hope she may recover again. Tell my sister and the children that it has been out of my power to write and is nearly so yet, which you can see by this. My love to them all and I do sincerely pray that the blessings of God may ever remain with them and that they may be prepared to meet their Saviour and God whenever his call may come. I wish you health and happiness and *all other blessings* here and hereafter.

Rachel O'Connor

P.S. I had to write Lambeth and Thompson for some articles. Those men being here at work caused me to need them earlier than usual. The sugar, I shall not need.

Ten months elapse before Rachel writes another letter. More and more her letters express resignation to the tribulations of this world and a longing for the blessings of the next. She warns nineteen year old Frances Weeks to be prepared for impending death.

Jan-ry 9th, 1839

My dear niece,

Since your last (from N. Orleans) I have written once to your mama and intended to have written to yourself ere this, but somehow have not done so until now I have undertaken to do so.

The weather has been so very cold that I scarcely could do anything. It is warm now and pleasant which raises a desire in me to move about and to try to do something again. My garden needs my attention. I had only one paper of the peas that you sent me planted the next day after they arrived. They are beginning to come up. I intent to sow some of the other seeds shortly. The pigeons are doing extremely well at this time. One of them has laid two eggs which I have put under a pigeon in the pigeon house. Those that you sent me are yet in the cage. I am afraid to put them with the others fearing they may drive them away. I have a large cage belonging to Mrs. Bowman that I keep them in as yet, but intend to have a large box fixed on a high pole for themselves so that they may have a little home of their own in which I hope that they may do well. They are so beautiful and so greatly admired that I should consider the loss of one, or more, of them greater than you can possible think. And more than even that, they keep you all ever in my memory, so that in praying for myself, I pray for you all.

And this morning I had more good luck. Charity has just been delivered of a fine daughter and is likely to do well for which I return many thanks to kind providence.

Mr. Davis has moved his people to his newly purchased plantation about 16 miles from here. Clarissa is at her brother William's at this time, but I expect she will go home shortly. Their little son is really a fine child. Charlotte is at home as well as can be expected. I have not seen her for some time and I can't expect her to come before April or May. Her little ones are all well. Julia Ann is in good health, but she seldom leaves her sister, to whom she is greatly attached; and great reason she has, for Charlotte is indeed a kind sister. She is like a mother to all her family. Your Uncle H. Flower and family are all in fine health. He has very lately received letters from his daughters, Maria and Harriet. They were well also. Mrs. Bowman and her children are in New Orleans.

I hope this may find you all safe at home enjoying all blessings and now and then some serious thoughts on the hereafter. Death must come and we know not the time. I need not ask you to be a comfort to your dear widowed mother. Your own goodness will teach you that obedience to parents is the only promise in the ten commandments of a long life, and if a parent ever experiences anything heavenly on earth, it is from dutiful children.

Forgive me, my beloved. It is love for you that guides my pen, not fear. I know you to be a good child and a happiness to all your relations. And sincerely do I pray that your brothers and sister may prove equally as good and that such goodness may guide you all, step by step, to that place of happiness where all sorrow ends. My love to your mama and your uncle and your brothers and sister, with much to yourself. I remain your most affectionate aunt,

Rachel O'Connor

Rachel is surprised to learn from Alfred Conrad that Mary is prolonging a visit with relatives and friends at New Orleans.

Jan-ry 13th, 1839

My dear sister,

Last evening I received a very friendly letter from your brother Alfred dated the 4th of this month. It brought the good news of his being in good health and all doing well in his affairs, but I was surprised to learn from it that you were not at home. I thought from the way that Frances wrote (or at least I understood it so) that you intended to start homeward instantly. Yet I blame myself for not being aware of your relations and friends prevailing on you to remain some time in the city with them as you had been gone from them so long. I feel almost as guilty as if I had acted wrong, and been unfeeling enough to neglect writing after I knew you had arrived in New Orleans. Indeed, my dear and only sister, I pray that you may not have ideas of that kind. I wrote the same night that I received my dear Frances' letter with the cage that contained the two pair of beautiful pigeons and a bundle of garden seeds which all came safe. The pigeons are doing finely. One has laid two eggs since they came. They are a show in the neighborhood. More people comes to see them than comes to see me which I delight in showing.

In my letter to you that I directed to New Iberia, you will find all the particulars. Perhaps yourself and the children may have started homeward before this. Your brother is on the lookout in every boat that arrives, or passes, with anxious expectations. I wrote to Frances a few days since; but directed it, as I did yours, to the Attakapas. Your brother has not mentioned the arrival of either, but I hope you may find them laid away for you. When I know where or to what place to direct my letters, I will write to Wm. and Alfred. They must not think I have forgotten them or any of you. Many hours have I laid awake and thought about you all while all others could sleep undisturbed. But I consider myself greatly rewarded in your safe return. I must write to your brother instantly. Should you continue any length of time in the city, do write to me which will let me know where you are and where to direct my letters, after which I shall be more particular to inform all particulars. My love to the children, not forgetting yourself. Your ever affectionate sister,

Rachel O'Connor

Rachel expresses the hope that Alfred Conrad will receive great reward both in Heaven and on earth for his goodness to her.

Jan-ry 16th, 1839

Dear Sir,

Three days ago I received your kind favor of the 4th instant for which my feelings of gratitude are more than I can find words to express. I sincerely hope that you may have great reward, both in Heaven and on earth, for all your kindness to me. You have received much, but none by me, much less by *Him* who sees and remembers all good acts and will surely repay you ten fold.

I have received the bottle of deaf medicine pr. Mr. Dunbar and am using it. I do not know that my hearing is any better, but my head is much relieved by it.

The sugar and molasses and the syrup that you sent are all come. The hogshead of sugar and barrel of syrup and two barrels of molasses were hauled home yesterday and the team has gone for more today. All come very safe. I shall not need any sugar next year should I live that time. What I have in the house at present will be a plenty for two years. I return many thanks for the syrup and all the rest.

Frances informed me of their safe arrival in New Orleans, and from the way she mentioned it, I understood from her that they intended to start home immediately, from which I wrote to my sister the same night and directed my letter to the Attakapas, and sometime after I wrote to Frances and directed it, as I did the other, but as soon as I found by your letter that they were yet in the city, I wrote to my sister again informing her of my mistake. She must have thought very strange of me after I'd heard they had come and not to write to her. I hope they may get home safe and then I shall make no mistake in directing.

I have all my papers in a bundle to show every part of business transacted since I saw you last. I was glad that you recollected to mention your two youngest sisters with their little children and that they are doing so well. From an early acquaintance with them, I have ever felt an interest in their welfare through life. Poor Mrs. Palfrey has experienced the feeling of deep sorrow by the loss of two children, which is common in this life. We have nothing else to expect. Mrs. Harding has had better luck. I hope it may last long.

I wrote to yourself some time ago, but as you did not mention it, I am afraid it never reached you, or perhaps its being so long, you had not taken time to read it yet. I cannot at all times write long letters, but I got so started when I wrote you last that I did not know when to stop.

My health is as good as I could expect, but I keep weak until of late. As soon as I recovered my health, my strength would return also, which I am very sorry to say is not the case now. All our friends over here are well. It is a general time of health. I do not know of one person being sick in the neighborhood. Joseph E. Johnson died the 22nd of December. I was told that more than three hundred persons attended his burying at Judge Dawson's.

Remember me to your sisters when you see them. Please to inform me when my sister returns home so that I may make no more mistakes in directing hereafter. I remain as ever your affectionate and grateful friend,

Rachel O'Connor

Jacob Germany, the former overseer who had left Rachel's service, became gravely ill on a visit to Evergreen Plantation. Rachel fills a letter to Frances Weeks with this news and optimistic plans for the coming year.

March 22, 1839

My dear Frances,

It has been so long since I have written to you that I feel at a loss how to begin. I received your last long since, but have been poorly several times—once for 8 or 10 days had a most painful time with the toothache. I am pretty well again now; but have so many changes, and so often, that I only think for the moment and not even dare to guess how my health may be on the morrow and try to live each day not knowing but it may be the last.

I have not seen Clarissa for more than two months. I hear of their being well and that their little boy grows finely, but has not begun to walk yet. I expect Charlotte has her babe by this time, but I have not heard whether or not. Otherwise they are all well. Her little daughter continues very pretty.

I have had such bad luck of late that I feel no heart to write. One pair of my beautiful pigeons died. I did not know anything was the matter with them until the white one fell dead on the ground. I sent up to see if the others were sick and found her mate nearly dead. They had one young one; but, being so young, it died also. I think they had eat something wrong that killed them. The other pair are well yet. They are setting. I hope they may do better than the others. My other pigeons are doing finely.

The Negroes are well excepting one woman who is poorly. I have three fine little ones born since the 17th of Nov-br. Poor Fanny is about yet. I expect her to be confined hourly. I think if that was over with, I should feel better contented. The plantation is in fine order—nearly all the corn planted and the cotton ground nearly all ready to plant. I hope and pray that a blessing may attend our work and that it may afford every satisfaction to all concerned.

Poor Germany is here very sick. They had moved to Jackson and he came here on a visit and has not been able to return home since and I am afraid he never will, he is so low. He can only walk a few steps at a time. Yesterday and today he has not walked any, and I fear the worst constantly. Mrs. Bowman has employed Dr. McKelvey to attend him at her own expense.

I have just got my new kitchen so that I can go into it. The old one had fallen down several weeks ago. I had to get brick from Dr. Bains for the chimney and Mr. Cook put it up for me. My garden looks very well. All the seed you sent me are growing excepting the beans and I will plant some of them soon. I am trying to do some good again. I feel better and sleep more comfortable after I have worked a while in the garden and attended to my other business as usual. I have got new pickets all round my garden. The rabbits cannot destroy it so bad now as formerly.

Remember me most affectionately to your mama. I often think of writing her, but my heart gets full and I pass it off by thinking about her. Tell all your brothers how dearly I love them and your sister Harriet also. Nearly every night I think of you all and pray that your journey through life may be happy and pleasant and that hereafter may be forever blessed.

My best respects to your uncle. I hope he may be fortunate in building the sugar house. Now, my beloved child, I must conclude for this time. I wish you every happiness and length of days and that you may continue a blessing to your good and well beloved mother through life. I remain your affectionate aunt,

R. O'Connor

LETTERS

In a letter to Frances Weeks, Rachel grieves for many deaths, including those of Mary's sister and Jacob Germany. Rachel again warns her young niece of the certainty of death and the need to be prepared.

April 21, 1839

My dear niece,

I received your letter last evening and felt great sorrow in reading over the *loss* and troubles you all had experienced. We little know the love we have for each other until finally separated during time; and whether we shall ever meet in an everlasting eternity or not is not for us to know during our stay on earth, but the hope of meeting our dearly beloved friends hereafter saves us from despair. I should not have expected (had I thought of such a thing) that the death of your aunt could have had such an effect on me as it really had. I thought of her and her little ones, and poor little Charley's dreadful attack and narrow escape, and the distresses of your dear mother, and you all, until I could find no rest during the night. Should I get into a doze, some disturbed dream would alarm and cause me to awake and to return to my former sorrowful reflections. I felt thankful to see daylight appear so that I might arise and walk about. I hope and pray that my dear little Charley may be spared and recover his former good health. My dear, dear children, one and all of you, consider the uncertainty of life and the certainty of death and try to be prepared to meet the awful call. Pray for yourselves and pray for me. The prayers of the good will not be refused. He that knowth all hearts will have mercy on us. He remembers we are but dust and will accept a sincere and contrite heart. Do all in your power to comfort your beloved mother. It will prove a blessing and joyful thought through life. Pardon the liberty I take. Did I not love you, I should not venture to write as I do. I am convinced of your love for each other. You always agree so well. Heaven is all love and mutual love is bringing heaven down to earth.

In my last I mentioned Mr. Germany being here very sick. He continued to get weaker even on until the night of the 24th of March at which time he died. He has left four poor little children; the eldest will be five years old the 2nd day of August next. Their mother is in low health.

Your Cousin Charlotte has a young daughter and is about again. Julia Ann has gone to Alexandria, Rapide, to see her old friends that live there. Clarissa is at her new home. I have not seen her since they moved home, which is more than three months. Wm. Swayze was here yesterday who informed me about his sisters. They are all well and doing their best to raise a crop. Mrs. Bowman and children are in good health. I am quite well myself and doing wonderfully. Poor Germany appeared surprised to see me doing better without him than with him. His state of health was too low to dissemble.

Fan had a son on the 18th instant and both doing well, which is four little babies born since the 17th of November last and all very well. A dreadful disease has been amongst the Negroes this spring. When it first came here we thought it to be the mumps. Their face and jaws swelled very much, but in a short time they were swelled from head to foot and had violent fevers. All are pretty well again but Julia, a mother of one of the young babes. Her child was born on 31st of Jan-ry and she had been in the field at work two weeks when attacked with this disease. We despaired of her recovery some time, but she is on the mend slowly. Her milk dried away so much that the others had to let her child suck and we feed it some. In this disease they lose the use of their limbs and cannot walk. Poor little Celeste was so badly swelled that I was afraid her skin would burst. I had to have her carried about in their arms. She appears stiff yet, but can walk.

Mr. McKoon has just left here. He lives in Jackson. He says that two brothers were living together in Jackson; one being drunk got angry with the other and shot seven buckshot into his heart, who died instantly. They have the other in jail. They are young men from Ireland and have five single sisters and several more brothers. Our world is filled with trouble.

My love to you all. You all have part in this letter. I have thought on every one of you in writing it, but you are so good in writing to me, I must direct it to yourself. You can see by the writing that my hand is very tired. My other pair of pigeons are well. They have set once, but their eggs rotted. They are setting again. I expect there are 100 pair of the others. It is beautiful to see them flying. I am, as ever, your most affectionate aunt,

Rachel O'Connor

In spite of the prolonged drought that has ruined her crops, in this letter to Frances Weeks, Rachel reiterates her faith in God's mercy to provide for her and her dependents as always.

June 4, 1839

My dear niece,

I received your more than kind letter of the 24th of May. I had indeed great uneasiness fearing some new distresses had happened; that through grief you were unable to write, when I opened a little book that had been laying on the table at the time I wrote my last to you in which lay my letter, sealed and directed, where I suppose I had laid it myself, but really thought I had sent it to the post office pr. George. You must have thought it strange to find it dated so far back. I concluded it the surest way to convince you that I had written when I had ought, and then unravel the mystery in my next, which I am endeavouring to do at present. The troubles you all had experienced, and the sincere sorrow I felt at the time I looked over your letter in order to answer it, caused me not to recollect any more about my letter until on opening the book, by mere accident, it fell out.

I am very thankful to learn that my dear little Charley is about again and able to attend school and that his little brother goes with him. I shall receive their letters with much joy should I be spared to see them arrive. If they are as good as their sister Frances has ever been, they will surely write. She fails not, let her be where she will.

We are all in great trouble throughout the neighborhood. As far as I have heard, we have not had any rain, more than a few drops at a time, 2 or 3 times, for more than three months. All the corn everywhere is ruined and the cotton looks bad. God only knows how we shall make out. My greatest comfort is trusting in his mercy. He has ever provided for me. I will not despair.

Your Cousin Charlotte's little babe is very pretty and the other continues as you saw it, but it cannot talk any yet. They talk of naming the babe either Rachel or Mary, but I have not heard which name they have given it. I have been so unfortunate through life that I should be afraid to have it named for me; still I had not ought to complain. My God has bestowed more mercies to me than I deserve.

Julia Ann has returned from the Red River, but I have not seen her since. During her absence, Mr. Doherty came in his carriage for me and I went home with him and stayed four days and then he brought me home again. I seldom see Clarissa. She has only come to see me once since they moved home. Her little son was a fine child then. Melinda and Wm. comes to see me oftener than any of them. She often asks about you. Their little ones all go to school.

The strange disease that came amongst the Negroes has disappeared. I thought that three had it here, but Dr. Denny says only two, and that the other was caused by cold. We had to make large poultices with corn meal and water, with saltpeter in it until the swelling left them. But all was guess work, for indeed we did not know what to do for it.

Give my love to your brothers and sister Harriet. The three eldest are growing large and will soon be grown. I hope they pray for themselves and me. I hope and pray that your good and kind mother may spend her days happy and contented in her beloved family. My kindest love to her. I think of writing to her often, but old age is so against me that I write but seldom.

My garden is all dried up; nearly all my flowers are dead.

I have got my house so well mended up and repaired it would surprise you to see it and a new frame kitchen built and the house yard railed in new timber, very comfortable.

Are you not coming to see me once more, my beloved children? I hope your mama will come also. Your ever affectionate aunt,

Rachel O'Connor

My pretty pigeons has hatched one little one since the other pair died. They have been setting again and I hope they have hatched, but I do not let anyone open the door of their little house so as to discover whether they will do better or not.

My beloved friend and neighbor, Mrs. Eliza Bowman, continues all kindness as usual. My God shows great mercies in bestowing me so faithful a friend.

A lapse of six months occurs before Rachel's next letter to Frances. She excuses this delay by relating a series of calamities. Yet, despite drought and sickness, she markets 130 bales of cotton.

Dec-br 2nd, 1839

My dear niece,

It has been so long since I have written to you that I feel guilty and scarcely can undertake to excuse what must appear to you like neglect. But after you know all, I hope to be forgiven.

In the first instance, I was quite unwell myself and several of the field hands were laid up, and on the 19th of Oct-br, old Mrs. Marbury came from Jackson to see me intending to stay a week or two. I never saw her in better spirits. The next morning, the 20th, as she was walking the gallery, through some mis-step, she fell out on the ground which broke her thigh bone, and only lived 13 days after. During her illness the house was continually full of her relations, which nearly tired me down. However kind providence gave me strength to be about to the end, for which I return many thanks. Had she lived until April next, should would have been eighty years of age. She was truly respectable and her death greatly lamented. I had been acquainted with her for more than forty years.

Shortly after the sorrow began to wear off, two strange men were passing in the night. One of their horses fell and broke the rider's leg. He was brought to the house in great pain. Dr. Denny set the bone, but the next evening his friends came for him. He was a son of old Dr. Lattimore who formerly lived in Natchez.

Poor Fan's little babe lays very sick. I much fear it will not recover. I was up with it last night. I never knew a child seven months to stand so much pain. I keep it in my room day and night to have every care taken of it while it lives. Dr. Denny thinks there is some hopes this morning. I am sorry for the child and sorry for its poor young mother.

I have been telling you much bad news and could tell much more (but not just at home). The yellow fever has been very bad in St. Francis Ville. More than eighty people died in that small place, and since it became healthy a man by the name of Hiram Grover stabbed Peter Jones several times near the heart, who died fifteen minutes after. Grover has stood his trial and gone clear, from its being made out he done it in self defense.

Your cousins are all well. I hear from them occasionally, but seldom see them. Mr. Davis stayed here on Saturday night last. Otherwise I have not seen any of them for three months, excepting Wm. Swayze and his wife. They come often.

I have sent 130 bales of cotton to New Orleans and have some picked and some yet to gather out of the field. The cotton crop holds out better than I expected. How it has done so well without any rain I cannot say. But corn is scarce. I shall have to buy until corn comes in again next year. I have taken what the Negroes raised; theirs being planted late done better than mine. Several horses died this year. I have bought four fine mules and a first rate riding horse—very gentle, all together cost seven hundred and forty dollars. And I expect I shall have to buy another pair of mules when plough-ing time comes to try for another crop should I live to do so. I really needed a horse to ride over the plantation and I think this one truly good and gentle. I have got Wm. Swayze to take him home and ride him awhile for the purpose of finding out whether he is really gentle or not. He is much pleased with the horse and takes good care of him.

In your next do inform me how your dear mama's health is. I am always thinking of her and praying she may live to see you all raised. She will be happy amongst her dutiful children and them with her. I am sorry for the loss of your two beloved aunts. Their be-loved little ones has lost their best friend, but we must trust in God who never fails to be a father to the orphan.

I often call you all to mind and, fearing that trouble or old age might cause forgetfullness, I keep your presents in view to assist my memory. My little nun is greatly coveted, but I have it still.

Give my kindest love to your dear mama and uncle and all your brothers and your sister Harriet, and accept much to yourself. I re-main your affectionate aunt,

Rachel O'Connor

I can assure you that it is long since I wrote as much before. I am quite surprised at my long letter.

Editor's note: The Nun mentioned near the close of this letter is a species of pigeon that has a veil of feathers almost covering its head.

Another six months pass before Rachel takes pen in hand to answer a letter recently received from her sixteen-year-old niece Harriet

LETTERS

Weeks. The letters received from David's and Mary's children are a source of comfort to Rachel.

May 23, 1840

My dear niece,

I received your last six days ago. It had been twenty days on its way. I do not know what detained it so long on its journey. I received one from your sister dated the 17th, and one from your brother Alfred dated the 14th of this month, today. They were all in good health. I have every hope that your brothers are in a good place. I do not know the Rev. Dr. Lacey, but am very well acquainted with the Rev. Mr. Ranney and believe him to be a good man. I sincerely hope they may benefit by being with them.

I am pretty well in health at this time, but the dry weather is much against the crops and my garden is all dried up. And all the new things that I begged about the neighborhood are dead, the drought has been so long and severe. There is not but very little in my flower garden; all are dried up.

The white fan tailed pigeon has hatched one little one and has raised it so that it can fly about. It is very pretty. She has two other younger, should they live. And the one that your sister and brothers brought me last has hatched two very pretty young ones which can nearly fly now and I expect she is setting again, is all the good news I have. I have just been answering your brother Alfred's letter.

My love to your mama, sister, and brothers. I will write to your sister after I rest awhile. Your affectionate aunt,

Rachel O'Connor

William and Alfred Weeks are attending boarding school at Baton Rouge. In reply to a letter from her fifteen-year-old nephew William, Rachel gives a detailed account of the fantail pigeons, a gift from the Weeks family. She invites William and his fourteen-year-old brother, Alfred, to accompany their tutor, the Reverend Mr. Raney, when he visits her during the summer.

June 15, 1840

My dear nephew,

I had the pleasure of receiving a very affectionate letter from you some time ago which I must acknowledge has been too long without being answered. I have been poorly several times since and there has been much sickness amongst the Negroes. Two little ones has died since you were here. My troubles still continues and I suppose will during life.

I was truly glad to learn from your letter that yourself and your dear brother Alfred were both enjoying good health and doing so well and that you intended to be so good in every other respect. You have every opportunity of obtaining the best advice. I know that my beloved friend (Mr. Ranney) will assist you in every part that is necessary for you to learn. I sincerely pray that his company may prove an everlasting blessing to yourself and your brother. I hope to see him in August, and that the good account he may bring of you both may cause my heart to overflow with joy.

We all have to die. The young may be taken unexpectedly. The old are aware of their time being short, according to the course of nature. Can you not accompany Mr. Ranney when he comes? I should be glad to see you and Alfred with him.

The crop is doing very well. The weather has been very dry. I feel quite uneasy about the corn. Your spotted pigeon has raised two fine young ones, more red than herself. They are flying all about, and has set and hatched again. She had one hatched yesterday and perhaps the other egg may hatch today. The white pigeon has one young pigeon as large as herself and did hatch another, but I do not know whether it lived or not. They are like the other white pigeons. Their tails are not much longer than the others. I can only know them when I see them flying with the mother.

My kindest love to my dear Alfred and yourself. May every blessing attend you, my beloved children, here and hereafter are the sincere prayers of your most affectionate aunt,

Rachel O'Connor

Please remember me most affectionately to Mr. Ranney—R.O'C.

On the same day as her letter to William, Rachel writes to Frances lamenting the ills of those on her plantation and throughout her small Feliciana world.

June 15, 1840

My dear Frances,

I have neglected answering your letter too long. It has been troubles that caused me not to write ere this. I have been unwell several times myself of late and the Negroes has been sickly. A great misfortune happened the 17th of May. Leven had taken a gun out to kill a wild turkey and had come in and was standing with the gun pointing to the ground which accidently went off and hit the earth and the shot bounced from the ground and hit three of the little ones. Two has recovered and one died. It was three years old the 17th of March, a fine healthy little girl. Charity has lost her babe, about fourteen months old. It had been sickly from its birth. Such troubles never fail to lay me up. A *death* and a burying lays me low.

I have written to your brothers since and mentioned two deaths, but did not tell them of one being shot. I have written to Wm. today. I am acquainted with the Rev. Mr. Ranney, who is one of their teachers and think him a fine man and a sincere Christian, and hope the boys may benefit greatly by his good advice. They are both pleased with him and always mention him in their letters to me. Heaven bless the dear children for their kind attention to me.

My garden is all dried up. It seldom rains. Corn cannot grow without rain. Cotton will do better, but it is small. Mr. Doherty's family has been very sickly for a long time, both black and white. A number of children have suffered with bowel complaints this season and many have died. It has been very troublesome amongst our little ones. It is hard to cure.

The railroad car has turned over nor far from Jackson, which has crippled many and killed some, about 40 in all.

Mrs. Bowman expects to start on Wednesday next for Browns Ville, Penn. to see Mr. B's parents. She takes her three children with her. I wish her a safe trip.

My kindest love to your dear mama and her children. Your ever affectionate aunt,

Rachel O'Connor

Field work comes to a halt during the warm days of early September as Rachel nurses the sick and buries the dead. She bears with

fortitude the deaths of five of her slaves during the spring and sum-
mer months, but pours out her grief to Mary over the death of her
faithful slave overseer, Leven.

Sept-br 4, 1840

My dear sister,

I have not written to you for a long time. I have often intended
doing so, but writing to the children to answer their letters has
caused my neglect. But now I feel in duty bound to inform you my
troubles and misfortunes. This year has proved a sad one to me indeed.

Jan-ry 26th, Ellen, 22 years old died; Amy, 3 years, shot by accident; Henrietta, one year old died June 3rd; Old Sam died July 6th.
All those above mentioned I bore with great fortitude. But now my
heart is nearly broke. I have lost poor Leven, one of the most faithful black man ever lived. He was truth and honesty and without a
fault that I ever discovered. He overseed the plantation nearly three
years and done much better than any white man ever done here and
I lived a quiet life. He died August 27th early in the night and his
little daughter, Clarissa, the latter part of the same night. Both are
buried together. No pen can tell you the distress I feel. I hope the
lord may be merciful to me, otherwise I must sink with grief. There
has been from 10 to 16 laid up for two months past. One girl about
14 years old lays speechless now for 7 or 8 days past. We hope she
is rather on the mend, but cannot talk or walk. Eben has been very
low. He can walk and that is all, and 8 or 9 others sick. Nancy and
Celeste has been at the point of death, but are recovering fast.

My dear sister, you can form an idea from what I have written
what my sufferings are. But after all you cannot know all, neither
can I describe all, but it is bad, bad indeed. Mrs. Bowman has lost
several. And the last time that I heard from Dr. Ira Smith, that out
of 148 field hands, he had only 14 able to work. Wm. Swayze has
lost one man and has one woman laying at the point of death and a
child also. He has been sick himself and his oldest son has been very
low. He comes to see me as often as he can be spared from home
and is really kind. Charlotte and Julia Ann has been very sick. Charlotte is not able to set up yet, the other is about again. The children
has been sick, the oldest daughter despaired of for a long time, but
she is recovering. Clarissa is in the family way again and is afraid to

venture down in this warm weather. Otherwise she would have been here to assist me.

Poor Leven left a promising crop. I have set Arthur to oversee. If the hands ever get able to work, I will try to have it gathered in.

Please to tell my dear Harriet that I have received her letter and will answer it when my mind gets more at rest, also one from my dear Alfred written in Franklin. The children are good, but it has not been in my power to return their goodness. But I hope I will should I be spared. My love to them all. I pray that God will be kind to you and that you may be spared from sickness and other distresses. Excuse all mistakes. I have written in a great hurry, amongst my calls from the sick ones. Pray for me, my beloved sister; pray the Lord to have mercy on me.

I remain your affectionate sister,

Rachel O'Connor

Do write and let me know how you are.

Numerous deaths and her constant concern for the welfare of her slaves bears heavily on Rachel's mind. She writes Frances that a requested visit from the Reverend Mr. Lewis, rector of Grace Episcopal Church, brings comfort to her burdened heart.

October 2, 1840

My dear niece,

I have received your letter dated the 14th of Sept-br, but the others that you mentioned has never come. A few days previous to the arrival of your last, I had written your mama informing her my distresses; but receiving no answer, I fear it has been lost or mislaid by the postmaster. This year has been dreadfully unfortunate so far. I feel broken hearted and can find no rest. Since the 26th of Jan-ry last, seven Negroes has died on this plantation. Poor little Willis died since I wrote to your mama, and six before, which I mentioned to her. The girl that I mentioned being speechless has got better and can talk a little and walk a few steps. I hope she may recover again. Eben has been very sick for three months, a part of the time not able to walk. He appears to be mending a little. Ginny has been much in the same way ever since Jan-ry. She is a little better now. Dave, Littleton, and Frank are all sick. They were taken very ill last week. Their fever has not been so severe today as before. There has been as many as seventeen confined to their beds at one time. Some died, and others are about again.

In my great troubles, I sent for the Rev. Mr. Lewis and requested him to pray for me. He came and promised to come again. I have felt better reconciled to my fate since and hope to bear all patiently as I had ought to do.

Wm. Swayze has lost two of his Negroes with the fever and many are sick. When I heard from Mr. Doherty's last, all were sick, black and white. Mr. Boone has lost one of his daughters a few days ago. She was taken sick at sunset, and died at 10 o'clock that night. Mr. Hargadine has had three of his Negroes die. Mr. Hanbleton has lost some, but I don't know how many. They are dying all around the neighborhood. Scarcely any place escapes.

It is a general time of distress. The worms has destroyed the cotton very much on many plantations and the storms has been equally as bad. But kind providence has most mercifully spared this place. Neither has been here yet. Mr. Doherty's crop has been severely injured by both; Mr. Davis' also, and many others. I am trying to get the cotton gathered, but sickness is much against it. I had to stop the gin so that the cotton might not be lost in the field. I have got 25 bales pressed. As soon as I get five more pressed, I will forward them to the city. So much wet weather is much against the corn. I shall have to buy what corn the Negroes has raised this year again.

I will write to your sister soon. She must excuse me. I would have written to her long ere this if I could have guided my pen. My heart was so sore that I had not the power to do so.

My kindest love to your dear mama, your brothers, and sister, and all other friends, if any, I have. I hope you all continue to enjoy good health. Kiss my dear Charley and David for me.

Your ever affectionate aunt,
Rachel O'Connor

In your next, please to let me know how old Sam and John are. Patience wishes to hear from her son very much since his poor old father died. And Sam's children keep asking about their father, more than usual since they lost their oldest brother Leven. He was everything to them—one of the best boys on earth; none more faithful and perfectly honest. My loss is great indeed.

*Two weeks later Rachel has more bad news. The worms are destroy-
ing much of the late cotton and wet weather delays the picking.
Rachel still laments the death of Leven. She writes to Mary late at
night so that she may shed her tears in privacy.*

October 16, 1840

My dear sister,

I received your kind and affectionate letter the same day that I
sent one directed to my dear Frances which caused me not to write
to you immediately, still hoping for something better to inform you
of.

The people are very sickly yet in many places. Mr. Blunt, who
lives near to Mr. A. Doherty's, had seven Negroes die in the course
of a few days, and in many other places the poor creatures die off
dreadfully. None of ours had died since poor little Willis who I mentioned in my letter to Frances. But they are very sickly yet; five are
confined to their beds with violent fevers, and several others just
beginning to get about again. I never had so many sick ones to
attend on at one time in all my days before. I feel heart broken at
the loss of Leven. I never knew so good a black man. I think that I
may say with safety, he was without a fault. All my neighbors say
the same, and lament my loss. I have not been sick since he died,
but I find myself much weaker and so discouraged that my time
passes sorrowfully. It is late at night. I cannot write to you without
crying my heart gets so full, and in the night I can be alone.

Arthur oversees the hands since Leven died and is doing as well as
could be expected considering the sickness of the Negroes. Sometimes
there are not more than 8 or 10 in the field. I keep all picking
cotton that is able. Only in wet weather the gin is running. If I can
get the cotton picked it can be ginned at any time. I have thirty-five
bales pressed and about 30 more picked that is not ginned yet. The
worms began about the middle of last month and in a few days eat
every leaf off the cotton bushes, and all the young bolls. If nothing
had befallen us this year we should have had the best crop by far
that ever was made on this plantation. And now I cannot say how it
will be. God only knows. We must trust in him and all will be
right.

Mr. Doherty's family are very sick. Julia Ann looks badly. She has
lost two of her Negroes. Our parish is everywhere in distress. Clar-

227

issa is far advanced in the family way. She expects to be confined in Jan-ry.

Give my love to all the children. I hope they will pray for their old afflicted aunt. And you, my dear sister, I hope and pray may never experience the severe trials that has befallen to my lot. You have seen trouble, but you still have six children to comfort you. Poor me has none. Excuse my bad writing and all mistakes. Much love to you, my only sister. May the blessings of God remain with you and yours are the prayers of your affectionate sister,

Rachel O'Connor

Louise Flower and Mr. Collins are to be married next month, so report says, which is all I know.

Rachel forgets her own health in her anxious concern for her sick slaves and friends. But despite sickness, wet weather, and caterpillers, she records pleasure in events such as Clarissa's small son kneeling to lisp his prayers.

Nov-br 28, 1840

My dear sister,

I much fear something has happened to you or the children from its being so long since I have received a letter from any of your family. I am never clear of trouble; yet in the midst of it, I can think of you and when I know you are happy, my heart rejoices in your happiness. But at present I feel distressed and uneasy until I hear from you.

I have not laid up one day for 8 or 9 months past and am constantly nursing sick Negroes. There has not been one day past for several months that there has not been more or less very sick. Two are sick now. On the 26th of last month little Sam died. He was seven years old on the 13th. O, my dear sister, no pen can convey to you my distresses. The loss of my little ones, with *Leven*, has nearly broken my heart. Mrs. Bowman has had 9 to die this summer and fall which don't appear to cost her a thought. Why cannot I be so? John Gray, who lives a short distance from here, buried three young men just grown in one day last week. As he did not own many slaves, it will nearly break him up. All around me are in distress at the loss of so many of their Negroes. A great many of the white people has died also.

Clarissa came down to see me last week and stayed ten days. She expects to be confined in Jan-ry. Her little son is a charming child indeed. Charlotte has been badly hurt by being thrown from a horse. He run away with her and she fell to the ground. What a mercy it is that she was not killed. Her four little ones and Julia Ann looks badly. It is thought by Dr. Denny that her liver is affected and that she ought to travel to regain health. But she don't appear to pay the least attention to his advice on the subject.

Wm. Swayze was here today. His health is very good and his children are all well, but his wife is very poorly and has been for some time past. I am sorry about her. She is a most lovely woman. Wm. and his wife are very kind to me.

It is reported that Louisa Flower and a Mr. Collins were married on Thursday, the 26th, but I am not certain of its being true. I have not heard it from any of the family.

Has William and Alfred returned to school? I have not heard from them for a long time. Your own letter is the last I have received. I should write oftener were it not for my troubles. For indeed there are times that I cannot write, particularly to you who are so near the heart.

I have sent fifty bales of cotton to Messrs. Lambeth and Thompson, New Orleans, and have 25 more pressed which I will send as soon as it can be hauled to the landing. I hope there will be as many bales as there were last year, although the caterpillers did destroy a number of cotton bolls. They were in the field when you wrote to me about it, but the death of the Negroes caused me not to know it for some time after.

My love to all the children. Tell my little sons, Charlie and David, to be good boys and to pray to God for themselves and me. Little James Davis has learned his prayers and on his little knees says them every night. Much, much love to you, my dearly beloved sister. May the Lord bless you and yours are the prayers of your affectionate sister,

Rachel O'Connor

As 1840 draws to a close, Rachel writes sixteen-year-old Harriet Weeks that the year has been a sorrowful one for her and her neighbors, but that a short time will place them all together in a better world. She cautions Harriet to be loving to her mother and to thank God for sparing Mary to care for her children.

Dec-br 11, 1840

My dear niece,

Your very welcome letter of the 8th of Nov-br only came to hand on the 8th or 9th of this month from which it must have been a month (at least) on its journey to this place. I was truly glad to hear from you all and that you enjoyed good health, but the unfortunate dance that caused your sister to be taken so ill must have been alarming and the danger very great indeed. I hope it may cause you both to be more cautious for the time to come.

Your Cousin Louisa Flower and Mr. Collins were married more than two weeks ago and are gone. They started on a journey the next day after they were married in the church at St. Francis Ville, but I did not know of it for some time after. Your Cousins James and William are well. Sidney lives so far away that I see him but seldom. David is in Jackson at school. Mr. A. Doherty's family has been quite sickly this summer and fall. He was very sick, but fortunately it did not last long. Your Cousin Charlotte has had several severe attacks at different times this year, the last one caused by a fall from her horse. She is so unfortunate. Their children are very sickly also. And your Cousin Julia Ann's health is far from being good. Mr. Davis and Clarissa and their son are quite well. They have not had near as much sickness in their family as the rest of us. My own health has been good, but the Negroes has been dreadfully sickly. This year has been a sorrowful one to me and to many others near about here. But a short time will place us all together in another, and I hope a better, world.

Be very kind and loving to your dear mama. She is your best earthly friend. Remember, return thanks often to God for sparing her to you. My kindest love to her and your sister and little brothers. Your brother Alfred has written to me since their return to Baton Rouge. Your brothers are both well and I expect quite happy.

May all and every blessing attend you, my darling child, are the prayers of your affectionate aunt,

Rachel O'Connor

LETTERS

Harriet Weeks, who is prolonging her stay with cousins at St. Mar-
tinville, writes regularly to her aunt. Rachel appreciates the atten-
tion of her young relatives and answers faithfully. She apologized
that her letters are now brief as she can no longer see well enough
to write lengthy letters by candlelight.

Feb-ry 17, 1841

My dear niece,

I received yours of the 31st of last month the evening before last.
I am always glad to hear from you, but must not complain of your
not writing often, as I let too much time pass without writing myself. My will is good, but I cannot write now as I used to do, by
candle light, and I have so much to look after all day that I scarcely
can spare the time to write. You are all young now and know very
little of the troubles of the world. You can at any time spare the
time to write if other amusements do not crowd to prevent. Youth is
the time to enjoy life. After that passes off and the cares of the
world commences, we see very little but distresses.

Poor me, I see my part. I have been on the lookout for better
than five weeks every hour expecting to hear of your Cousin Clarissa's confinement, but she is about yet. I am so uneasy about her that
I cannot say whether I am sick or not, for I do not think I know.
Her sisters has been expecting to be sent for and prepared to start at
the moment's warning for such a length of time that I much fear
their fatigue of mind may lay them up. If I thought it was possible
for me to stand the journey, Mr. Doherty and Charlotte would come
and take me to Mr. Davis', but I am afraid I should not live to
come home again. My good and comfortable old *home* is so precious
to me that when my time comes, it is my desire to die here. Others
might not think as I do, but no other place could be a home for me
at this age. Often do I return my grateful thanks to my God and
good friends for my pleasant comforts of life which are much greater
than I deserve. But it is the mercy of God to bestow it to me.

I spent a pleasant time with your good brothers while they remained with me. Your brother Alfred has written me since their
return to Baton Rouge. He was formerly considered wild, but I now
think him a most gentle and charming youth. I was a little poorly
while they were here, and I felt surprised to find them so attentive
to me as they were. They have grown very much and continue to
grow prettier. I am almost glad that your mama thinks of taking

them to the North to finish their education, fearing they might fall
into bad company in La. I know but little about Baton Rouge, but I
fear Jackson will cause many a mother the heartache. There is a
number of good people living there and as many far from being so
good.

The roads are so wet and muddy that a horse can scarcely travel.
Nothing else attempts it. All the people agree in saying they never
knew so much wet and rainy weather. Julia Ann's tiny sewing girl
lays extremely low; that is, if she is alive. She was expected to die
the day before yesterday.

I have not got all the cotton pressed yet. I hope it may hold out
to make a hundred and forty bales, which is more than I expected
after the worms came and destroyed it as they did and the sickness
and deaths made it worse.

My love to your dear mama and your sister Frances and your two
little brothers, Charley and David. As every I remain your affectionate aunt,

Rachel O'Connor

I write this to you all, for if my poor Clarissa should meet bad luck,
or not recover it may be long ere I shall be able to write again, if
ever.

*On a rainy March night, Rachel sits and writes by candlelight a
melancholy letter to Frances. In the only cheerful portions, she mentions a good cotton crop and praises the conduct of her nephews
Alfred and William Weeks.*

March 10, 1841

My dear niece,

I received your letter some days ago. I don't know the cause of
letters being so long on their way as they generally are now.

I am glad you all enjoy such good health. Many are sick in our
parish. Your cousins Charlotte and Julia Ann are in bad health and
look bad. They do not lay up, but are fallen away very much. I feel
uneasy about them. Poor Clarissa's little daughter was born the 21st
of Feb-ry and died the 28th of the same month. I am very sorry for

her and Mr. Davis. They lament their loss greatly. I have only seen him since. Clarissa is not able to come down here yet. Their little son is well.

I often feel poorly of late. The weather is so uncommonly wet. It rains every day or two so that the ground is all in a slop. The roads are so bad that the people seldom travel in a carriage. They say that it is even hard to ride on horseback. I am sorry to inform you that I had no flowers in my little garden. Some few shrubs bore seed without any care being taken. The hands were so sickly and died so fast that I never had time to work in the garden. Perhaps I may do better this summer with flower seed. If so, I will save you some, if I should have any plants to save from. Mrs. Bowman has given me some flower seed which I have planted some time ago, but they have not come up yet. I bought a few previous to that. Some of them are growing. I sent to get some of the same for you, but they were all sold.

The crop of cotton amounted to 135 bales. The worms done much harm and the sickness caused much to be lost in the fields. I always have the seed of the cotton that is ginned last saved to plant.

My garden looks bad. The rains caused the seed to rot in the ground and sometimes after they begin to grow.

You wish to know how your brother Alfred conducted himself when last here. I am at a loss for words to bestow praises equal to his goodness. I entertain no fear of his not being amongst the best. And since his return to school, he has written twice to me. Alfred is very young to have so much good sense. Your brothers are both good and I hope may be a blessing to us all. I rejoice in the happiness of your dear mama having a family of such amiable children.

I am writing by candlelight. I am afraid you cannot make it out it is written so bad. Remember me most affectionately to your dear mama, and your sister Harriet, and your two little brothers Charlie and David. I remain as ever your most affectionate aunt,

R. O'Connor

Late at night by a dim lamp, Rachel writes a brief letter to Harriet Weeks. Having no overseer except the slave Arthur, Rachel has

many demands upon her time and cannot often indulge in letter writing. Old Sam, a slave whom David had removed from Rachel's plantation ten years earlier, has been returned to Evergreen Plantation and is reunited with his children much to everyone's joy.

April 12, 1841

My beloved niece,

I received your letter several days ago and have intended to answer it every day since, but something continually happens to prevent. I am so busy all day that I scarcely get time to write and when night comes I feel so tired that I have to lay down to rest and so fall into a sleep. I have no overseer but Arthur and have many things to attend to which keeps me very busy. The crop is nearly all planted and the work going on very well. I sincerely pray for a blessing to attend it.

Old Sam Brock has arrived safe. The poor old man mourns the death of his son Leven and his daughter that died last year. Otherwise his joy would have no bounds. I felt much overcome at seeing him and his children meet. George has been sick five of six weeks. He is very low. I am afraid he cannot recover. He can scarcely walk he is so very weak. The others are well.

Mrs. Bowman is in New Orleans, and I expect married ere this to a Mr. Lyons. God only knows whether it may add to her happiness or not, but I sincerely pray that it may.

Does your mama intend going to the North this year with her children or continue at home? Last year was so sickly with us that I live in constant dread of something happening. If a child cries, I am afraid it is sick; and if sick, I am sure it is going to die. I will trust in my God and do the best I can. Six babies were born on the place last year which are yet alive and very well. And Old Sam thinks the place greatly improved since he left here ten years ago. I felt pleased that anyone, even him, thought I had done justice through the help of my God.

My darling child, it is late at night and my lamp is getting dim. I must conclude for this time. I hope to be better hereafter. Your ever affectionate aunt,

R. O'Connor

LETTERS

Twenty-one-year-old Frances Weeks has been lately wed to young Augustin S. Magill and, in accordance with the custom of the time, is making a series of bridal visits. Rachel urges Frances and her new husband to pay their promised visit soon.

Dec-br 17, 1841

My dear niece,

I received a letter from you about the first of this month saying you expected to be here at that time. But as you have not come, I begin to fear some of you are sick. You mentioned in your last that your dear mama had long been troubled with a bowel complaint, but that she had mended much after her return home, from which I hope she may be perfectly restored to her usual good health ere this time. If not, the enclosed receipt is considered a sure cure for that disease. I hope she will try it as it is directed to be taken. I just procured it from Dr. Denny who has long used it in that disease.

If your mama is sick, or any other in the family, do write and let me know. I had written to you near the same date of your last and directed it to Nova Iberia, Attakapas, which I hope you have received long since. I am poorly so often that I am seldom able to write. I have been pretty well for the last three days, otherwise I cannot say when I have been able to be about before.

I am still expecting yourself and Mr. Magill every day. The weather is so cold that I can scarcely make out to write at this time. When you write to your dear brothers, do let them know that it is sickness that prevents me from writing to them and not willful neglect. You must excuse my short letter. The cold weather and weakness together prevents me from writing more at this time. My love to all our dear friends. I remain as ever your ever affectionate aunt,

Rachel O'Connor

A second marriage has taken place in the Weeks family before Rachel writes again. David's widow, Mary, has wed Judge John C. Moore, a prominent planter and politician of the Attakapa area. Rachel's "guardian angel" (Alfred Conrad) has resigned the business

management of Evergreen Plantation in favor of Frances's young husband, A. S. Magill. Magill attempts a systematic reorganization of Rachel's plantation affairs. Rachel tactfully asks Mary to intercede for her.

May 23, 1842

My dear sister,

I had intended writing to you ere this, but being so often unwell and much to attend to at all times often causes me to let more time slip off than I wished or intended, which is really the case now.

I am very poorly and have been so since Saturday last with a very bad bowel complaint which is very common (at this time) all over the parish. Mr. Hargadine, a near neighbor of mine, lays at the point of death and several of his family are quite sick with it. Also some of our Negroes have the same disease, but not dangerously ill yet. One woman has been laid up four days, quite sick, but the Dr. thinks she is rather on the mend this evening.

I was so surprised to receive a letter a few days ago from Mr. A. S. Magill, dated the 28th of March last. The postmark was Fort Adams, Mississippi, April 10th. I am at a loss to know what could have detained it so long on its way here.

The price of corn has begun to rise, being in great demand. I concluded it to be best to give a draft on Messers. Lambeth Thompson and Co. for three hundred dollars which I paid for the corn. And after that I wrote to them for iron and a barrel of tar for the use of the plantation, which could not be done without unless I sent the work to a shop from home which would cost ten times as much as at home where I hire a blacksmith at two dollars pr. day. He belongs to Mr. Bains. They send the iron and tar which is all that I have written for as yet. Mr. Magill directs me to apply to Messrs. Follain Belloq and Delos. I have not written for any provisions for the Negroes yet. I wish Mr. Magill would order twenty barrels of good Miss. pork to be sent to the care of Mr. I. Holmes at the Bayou Sara landing for the use of this place and direct how the freight is to be paid, which must be paid as the articles are delivered. And I must have six sacks of salt. The stock must be salted. And after a short time the bagging and cordage and sewing twine will have to be procured, and cloth for the Negroes' winter clothing. I should like to have the cloth sent before the weather gets very cold so that I may get my part of the work done when I am able to work. The cold weather causes me to have pains in my bones and joints from which I have to pick my time and get along by degrees as I am able. Perhaps there may be medicine needed this summer; I do not know.

I have workmen making a new press; the old one being worn out before the cotton was done pressing. I really am as saving in every respect as I know how to be. When my account will be called for by the great giver of all good, I hope to be found faithful in all things, as far as I know. I have the place in fine order—good outhouses, all new. All the old ones are rotting down and I had to get new ones built. The Dr. that was called in to assist Dr. Denny during my last illness last July and August charged sixty-one dollars and I had to give him a draft on Messrs. Lambeth Thompson and Co. for that amount which is the most, or nearly all, that I cost the estate last year myself. Very little will do me and I shall not need that little long.

I have been called on for the state and parish taxes which amount to one hundred and nineteen dollars and ninety-six cents in all, for which I gave a draft on Messrs. Fallain Belloq and Delos which I hope they will settle. I forgot to mention a keg of nails that I sent for with the iron and tar.

Your sons William and Alfred are well. I received a letter from my dear, dear Alfred dated the 4th instant. His letter is so affectionate that tears of joy roll down freely whenever I read it. He speaks of living with me, should I be spared until he returns home, which is my most earnest prayer. On many accounts, the boys has a faithful friend in a widow lady who I hope may be long remembered by them. She is a sincere Christian and is taking great pains to make the road to heaven plain to them.

My beloved Alfred writes a beautiful letter and truly affectionate. I am surprised that he feels so much love for me. All my earthly happiness is in him. He is in my thoughts day and night. He is a sweet youth and I hope very pious. It is out of my power to say how dearly I love him. He mentions his sister Harriet—that she was well and perfectly contented and that she wrote to him often.

I hope this may find Mr. Magill and my dear Frances and their little son enjoying good health. I long to see you all again. I expect my dear Charlie and David are nearly grown. My kindest love to them and to you all. When any of you write to me, let me know the babe's name and how all your healths are. Should the Judge be at home, remember me most affectionately to him.

Poor Clarissa has got through her troubles pretty well and is more loving and kind to me than she ever was. She spends one week in every month with me and sometimes more. Their small son is a fine child. Mr. Davis is very industrious and I hope may meet the payments of the land that they live on. After that they will be very comfortable again.

My dear sister, I hope and pray that this may find yourself and family all well and happy. Don't let the hard times distress you. Trust in God and there is no danger. Your affectionate sister,

Rachel O'Connor

If I must send the cotton to any others, please to tell Mr. Magill to write to Messrs. L-T and Co. and inform them his reasons for causing me to leave them. Their friendships are dear to me.

In a blunt, but conciliatory, letter to Frances's husband, Rachel reiterates the terms of the transfer of her property to David and demands that Magill adhere to those terms.

June 4, 1842

Dear Sir,

I have been called on for the amount of the taxes, being $119.96, for which I gave a draft on the merchants that you directed me to apply to for the expenses of the plantation, which you will see by the enclosed letter has been protested, which I am afraid will cause me some trouble unless you order it paid instantly.

Your last letter being so long on its way here that I become alarmed fearing I might be disappointed in getting the corn which caused me to write to Messrs. Lambeth and Thompson and request the favor of them to accept a draft from me for the amount the corn might come to, which they done, and also sent me some iron and a barrel of tar which I wrote to them for, which is all that I have sent for as yet. I have not sent for one barrel of pork for the Negroes to live on, or anything else toward their support, which you know is not doing either them or myself justice. However I am willing to do almost any way for *peace* sake. But it is out of all reason to expect a crop to be raised without provisions to feed the Negroes on. As for myself, I can make less do me than most any other person living, were it not for the people saying so much about it, all knowing that I have, and still do, serve out my days faithfully and had ought to have a peaceful and quiet life now in my old days.

Since I have a draft for the taxes, I wrote a long letter to my sister (Mrs. Moore) which I hope you have received and opened, as it would explain all respecting the expenses of the farm and afford every satisfaction to you all. I was at that time poorly, but have been very sick since—not able to rise from my bed without assistance, but I feel better and hope to recover my health again.

Please write to me as soon as you get this and let me know what I must do to run through the year (*should I live that long*). Times are hard with me now and I live in trouble day and night. I hope after my time on earth is over, I shall be taken to a happier world where all sorrows end. If you do not wish me to send the cotton to Messrs. Lambeth and Thompson after it is ready for market, you must write to me to that effect, so that I may excuse myself to them. They have been extremely kind to me, for which I am ever ready and willing to acknowledge the gratitude I feel for past kindnesses. My trials in life has been very great, which has learned me the value of a *friend*. Whoever I send the cotton to must consider themselves bound to send me such necessaries as I write to them for, and to pay any drafts that I may draw on them to enable me to carry on the farm. Otherwise my liberties would be less than a common overseer. Besides, I have in my brother's own handwriting acknowledging that I am justly entitled to anything that I may want for myself or for the use of the plantation during my life, out of what is raised here with me on the place. And I really think his heirs should feel a pleasure in fulfilling their good father's desires.

During my sickness I received a letter from my dear Frances saying that she had named her little son David Weeks. I am much pleased with the name. It is the name it had ought to have, and I hope all blessings may attend it. I am quite weak, but as soon as I am able, I will answer her kind letter. My kindest love to her and yourself and you both must kiss my little David Weeks for me. I should be glad to see you and him. Your ever affectionate aunt,

Rachel O'Connor

*The day following her letter to Magill, Rachel writes a loving letter
to Frances urging her to persuade her new husband to amend his
orders. In the letter Rachel also refers sarcastically to the former
Mrs. Eliza Bowman's quick recovery from her inconsolable grief over
her late husband's death and her pride in her new husband and her
possessions.*

June 5th, 1842

My dear niece,

I received your kind letter dated the 22nd of May several days
ago, which I was fearful (at the time of its arrival) I should never be
able to answer, as I was laying very sick and had become so weak
that I could not rise from my bed without help. It was a bowel
complaint that brought me so low, a disease quite prevalent in our
parish for several weeks past. Numbers died of it. But thanks be to
kind providence for all his goodness to me in raising me again from
so low a state, I begin to find myself recovering fast—only extremely
weak. My own dear Clarissa was my constant nurse. She stayed with
me three weeks. She started home this morning, but intends to return
in 3 or 4 days to stay a week or two longer with me. She was
dreadfully alarmed and wanted to send for Dr. Forsythe to assist Dr.
Denny; but as I did not consent to it, she did not send for him. The
physicians charge so high with us that I was afraid to let her send
for any. They sent for Dr. Forsythe last July when I lay senseless. I
believe he done much good, but his bill came to sixty-one dollars for
which I had to give a draft on Messrs. Lambeth and Thompson, N.
Orleans. Your Cousin Clarissa tried to write to you, but she had so
much to do, and her distresses were so great that she could not. She
desired me to send her love to you and wish you joy in your dear
little son. We parted in tears this morning, but hope soon to meet
again.

I am sorry you have been so poorly since your confinement, but
hope the worse is over and that your health will be good again. I
am thankful to yourself and Mr. Magill for the name you have given
your son. When you come over to see me, you must get Mr. Lewis
to baptise your babe.

You wish to hear something of Mrs. Bowman (now Mrs. Lyons).
She is at home, sometimes, but uncommonly gay and enjoys the pleasures of this life beyond all others that I ever knew, pays several
visits (almost every day), and has 4 or 5 carriages. Sometimes they

both ride in one and at others they take one for each and ride by themselves. Their pride appears to know no bounds. I wish it may not fall. She expects to be confined in August. Don't mention in any of your letters that I have written a word about her to you.

Your Cousin Charlotte had a son born the 3rd of March last. They call him William. They were all well when I last heard from them. Your Cousin James Flower and his wife came to see me during my illness. She is really a charming sweet little woman. You will be pleased to see her.

I wrote to Mr. Magill yesterday. I am in great trouble about getting the taxes paid and getting provisions for the Negroes. Do, my dear child, prevail on Mr. Magill to arrange matters so that my drafts may not be protested. I am very willing to give an account of myself to any that may wish me to do so. If there is no danger of Messrs. Lambeth and Thompson failing, I would rather send the cotton to them, but am willing to do any way for the best and safest.

Please request of Mr. Magill to write me the moment he receives my letter, for I am distressed in mind. We have not had any rain for seven weeks. The crop is in fine order, but needs rain. I hope that your dear mama and your brothers has arrived safe and are well. Do let me know when you write.

My love to Mr. Magill and yourself. Heaven bless you and yours are the prayers of your most affectionate aunt,

Rachel O'Connor

I am very tired.

Rachel is becoming increasingly deaf but strives to accept her affliction as ordained by God for her benefit. She writes a sad but loving letter to Mary.

July 12, 1843

My dear Sister Mary,

Scarcely a day or night passes without thinking of you and your family. I often wonder you do not write. I hope you are well now. My dear Frances mentioned in her last letter that your health had improved very much from which I concluded your hand had got well and if so, do write.

My hearing is nearly lost. I find it hard to understand anything that is said. It is a great punishment, but *God's* will must be done; and I hope the time will come when I shall find that it was good for me to be afflicted. I try to feel resigned to my fate, yet it cannot be so, for I continue to lament and mourn the loss of my family and my brothers and sisters, and dream of them—my dear mother in particular. But I must not distress you with my sorrows and will say no more on that subject.

My health continues very good. I am up very early every morning attending to my business and getting along very well. I have not hired an overseer for several years and find the place much improved by not having any. It has been a strange season to raise a crop—the first part so very dry that nothing could grow, and then so wet that all appeared drown out. Yet I hope the crop will be pretty good. About a month ago my corn give out and I bought two hundred barrels at forty cents pr. barrel from Mr. Henderson, a neighbor of mine. I borrowed forty dollars and paid for one hundred barrels and gave a draft payable in October next for the other hundred barrels. The two hundred barrels came to eighty dollars which must be paid out of the first cotton sent to market.

I have had a good garden all the spring and summer and hope to have it so in the winter, or at least I will do my best. I find it a great help in feeding the little ones. It takes a great deal to feed so many children, still it is my greatest pleasure to take care of them and to see them look well. At this time they are all very well.

Last winter was so very cold that nearly one half of the stock died. It was the case throughout the neighborhood.

I am sorry to inform you of the great loss that Mr. Doherty and Charlotte met of late. On Friday, the 30th of June, their daughter Julia Ann died. She was six years old the second day of the same month that she died. Charlotte has had seven children, and only two left alive. Her eldest son and her youngest son are all that she has left. Their daughter was sick on Sunday and only lived four days. She was a beautiful child and generally very healthy. It is thought to have been worms that caused her death. Clarissa has only one child alive. So far as I know they are all well. They don't visit me often. I am so very deaf that it can be no pleasure to them to see me.

My kindest love to my dear Charles and David and my beloved Frances and her sweet babe. My best respects to the Judge and Mr. Magill and much, much love to yourself. I remain your very affectionate and ever grateful sister,

Rachel O'Connor

If you do not write the disappointment will be very great indeed.

In this letter Rachel is full of her usual busy plans for harvesting the plantation crops. The slave Arthur has again become overseer, and Rachel compliments him and Dr. Denny for their services. In a letter reminiscent of her old style, she writes Mary telling of the purchase of a new cotton gin, recommending an unusual treatment for Mary's sore hand, lamenting a steamboat disaster, reiterating her esteem for Judge Moore, and urging Charles and David never to forget their duty to him.

Sept-br 19th, 1843

My dear sister,

I have received your kind and affectionate letter of the 23rd of August long since. I should have answered it much sooner had I been able. I have been sick and am just beginning to recover so that I can attend to my business once more. It has been dreadful sickly throughout our neighborhood. Many has died both white and black. None of ours had died yet, but several has been despaired of. But the disease took a favorable turn and some has got able to work a little and others are recovering.

Dr. Denny has done a good part by the sick ones this year. I feel truly grateful to him for the attention he bestowed them. In my distress a part of the time I was not able to see that they were taken care of. Arthur was only sick a few days from which he was able to look after them and take care of the farm. He has behaved himself extremely well and manages as well as any of their white overseers with a driver to wait on them. The corn is pretty good and the cotton equal to any of the best farmers.

I have to get a new gin. I expect it every day. It is called Butler's gin. He lives up on Red River. They are highly spoken of. The first cost is two hundred dollars and some other expenses attending it. I did not know that the old gin was past mending until I got a workman to examine it, which makes it late in applying for a new one. I sent for my nephews, James and William Flower, and had their advice on the subject. They are two worthy young men and can be depended on.

I am sorry for you, my dear sister, to suffer so much with your hand. Perhaps my dear Frances forgot to tell you to have a beef killed and to have the maw cut open as soon as possible and run your hand into the middle of it and keep it there until entirely cold. I think if you would try that a few times it would draw all the humour out and you would get well. However I will enclose a paper that is wrapped round little tin boxes of salve called Dalley's Magical Pain Extractor, in which I have great faith. Do try it. Your hands and all the rest of you are dear to my heart. Do try everything until you find a cure—for my sake.

I answered Judge Moore's kind letter directly, but could not explain to him the thankful feelings of my hearts. The children and yourself has long since informed me of his kindness to you all. It is no new thing to me to love him as one of my best friends. Tell my dear Charley and David they must never forget to love, honour, and obey so good a father. The others are older. They know all this themselves. Tell Frances to come over with Harriet. I want to see them together. I have a promising crop of red peppers coming on.

O, my dear sister, I was just going to thank you for writing about the molasses and bad news spoiled all. The boiler of the Steamboat Clipper burst this morning and has killed 100 people, many that lived in St. Francis Ville and one of John Dawson's family and twenty poor black slaves that their master was sending to pick cotton on the coast.

My love to you all. I remain your ever affectionate sister,

Rachel O'Connor

Just as Rachel was regaining her strength, a double tragedy befalls her in the unexpected deaths of two beloved nephews (James Flower, son of Henry and Pamela Flower, who died in young manhood, and nine year old David Weeks, Jr.). The ranks are thinning and Rachel's world is becoming smaller as she writes this letter to Judge John C. Moore, Mary's new husband.

Dec-br 22nd, 1843

Dear Sir,

In the first instance, I feel in duty bound to apologize for my long delay in answering your very friendly letter. It is a fault that I am seldom guilty of unless sickness has been the cause. I am not very well, but not laid up.

But a sore heart is a sad complaint, which is my disease at present. The loss of my two nephews has almost broke my heart. Their deaths were both unexpected and sudden, which shows the need of being prepared, which I hope they were, this fact being my greatest comfort. I have an anxious desire to hear how my dear sister is and sincerely pray that her three lovely children may prove a great comfort to her in her present distresses.

It appears very sickly throughout this neighborhood. David Johnson, Samuel Dalton, James Flower, Dr. Bains, Mr. James Turner, and Mr. Samuel McCaleb all died very lately and many others that I do not know. Indeed it appears to be a general time of mourning in our parish. I shall send this to the post office in the morning at which time I hope to receive good news from you all.

This is the first dry day we have had for two weeks past. The roads are in dreadful order. I have sent sixty-five bales of cotton to Mr. Thompson, New Orleans, and have fifteen more pressed ready to send when the roads can be travelled. This last new gin makes beautiful cotton. I have not heard anything from Mr. Butler, the man that I bought the other new gin from. Poor James Flower would have attended to that had he lived to do so, but I will do the best I can to have it returned. My nephews Wm. and Alfred can inform you the particulars respecting the gins. We are not quite done picking cotton yet.

When the children were here, and about that time I was afraid I should have to hire an overseer, but I am now doing very well and hope to do without. My deafness is much against me. The most that I can understand is by signs and nods. But I am contented and thankful that I am not worse punished. When my health is good, I can attend to my business with ease and take a pleasure in doing so. I was raised to industry, one of the greatest duties of parents.

My kindest love to my beloved sister and her children. May they live long and prosper, and yourself to whom I feel under so many obligations. If my prayers are heard, you will enjoy all blessings, now and ever, for the goodness you bestow in your family. Please to accept my best wishes for your health and happiness. Your ever grateful and affectionate friend,

Rachel O'Connor

Mary Weeks Moore and the judge are enjoying their new found happiness and often travel away from New Town for extended periods. The Weeks heirs are growing to adulthood and are looking to the future uses of their father's several properties. Frances's husband, Augustin Magill, wants to take over the management of Rachel's plantation. William Weeks informs Rachel of Magill's seeming surprise that she should object to changes.

Feb-ry 3rd, 1844

Dear William,

Your letter dated the 22nd of last month came to hand this evening and I am trying to answer it by candlelight. I am glad to hear of all your good luck and I hope it may continue, but very sorry to learn of your Uncle A. T. Conrad's bad health and other troubles. I had ought to know how to pity him from my own sad lot. Few, very few, has had the experience that I have had, and I fear it is to last until my breath is gone. After that I hope to be in better hands.

I am greatly surprised at Mr. Magill's alarm. Your poor father was perfectly pleased with all he done and with all Judge Dawson done. And from the time your father began to despair of his recovery, he strictly charged me against signing any more papers respecting that business, and after that he wrote to me to take care of myself which I will try to do. Nothing will induce me to sign another paper. I must have a home. I am too old now to go about like a wandering Jew. I never received one dollar in payment for the property. I had some notes on your father, but gave them to your mother for her children, which your Uncle Alfred saw me do. I only wanted to live. Your father willed me the property during my life, which

246

was enough for me; and after my death it belongs to his family. They have had all that I could make excepting a support that the plantation and Negroes required. You are very young, but do you really think that I should turn myself out of house and home at this age? I don't think Mr. Magill would like to see his old mother turn herself adrift in that way. But let it be as it may, I now declare that I will not sign any more papers. I cannot part from my Negroes. I have raised all but a few and I love them. They have their faults and I have mine. All living has faults. None is clear of sin. The merciful is to find mercy. I must try to be merciful and to forgive that I may hope to be forgiven.

If your poor father was alive he would not wish me to be tormented, not for ten times as much as is here. He knew too well how to make a living for his family to take any advantage of a poor old deaf widow woman. If my own dear sons can see the situation they have caused their old and friendless mother to be in, they cannot but mourn my lot.

My dear son, I sincerely pray that you may ever be happy and to know no sorrow and to be merciful to all that you may ever find mercy, now and ever. So be it.

Your affectionate aunt,
R. O'Connor

P. S. The 13th of next month, if I should live that long, I shall be seventy years of age. Have patience, I cannot be long here to be a trouble to any person. The time may come, when you think of it, you will value the peace you caused me to have more than thousands of money or moneys worth.

Tell my beloved Alfred to pray for me. I hope God will hear his prayers. I think he is a godly youth.

In her next letter to her twenty year old nephew William Weeks, Rachel regrets that her recent letter had caused him unpleasant feelings, but she assures him that when he himself reaches her own seventy years, he will see the matter in a different light.

Feb-ry 24, 1844

My dear William,

Your letter dated Feb-ry 15th is now laying before me. I received it about an hour ago. I am sorry to find that my letter, written on the 3rd instant, gave or caused you any unpleasant feelings. You will not see as you now do, should you live fifty years longer, which will bring you to the age of myself at this time. I can safely declare to you that I did not doubt your honour nor any one of your brothers' or sisters', nor your dear parents'. Your best of mothers has ever been all kindness to me, which I can assure you has not been thrown away on a careless thoughtless being. Her health and happiness are dearer to me than I have words to express or convey to you the real feelings of my heart.

But from the treatment I have received from numbers, since I arrived at the age of fifty years, has caused me to fear my own shadow. You left me as happy as I ever expected to be in this life from yourself, your brother and sister appearing to be so perfectly satisfied with all that I have done. I informed you of every circumstance *so that you would have confidence in me* which from your letter previous to this last one, I had a dread of it not having the effect I so sincerely prayed for. I had a fear of some person trying to lead your young mind astray.

As you are well aware, I have ever done all business of every kind in the name of, and for the estate of, my brother David Weeks, and not in my own. So that yourselves and all the world and all the people in the world might see that I only acted as an agent for this part (now under my care) belonging to your father's estate, which at my death belongs to his heirs, I now declare that I sold to him in my perfect senses, and with my own free will and consent, and have not since repented of doing as I most justly acknowledge I done. The same evening after the sales were made before Judge Dawson, my brother David Weeks wrote in the form of a will certifying that he left all the property that he had bought from me to me during my life, and after my death, it would be his, or his heirs, which I acknowledge to be true and just and that it is my will, and wish, it should be so, to which I add my A-men. So be it.

Now, my dear son, I have written the above with my own hand which is well known, being an old written handwriting and different from the way people write at this time, and I have much writing to do, which considering all, I think is sufficient to prove that I do not consider this property now with me, as belonging to myself, but lent to me by your dear father, and to be supported from it during my lifetime, and after my death, it belongs to his heirs.

Your affectionate aunt,
Rachel O'Connor

Feb-ry 24, 1844

My dear nephew,

I enclose to you to let you know how the affairs of the plantation are going on. In the first place the whole place is in good order and nearly ready to plant were it not too early in the season. My gardens never were as promising before Should no misfortune happen, I expect to nearly feed the little ones out of it.

I had to buy four mules at seventy-five dollars each and traded off one old mule that was of no account and gave thirty dollars into the bargain, which altogether amounted to three hundred and thirty dollars. They are fine large mules and work very well already. I have my orchard planted with better than four hundred young fruit trees. I did not think I had so many friends. The people sent me trees from all quarters until the ground was filled. It adds much to the beauty of the place. The molasses you mention is a plenty, and the sugar also, if the Negroes should not be sickly again.

Do please to not mention your cousins to me in your letters in the same way. I has a wish to set you on your guard, but not to make it a subject in writing. I have never expected anything from them but hard thoughts, nor them from me—only in the way I told you of. They are all low enough in the world and need pity, rather than otherwise. I done worse in speaking. Their necessities are greater than I knew of, but time will put all on a footing. We came from dust and must return to dust again.

Editor's note: An extant document of Rachel's (now missing from the Weeks papers) is quoted, in part, by Avery Craven in *Rachel of Old Louisiana*, pp. 100–101. It constitutes a touching appeal for the welfare of her slaves, whom she realizes soon must be entrusted to others. Craven states that Rachel followed this appeal with the names and birth dates of all her slaves. This last (which is found in the Weeks papers and included here) is dated March 15, 1844, and is followed by a note to Mary. In compiling the list, Rachel uses the abbreviation do. for ditto instead of writing the word "born" beside the name of each slave.

My dear sister:

I send to you by your son and my beloved nephew Alfred C. Weeks a list of Negroes names and the family they come of, which I pray you and your sons to take care of for my sake after I am in my grave—Charity is a yellow woman born the 25th day of December, 1812—she is the grand daughter of Old Daniel and Leah and a daughter of old yellow George and Henny. Henny was a daughter of the above Daniel and Leah, and a sister of Arthur the present driver. She has ever since her birth been a good girl but I did not know her worth until since my severe spell of sickness in July and August 1841. Since that time I trusted her in all my housekeeping affairs. In the first instance my low state of health and weakness obliged me to do so and from finding her so very honest during that time, I have continued to trust her and as yet she has not showed any wish to deceive me—I love her as a mother loves her good child—pray, pray my beloved friends don't let her and her children fall into cruel hands. She has five daughters, Viz. Nancy, Margaret, Frances, Mary, and Elizabeth and perhaps may have another in 6 or 7 months from this time; old Patience has been my cook for thirty-eight years, the only one I ever had. I expect she is now sixty years old at least, but I pray you be kind to her for the good she has done; she has five daughters. The oldest have children and grand-children. Pray do the best you can for all of old Patience's children—Eben is Fanny's husband. Harry and Songy are old Patience's sons. Songy is the best disposed and his wife Hetty is a fine girl. She was born on the 30th of July, 1828. She is a sister to Charity. Eben is truly a good man and very trusty. He was born the 26 of Janry, 1812. Arthur is a good slave and valuable, either 43 or 44 years old. We bought him with his father and mother, old Leah's youngest son. I expect his mother is nerly seventy years old and poor old Milly eighty-five or six. Please to have them taken care of, for the good they have done. They have served their time faithfully and are doing good yet. They were all born mine or here with me and raised chiefly in house with me while small.

March 15, 1844

Old Milly, about 85 or 86 years old

Old Leah, about 70 or 72

Old Patience, 60. Her daughter Pless is 42

Old Minty, 65 years old

Old Dinah, 60 years old

Arthur, about 43 years old

Eli, at least 60 years old

Mark, 50 years old

Bob, 45 years old

Mary, 47 years old

Pless, born August 29, 1802

Harriet, do, Sept-br 13, 1804

Little Milly, do, Dec-br 11, 1804

Sampson, do, Sept-br 3, 1807

Lydia, do, Sept-br 11, 1808

Caroline, do, Dec-br 14, 1809

Sarah, do, Feb-ry 11, 1810

Dave, do, Dec-br 31, 1810

Harry, do, Jan-ry 19, 1812

Eben, do, Jan-ry 26, 1812

Charity, do, December 25, 1812

Littleton, do, July 14, 1813

Genny, do, Jan-ry 7, 1814

Little Minty, born June 1, 1833

John, do, October 7, 1834

Henry, do, October 8, 1834

Little Patience, do, Feb-ry 21, 1835

Sylvia, do, July 31, 1835

Frances, do, June 6, 1837

Louisa, do, June 6, 1837

Mary Ann, do, Oct-br 29, 1837

Martha, do, Nov-br 5, 1837

Celia, do, Nov-br 17, 1838

Bridget, born Jan-ry 24, 1814

Frank, do, March 26, 1815

Joe, do, May 25, 1815

Songy, do, Jan-ry 12, 1816

Julia, do, Sept-br 19, 1817

Eliza, do, Jan-ry 11, 1818

Maria, do, June 11, 1818

Matilda, do, May 28, 1820

Amos, do, August 7, 1820

Ann, do, July 2, 1822

Peter, do, Sept-br 10, 1823

Fanny, do, March 2, 1824

Lewis, do, August 7, 1826

Little Leah, do, November 18, 1826

Ephraim, do, March 31, 1827

Hetty, do, July 30, 1828

Rhoda, do, Feb-ry 26, 1830

Rose, do, June 16, 1830

Nancy, do, Feb-ry 7, 1831

Henry, do, Jan-ry 2, 1832

Celeste, do, Jan-ry 15, 1832

Betty, do, April 14, 1832

Margaret, do, Jan-ry 19, 1833

Rixum, born August 12, 1840

Little Mary, do, October 13, 1840

Polly, do, Dec-br 24, 1840

Leven, do, Jan-ry 26, 1841

Biddy, do, July 6, 1841

Little Arthur, do, July 22, 1841

Winny, do, Oct-br 24, 1841

Alfred, do, Dec-br 23, 1841

Nelly, do, May 25, 1842

Luther, do, Sept-br 8, 1842

Essex, do, Jan-ry 31, 1839   Little Harriet, do, Jan-ry 5, 1843
Ben, do, April 18, 1839   Elizabeth, do, Feb-ry 26, 1843
Cathrine, do, Nov-br 17, 1839   Writta, do, March 30, 1843
Lucinda Jane, do, Dec-br 25, 1839 Little Joe, do, April 2, 1843
Delphine, do, July 28, 1840   Emily, do, April 27, 1843
                            Little Caroline, do, March 15,
                            1844

My dear sister,

I send you the numbers of all the slaves on this place—their names and ages. You find that there is only sixteen men. The four that is first on the list were not born here on this place. All the rest of the males were and there is eighteen women that are young enough to be good hands. The oldest of the 18 is forty-seven years old, and Hetty, the youngest, is 16 on July 30th, Rhoda and Rose about two years younger, and Nancy three years younger, which makes 21 in all, and two little boys, Harry and John. Patience cooks for me. Old Milly raises poultry, Old Leah spins wool, Old Dinah is nearly blind, but churns and feeds the cows and helps about all she can see to do. Charity is washer and attends about the house. I have a large garden and truck patch and a nice little orchard which takes Mary and Pless nearly all their time to work it all—which takes three women from the 21 mentioned as able to work. Arthur has to oversee the hands which leaves 15 men to work and 18 women counting the three young girls, and altogether 32 hands in the field and several small children what can pick cotton and assist a little. You will know all about them when you look over their ages. Sampson, you know, is worth very little—. My beloved nephew will be able to inform you all particulars. Your ever affectionate sister,

                                          Rachel O'Connor

Rachel's mind turns toward the hereafter, yet her fighting spirit and courageous heart determine her to cling tenaciously to her plantation and her slaves for as long as she lives. She urges young William Weeks to devise a legal contract securing Evergreen Plantation for David Weeks' heirs after her death. She gives a lengthy account of plantation affairs, describing especially the planting of her new orchard; and she reiterates that, to the best of her ability, she has done her duty towards God and man.

March 23, 1844

My dear nephew,

I received your letter dated the 6th of this month. I expect it had been in the post office some time. It has been two weeks since I sent to inquire for letters until this evening I concluded to send down.

I am very glad to receive your letter and will do all in my power to make you all safe. I have never had the smallest doubt of your honour or the honour of any one of your family. But the time makes alterations in our ideas. Could you not have a will written for me to sign that would suffice to secure to you any claim that may be mine or that any person may wish to make it mine? I am willing to sign anything that you wish me to so that it may all and every part belong to your family after I am no more. But at present you are all under age and it would be useless to sign anything. You have many relations and friends to advise you. Do try to get a will written that would stand good in law and I will sign it before as many witnesses as you wish me to.

But pray don't make me sign anything that will ruin the peace of the few days that I may yet be spared on earth. I am alone in the world. I have no one to save me from falling. To call on you would be taking you from your own business to attend mine. I cast all my cares on my God hoping he careth for me. I am so distressed that I seldom sleep any. I want to do what is right and to give peace and have peace myself. I hope and pray that a will may do.

I can safely declare to you that my conscience is clear. I do not recollect one act that I would not be willing to tell you every particular, and I hope ever to do so during life. I will constantly pray to be directed from above and will ask you to pray for me.

Tell your dear mama that I do not know anything about the sales of the land, that I did not know of it until your poor father informed me that he had bought my son's claim on the island. I never knew or heard anything about Mr. Hopkins' or what was done respecting it. I do not know how she will find out, as I scarcely think there was any account kept of it, or at least I never heard of any.

I really have the prettiest garden that I ever had—all planted and growing beautifully. I never took so much care of it as I have done

253

this winter and spring. But perhaps one severe frost may spoil all my work for three months past. I was glad to find that she (your mother) had taken so much care of her garden. It will add to her health. I have got my little orchad nicely planted since you left me which makes the place much prettier. My neighbors sent me trees from all quarters. I was surprised at so much goodness. I have 400 trees planted in it. It is very late at night. I will pray the Lord to bless you and bid you goodnight. Your affectionate aunt,

My love to you all.

R. O'Connor

Direct your letters to Wm. Flower, St. Francisville. He will surely get it there. He is a charming young man, and very kind to me. I have received your molasses and sugar which I thank you for. Mr. Butler has taken his gin back again without giving me any trouble. *Poor Wm. Flower* wrote to him for me and got him to take it back again. The gin is for sale, I expect Bains, the carpenter, has the selling of it.

The plantation is in first rate order and nearly all planted. The corn is up and growing very pretty. The hands were sowing the cotton seed all this week past. I hope a frost may not destroy it. All my neighbors are planting, but my orchard is my *idol.* I am afraid I think too much of it and that God will punish me for letting my heart cling to earthly treasures. I am not afraid to love the little black children. Christ suffered on the cross for us all and it is my duty to take care of all that he has seen proper to place under my charge, for his sake, which I do, and love to do. Their mothers were all raised under my care.

The scarlet fever is at this time in St. Francis Ville. A man died with it this morning near the river. The Rev. Mr. Lewis and Harriet Collins were married not long since. She is your cousin and appears to be a good girl. They came to see me once since their marriage. I trust in God that her choice is good and that her happiness has commenced on earth. I believe Mr. Lewis is a good man. He is greatly beloved by all that is acquainted with him. He has bought the place that formerly belonged to Dr. Barton.

It is love for the place and the people on it that causes all my earthly trouble. The name of riches has no value with me. That has long since been buried in the graves of my relations and friends. *But God is all love* and has placed love in my heart for all, particularly such as his judgment placed under my care and has given me a willing mind to do my duty in all things so far as I know. I have long since been nothing but a trouble to my friends. What am I, or what must I do? My son, lean to the side of mercy.

Grave illness takes its toll of Rachel's waning strength. She arises from her sick bed to answer two urgent letters from Alfred Weeks seeking information she may have concerning titles to Weeks property at Grand Cote. On the outside of her letter, she directs a note to the postmaster requesting him "please to forward this with all possible speed which will greatly oblige a friend and relieve much anxiety."

April 17, 1844

My dear and beloved nephew,

I have this moment received and read your two kind letters dated the 25th and the 28th of March. Everything has been very busy getting the crop planted, and I have been entirely confined to my bed for thee weeks past with a violent pain in my back so bad that I really could not get out of bed myself nor let any person help me to raise up. I have not words that could convey to you the pain I suffered, but I am about again and hope soon to be well. Your Cousin Clarissa came and stayed two weeks with me, and was all kindness, as she has ever been whenever I have been sick. I am sorry you will have to wait so long ere you will receive an answer to your letters, but I could not have written until yesterday if your letters had arrived. As soon as I found that I could set up, I sent to the post office to find if any letters were there for me.

I am surprised and sorry to find that your brother Wm. has not received my answer to his last letter which I wrote the same day that his arrived to let your mama know all that I could inform her respecting the land on your island.

I am glad that you are coming to see me soon. I want to have some talk with you. In my last letter to your brother Wm., I requested of him to inquire if a will signed by myself before witnesses would not secure all the property now under my care to your father's heirs; and, if so, to get one written for me to sign. But I hope to see you soon and then I will tell you all. It is my sincere wish to let you know all and you will find it so when you come. I never felt a greater desire to do for my own children than I now feel for you all, and have ever done since their deaths. I have not failed in one promise I made to your father. I hope to meet him in a happier world and to meet with the same pure love that we ever lived in this. We never quarreled nor had any angry feelings towards each other, and of course I love his children.

I have a good garden and all doing well. The Negroes go on with the field work very well. I have nothing to complain of in that respect. I much conclude my letter and write all I can remember about the island. I hope it may not be too late. I will send this to the post office in the morning. My love to your dear parents, brothers, and sisters. As every, your affectionate aunt,

Rachel O'Connor

My son, it is late at night. I have just finished writing to your mama. I am writing by the light of a lamp. You will find it badly done, but I have done my best. I am truly sorry about your brother's not getting my last letter, but I am not to blame. I send it to the post office by Arthur. Please to show this to your dear mama that she may know that my wishes are to do right so far as I know.

Yours, etc., *R, O'C.*

Rachel encloses this memorandum to Mary Weeks Moore in her letter of the same date to Alfred Weeks, stating her recollections of the early settling of her relatives at Grand Cote.

April 17th, 1844

My dear sister,

I have written in a great hurry to my nephew A. C. Weeks, and at his request I will inform you all I know respecting the first settling of Grand Cote Island.

My son, Stephen Bell, went to the Grand Cote Island with the intention of living there sometime in the spring of 1814 or 1815 and remained there several months, but the place being so lonesome, and my being so uneasy about him, he concluded to return home. He had taken two Negro men of our own and a few belonging to his Uncle David Weeks (I do not recollect the number) to raise corn so that they could take more hands the year following. The Negroes belonging to my brother that were taken there remained on the island, but my own two sons went and brought our two men home again, but my brother continued to improve and settle the land and raise crops even on until he moved to the Attakapas. After that time you know more about it than I do. If ever his Negroes were brought away after being taken there, I must have forgotten it. The last letter that I received from my nephew Wm. F. Weeks mentioned something about the land on the island, but I did not understand by it that you was likely to have any trouble. I concluded that you and your children were making some arrangements amongst yourselves. I answered his letter instantly and sent it to the post office by Arthur. I am surprised at his not receiving it, but I hope this may reach you before it is too late. I did not receive Alfred's letters until this evening and you can see that I have lost no time in answering them.

Please remember me most affectionately to the judge and your children. Your ever affectionate and grateful sister,

Rachel O'Connor

The property owned by her deceased son at Grand Cote is still in question, and Rachel writes again to Alfred Weeks concerning the matter. She reiterates her desire that a legal document be drafted giving titles to David's heirs upon her death.

April 26, 1844

My dear nephew,

Your kind letter dated the 28th of March last is now laying before me. I will try to answer it again, from my being entirely confined to my bed for several weeks previous to its arrival (or I may say) before I received it. I expect both your two last letters were in the post office some days ere I sent to inquire for letters, owing to my entire confinement from a severe pain in my back. I could not raise myself out of my bed or turn myself in my bed, nor suffer any person to assist me, the pain and the soreness in my back was so great, and it lasted for such a length of time, and is not well yet. I can walk about and lay on a bed without much pain, but when I set up, my sufferings continue very great. When I wrote my first answer to your two letters and enclosed one to your dear mama within yours, I had to have a large cotton cord laced round me a number of times to obtain strength to set up to write. I am now much better, but far from well.

I hope your brother William has received my answer to his last letter. I wrote to him instantly on receiving it so that I might answer his and your mama's inquiries respecting the land of the island. I did not understand by it that there was any danger of old claims being brought against her respecting the island, but merely concluded that some arrangements were taking place amongst yourselves. In my letter to your mama and yourself I said, so far as I knew, or could recollect, I do not know the time when your dear father and my son Stephen Bell made their bargain for our part of the island, which if I do not forget was 400 acres. I had given it to my son and him and your father made their own trades. Your father informed me after the death of my son that he had bought the land on which is all that I ever knew about it—which I now wish that I had been more particular, but I was afraid he might think that I had some selfish views should I ask him any questions and I did not do so. His word was always sufficient to afford me every satisfaction—and I now declare to you that I would not have given him cause for one hard thought for twice the value of the 400 acres of land, so sincere was my love for him.

My son Stephen went to the Grand Cote Island with two of our Negro men, Sam and George, and your father sent a few hands at the same time to settle there and raise some corn in the spring of the year 1814 or 1815. I cannot remember how long he remained there. I remember his often speaking about some orange trees that he planted and appeared sorry to leave. I do not know whether he planted the seed or got some young trees to set out; but as well as I can recollect, your father's Negroes remained there, but our two men were brought home.

Tell your brother William when he writes his letter to his cousin to direct it to William Flower, St. Francis Ville. I had informed him in my last to him. I would write to your brother at this time if I could set up to do so. You observed that you felt certain that I would be the last one that would wish to wrong your father's children. In that you are right, for I can truly say that I never felt a greater desire to do for my own children than I do for his, which you will see when you come.

If Mrs. Dawson's being one of the witnesses to the sale of the property is not lawful, we can have the same writing witnessed by men if that will answer, or I am willing to sign a will making it all your own at my *death*.

Your ever affectionate aunt,
Rachel O'Connor

Rachel has received affectionate letters from the Weeks heirs Frances, William, and Alfred. In this letter to Mary Weeks Moore, she states that she will answer the children's letters as soon as health permits and will send a requested writing. She adds that several of the Feliciana planters are troubled by runaway slaves but that her own slaves remain quiet and peaceful.

May 7, 1844

My dear sister,

This morning I received three letters—one from Frances, one from William, and one from Alfred. I am very thankful to learn from their letters that you are all in good health and I hope doing well. I have suffered more this spring from a pain in my back than I ever did with all the pain that I ever had in my life. I could not walk nor raise up nor let any person assist me on my feet. It is useless for me to undertake to inform you of my sufferings, for that is out of my power. I am not well yet, but much better and able to attend my business.

The crop is in good order, but needs rain very much. I have a good garden—peas and beans and beets in abundance, and potatoes in blossom. I expect I may blame the garden with all my pain. The weather was so fine for gardening that I could not keep out of it, but followed it constantly from morning until night without once thinking of old age.

I write this merely to let you know that I have received the children's letters and will answer them and do the other writing, as they request me, as soon as I am able and enclose it to you and them. My back is still so weak and painful that I cannot set to write long at a time. The children need not apprehend the least danger. I am more anxious to do for them than they are to do for themselves. I now feel so happy to find all can be done in perfect friendship. It is my greatest desire on earth.

Charlotte expects to be confined next month. Clarissa is quite well. I have not seen the others since August, 1841.

Our neighborhood is much troubled with runaway Negroes from different parts. A number of the neighbors has turned out and taken 7 or 8 and shot one dead not far from this place. Mr. Daniel Turnbull had ten runaways at one time. They have taken most of them.

When I write you again, I shall write you a long letter and send you a list of all my little ones, younger than my poor little Issac—or least born since he was. They are at this time a fince parcel of healthy little children—one born since your children left me last.

My love to all your dear children. My best respects to your good and worthy husband. May he long live to keep you all happy. I remain your affectionate sister during life,

R. O'Connor

Excuse all mistakes, blots, and bad writing. I have to turn and twist about so much with uneasiness in my back that I almost forget what I am doing.

Two days later Rachel writes and mails the confirmation requested by David Weeks's heirs. A note written on the outside of the envelope directs the postmaster to forward the letter with great care and speed.

May 9th, 1844

My dear sister,

I have this day finished the writing I have been requested to do. It is perfectly right that it should be done and I pray that it may prove a blessing to you all. It has been a melancholy day's work, but I considered it my duty and feel thankful to get through with it. I am yet poorly and cannot write you the long letter that I promised to write you in my last, but will write it should I live to get well. I feel in a hurry to get this and the enclosed safe to you. We know not what a few hours may bring forth. A little delay might cause it to be forever too late. I have every confidence in you *all* without one doubt of all your good wishes towards my happiness and peace of mind, and I sincerely pray that the God of Heaven and earth may forever bless you and yours. Your ever affectionate sister,

Rachel O'Connor

Editor's note: Copy of the above mentioned enclosure:

In the name of God, a-men. I, Rachel O'Connor, of the Parish of West Feliciana and State of Louisiana, being advanced in age, but of sound mind, take occasion, while so, to express these last wishes. I trust in the Redeemer, pray to God to take my soul, and desire a Christian burial.

I recognize as valid, and hereby confirm and ratify the sales of property made by me to my late brother, David Weeks, by acts passed before John B. Dawson, Parish Judge, on the 16th day of March 1830, and before Robert C. Wederstrand, Notary Public, on the 23rd day on March, 1830, having received value therefor as expressed, and it is my desire and wish that the property therein described, together with the increase and profits, be delivered over according to the tenor of said acts after my decease.

Written, dated, and signed by me in the said parish this ninth day of May, one thousand eight hundred and forty-four.

Rachel O'Connor

Despite increasing weakness Rachel continues active management of plantation business. The death of Lewis Davis, husband of her beloved niece Clarissa, is a sad blow. Rachel writes Mary of other troubles. Clarissa herself lies at the point of death and Rachel herself suffers a painful lump in her breast.

Nov-br 28, 1844

My dear sister,

I have set myself down to try if possible to write you a few lines. Troubles crowd so heavily that my poor heart is nearly broken. To-day poor Lewis Davis will be buried. He died yesterday a little after daylight in the morning. He had not been able to rise or even to get out of his bed for five or six weeks. Wm. Swayze wrote to me this morning that poor Clarissa lay nearly senseless and her little son quite sick. All I can do for them is pray to God to have mercy on them. I much fear she will die; I am told she has wasted away to a shadow from being up night and day attending on her husband. They all say that she was a faithful nurse, and I am sorry to say she is far advanced in the family way, *if she lives*. I expect she will be confined in Feb-ry.

I should be quite well now if my breast was well. The lump is getting larger and more painful. How it will end, God only knows.

A few days ago I received two letters—one from my dear William and one from my dear Harriet, which was the first that I had heard of your being at home. I had been looking for you to call here on your way home for a long time. I received all the letters that you and the children wrote to me and answered them instantly, and got Dr. Denny to direct them so that it might be done right. The first that I wrote to you was before any from you had come. I have written to my dear Alfred and directed it as well as I knew how. When you or the children write again, please to let me know how to direct my letters to him so that they may not be lost.

I feel very sorry that you did not receive my letters that I wrote to yourself and the children while gone. But you must not think hard of me. You are the last person I could possibly neglect (now alive). I am very thankful that dear little Charlie has benefited so much by the trip.

Mrs. Lyons (former Mrs. Bowman) said that you all looked well. I have sent one hundred bales of cotton to Mr. Thompson, and have eighteen more pressed, and I expect there is five or six more to pick out of the field. When all is pressed, I will let you know the number. The corn is middling, but some will have to be bought in the summer.

When I looked over what I had written, I felt ashamed of it, but my mind is in such a way that I cannot do better at this time. Should I ever feel better, I will write you a long letter and answer those that I have lately received from my dear children. My best respects to the judge and love to all your children, and much, very much, to yourself. Oh, my beloved sister, you can have no idea how dear you are to me. I think of you daily, and if I should say hourly, I do not think I would say wrong. Your ever affectionate sister,

Rachel O'Connor

Though still ailing, Rachel is careful to answer every letter she receives. She writes Harriet Weeks of the kindness of her slave women who care for her and she looks forward to vists from her relatives.

Dec-br 4, 1844

My dear niece,

I received your kind letter several days since which trouble prevented me from answering as I would otherwise have done. I have written to your brother William. His letter can inform you all I know about Mr. Davis during his sickness and how he died which took place the 27th of November early in the morning. I hope he is happy. He is buried at Mr. A. Doherty's. I cannot get him off my mind. I loved him dearly. I feel as if I had lost another son. He has ever been kind to me. I have not seen poor Clarissa since Mr. Davis took sick. They say she looks dreadfully bad and her little son very poorly. Charlotte was here when Mr. Davis died and went from here to his house in the rain. Charlotte has had much sickness this summer and fall past. She looks worse than I ever saw her before. Her babe is a fine fat child. They call him Anthony. She has only three left alive out of eight. All three are sons.

I am afraid your mama and yourself did not receive my letters that I wrote you both during your stay at the springs in Ky. Dr. Denny directed them all. I thought perhaps he could direct them better than myself. In one I pasted a little piece out of the red paper to show how bad the caterpillars were amongst the cotton. I was sorry that you and your mama could not call. I had been poorly so long I did not expect to get well any more, but I am now quite healthy only this bad lump on my breast. It is troublesome and painful. I do not know of anything that should have caused it to me. I was afraid at first it might prove to be a cancer, but I don't think so now.

My being so sick all last summer has caused my garden to look bad. I was a long time not able to walk that far, and of course did not see it. What few were well had to nurse the sick. However they were kind to me. Charity, Mary, and Pless stayed with me day and night. They had to lift me about like a child. A part of the time I do not recollect of. I had no white women with me but Miss Swift a few days. And her sisters got sick and had to send for her. All the people everywhere was sick.

I wrote to your brother Alfred yesterday and to your brother William today, and now to you which will show that I am pretty well. You must give my love to my dear Frances and kiss her little ones for me. I hope to live to see you all again. Tell your brother Charley he must grow fast so that he may come to see me. I have the doll that he sent me 3 or 4 years ago, so he may be sure I have not forgotten him, but think of him often.

Now, my dear and beloved child, I must say farewell. Remember me most affectionately to your dear parents and to your brothers and sister. I remain your affectionate aunt,

Rachel O'Connor

Rachel follows her letter of the previous day with a long letter to Mary. Although increasingly ill and almost completely deaf, she retains her lifelong interest in the affairs of her family and friends.

Dec-br 5, 1844

My dear sister,

I have just written William, Alfred, and Harriet and now I have set myself down to write the long epistle that I have been promising you.

In the first place I must mention my fear of your not receiving my letters that I wrote you yourself and Harriet while you were at the springs. I wrote once to you ere I received any from you, and twice afterwards, and one to my dear Harriet. Dr. Denny directed them all, as I thought he might know better how to direct them than myself.

The lump that has come on my right breast (which you so kindly mentioned in one of your letters to me) continues an ugly looking swelled place and painful, moreso at night than in the daytime. My mind is distressed on account of it, but I trust in my God who does all things well. If it were not for the best, it would not be so. I keep a thin plaster of quicksilver ointment on it now for some time past and at times I venture to hope that the swelling gets smaller, and then (again) I give away to despair.

I am truly sorry for Mrs. Conrad. I think of all that I ever knew she is one of the most innocent women; appears to know nothing but goodness. I had so much sickness during the sickly season this year. A part of the time I could not rise out of my bed without assistance, and some part of the time I don't recollect. Miss A. Swift came and stayed a few days and would have remained longer had not her sisters taken sick and had to send for her, but I have every reason to be thankful to my God for all his goodness to me in opening the hearts of those women about the house to be so very attentive to me. I all my sickness they stayed by me day and night and a part of the time were quite sick themselves. Yet they stayed by me. Charity was sick all the time, but did not leave me.

Mr. A. Doherty and family were dreadfully, dreadfully sick indeed. Charlotte was despaired of for a long time and had her child born during the time, which made times worse than it would have otherwise been. She looks worse now than I ever saw her before. She has a fine child and has called him Anthony. He was born the 20th of July. She has only three children, out of eight, alive, all sons. Wm. Swayze and his wife has six—three sons and three daughters. They never lost any yet, but they were all very sick. Melinda has some kind of spasms. They all looked very bad, but had begun to mend ere I seen any of them. Clarissa was sick but not as bad as the others. But poor Mr. Davis suffered more than all the others. His feet and legs continued warm, but otherwise than that, they were dead. He could not move his toes or feet, but he could use his hands and arms. His senses remained good to the last moment. He was a good young man. I hope and pray that his precious soul may be happy. They buried him in they burying ground at Mr. Doherty's.

All the Negroes far and near were very sickly. Numbers died, but none of ours. They were very sick and some despaired of, but they all recovered. Charity had a child born the 6th of Nov-br, which only lived four days. It was a poor little thing. She was sick three months before it was born. She is about now, but looks very poorly. There has been three born since Charity's—one the 16th of Nov-br, one born the 1st of Dec-br, and one born today, the 5th of Dec-br. The one that was born the 1st of Dec-br is the least poor little thing that I ever saw, but I hope it may live. Its mother was sick with severe fevers for a long time. I had but little hopes of her ever getting well again. I was afraid all these last ones would be poor puny things, their mothers were so sick last summer and fall.

I had like to forget to tell you that I have a watch that belonged to my sons, first one and then the other, which I look at sometimes. But I have not carried it about with me for 17 or 18 years.

There are four children that are living now that has been born since my beloved Alfred and young Mr. Towles were here. The first was born the 4th of June, named Susan. Should I live until they name those last three, I will write and let you know their names and ages.

My beloved sister, I have written this with a heart full of love and praying for your everlasting happiness. I remain your affectionate sister,

Rachel O'Connor

Please to remember me kindly to your dear and good husband. I have no words to express my thanks to him for his kindness to yourself and your dear children. My deafness is getting worse. I can scarcely understand anything that is said to me; all has to be written. I have a small slate for that purpose.

118 bales of cotton are pressed and there is a little to gin when we get it dried. The weather is very rainy. The corn about as much as usual. We have thirty children now alive born since the year 1837. Poor Clarissa Davis is in the family way; expects to be confined in Feb-ry. I am dreadfully troubled about her. I wish I could care as little for her as she appears to care for me.

I have to pay four dollars to an old midwife for each of those little ones. She belongs to Mr. Stephen Henderson very near here and has had very good luck so far. The old woman will soon get rich. I have paid her 16 dollars since the 6th of last month, but she has done very well. It is better to pay that than to run any risk.

Farewell my best of sisters,

R. O'C.

I have not seen Clarissa since the death of her husband. How that may affect her heart, I know not. I blame her sisters for weaning her heart from me. I hope they may repent of it ere it is too late. Henry Flower's children are all clever to me. Even poor Mr. Handy showed all the love that child could do to a mother. On the 28th and 29th of last month was the first time that I had seen him since poor Harriet died, which happened the 4th of July. Don't mention the above to Caleb Swayze.

An outside doctor has diagnosed Rachel's tumor as very serious. Probably with a premonition that the end is near, Rachel writes begging Mary to come to see her.

Feb-ry 3rd, 1845

My dear sister,

I received your very kind letter so long since, but have been poorly ever since that I could not answer it. My breast is in a dreadful situation. Dr. King says it is one of the worst kind of tumours, and is very doubtful respecting it. He is doing all he can for me. You must come to see me if possible. I have received my dear William's letter, but am not able to answer it.

The 14 barrels of molasses and one barrel of sugar has come and I have all at home.

Clarissa had a son born on the first day of this month. Both are well yet. She is at Mr. A. Doherty's. Lewis Davis died with the liver complaint.

You must excuse my short letter. I am not able to write any more. Remember me most affectionately to your beloved husband and children. Your ever grateful and affectionate sister,

R. O'Connor

267

Mary has paid the requested visit to Rachel, whose condition had become so critical that doctors stated she could not recover without surgery. Rachel then resigned hereself to die. But the doctors, together with her nephew William Swayze, prevailed on her to have the tumor removed. Frightened and suffering, she looked on as the doctor cut the tumor from her breast. Weak but recovering, she writes Mary fives weeks after the operation.

Editor's note: She withstood the surgery without benefit of anesthesia, the use of which, however, had been demonstrated three years earlier in Georgia by Dr. Crawford W. Long.

June 20, 1845

My dear, dear sister,

This is my first attempt to write since you left me. I have been greatly afflicted; indeed I never expected to write again. My breast was so sore and painful, from which I became so weak and discouraged, that I felt lost and without any comfort. I thought if only I had you with me again I could bear all my troubles so patiently. But after Dr. Stone came and told me it was impossible to cure my breast without cutting a part of it off, I said I must die, and felt resigned to my fate. But Dr. Stone and Dr. King and Wm. Swayze talked to me so seriously that I consented to let it be done, and on the 11th of May, the Dr. cut away between 2 and 3 ounces from my breast. It looked like a pig's heart cut open and bled dreadfully. I cannot tell you how great my sufferings were. I was nearly scared to death, but I am very glad now. My breast is all healed and well, but I remain very weak.

Charlotte and William and Clarissa has been very kind to me, and Melinda also. Poor Charity and Fanny stayed by me day and night during my sickness and distress. I feel as if them two girls were a part of myself from their goodness to me. It must have been ordered by my God himself.

I am truly sorry for you to have so much sickness in your family. I received a letter from my dear William dated the 4th of June. My dear little Charley was then sick, but I hope he is well now. I am afraid to ask you to come to see me now as the weather is so warm it might cause you to get sick. I have received my dear Harriet's letter and William's also, but am too weak to answer either of them.

I have received two letters from yourself which I could not answer, which made me feel unworthy of so good a sister. But if I live long enough an my strength returns, you will find that my heart overflows with gratitude for all your goodness to me.

Please to give my kindest love to your beloved husband. He has a great share in my heart. I am very tired and must conclude my letter with much love to yourself and my dear nephews and nieces. Your ever grateful and affectionate sister.

Rachel O'Connor

I have five little dogs for William. I hope they may live.

Mary and Judge Moore, together with Harriet and little Charles, are again on an extended vacation. Rachel writes Mary that she has found it expedient to hire an overseer to replace Arthur.

July 25, 1845

My dear sister,

I am getting quite uneasy about you and your family. I have sent to the post office several times to find if any letters had arrived, but as yet none has come. I intend to send Eben to tomorrow morning. Perhaps there may be some by this time.

My health is improving as fast as I could expect, but I continue weak. I walk about in my garden every morning and evening trying to gain some strength. I hope the weather may not be so warm where you are. It is dreadfully warm here, and many places very sickly. Mrs. Lyons had one of her little Negroes die yesterday and one of Wm. Flower's Negro men died last week.

Mr. Hargadine has hired an overseer for this place. He commenced overseeing the 11th of this month at five hundred dollars pr. year. He was overseer for Mrs. McDermit six or seven years before she died. She was very well pleased with him. She made him a present of a fine watch during the time he overseed for her. He is a middling old man and is said to be very industrious. The Negroes has behaved very well. I hear no complaint. Old Milly is laid up with a sore leg. I hope it may not last long. She is so old that I tremble for her when anything ails her. Joe's leg is mending. He walks a little with a staff. His doctor charges 25 dollars for seeing his leg.

Charlotte Doherty has not been down since you left me. Her babe is sick.

Your must excuse my letter. I can do anything better than write. I hope you are all enjoying good health. My love to my dear Harriet and Charley, and best respects to the judge. If you are all well, you must be happy. So kind a husband and father would cause happiness in any family. May the blessings of God remain with you and yours are the prayers of your affectionate sister,

Rachel O'Connor

Rachel has accepted Mary's second husband, Judge John C. Moore, from the beginning. But in this touching letter to him, Rachel is so filled with gratitude for his kindness to her and her family that she acknowledges that she has come to love him as dearly as she had loved her own brothers.

Editor's note: After her breast operation, the glands under Rachel's right arm are swollen and she is unable to write. She asks Dr. Denny to relate this information to Judge Moore. Dr. Denny sent the following message on September 11, 1845:

". . . Mrs. O'Connor desires me to let you know Dr. Stone's opinion of the swelled gland under her arm. He thinks it is nothing more than a common ordinary swelling of the gland, which by an application of hemlock, would soon disappear. . . .

Accept a Benjamin's portion from, Yours, etc., W. L. Denny"

August 15, 1845

My dear friend,

I have received two letters from you since you left the Bayou Sara, one dated the 9th of July and the second the 22nd of the same month, for which I return you many thanks. You have proved yourself to be a good husband and father, and now one of the best of brothers. I sincerely wish it may ever be in my power to return the favors you so richly deserve. My being deaf causes me to feel more unworthy of your kind attention than I should otherwise do. I have had the pleasure of seeing you, but the gratification of hearing you speak is out of my power. I find it a great loss, but God's will must be done, who does all for the best.

I am truly thankful to learn from your letters that you and the family enjoyed the trip as you did. I am always uneasy when any of my friends are travelling on board of the steamboats, fearing some misfortune may happen. But I hope kind providence may guard you and that you may return safe. I am glad to learn that you expect my dear Alfred and his wife to meet you and return home in company with you and his dear mother, sister, and brother. It will be happiness itself. Please to give my dearest love to them. His dear mama can inform him the reson why I could not write to him, and all my sufferings since I saw him last which will excuse all that must have appeared as neglect. I have received one letter from my beloved Frances since you left me. They were all enjoying good health and doing very well. My dear William Weeks has not written since he left me, but I hope all is well with him.

I have written to you once ere this before I received either of yours. It was badly done. I was very poorly at that time and not very well yet, but mend slowly. Your kind letters raised my spirits greatly. I have attended better to my garden since that, which is now doing pretty well for this time of the year.

Mr. Hargadine has hired a most excellent overseer, one of the most industrious overseers that I ever knew. (He is a whimsical being.) I have to humour him like a child, which I am very willing to do as long as he attends to his business as he has since he commenced here. Mr. Hargadine and family are all in good health and Dr. Denny also. The neighborhood near me has been quite sickly. The weather has been extremely warm; most of the people think it is more so than they ever knew it to be before.

My dear sister must not think that I have not written to her or her children. I intend this for you all. It still goes hard with me to write, and Dr. Denny will not write for me. The Negroes behave very well under their new overseer. Arthur has worked with the others without giving any trouble. Several of them has been very sick. Old Milly has been laid up ever since you left here with a sore leg.

My love to my beloved sister and my dear Harriet and Charley, hoping your healths may all prove good. My dear friend, I feel at a loss for words to express my feelings toward yourself for all your goodness towards myself and my family. I do not consider myself as

I once did since my brothers died. I feel that God has given me a
brother in you, and I love you as I did them.

Most affectionately yours,

Rachel O'Connor

*Death hovers closely over Rachel as she writes this letter to Mary. A
strange looking rising has again erupted on her breast and causes
her final sickness. Her mind wanders and she asks forgiveness for
failing to answer letters. Proceeds from cotton sales are in the hands
of her trusted broker, W. E. Thompson; but her beloved nephew
Alfred Weeks must come and attend to the disposition of the money,
leaving her only enough to supply the Negroes and the plantation.
Her overseer has proved deceitful, and her neighbor William Hargadine will attend to hiring another in the future.*

November 14, 1845

My own dear sister,

I have been sick, very sick, ever since I wrote to you last. And in
a few days after, I had fevers which affected my poor weak head in
such a manner that I could not write for fear of making mistakes. I
was continually dreaming, or perhaps imagining, I was writing or had
written to you, which I am now convinced could not be the case as
I could not set up, only a few moments at a time. I recollect having
a great desire to answer my beloved Alfred's letter, and at times
thought I had, which would comfort me while the idea would last.
But as soon as I could be able to reflect a moment, I knew that I
had not been able to write. He must forgive me and not have one
hard thought, and all of you must do the same. We shall all meet
when the great day comes, at which time you will know that my
heart is true, and that I wish to do every justice as I promised my
brother I would do. You have all been kind, very kind, to me for
which I hope and pray that your rewards may be great in Heaven
and earth forever and forever. Remember me most affectionately to
your beloved husband. I return him many sincere thanks for his kindness to me in writing to me.

My nephew Wm. Weeks wrote me and advised me how to act respecting the money now in Mr. Thompson's hands, but my situation would not admit of my attempting to do any business for fear of making some mistake. I expect my dear Alfred will come to see me ere long and assist me in doing all things right. Mr. W. E. Thompson has ever been so kind and obliging to me that I am so fearful of offending him through ignorance or want of experience in business that I dare not even write to him on that subject. Alfred must come here and then go to see Mr. Thompson and explain all to him. I only want enough secured to me to supply the wants of the plantation and the Negroes on it. There is a fine parcel of fine looking little children and my heart desires to take care of them. I have all, young and old, well clothed at this time.

Some strange looking rising came on my breast again which caused all my late sickness. It is getting better and my fever has left me. I have gained strength so that I can walk in the garden and see a little to it. Dr. Stone came up to see his wife's parents and came to see me. He promised to send me something for my sore breast from N. Orleans, but Mr. Hargadine says he is to return in a few days, at which time I hope he will remember me.

The old overseer that Mr. Hargadine hired a few days after you left me has gone away. He was displeased with Mr. Hargadine. I felt glad that I was out of the scrape. He was an excellent manager on a farm, but as deceitful as sin. I was really sorry to discover so much meanness in a being that has a white skin. But I did not mention it to any person, not even to Mr. Hargadine. Mr. H. has been talking to another that he thinks will do better. He has not come yet. He is to come the 1st of Jan-ry. Mr. Hargadine says he can make Arthur gather the crop by attending to his management himself. No person ever was a better neighbor than Mr. Hargadine is to me. If he was my own child, he couldn't be kinder and all his family are equally so. His family has been very sickly this year, yet they never neglected me in my sickness.

I am getting tired and my paper is nearly all scratched over. I must conclude for this time. My love to you all, my beloved friend. Your affectionate sister,

R. O'Connor

I wrote a long letter to my dear Frances in answering hers, but never heard that she received it. I hope they are all well. I want my dear Alfred to bring his wife to see me and his sister-in-law also. I can only see them. My deafness remains as it was when you were here, but my little slate is whole yet. I expect my dear Harriet has forgotten me. Isabele Bowman told me that she was killing some of her young men in Ky., but she did not say that they were killing her, so I hope she will remember her old friend yet. My love to all the children. I hope my dear Charley is quite well. I have hope that you can come over here in the spring. I will try to have a good garden should I be spared that long. I am much fallen away since you left.

I write to you all, being too weak to write more at present. I have one hundred and two bales of cotton pressed which will be in N. Orleans by the time your receive this.

AFTERWORD

"I'm getting tired," wrote Rachel in the last paragraph of her last letter, "and my paper is nearly all scratched over." An added postscript to that final letter stated, "I have one hundred and two bales of cotton pressed which will be in N. Orleans by the time you receive this."

Rachel's tiredness might symbolize the heavy load she had always carried. Her paper being nearly "all scratched over" might indicate that her life was nearly over. The 102 bales of cotton en route to market show her constant attention to duty. She had lived to see cotton become a vital part of the economy of antebellum Louisiana. She had supervised plantation operation and had solved plantation problems. Planting, chopping, picking, pressing, and marketing were ever present in her mind and efforts. She had lived so long among fleecy white fields and Negro slaves that they had become a part of her life.

Rachel last letter still showed the warm interest in family, friends, and slaves that her earlier letters had exhibited. But her very last days present a question. Why should Rachel (who had loved her home so much that she had expressed a desire to live out her days and die there) take to the river and embark upon a long journey? On several occasions she had expressed her fear of steamboat accidents. Evidence suggests that she had never before travelled a greater distance than the sixty-odd miles lying between Attakapa, the place of her birth, and Feliciana, the place of her long residence. Her kind heart and willing hands rested in her "comfortable old home." Why should she leave it when she realized that her end was near?

The reason for the journey was her will to live. She must have heard of the skill of a doctor at Memphis, Tennessee, who she believed could restore her health. A letter of Mary Weeks to a relative reveals Rachel's decision to go to Memphis. Although she had often expressed her

275

acceptance of the will of the Almighty, "who giveth and taketh at pleasure," Rachel felt that God had placed a heavy responsibility upon her for the welfare of her slaves. With restored health she felt that she could continue to attend to the needs of plantation and slaves. So the journey was made.

On that first, and last, far journey, Rachel was accompanied by William L. Denny, her faithful plantation doctor, who had saved so many of her slaves and had often restored her own health. On May 12, 1846, Dr. Denny addressed from Memphis a letter to John Moore at Attakapa describing the treatment of Rachel's "diseased breast" administered by Dr. Samuel Gilbert. Denny's address was "Care of Mr. Shaw of the Wharf Boat, Memphis, Tennessee." Rachel died ten days later on May 22, 1846. The following day a bill from the Gilbert Infirmary at Memphis was directed to Alfred Weeks. It included a "medical bill for Mrs. O'Connor" amounting to three hundred dollars and board for two months at twenty dollars per month for Rachel and Dr. Denny. Their total board bill came to eighty dollars for the two months they spent at Memphis. "Articles for burial" listed on the bill included eight yards of jaconet, eight yards of fine cambric, a quantity of book muslin, one pair of silk gloves, one pair of cotton hose, one coffin (wood), and one outside box. The silk gloves cost one dollar, the cotton hose fifty cents, and the coffin and outside box came to fifty-nine dollars. The statement recorded $120 paid by cash, leaving a balance against Rachel's estate of $376.45. An added note read, "Draft on sight will answer the purpose." (It is interesting to note that in 1846 the entire expenses for a hospital stay of two months for a patient and an attendant, together with physician's fee and burial expenses, came to a total of only $496.45.) So Rachel was buried with her hands clad in silk gloves and with the cotton she helped produce covering her feet and legs.

Dr. Denny was with Rachel at the end and (as her estate was being settled) it was he who made a deposition stating that "Mrs. Rachel O'Conner, late of the Parish of West Feliciana, departed this life near the town of Memphis, Tennessee, on the twenty-second day of May, 1846, the said witness being with the said Rachel O'Connor at the time of the death." This deposition, Dr. Denny's letter to John Moore, and the bill from the Gilbert Infirmary provide a brief account of Rachel's last days.

On June 4, 1846, a public inventory was made of her property. Her land, slaves, and personal property were appraised at $33,029, a sizable sum for 1846 and a testimony to her thrift and courage. On October 23, 1846, Alfred Weeks arrived at Evergreen Plantation to transport her slaves to the Weeks's Attakapa plantations. On the morning of November 11, 1846, friends and neighbors gathered at Evergreen Plantation and her personal property was sold at auction. (A copy of the sale is in the appendixes.)

The story of Rachel's activities ends with her last letter. But readers who feel that they have come to know the relatives and friends that she loved may be interested in knowing something of their future lives.

In 1847, the year after Rachel's death, Mary Weeks Moore and her sons formed a partnership for the management of David Weeks's estate. The organization, chartered as William Weeks and Company, administered the properties belonging to all the heirs of David Weeks. They lived at an exciting time in Louisiana. All of them contributed to their economic, social, and cultural era. Two married their cousins, thus adding more land to their already extensive estates. David's sons became planters and his daughters lived in the grand manner. All went regularly to New Orleans during the winter to visit, to shop, and to attend the concerts and balls. During the summer all visited the springs of Virginia or the watering places off Louisiana's coast.

Frances Weeks, David's oldest daughter, married her cousin Augustin Smith Magill and bore three children, David Weeks; Mary Ida, and Augustin, Junior. Following the death of Magill and after a suitable period of mourning, Frances married Dr. Buford Prewitt and played a prominent role in plantation society. At age thirty-six, Frances, together with her two younger children, died (along with hundreds of others) in the tidal wave that swept over and destroyed Isle Dernier off the Louisiana coast on August 10, 1856. Frances' death left her minor son, David Weeks Magill, as sole heir. An inventory of Frances's estate made on September 3, 1856, revealed that her land, slaves, and chattels amounted to $142,127. Mary Weeks became her young grandson's executrix.

Harriet Weeks, the younger daughter, was a plantation belle much sought after as she accompanied her mother and step-father on their travels. Young men "addressed her" with proposals of marriage. She wed Dr. David E. Meade of St. Louis, Missouri, and they lived at Fair Hope Plantation in St. Mary Parish, This plantation was located near the present town of Centerville, Louisiana. On the death of her husband in 1854, Harriet with the help of her brothers continued to operate the plantation until her death in 1894. She was survived by her son, Edward Meade.

In 1845 Alfred Weeks, aged nineteen, married Nannie Hunter, who was several years his senior. Rachel in one of her last letters showed much interest in the newlyweds. They were kind to her and lived for extended periods at Evergreen Plantation during her last illness. Following her death they moved to Attakapa. Their baby son died and was buried in the family tomb at St. Martinville. Alfred died in 1864.

Charles Weeks, sickly and frail throughout childhood and early manhood, outlived all his brothers and sisters, dying in 1900 at the age of sixty-eight.

William Weeks, the oldest son of David and Mary, carried on the plantation tradition of his family. He added several tracts of land to those inherited from his father. William was beloved by family and respected by friends and business associates. He was attentive to the needs of his widowed sisters and considerate of his many slaves. He married his first cousin Mary Gorham Palfrey, daughter of John T. Palfrey and Sidney Conrad Palfrey, and became the father of two beautiful daughters, Harriet and Lily. Harriet married Walter Torian and went to live at his home in New Orleans. Lily married Major Gilbert Hall (a New Yorker who fell in love with the South as well as with the beautiful Lily) and became the mother of Weeks Hall. Weeks Hall, the great-grandson of David and Mary Weeks, survived all his family and became the sole heir to the Weeks estate. He was one of the most fascinating characters of early twentieth century Louisiana. He lived for many years in Paris, where he studied art. He was a unique individualist with a mighty sense of humor. Hospitable, talented, and a brilliant conversationalist, he drew friends from all walks of life. After living abroad for many years, he returned to the home that David Weeks had built so many years earlier. To restore that home to its original beauty became his last project. Before his death in 1958, he willed it to the National Trust for Historic Preservation. The mansion house, now known as Shadows-on-the-Teche, is known throughout the country as a showplace of antebellum architecture.

During the Civil War, General N. P. Banks took Shadows-on-the-Teche as his headquarters. Judge John Moore and Mary's sons gathered their slaves and fled to Texas. But Mary Conrad Weeks Moore, refusing to leave her beautiful home, retired to her attic and closed her curtains to blot out the sight of Federal soldiers. Following a few months of self-imposed imprisonment, Mary died during the fall of 1863. War conditions precluded burial in the family tomb at St. Martinville. She was buried in the garden of Shadows-on-the-Teche. Judge John Moore did not long survive her. He died in 1866.

The descendants of Mary's brother Frederick Conrad to this day own the site of The Cottage Plantation located at Conrad Point on the Mississippi. Unfortunately, the mansion house itself was destroyed by fire in the spring of 1960. It was on that plantation that five of Rachel's slaves (lent to help harvest sugarcane) had been so unhappy in 1833. Decendants of the Conrad and Palfrey families continue to play an important part in the economic and cultural life of south Louisiana.

Mrs. James Pirrie's fine house (that Rachel noted being occupied by an overseer in 1833) has been completely restored and is now known as Oakley Plantation. It has been designated by the state of Louisiana as a park in memory of John James Audubon, who once lived and worked there. Descendants of the Reverend William Robert Bowman and Eliza Pirrie Bowman inherited Rosedown Plantation. Their son married Sarah Turnbull of Rosedown. Descendants lived at Rosedown until past the middle of this century. Rosedown Plantation, now restored, is considered by many to be the most beautiful antebellum home in Louisiana.

Evergreen Plantation has changed hands several times since the death of Rachel O'Connor. Since 1964 the site has been the property of the David Howell Jackson estate. Today the place still retains some of the charm that Audubon found there more than a century ago. He appreciated the natural beauty of his surroundings. That same natural beauty remains a chief characteristic of the area. It is still remote and apart from the changes taking place around it. Standing on the house site of Evergreen Plantation and looking through the dense foliage, one can see an old trace that appears to be the original carriage drive connecting Evergreen with Oakley Plantation. Along it Audubon rode to the deathbed of Hercules O'Connor in 1820. And Rachel herself often travelled it on her way to administer to the ailing Mrs. Pirrie, Eliza Bowman, and the Reverend Mr. Bowman. Rachel's frame house is gone and a modern brick residence stands on the site. But memories of Rachel live in the centuries-old oak trees, the row of ancient crape myrtles she planted, and the profusion of old shrub roses and jonquils that appear each spring and multiply as the years pass. Additional bulbs and roses bloom several hundred yards from her house site at a spot assumed to be the location of her overseer's house or the slave quarters.

In essence Rachel's life, as revealed in her letters, presents a panorama of the plantation system at its apex of prosperity and growth. Twenty years after her death, all that world (of which Evergreen Plantation was a microcosm) would be shattered and her way of life forever changed. One feels that Rachel, as the reader has come to know her, would never have let the calamity of a civil war defeat her. Her indomitable will would have enabled her to adjust to whatever conditions her God had seen fit to impose upon her.

Rachel's letters were never intended for publication and never before have been published. In them she reveals her inner self, vulnerable to the unscrupulous through her faith in God and man, yet at the same time strong and self-reliant. These letters permit the reader to share her very personal life story. From her letters Rachel emerges as a combination of the traditional southern woman and a forceful personality in any age.

APPENDIX I
Last Will and Testament

Copy of will of Rachel O'Connor, November 27, 1845, in West Feliciana Parish Probate Court records. Document filed June 20, 1846.

Parish of West Feliciana

br
Nov-- 27, 1845

Blessed be the Name of God, Amen.

I, Rachel O'Connor, of the Parish of West Feliciana, State of Louisiana, considering the uncertainty of this mortal life, and being of sound mind and memory (Blessed be the name of Almighty God for the same), do make and publish this my last will and testament, hereby revoking all former wills and testaments by me made or signed.

First, I give and bequeath unto my beloved sister-in-law, Mary C. Conrad, widow of my late brother, David Weeks, deceased, of St. Martins Parish of Louisiana, and now wife of Judge John Moore of the Parish of St. Martins, State of Louisiana, seven undivided twelfths (7/12) of all my property, real or personal, consisting of the plantation on which I reside, and all the appertenances thereto belonging, all the slaves, movable property, etc.

Second, I give and bequeath unto my beloved nieces and nephews, Frances M. Weeks, wife of A. S. Magill of St. Martins, State aforesaid, William F. Weeks, Alfred C. Weeks, Harriet C. Weeks, and Charles C. Weeks, of the Parish and State aforesaid, each one undivided twelfth (1/12) of all my property, real or personal, consisting of the plantation on which I reside situated in this Parish, and all the appertenances thereto belonging, all the slaves, movable property, etc.

I do hereby appoint my beloved nephew, Alfred C. Weeks, to this my last will and testament.

In witness, I have wholly and entirely written this in my own handwriting and do affix my own name this 27th of November, A.D., 1845.

Rachel O'Connor

APPENDIX II
Inventory of Rachel O'Connor's Property
June 4, 1846

Copy of sale of personal property belonging to the estate of Rachel O'Connor, deceased, conducted by Seymour H. Lurty, Sheriff of West Feliciana Parish, on November 11, 1846.

State of Louisiana
Parish of West Feliciana

On the eleventh day of November, 1846, I attended the residence lately occupied by Mrs. Rachel O'Connor, deceased, at the hour appointed, and according to law, I offered for sale to the highest bidder for cash all the personal property belonging to the succession of Mrs. Rachel O'Connor, deceased, and the same was purchased as follows:

Wm. S. Swayze, one side board (marble top)	$ 19.00
James I. Weems, one waiter and glasses, five dollars	5.00
James I. Weems, two candle shades, two dollars	2.00
James I. Weems, one castor, nine dollars	9.00
Wm. S. Swayze, one pair card tables, fifteen dollars	15.00
James R. Dupree, one book case, fifteen dollars	15.00
James I. Weems, one lot of books, seven dollars	7.00
Wm. S. Swayze, one mantle glass, seven dollars	7.00
Wm. S. Swayze, one lot of fire irons, fourteen 50/100 dollars	14.50
L. B. Johnson, shovel and tongs, fifty cents	.50
James I. Weems, one sofa, twenty-five dollars	25.00
Henry W. Lyons, one secretary, twenty dollars	20.00
Jas. R. Dupree, ½ dozen cane chairs, six dollars	6.00
Wm. Selby, three curtains, three dollars	3.00
Wm. Selby, one carpet, eight dollars	8.00
B. F. Brooks, two maps, fifty cents	.50
James I. Weems, one mahogany bed stead, sixty dollars	60.00
Wm. Selby, one armoire, fifty-five dollars	55.00

John L. Lombard, one old desk, one dollar	1.00
Wm. S. Swayze, one mantle glass, eight dollars	8.00
James I. Weems, one old arm chair, four 50/100 dollars	4.50
Wm. S. Swayze, one pair small fire irons, one dollar	1.00
L. B. Johnson, one trundle bed stead, one 12/100 dollars	1.12
James Lindsey, one bed stead, bed and bedding, thirty-three 50/100	33.50
Hardy Perry, one bed stead, bed and bedding, fifteen 50/100	15.50
G. W. Purnell, one bureau, nine dollars	9.00
Wm. Sullivan, one old bureau, two dollars	2.00
Richard Hammer, one toilet glass, one 87/100 dollars	1.87
G. W. Purnell, one old carpet, six dollars	6.00
Wm. Selby, one bed stead, bed and bedding, fifteen dollars	15.00
Hardy Perry, one trundle bed and bedding, seven dollars	7.00
G. W. Purnell, one wash stand, one 50/100 dollars	1.50
Henry W. Lyons, one old clock, four dollars	4.00
Patrick Flinn, one side board, eight 50/100 dollars	8.50
George W. Purnell, one wire safe, nine dollars	9.00
Patrick Flinn, one setee, five 50/100 dollars	5.50
Wm. Sullivan, two dining tables, seven 50/100 dollars	7.50
G. W. Purnell, one armoire, eight 50/100 dollars	8.50
James I. Weems, one sofa lamp, ten dollars	10.00
Wm. S. Swayze, one glass lantern, two dollars	2.00
Patrick Flinn, one pair lamps and candlesticks, two 25/100	2.25
L. B. Johnson, one pair andirons, two dollars	2.00
James I. Weems, one lot of silver spoons, one hundred dollars	100.00
G. W. Purnell, one mule (Cash), sixty dollars	60.00
John M. Gray, one mule (John), fifty-six dollars	56.00
G. W. Purnell, one mule (Adolphus), seventy-one dollars	71.00
John M. Gray, one mule (Tom), sixty-one dollars	61.00
James R. Dupree, one mule (General), sixty-five dollars	65.00
Henry W. Lyons, one mule (Ruffin), sixty-five dollars	65.00
G. W. Purnell, one mule (Tan), eighty-three dollars	83.00
G. W. Purnell, one mule (Bill), sixty-five dollars	65.00
Paul Fulsom, one mare (Peg), twenty-four dollars 50/100	24.50
John Lombard, one horse (Fox), four 25/100 dollars	4.25
Wm. Finley, one horse (Jim), seventeen dollars	17.00
Patrick Flinn, one horse (Arthur), two 13/100 dollars	2.13
A. McKinney, one horse (Charley), thirty-five dollars	35.00
Henry W. Lyons, one horse (Bluster), forty-one dollars	41.00

L. B. Johnson, two horses (Ball and Wap), one 06/100 dollars   1.06
H. W. Lyons, 70 head of sheep, 6/ per head   52.50
H. W. Lyons, 13 head of hogs, three 12½/100 dollars per
head   40.62
G. W. Purnell, two yoke of oxen, forty-eight dollars   48.00
James R. Dupree, two yoke of oxen, eleven 25/100 dollars   11.25
Hardy Perry, one yoke of oxen, eleven dollars   11.00
G. M. Purnell, one yoke of oxen, twenty-two dollars   22.00
John Lombard, one yoke of oxen, seven dollars   7.00
James I. Weems, one wagon, thirty dollars   30.00
James I. Weems, three chains, five dollars   5.00
Henry W. Lyons, one ox cart, twenty-four dollars   24.00
G. W. Purnell, lot of hogs, sixteen dollars   16.00
Henry W. Lyons, one market cart, fifteen dollars   15.00
G. W. Purnell, one scrap iron, one 50/100 dollars   1.50
A. McKinney, one lot of hides, one dollar   1.00
Henry W. Lyons, 600 barrels of corn, fifty cents per barrel   303.00
Patrick Flinn, one lot of fodder, thirty-nine dollars   39.00
A. McKinney, one lot of fodder, thirteen 50/100 dollars   13.50
Henry W. Lyons, one lot of hay, two 50/100 dollars   2.50
Henry W. Lyons, nineteen cows and calves, sixty-three dollars   63.00
Wm. Selby, 1st choice of ten cows, thirty dollars   30.00
James I. Weems, 2nd choice of ten cows, sixteen dollars   16.00
H. W. Lyons, all the balance of the cattle, thirty-six dollars 36.00
H. W. Lyons, one bull, one dollar   1.00
G. W. Purnell, one lot of harness, one 50/100 dollars   1.50
Richard Hammer, one lot of ploughs, two 50/100 dollars   2.50
Jas. I. Weems, one lot of plough gear, nineteen dollars   19.00
G. W. Purnell, the blacksmith tools, twenty-one 50/100 dollars 21.50
H. B. Benjamine, one lot of iron oil, one 50/100 dollars   1.50
H. B. Benjamine, one lot of coal, fifty cents   .50
James I. Weems, one lot of hoes, two 50/100 dollars   2.50
H. B. Benjamine, three spades, one 40/100 dollars   1.40
John Lombard, one pair of weights, three 25/100 dollars   3.25
G. W. Purnell, one box axes, hoes, etc., five dollars   5.00
James I. Weems, two small tables, one dollars   1.00
G. W. Purnell, two washstands, four 25/100 dollars   4.25
G. W. Purnell, one lot of crockery ware, fifty-one dollars   51.00
John Lombard, two settees, one dollar   1.00
Patrick Flinn, one settee, eighty-eight cents   .88

Wm. S. Swayze, one lot of chairs, six dollars   6.00
James I. Weems, one lot of kitchen furniture, eleven dollars   11.00
Wm. Selby, one bed stead and mattress, four 50/100 dollars   4.50
Wm. S. Swayze, one lock, two 88/100 dollars   2.88
G. W. Purnell, one lot of bedding, thirty dollars   30.00
James I. Weems, one basket, one-half dollar   .50
Wm. S. Swayze, two lambs, twelve 50/100 dollars   12.50

There being no more personal property, I closed the sale. Total amount of the sale was twenty-one hundred and forty-four 10/100 dollars.

(Signed) Seymour H. Lurty
Sheriff, West Feliciana Parish

APPENDIX III
Letter of Rachel O'Connor to David Weeks
February 28, 1830

February 28th 1830

My Dear Brother

I hope, ere this, you have received my last, and if so you are no stranger to my distresses, nor the anxious desire I have of seeing you. To Pray my good Brother, make every haste to get here, that is in your power. Harry has behaved so meanly towards myself, and those orphan children of our Brother Stephen's, that I look on him, as great an enemy, as his brothers. They know I have written to you, and that I expect you to come, but they don't know, that I had any other reasons, only that of Harry's suing me. Mr Handy was here, the day before yesterday, and asked me if I expected you. I answered (him in a very careless manner) yes, that I look for you to come, in ten or twelve days. He asked me if I had written for you I said yes. He asked what hurried, to which, I carelessly answered, nothing, only the suit that H.F. had (of late) entered against me

If you can come, we can secure all, out of there power, with the greatest safety, I know you will feel afraid of there having a claim against you, for the debts, but indeed they cannot. I would not ask you to come, to bring you into trouble— Mr Swift stayed here last night and we had a long talk, on the subject of those two suits, and the danger of there going against me. But said, if you came in time it could be easily secured, out of there power, or any others, whatever and then they would be glad to compromise, and settle on easy terms and what we were willing to give—If you should be afraid, to let me make it over to you, and take my receipt in full. I will not insist on your doing so, only come and see it done, the other will undertake it, if you are present— When you come should you see H.F. or Handy, don't let them know, that you had heard of the suits being returned, or any thing about it, but I hope to see you before them and have our talk first — I cannot bear the idea of H.F. and his friends, enjoying the pleasure of braking me up, which I am convinced is there mutual wish—what a fool Harry is, to bite his nose off to spite his face

287

the Plantation is in good order & under good farmer. all doing well. Caroline had a young child the [day] before yesterday. and I expect Harriet to have one [hourly] and Bridgets only eight months old, the 6 of next month. which has the appearance of doing well — O dear me, how I want to see you. I am writing. but cannot explain half my desires. However if you can save the property together, and I should be spared and have my health. I hope to convince you, that my views were not selfish — Give my love to my Dear Frances. tell her, that I am so troubled, that have not written to her for some time. but that I will soon — She must kiss her little Brothers and sister for me. Remember me very affectionately to My Dear Sister Marg. whose health, I hope continues to mend — I remain your
affectionate Sister

R. O'Connor

GENEALOGY

Rachel Hopkins (d. 1790?)

m. 1st: Stephen Swayze
Children
1. William S. Swayze (d. 1820)
   m. 1st: Melissa Smith
   Children
   Julia Ann Swayze m. James Scott
   Charlotte Swayze m. Anthony Doherty
   Clarissa Swayze m. Lewis Davis
   William S. Swayze, Jr., m. Melinda Harbour
   m. 2nd: Maria Jefferson
   Children
   Stephen Courtland Swayze
   Love Swayze m. Charles Hoffman
2. Rachel Swayze (1774–1846)
   m. 1st: Richard Bell (d. 1792)
   Child
   Stephen Bell (1790–1821)
   m. 2nd: Hercules O'Connor (d. 1820)
   Child
   James O'Connor (1807–1822)

m. 2nd: William Weeks (1743–1819)
Children
1. Pamela Weeks m. Henry Flower
   Children
   James Flower
   William Flower
   Maria Flower
   Harriet Flower
   Sidney Flower
   David Flower
   Louisa Flower
   Stephen Flower

2. Caleb Weeks (d. 1798?) wife unknown
   Children
   William D. Weeks
   Anne Weeks

3. David Weeks (1786–1834) m. 1st: Mary Conrad (1796–1863)
   Children
   Frances Weeks (1820–1856) m. 1st: Augustin Magill
      Children
      David Weeks Magill
      Mary Ida Magill
      Augustin Magill, Jr.
      m. 2nd: Buford A. Prewitt
   Harriet Weeks (1824–1894) m. David E. Meade
      Child
      Edward Meade
   William Weeks (b. 1825) m. Mary G. Palfrey
      Children
      Harriet Weeks m. Walter Torian
      Lily Weeks (1851–1918) m. Gilbert Hall
         Child
         Weeks Hall (1894–1958)
   Alfred Weeks (1826–1864) m. Nannie Hunter
   Charles Weeks (1832–1900)
   David Weeks, Jr. (1833–1843)

Who's Who in the Life of Rachel O'Connor

Barrow, Robert Hilliard: oldest son of Eliza Bowman

Bell, Richard: Attakapa farmer; first husband of Rachel O'Connor

Bell, Stephen: son of Richard and Rachel Swayze Bell; oldest son of Rachel O'Connor

Bowman, Eliza Pirrie: daughter of James and Lucy Pirrie of Oakley Plantation; first husband was Robert Hilliard Barrow; second husband was the Reverend William Robert Bowman; third husband was Henry E. Lyons

Bowman, William Robert: Feliciana planter; rector of Grace Episcopal Church at St. Francisville; second husband of Eliza Pirrie

Caskadin, ?: merchant at St. Francisville

Chinn, Thomas Withers: Feliciana planter and judge

Collins, Louisa: youngest daughter of Henry and Pamela Weeks Flower

Collins, Maria: oldest daughter of Henry and Pamela Weeks Flower

Conrad, Alfred: brother of Mary Weeks; New Orleans lawyer; superintendent of David Weeks's estate for several years following David's death

Conrad, Ann: sister of Mary Weeks; wife of Dr. John Towles

Conrad, Charles: brother of Mary Weeks; secretary of war in President Millard Fillmore's cabinet

Conrad, Elizabeth: sister of Mary Weeks; wife of Mr. Harding

Conrad, Frederick: brother of Mary Weeks; master of The Cottage Plantation

Conrad, Mary Clara: wife of David Weeks; mother of Frances, Harriet, William, Alfred, Charles and David Weeks; sister-in-law of Rachel O'Connor; second husband was Judge John C. Moore

Conrad, Sidney: sister of Mary Weeks; wife of John T. Palfrey

Davis, Lewis: Feliciana farmer; husband of Clarissa Swayze

Dawson, John: judge, West Feliciana Parish

Denny, William L.: doctor in residence, Evergreen Plantation

Doherty, Anthony: Feliciana farmer; husband of Charlotte Swayze

Dunbar, K.: St. Francisville merchant

Flower, David: youngest son of Henry and Pamela Weeks Flower

Flower, Harriet: second daughter of Henry and Pamela Weeks Flower; wife of Mr. Handy

Flower, Henry: Feliciana farmer; husband of Pamela Weeks; father of David, Harriet, James, Louisa, Maria, and William Flower

Flower, James: oldest son of Henry and Pamela Weeks Flower

Flower, Louisa: youngest daughter of Henry and Pamela Weeks Flower; wife of Mr. Collins

Flower, Maria: oldest daughter of Henry and Pamela Weeks Flower; wife of Mr. Collins

Flower, Pamela Weeks: wife of Henry Flower; sister of David Weeks; half sister of Rachel O'Connor; mother of David, Harriet, James, Louisa, Maria, and William Flower

Flower, William: second son of Henry and Pamela Weeks Flower

Flower, William: New Orleans merchant who sued Rachel O'Connor for her deceased son's debts

Germany, Jacob: overseer, Evergreen Plantation

Hall, Weeks: last heir to Weeks estate; prior to his death in 1958, he willed Shadows-on-the-Teche to the National Trust for Historic Preservation

Handy, ? : farmer and storekeeper at St. Francisville; husband of Harriet Flower

Harbour, Melinda: wife of William Swayze, Junior; mother of Caleb and David Swayze

Harding, Elizabeth: sister of Mary Weeks

Harraldson, ? : lawyer hired by William Flower in his suit against Rachel O'Connor

Heaton, Anthony: host of David Weeks at New Haven, Connecticut

Hunter, Nannie: wife of Alfred Weeks

Lambeth and Thompson: New Orleans commission merchants

Linton, ? : New Orleans merchant

Lyons, Henry E.: third husband of Eliza Pirrie

Magill, Augustin Smith: Attakapa lawyer; first husband of Frances Weeks

McCausland, Robert: veteran of Revolutionary War and War of 1812

McVey, ? : St. Francisville merchant

Milladon, ? : New Orleans cotton factor

Moore, John C.: second husband of Mary Weeks; United States Congressman; judge in St. Mary Parish

Mulkey, ? : overseer, Evergreen Plantation

Murrell, John A.: leader of outlaw gang

O'Connor, Hercules: Irish immigrant; settled in Feliciana in 1790's; husband of Rachel Swayze Bell

O'Connor, James: son of Hercules and Rachel O'Connor; died at age of fifteen years

O'Connor, Rachel: mistress of Evergreen Plantation; daughter of Stephen and Rachel Hopkins Swayze; wife of Richard Bell; later married Hercules O'Connor; mother of Stephen Bell and James O'Connor

Palfrey, Sidney: sister of Mary Weeks; wife of John T. Palfrey

Patrick, Simpson: overseer, Evergreen Plantation

Percy, Robert: Feliciana planter; master of Beechwoods Plantation

Pirrie, Lucy: widow of James Pirrie; mother of Eliza Bowman and Mrs. Ira Smith; mistress of Oakley Plantation

Rhea, ? : judge, West Feliciana Parish

Scott, James: planter at Rapide Settlement on Red River; husband of Julia Ann Swayze

Smith, Boyd: superintendent of David Weeks's estate; tutor of Weeks children

Smith, Ira: Feliciana medical doctor; son-in-law of Mrs. James Pirrie

Stinson, ? : tutor of Weeks children

Swayze, Charlotte: niece of Rachel O'Connor; wife of Anthony Doherty

Swayze, Clarissa: niece of Rachel O'Connor; wife of Lewis Davis

Swayze, Julia Ann: niece of Rachel O'Connor; wife of James Scott

Swayze, William S.: brother of Rachel O'Connor; husband of Melissa Smith; father of Julia Ann, Charlotte, Clarissa, and William S. Swayze, Junior; later married Maria Jefferson and fathered Stephen Courtland Swayze and Love Swayze Hoffman (wife of Charles Hoffman)

Swayze, William S., Junior: nephew of Rachel O'Connor; husband of Melinda Harbour

Swift, John: St. Francisville merchant

Towles, John: medical doctor; master of Rickahoc Plantation; husband of Ann Conrad

Turnbull, Daniel: master of Rosedown Plantation

Turner, John: St. Francisville lawyer

Weeks, Alfred: son of David and Mary Weeks; husband of Nannie Hunter

Weeks, Caleb: oldest son or William and Rachel Swayze Weeks; half brother of Rachel O'Connor; father of William D. and Anne Weeks

Weeks, Charles: son of David and Mary Weeks

Weeks, David: youngest son of William and Rachel Swayze Weeks; husband of Mary Conrad; half brother of Rachel O'Connor; father of Frances, Harriet, William, Alfred, Charles and David Weeks; builder of Shadows-on-the-Teche in New Iberia

WHO'S WHO IN THE LIFE OF RACHEL O'CONNOR

Weeks, David, Junior: youngest son of David and Mary Weeks

Weeks, Frances: oldest daughter of David and Mary Weeks; wife of Augustin S. Magill; mother of David Weeks Magill, Mary Ida Magill, and Augustin Magill, Junior; second husband was Buford A. Prewitt; she and her two younger children died in the Ile Dernier tidal wave, August 10, 1856

Weeks, Harriet: youngest daughter of David and Mary Weeks; wife of David E. Meade

Weeks, William: oldest son of David and Mary Weeks; husband of Mary Gorham Palfrey; father of Harriet and Lily Weeks; grandfather of Weeks Hall

Weeks, William: patriarch of Weeks family in Louisiana; acquired land grants in Attakapa and Feliciana from Spanish government; husband of Rachel Swayze; father of Pamela Weeks Flower, Caleb Weeks, and David Weeks

Weems, James: West Feliciana Parish planter and judge

Winderstrandt, Robert: West Feliciana Parish notary public

BIBLIOGRAPHY

Baton Rouge, La. Dept. of Archives, Louisiana State University. Weeks family papers.

Butler, Louise. "West Feliciana: A Glimpse of its History." *Louisiana Histroical Quarterly* 7, 1 (January, 1924): 90–120.

Cox, Robert R. "The Gardens of the Shadows on the Teche," MA thesis, Louisiana State University, 1978.

Coxe, Tench. *A Statement of the Arts and Manufacturers of the United States for the Year 1810.* Philadelphia: A. Cornman, 1814.

Craven, Avery O. *Rachel of Old Louisiana.* Baton Rouge: Louisiana State University Press, 1975.

Davis, Edwin A. *Louisiana: A Narrative History.* Baton Rouge: Claitor' Book Store, 1965.

Gueymard, Ernest. "Notebook," Baton Rouge *State Times*, October 12, 1981.

Kane, Harnett T. *Plantation Parade.* New York: William Morrow, 1945.

Louisiana Historical Association Newsletter 5, No. 2 (March, 1979).

Norton, Leslie. *Readings in Social Science: Louisiana, 1699–1876.* Baton Rouge: Louisiana State University Press, 1935.

St. Francisville, La. West Feliciana Parish Courthouse. West Feliciana Parish Records.

Scroggs, William O. *The Story of Louisiana.* New York: Bobbs-Merrill, 1936.

U. S. Census Office. *Census of the United States, 1800–1850.*

U. S. Congress. *American State Papers*, Public Lands, vol. 1, 9th Cong., 1st sess., 1805, document 113.

U. S. Works Progress Administration of Louisiana. Survey of Federal Archives in Louisiana, *Greenburg Land Claims*, U. S. Land Office, Baton Rouge, Louisiana.

INDEX

Acadians, xv
Adams, Arthur, 39
Alexander's Creek, 95, 187
Allouez, Claude Jean, xi
Alstone, Solomon, 56
Ambrose, Thomas, 9
Amos (Slave), 140
Anders Boarding School, xxii, 55
Anesthesia, 268
Archives, Louisiana State University, ix
Arpents, xiii, xvi, xxiv, 42
Arthur (Slave), 11, 16, 33, 75-80, 87, 92,
    101, 107, 122-123, 126, 129, 132, 134,
    140, 143, 170-174, 225, 227, 233-234,
    243, 250, 252, 256-257, 269, 271, 273
Ashland Plantation, 93
Attakapa, xv-xvi, xviii, xxi, xxiii-xxiv, xxvi,
    53, 83, 106, 145-146, 161, 170, 196,
    211-212, 235, 257, 275-278
Audubon, John James, xiv, xxiv-xxv, 279

Baines, Dr. H., 195, 214, 236, 245
Baltimore, Md., 107, 111
Banks, x, xxi, 12, 15, 32, 43, 55, 68
Banks, Nathaniel P., 278
Barleycorn, John, xxv
Barrow, Boatner, 93, 145
Barrow, Robert, 62, 74, 180
Barton, Dr., 3, 254
Bastrop, Baron de, xv
Baton Rouge, xvi, xviii, 3, 32, 41, 66, 92,
    122, 126, 139, 181, 199, 221, 230-232
Bayou Boeuf, 166
Bayou Sara, 8, 12, 15-17, 21, 28, 59,
    67-76, 163, 168, 236, 270
Bayou Sara, 166, 168, 171
Bayou Teche, xv, xxi, xxiii, 96
Bayou Tunic Plantation, 3
Bedell, James, 96
Beef, 36, 244

Bell, Jane, 66, 72
Bell, Richard, xxiv
Bell, Stephen, xxiv-xxvi, 21, 26, 91, 104,
    142, 186, 247, 253, 256-258, 266
Bell, Dr. William, 93, 107, 109, 111, 125
Bernard, Joseph, 59
Bernard, Lucy, 99
Bienville, Jean Baptiste Lemoyne, Sieur de,
    xi-xii
Blacksmiths, xxi, 109, 133, 188, 195, 236
Bore, Etienne de, xvii-xviii
Bowman, Eliza, xiv, 12, 16, 48-49, 52, 87,
    89, 119, 121, 124, 152, 174, 176-180,
    183, 191, 193, 196-198, 200-201,
    204-206, 209-210, 214, 216, 218,
    223-224, 228, 233-234, 240, 262, 269,
    279
Bowman, Isobel, 274
Bowman, James Pirrie, 89, 193-194
Bowman, William Robert 36, 38, 44, 52,
    57, 67, 71, 73, 99, 102-103, 108,
    115-116, 119, 121, 124, 146, 175-177,
    179, 193-194, 204, 223, 279
Bradford, David, 11
Breast Tumor, 261-263, 265, 267-268
Bridget (Slave), 33, 37, 46, 73, 95, 117,
    140, 194, 202, 288
Brock, Sam (Slave), 234
Brown, Acy, 79
Brown, Dr. David, 111
Brownsville, Pa., 111, 205, 223
Burial Expenses: for Rachel O'Connor, 276
Bushnell, Judge, 79

Caleb, M., 71
Cash, Craven, 9, 76, 123
Caskadin (Merchant), 125, 143, 145
Casket Girls, xii
Cattle, 18, 73, 92, 112, 155, 167, 175, 252
Cattner, Ann, 61

Celeste (Slave), 216, 224
Centerville, La., 277
Chaney, Mrs., 89, 92
Chaney, Tom, 24
Charity (Slave), 92, 110, 140, 204, 210, 250, 252, 264–266, 268
Charles iii, xiii
Charlevoix, Pierre Francois, xi
Chew, Dr. Edward, 4
Chinn, Thomas Bolling Robertson, 9
Chinn, Thomas Withers xiv, 9, 32
Cholera xx, 72–74, 80–87, 89–90, 97, 100, 102, 104–106, 108–109, 111–113, 115, 122, 128–131, 151, 153, 155
Cincinnati, Ohio, 58–59
Clark (Surveyor), 23, 168
Clinton, La., 34, 39, 49–50, 100, 111, 123
Clipper, 244
Cocoran, F. H., 134
Coffee, 119, 121, 131, 145, 166, 180, 187
Collins, Harriet, 254
Collins, Louisa, xxii, 10, 29, 41, 44, 56, 61, 65, 228–230
Collins, Maria, xxii, 8, 10, 14, 16, 56, 84, 210
Collins and Cash, 7
Coltders Boarding School, 44
Columbia, 125
Company of the Indies, x
Conrad, Alfred T., xvi, 4, 21, 30, 32, 54–55, 87, 114, 147, 149–152, 155–157, 159–166, 168–170, 172–173, 175, 177–179, 182–186, 188–189, 192–193, 195–196, 198–202, 204, 206–208, 210–211, 214, 220, 235, 246
Conrad, Charles M., xvi, 62, 132
Conrad, Frances, Thurston, xvi, 4
Conrad, Frank, 207
Conrad, Frederick, xvi, 122, 125–126, 128–130, 132, 139, 279
Conrad Point, 279
Corn, xvii, 12, 23, 25, 32–33, 35–36, 49, 59, 66, 68, 72, 89–90, 92, 95, 97, 100, 102, 108, 119–120, 124–125, 127, 131, 140, 143–146, 151, 159, 164, 166, 168–169, 174, 179, 182, 185, 187, 204–206, 214, 217, 220, 222–223, 226, 236, 238, 242–243, 254, 257–258, 262, 266
Corrie, James, xxiv
Cottage Plantation, xvi, 122, 279
Cotton, xvii–xix, xxiv–xxv, 4, 7, 11–12, 23, 29, 32–33, 39–40, 44, 49, 53–55, 58–59, 62–63, 66, 72–73, 75–76, 78, 81, 84–86, 91–93, 95, 97, 100–102, 104–109, 116–117, 119–121, 123, 125, 127, 131, 134, 140–141, 145, 151, 159, 162,
167–168, 179–182, 184–185, 187, 190, 196, 198, 204–205, 208, 214, 217–218, 220, 223, 226–227, 229, 232–233, 237–239, 241, 243–245, 252, 254, 262–263, 266, 274–275
Cotton Gins, xvii, xxiv, 7, 11–12, 39, 53, 73, 117, 121, 167, 196, 208, 226–227, 243–245, 254, 266
Craven, Avery, O, 249
Crawford, H., 7, 8
Crozat, Antoine, x
Cypremont Plantation, xiii
Cypress Hall Plantation, xiv
Cypress: Lumber, xviii, xxv, 96, 174; Swamps, xiii, xviii

Dalley's Magical Pain Extractor, 244
Dalton, Samuel, 245
Dangerfield, Mrs., 4
Daniel (Slave), 17, 21, 33, 36, 47, 68, 81, 95, 99, 101, 104, 109, 113, 116, 122, 143, 250
Dave (Slave) 122, 129, 132, 140, 226
Davis, Clarissa, xxii, 7, 9, 16, 18–20, 27, 29, 31, 34, 37, 40–42, 44–45, 48, 50, 52–54, 58, 61–62, 64–67, 69–72, 74, 79, 81–82, 84, 86, 88, 91–93, 102–104, 111, 115–116, 123, 130, 133, 139, 142–143, 148–149, 151–152, 159, 161, 168–169, 172–174, 176–177, 179, 184, 193, 199, 205, 207–208, 210, 213, 216, 218, 224, 228–232, 238, 240, 242, 255, 260–263, 265–268, 287
Davis, Green, 55
Davis, James, 228–229, 238, 262–263
Davis, Lewis, 40–41, 45, 48, 50, 52, 54, 59, 61–62, 67, 69, 74, 79, 86, 88, 92, 99, 102–104, 111, 115, 119, 122–123, 133, 141, 144–145, 149, 152, 159, 161, 164, 168, 172, 177–178, 180, 184–186, 193, 207, 210, 219, 226, 230–232, 238, 261, 263, 265, 267, 287
Davis, Robert, 53, 134
Davit, Jessy, 67
Dawson, John B.37–38, 62, 71, 106, 109, 164, 213, 244, 246, 248, 261
Deafness, 212, 241–242, 245, 247, 264, 266, 270, 272
Denny, Dr. William L., 37, 44, 50, 58–59, 62, 66, 69, 73, 84, 88, 90, 98, 101, 103–105, 107–111, 114, 121, 124–125, 129–130, 133, 138, 140–141, 146, 166, 168, 262, 264, 270–271, 276
Distemper, 73, 112, 194
Doherty, Anthony, 53, 54, 56, 61, 66, 70, 88, 91–92, 94–95, 99, 102, 113, 132–133, 135, 137, 139, 141, 145, 149,

156–157, 160–161, 170, 172, 174,
177–181, 183, 185, 193, 204–205, 217,
223, 226–227, 230–231, 242, 260, 263,
265, 267

Doherty, Charlotte, xxii, 5, 7, 9, 19, 24–25,
27–29, 31, 37, 40, 42, 44, 50, 52–54,
56–57, 61, 64–66, 74, 86, 88, 91–92, 94,
98, 102, 110–111, 113–114, 116, 128,
135, 137–139, 142–143, 148, 156, 159,
160–161, 168–170, 173, 178–179, 183,
193, 199–200, 205, 207–208, 210, 213,
215, 217, 224, 229–233, 241–242, 263,
265, 268, 270

Doherty, Julia Ann 242

Doherty, Robert Hail, 66, 156, 199

Doherty, Samuel, 161

Doherty, Stephen, 200

Dorch, Thomas 143

Douglas, A. H., 112

Downs, J., 75, 77–78, 80, 91, 111, 120,
124, 128

Doyle, Jamees, 4

Duer, Dr., 6, 22, 32, 90

Dunbar, K., 167, 188–189, 193, 195–196,
205, 208, 212

Dunbar, Samuel, 121, 129

Dunn, Mrs., 38

Duplantier, Fergus, 66

Earthworms, 61

East Baton Rouge Parish, xv

East Feliciana Parish, xv, xvii–xvii, 3, 35,
74, 80, 110–112, 114, 174, 185, 191, 236

Eben (Slave), 122, 127, 129, 132, 140,
224–225, 250, 269

El Camino Real, 175

Empresario System, xv

England, xi, xiii, xix

Esneault, L., 43

Evergreen Plantation, xxiv, 133, 136, 138,
142, 160, 198, 213, 234, 236, 252, 254,
277–280

Explorations: French, x, xi; Spanish, x, xi

Fair Hope Plantation, 277

Federal Soldiers, 278

Feliciana, ix–x, xiii–xv, xvii, xxii–xxiv, xxvi,
101, 110, 175, 222, 259, 275

Fillmore, Millard, xiv

Finley, Jo, 12, 15, 36, 114

Flour, 119, 144, 180, 205

Flower, David, xxii, 8, 24, 51, 65, 90, 230

Flower, Henry, xxii, xxvi, 6, 8, 12, 15, 21,
23–24, 26, 28, 31, 33, 35–36, 42, 45–47,
49, 51, 56, 61, 65–68, 70, 72, 74, 76,
81, 91, 101, 103–104, 135, 210, 244,
267, 287–288

Flower, James, xxii, 6, 10, 12, 23–24, 44,
56, 59, 65, 79, 81, 84, 91, 106, 109,
111, 118, 132, 170–171, 177, 192, 194,
199, 205, 230, 241, 244–245

Flower, Pamela, xxii, xxvi, 8–9, 14–18,
22–24, 26, 28, 30, 32–33, 35–36, 39–42,
44, 46–47, 50–52, 54, 67, 76, 93, 244

Flower, Sidney, xxii, 55, 57, 64–65, 90,
135, 230

Flower, Stephen, xxii, 6

Flower, William (Nephew of Rachel
O'Connor), xxii, 24, 55–56, 59, 65, 81,
109, 118, 121, 125, 135, 230, 244, 254
258, 269

Flower, William (Merchant), xxvi–xxvii, 8,
21, 24–25, 28, 31, 47, 52, 57, 60, 66,
75, 79, 86, 96, 108

Follian Belloq and Delos, 236–237

Fontainebleau, Treaty of, xiii

Forlorn Hope Plantation, xvi

Forsythe, Dr., 240

Fort Adams, 236

Fort Saint Jean Baptiste, xii

Frank (Slave), 122, 129, 132, 226

Franklin, La., xvi, 87, 131, 146–147, 225

Fuergirola, Spain, xvi

Gaitre, Mrs., 38

Gallatin, Tenn., 112

Garnet Boarding School, 181

Gayoso de Lemos, Manuel, xxiv

Germany, Jacob, 119–120, 124, 127–128,
130–131, 133–134, 137–140, 143–145,
148, 151–153, 155, 162, 164–165,
167–168, 174, 176, 178–183, 185, 187,
189–190, 194–197, 199, 202, 204, 208,
213–216

Gilbert, Infirmary, 276

Gilbert, Dr. Samuel, 276

Grace Episcopal Church, xiv, 193, 225, 230

Grand Cote, xxiii, xxv–xxvi, 255–258

Greek Revival Architecture, xviii, xxv

Grey, John, 228

Grey, Mayo, 97

Grover, Hiram, 7, 219

Hail, Robert, 183, 185, 187, 189–190, 199,
203, 206

Hall, Gilbert, 278

Hall, Weeks, 136–278

Handy, Mr., xxii, 27–28, 30, 32–33, 39,
45–47, 53–54, 56, 59, 65, 68, 81, 86, 88,
90, 111, 116, 124, 156, 267, 287–288

Handy, Emily Pamela, 58

Handy, Harriet, xxii, 10, 13, 20, 27, 30,
32–33, 37, 52, 54, 58, 60–61, 64–65,
67–68, 73, 81, 87, 90, 111, 114, 121,

131, 135, 139, 148, 156, 159, 199, 210, 267
Handy and Scillman, 47
Handy and Waddle, 47
Happy Land (Feliciana), ix, xiv
Harbour, John, 29
Harding, Elizabeth, xvi, 4, 8, 17, 20, 27–28, 37, 52, 54, 62, 155, 158, 212
Hargadine, William, 226, 236, 269, 271–273
Harraldson (Lawyer), 31, 79, 86, 93
Harriford, Dr., 90, 172
Harry (Slave), 122, 129, 132, 161
Heaton, Mr. and Mrs. Anthony, 150, 152, 157, 159
Henderson, Stephen, 242, 266
Henny (Slave), 250
Higgingbotham, Mrs., 34, 39
Hoffman, Charles, xxii
Hogs, 65, 68, 90, 92–93, 112, 131, 151, 171, 187, 190, 194
Holmes, I., 236
Hopkins, Mr., 253
Horses, xx, 18–19, 29, 50, 55, 59, 66, 70, 73, 81, 84, 86, 92, 101, 103, 108, 112–113, 120–121, 123–124, 129, 131, 133–134, 143, 145, 151, 153, 155, 161, 164, 166, 175, 180, 187, 190, 196, 219–220, 232–233; Race Horses, 62, 66, 69, 89–90, 94, 103, 141
Huff, Dr., 4
Hull, Mr., 7
Hunter, Nannie, 278
Huntsville, 166

Iberia, 164
Indentured Servants, xii
Indians, x, xi–xiii, xxiii, 194; Algonquin, xi; Attakapa, xv; Choctaws, xi; Natchez, xii
Inventory, 276–283
Ireland, xxiv, 42, 216
Isaac (Slave), 58, 78, 96, 108, 140, 170–171, 185, 194, 196, 208, 260
Isle Dernier, 277
Islenos, xv

Jackson, David Howell, 279
Jackson, La., xxii, 23, 35, 42, 55, 61, 65, 77, 80, 88, 90, 108, 134, 143, 214, 216, 219, 223, 230, 232
Johnson, David, 245
Johnson, Isaac, 61
Johnson, Joseph E., 23, 213
Johnson, Richard, 22
Johnson, William G., 22
Jones, Peter, 219
Journal, St. Francisville, xv

Kendrick, Benjamin, 121, 131
Kenner, Duncan, 92–94
King, Dr., 267–268
Kitsatchie, 174–175

Lacey, Dr., 221
Lambeth and Thompson, 195, 209, 229, 236–241, 245, 262, 272
Land, xiii–xvi, xviii–xix, xxi, xxiii–xxiv, xxvi, 12, 31, 42–43, 57, 68, 71, 82, 90, 108, 170–171, 178, 180, 182–183, 185, 190, 238, 253, 255, 257–258, 261, 276–277
Lastly (Overseer), 7
Lattimore, Dr., 219
Laudanum, 83
Law, John, x
Leeks, 5
Legendre, Mrs., 70
Leonid Meteor, 126
Leven (Slave), 166, 223–224, 226–228, 234
Lewis, Rev., 225–226, 240, 254
Lid (Slave), 134, 139, 140
Lime, 74
Linton, Mr., 75, 104, 116, 125, 131, 134, 145
Littletown (Slave), 122, 129, 132, 140, 181, 226
Lobdell, Mr., 91
Long, Crawford W., 268
Looms, xxi, xxiv, 100–101
Los Adaes, 175
Louis, xv, x, xiii
Louisville, Ky., 201
Lurty, Seymour H., 283, 286
Lynch Law, 177
Lyons, Mrs., 31, 37, 163
Lyons, Henry E., 234, 240

Madison, James, xv
Madison Parish, 177–178
Magill, Augustin Smith, 235–238, 240–242, 246–247, 277, 281
Magill, Augustin Smith, Jr., 277
Magill, David Weeks, 239–240, 242, 277
Magill, Ida, 277
Maison Rouge, Marquis de, xv
Manufacturing, xxi
Marburg, Mrs., 219
Marburg, William, 72
Mardi Gras, xi
Mark (Slave), 36
Marshall, B., 195
Mathews, Judge George, 90, 121
Maxwell and Hudson, 54
McAllister, Samuel, 99

McCaleb, Samuel, 109, 115, 118–119, 124, 245
McCausland, Gen. Robert, xiv, 42, 161
McDermit, John, 16, 269
McKelvey, Dr. S.B., 195, 214
McKoon, Mr., 216
McVey, John, 4, 7, 12, 42, 44, 58
McVey, John Cabot, 42
Meade, David, 277
Meade, Edward, 278
Meal, 81, 119, 137
Measles, 38, 191–194, 199
Medicines, xx, 67, 70, 73, 81, 104–105, 107–108, 155, 212, 218, 237, 265, 270
Memphis, Tenn., 275–276
Mexico City, 175
Midwife, 266
Milladon, Mr., 7, 11
Missah Sippah, xi
Mississippi River, xi–xii, xiv–xviii, xxv, 16, 54–66, 71, 76, 80, 82, 86, 90, 95, 109, 128, 145, 157, 275, 279
Molasses, 28, 99, 189, 195, 208, 212, 244, 249, 254, 267
Monroe, La., 119
Moore, John C., 235, 238, 243–246, 257, 260, 263, 266–267, 269–270, 272, 276, 278–279, 281
Morris, John C., 195
Mortgages, 15, 46, 68, 71
Mosquitoes, xx
Mulattoes, 34, 68
Mules, 220, 249
Mulhollen, Charles, 166
Mulhollen, John, 36, 97
Mulkey (Overseer), 71, 73, 78, 81, 84–85, 89–92, 95–96, 99–102, 104, 106, 108–109, 114, 117–120, 122–125, 127–128, 131, 135, 140–141
Mullallen, Sarah, 12
Mullford, Captain, 3
Mumps, 199, 216
Murrell, John A., 173–176

Natchez, xviii
Natchitoches, xii
National Trust for Historic Preservation, 136, 278
New Haven, Conn., 112, 150, 152
New Iberia, xvi, 96, 211
New Orleans, xi, xiv, xvi–xxiii, xxvi, 4, 7–8, 10, 12, 16–17, 23, 28, 32–35, 38–40, 42, 44, 52, 61, 63, 65–66, 71, 78, 80, 82, 84, 87, 91, 94–95, 99–100, 103–107, 117, 121, 128, 132, 141, 143, 145–146, 159–160, 162, 170, 179, 182–183, 185, 188, 191–192, 197–198,

201–202, 209–212, 220, 229, 234, 240, 245, 273–275, 277–278
New Town, xvi, 13, 80, 96, 100, 108–109, 111–112, 246
New York, N.Y., 7, 8, 16, 81, 110, 114, 278
No Man's Land, 174–175
Nouvelle Orleans, xi
Nova Iberia, xvi, 235
Nubling, Mr., 59

Oakley Plantation, xxiv, 279
Oats, xvii, 90, 108, 144, 194
O'Connor, Hercules, xiv, xxiv–xxvi, 198, 279
O'Connor, James, xxiv–xxvi, 11, 14, 23, 97, 142, 247, 256–257, 266
Orange Trees, 258
Orchard, 249, 252–254
O'Reilly, Don Alexandre, xiii
Ouachita River, xiii, xv
Overseers, xx, xxiii, xxviii, 6, 27, 29, 62, 67, 69, 71, 81, 85, 88, 90, 97, 102, 110, 116, 119, 121, 123–124, 127, 129, 131–132, 152, 160–162, 166, 175–176, 180, 187, 201, 224, 227, 233, 239, 242–243, 245, 252, 269, 271–273, 279
Oxen, 7, 66

Palfrey, John, xvi
Palfrey, John T., xvi, 27–28, 32, 51–52, 62, 87, 160, 278
Palfrey, Mary Gorham, 278
Palfrey, Sidney, 4, 9, 17, 20, 28, 51–52, 54, 62, 87, 155, 192, 212
Panic of 1829, 35
Panic of 1837, xvii, 206–207
Parc Perdu, xxiii
Paris, France, 278
Patience (Slave), 18, 170, 194, 226, 250, 252
Patrick, Simpson, 33, 36, 43, 49–50, 53, 55, 58, 62, 66, 68–71, 89, 92, 97, 119–120, 127, 180, 200–201, 204
Pauger, Adrien de, xi
Percy, Mr. and Mrs. Robert, 55, 60–61
Phoenix, St. Francisville, 82
Pigeons, 209, 211, 213–214, 216, 218, 220–222
Pirrie, Lucy, (Mrs. James), 3, 4, 16, 35–36, 39, 44, 56, 61–62, 71, 73–74, 87, 89–90, 94–95, 99–100, 102–103, 108, 116, 180, 197, 279
Place d'Arms, xi
Plains, 37, 74, 82, 112, 120
Plaquemine, La., 79, 93, 168
Ploughs, 59, 92, 134, 164, 166

Point Coupe Parish, 84, 89, 201, 204
Pope, Dr., 9, 182, 201, 204
Population: of Feliciana (1820), xviii; of Louisiana (1762), xii, (1810), xvii; of New Orleans (1721), xii, (1762), xii, (1820), xvii
Pork, 55, 99, 143–144, 170, 187, 189–190, 196–197, 236, 238
Port Gibson, 166
Potatoes, 72, 97, 100, 102, 106, 120, 140, 143, 145, 259
Poultry, 55, 57, 62, 69, 102, 169, 191, 199, 252
Powell, Dr. 174
Prewitt, Buford, 277
Pritchard, Walter, xix
Prostitutes, xvi

Rabbits, 44, 214
Rachel of Old Louisiana, 249
Ranney, Mr. 221–223
Rapide Settlement (Alexandria, La.), xxii, 27, 73, 88, 106, 168, 170, 215
Red River, xii–xiii, xvii, xxii, 217, 243
Rhea, Judge John, 6, 12, 32, 118
Rheumatism, 1, 39, 136, 138, 144, 189, 191–192, 196, 199
Rice, 145, 202, 205
Richardson, Wade, 153
Rickahoc Plantation, xxiii
Ringworms, 111
Rio del Espiritu Santo, xi
Rio del Flores, xi
Rosedown Plantation, 279
Runaway Slaves, 35, 37, 53, 99, 103, 106, 132, 207, 259–260
Rye, xvii

St. Denis, Luis Juchareau de, xii
St. Francisville, x, xiii, xv, xxii, xxiv, xxvi, 4, 21, 23, 26, 38–39 42, 44, 47, 49, 51, 54, 56, 64, 66, 72, 77, 80, 82, 84–85, 90, 100, 102, 106, 108–109, 122, 124, 160, 170, 183, 186, 189, 193, 195, 201, 204, 219, 230, 244, 254, 258
St. Helena Parish, xv, 11
St. Louis, Mo., 277
St. Martin, 123
St. Martinville, 109, 231, 278–279, 281
St. Mary Parish, 277
St. Tammany Parish, xv
Salivation, 70
Salt, 74, 236
Sam (Slave), 36, 142, 226, 258
Sampson (Slave), 56, 104, 130, 142, 252
Saw Gin, xvii
Scarlet Fever, 143, 254

Scott, James, xii, 25, 29, 31, 35, 37, 40, 42, 73, 88, 91, 156
Scott, Julia Ann, xxii, 7, 29, 40, 42, 52, 54, 64, 66, 73, 81, 86–88, 91, 102, 111, 114, 143, 148–149, 151–153, 156, 159, 161, 168, 170, 172, 177–179, 189–190, 193, 199–200, 205, 207, 210, 215, 217, 224, 227, 229–230, 232
Shadows-on-the-Teche, 96, 98, 137, 153, 278–279
Sheep, 187, 190
Sheriff Seizures, 70–71, 75, 77–79, 85–86, 96, 103–107
Shipp, William, 99
Shrubs and Flowers, 70, 87, 94, 96, 98–99, 136–138, 202, 233, 279
Skipwith, Fulwar, xv
Slaugher, Dr. 4
Slaves, xiv, xvii–xviii, xix–xxi, xxiii–xxiv, xxvi–xxvii, 6, 13, 18, 24, 29–32, 36, 41, 43–44, 49, 56, 58, 62–63, 70–72, 74, 77–78, 84–86, 89, 93, 95–96, 99–100, 102–103, 105–106, 108, 113–115, 121, 128–130, 135, 137, 140–142, 145–146, 149–151, 153, 161, 164–167, 169–170, 175–177, 179–180, 183, 185–187, 189–190, 192–193, 196–197, 199, 202–206, 214, 316, 218–219, 222–223, 225, 228, 230, 233, 238–239, 241–244, 247, 249–252, 254–258, 260, 263–265, 269, 271–273, 275–279, 281; births, 30, 68, 202, 216, 266; clothing, 62, 64, 100–101, 165, 167, 182, 236, 273; crops, 66, 176, 182, 195, 220, 226; discipline, 127, 197–198, uprisings, xxviii, 62, 173, 184, 186
Smith, Beverly, 66, 170, 173, 188, 195, 200, 202
Smith, Boyd, 159, 165–166, 170, 173
Smith, Courtland, 71, 84
Smith, Courtney, 50, 108, 174
Smith, Ira, 16, 44, 48, 58, 72, 81, 87, 89–90, 94, 108, 116, 174, 224
Smith, Isaac, 9, 59
Smith, Luther, 6, 29, 108, 131
Snow Hill, 73
Spanish Trail, xv, 96
Spinning Wheels, xxi, 99–100
Squatters, xviii
Steamboats, xxvii, 4, 84–85, 87, 108, 121–122, 128, 132, 145, 181, 205, 211, 243, 271, 275
Stinson, Mr., 170, 173, 184–185, 188, 191–192, 195, 197
Stirling, John, 195
Stirling, Lewis, 56, 103
Stirling, Ruffin, 123

Stokes (Overseer), 21, 33, 34, 70
Stone, Dr. Warren, 58, 268, 270, 273
Sugar, xvii–xviii, xix, xxi, xxiii, xxv–xxvi, 4, 15, 23, 28, 32, 38, 43, 84, 91–92, 99, 108, 119, 121–122, 126, 131–132, 135, 137–139, 180, 182, 187, 189, 195, 208–209, 212, 214, 249, 254, 267, 279
Sulphur, 13
Swayze, Caleb, 31, 133, 137–138, 145, 163, 191–192, 267
Swayze, David, 31,. 163
Swayze, Love, xxii
Swayze, Maria, xxii
Swayze, Melinda, 34, 40, 53–54, 64, 218, 229, 265, 268
Swayze, Melissa, xxii
Swayze, Rachel Hopkins, xiv, xxi–xxii, 18, 166
Swayze, Stephen (Father of Rachel O'Connor), xxi, xxiv
Swayze, Stephen (Brother of Rachel O'Connor) xxi–xxii, 18, 30, 45, 64, 67, 91, 102, 193, 272, 287
Swayze, Stephen Courtland, xxii
Swayze, William, 8, 24, 29, 31–32, 34, 37, 40, 49–50, 52, 54, 73, 138, 156, 169, 174, 177, 204, 210, 216, 218–220, 224, 226, 229, 262, 265, 268
Swift, Miss A., 265
Swift, John, 3–4, 7, 12, 21–23, 28, 30, 32–33, 35, 39–40, 42, 44–45, 47, 49–50, 54–56, 58–61, 66, 71–72, 81–82, 84–85, 90, 94, 99, 104–107, 114, 134, 154, 179–180, 184, 187
Swift and Crenon, 106
Syrup, 99, 205, 212

Taxes, 82, 196–197, 237–239, 241
Tea, 189
Telegraph, 79
Territory of Orleans, xv
Thomas, David, 141
Thompson's Creek, 59, 185
Tobacco, xvii
Torian, Walter, 278
Towles, Ann, xvi, 87, 156
Towles, John, xvi, 32, 87
Town, Farm, xxiii
Turnbull, Daniel, 39, 260
Turnbull, Martha, 67, 112
Turnbull, Sarah, 279
Turner, James, 245
Turner, John, 21–22, 25, 33, 49–50, 56, 59–60, 69–73, 75–81, 85–87, 89, 99–100, 104, 106, 121, 123, 129, 153–154, 203

Ulloa, Antonio de, xiii

Unzaga, Luis de, xiii
Ursulines, xii

Varney, Dr., 113
Vermillion, 145

Watts, Mr., 4
Weather, 7, 25, 39, 52–53, 57–58, 61, 67–68, 72, 79, 87, 92–96, 98–99, 101–102, 106, 108, 110, 113, 119–120, 131–133, 136–138, 145, 149, 152, 155, 157, 159–160, 167, 171, 179, 181, 186, 188–189, 192, 196, 198, 200, 202, 205–207, 209, 217–218, 221–223, 225–228, 232–233, 235–237, 241–242, 245, 254, 259, 260, 268–269, 271, 277
Weathers, Mr., 32
Weeks, Alfred, 20, 25, 37, 52, 87, 111, 118, 120, 122, 150, 152, 163, 173, 186, 191, 195, 201, 204, 207, 211, 221–222, 225, 229–233, 237, 245, 247, 250, 252, 255–257, 259, 262, 264, 271–273, 276–278, 281
Weeks, Ann, xxiii, 22, 32
Weeks, Caleb, xxii–xxiii, 18, 32, 93
Weeks, Charles, 87, 101, 111, 163, 166, 173–174, 191, 198, 201, 215, 217, 226, 229, 232–233, 237, 243–244, 262, 264, 268–271, 274, 278, 281
Weeks, David, xvi, xxii–xxviii, 3, 5–7, 10, 14, 17–20, 22, 24, 27–28, 30–31, 35, 38, 40–41, 43, 46–49, 52–54, 57, 60–62, 65–67, 70–72, 75–77, 79–80, 82, 84–85, 89–92, 94–96, 98, 100–105, 107–108, 110, 112–116, 118, 120, 122–123, 126, 128, 130–131, 133, 135–136, 138–139, 141, 144, 146–148, 150–154, 156–162, 180, 203–204, 221, 238–239, 246–249, 252–253, 255–261, 267, 272, 277–278, 281, 287
Weeks, David, Jr., 134, 136, 155, 163, 166, 168, 173, 191, 201, 217, 226, 229, 232–233, 237, 243–245
Weeks Family Papers, ix, xxvii, 249
Weeks, Frances, 5, 8, 9, 17–19, 25, 29, 31, 37, 40, 46, 52, 54, 56–57, 62, 68, 87, 89, 101, 103, 108, 111, 116, 132,135, 137–138, 150, 152, 155, 162–163, 167–168, 171, 174, 176–178, 181–182, 184, 188, 191–192, 197, 199, 201, 205–206, 209, 211–213, 215, 217–218, 221–222, 225, 227, 230, 232, 235, 237–241, 243–244, 259, 264, 271, 273, 277–278, 281, 288
Weeks, Harriet, 20, 25, 27–28, 37, 40, 72, 87, 111, 116, 151, 163, 172–173, 179, 182, 191, 194, 200–201, 214, 218, 220,

225-226, 230-231, 233, 237, 244,
262-264, 268-271, 273, 277-278, 281,
288
Weeks Island, xxiii, 43, 53, 78, 80, 82, 85,
108, 130, 161, 166, 197, 255-256
Weeks, Lily, 278
Weeks, Mary, xvi, xxiii, xxvi, 5, 8, 10, 13,
15, 17-18, 20, 22-23, 27-29, 31, 35, 37,
40-41, 43, 46, 48-49, 51, 59-63, 66,
68-70, 72, 74, 76, 82, 85, 88, 90-91,
93-94, 96-97, 101, 105-106, 108, 110,
112-113, 115, 117-118, 120-121, 123,
126-127, 129-130, 132, 134-136, 139,
141, 143, 146-151, 154-155, 157-158,
161-163, 165-166, 168-169, 171-173,
176-177, 179, 181, 184, 188, 190-192,
196-198, 200-201, 203-210, 213-215,
218, 220-221, 224-228, 230-236, 239,
241, 243, 246, 248-250, 253-256,
258-261, 263-264, 267-269, 271-271,
275, 277-278, 281, 287-288
Weeks, William (Nephew of Rachel
O'Connor), 15, 20, 25, 29, 37, 87, 111,
128, 132, 134-136, 139, 143, 146,
154-155, 163, 173, 182, 190-192, 194,

201, 211, 221, 223, 229, 231-232, 237,
245-248, 252-253, 255-249, 262-264,
267-269, 271, 273, 278, 281
Weeks, William (Patriach of Weeks Family
in Louisiana), xiv, xvi, xxii-xxv, 166
Weeks, William David, xxiii, 10, 17-18, 22
Weems, James, 171, 181
West Feliciana Parish, xiv, xv, xxiv,
xxvi-xxvii, 1, 13, 35, 42, 82, 110, 114,
261, 276, 281, 283, 286
West Florida, xiii
West Florida Republic, xv
West Point, 10
Whitney, Eli, xvii
Whooping Cough, 122
William Flower vs. Rachel O'Connor, xxvi,
4, 20, 25-26, 33-34, 39, 42, 47, 59, 61,
69-70, 73, 85, 96, 132
William Weeks and Company, 277
Williams, James, 119
Winderstrandt, Robert C., 71, 118, 261
Woodville Bank, 55
Woodville, Miss., 100
Workman, Judge John, 39

Yellow Fever, xx, 3, 4, 38-39, 219